Dale Peterson

STORYVILLE USA

THE UNIVERSITY OF GEORGIA PRESS   ATHENS

Published by the University of Georgia Press
Athens, Georgia 30602
© 1999 by Dale Peterson

Set in Electra by G&S Typesetters, Inc.
Printed and bound by Maple-Vail
The paper in this book meets the guidelines for
permanence and durability of the Committee on
Production Guidelines for Book Longevity of the
Council on Library Resources.

Printed in the United States of America
03 02 01 00 99 C 5 4 3 2 1

Library of Congress Cataloging-in-Publication Data

Peterson, Dale.
Storyville, USA / by Dale Peterson.
p.   cm.
ISBN 0-8203-2151-6 (alk. paper)
1. United States — Description and travel.   2. United
States — History, Local.   3. Cities and towns — United
States.   4. Names, Geographical — United States.
5. Peterson, Dale — Journeys — United States.   I. Title.
E169.04.P48   1999
973 — dc21   99-20132
CIP

Lyrics in the chapter "Alligator" are reprinted from
"I Just Want to Make Love to You," written by
Willie Dixon, © 1959, 1987 Hoochie Coochie Music
(BMI) / Administered by Bug Music. All rights reserved.
Used by permission.
Quoted passages in the chapter "Wounded Knee" are
reprinted from Black Elk Speaks by John G. Neihardt
by permission of the University of Nebraska Press.
Copyright © 1932, 1959, 1972 by John G. Neihardt,
copyright © 1961 by the John G. Neihardt Trust.

This book is dedicated to the people of Storyville, USA:
Good Samaritans all.

Contents

Leg 3

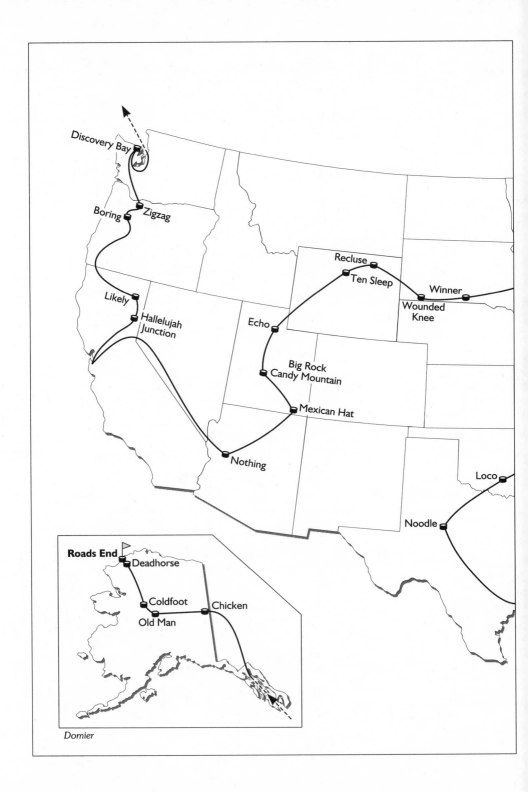

Domier

Storyville, USA

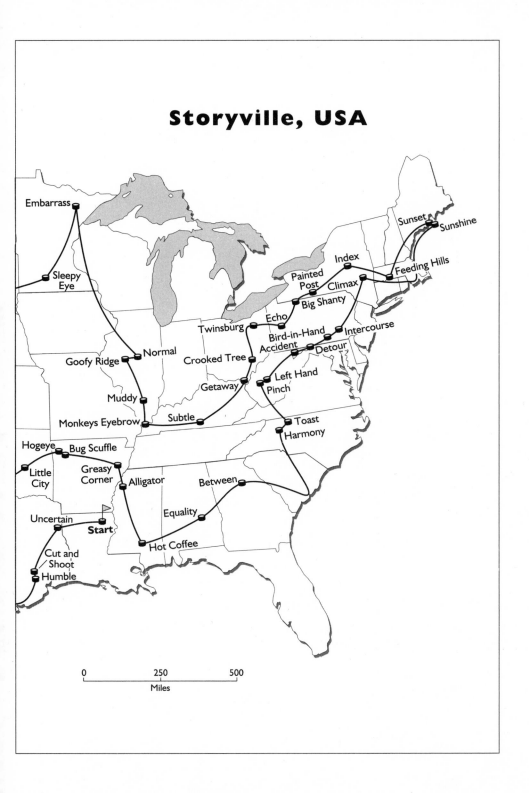

How It All Began

ne day my son said to me, "There aren't any more open spaces or wild places left in the United States, are there. It's all used up, isn't it."

We live near Boston now, in an urban conglomeration on the very edge of the continent, where indeed there are not many open spaces or wild places left to speak of. The population explosion has already happened here. But I know there are spaces and places farther out. You can see them on the map: between towns.

For me, open spaces and wild places are what surround small towns. And since I myself grew up in a wonderful small town, it seemed that we ought to pack ourselves — me, my son (Bayne, age eleven), and my daughter (Britt, age fourteen) — into a car and find the small towns. So we invented the travel game called "Storyville."

A Storyville is a place whose name you find on a map — for example, Intercourse, Pennsylvania, or Monkeys Eyebrow, Kentucky — and you say to yourself: *Now what is the story behind that name?* Then, having wondered, you get in your car and go to the Storyville, where somehow or other you find out what the story really is.

I thought we could start in Start, Louisiana, and end, maybe, at Roads End on the other side of the continent. I decided that our rule book and grand arbiter would be the *AAA Road Atlas,* since that looked pretty darned complete.

I also figured it would be a good idea to write a book about our trip. That way, for one thing, income-tax-wise (and I am asking you to keep this just between you and me), we might be able to write it off. For another thing, Britt and Bayne could become more than mere passive travelers or remote observers. They would serve as my eyes and ears. I would pay them a certain amount, neither exorbitant nor exploitative, and they would be transformed into my Research Assistants.

That was the deal. We signed a contract. I agreed something for services rendered thereto and thisfor. They agreed something for services rendered wherewith and whatnot. Also not to pester me about watching television in our hotel room at night.

So, a Storyville is a town with a name that evokes a story. But the name has to suggest an actual story. For the sake of simplicity, the name ought to work

1

in English. And it ought to imply a story not immediately obvious. If it seems too obvious — say, State Line, Louisiana — that's not really a story, and the place is not really a Storyville. General or sentimental names don't count. Friendship, Maine, or Felicity, California. They probably don't have real stories behind them. Someone just pulled them out of a book.

Nor do accidental puns. Naturally, one must be realistic about this whole matter. Most puns are bad jokes, but where would the world be without puns? Puns are there. You can ignore them and pretend they don't exist, but the fact remains that puns do stumble across one's path from time to time when one isn't looking. What if, for example, you were bound for Grindstone, Maine, and on the way, you found a place called Nose? How could you avoid it?

Storyvilles are almost always small towns. Who knows why? Maybe because population centers destined to grow into big cities sooner or later acquire grand, abstract, or Old Worldian names, appellations of ancient anchor that announce destiny, grandeur, and power: New York City! Sure, that advertising wonk on Madison Avenue will (for a fee) invent and promote some quaint, reassuring Storyname for the place: Big Apple. And people do fall for that. Nervous tourists from the Midwest do seem to believe that no one in a town called "Big Apple" would dare stick a knife in their back. But New York is still just New York. And if the place had really been called Big Apple, surely some sober city father would have changed that tag long ago. Let me put it this way. Can you imagine an international center of commerce called Zap? Nothing? Hazard? Ono? Accident? Crapo? Detour? Wanker's Corner? For one thing, no airline in the world would fly to a place with a name like that.

Some Storyvilles give the earnest Storyviller a choice. Will you visit Normal, Alabama, or Peculiar, Missouri? Do you wish to see Dog Town, Alabama, or Cat Creek, Montana? Drytown, California, or Raintown, Indiana? Shorter, Alabama, or Longtown, Missouri? Why, Arizona, or Whynot, North Carolina? Frost, Ohio, or Frostproof, Florida? Tallman, Michigan, or Dwarf, Kentucky? Top Most, Kentucky, or Bottom, North Carolina?

Though Twinsburg, Ohio, doesn't particularly, other places promote their own missing siblings. Battiest, Oklahoma, for example, calls out for Belfry, Kentucky. And is it fair to visit Guys, Maryland, without spending equal time in Ladiesburg of the same state? Home, Pennsylvania, ought to be followed two or three thousand miles later by Sweet Home, Oregon. What is Loudville, Massachusetts, without Racket, Missouri? And who could possibly visit Mousie, Kentucky, without directly proceeding to Eek, Alaska? Fortunately, the road runs straight and short between Mutual and Climax, both of Ohio. But to proceed with grace from Intercourse, Pennsylvania, to Climax, New York is not so trivial a feat.

Many Storyvilles broadcast an optimistic inclination, but it is necessary to distinguish between bland boosterism and original positive thinking. Boosterism results in all those names invented during a sleepy Kiwanis afternoon, so predictable they have become as meaningless as an old shoestring. The positive-thought Storyvilles, by contrast, still make you wonder. There must be a story there: Alert, North Carolina; Fearnot, Pennsylvania; Good Intent, Pennsylvania; Pep, New Mexico; Pluck, Texas; Rough and Ready, Pennsylvania; What Cheer, Iowa; and Winner, South Dakota.

Yet the low-self-esteem Storyvilles are, to my mind, intrinsically more interesting. These are the pathetic underdogs, the sad sacks of small-town America. Places like Bland, Missouri; Boring, Oregon; Burden, Kansas; Coward, North Carolina; Craven, South Dakota; Cut Off, Louisiana; Downer, Minnesota; Drab, Pennsylvania; Droop, West Virginia; Dry Prong, Louisiana; Fickle, Illinois; Grimville, Pennsylvania; Hardscrabble, Delaware; Low Point, Illinois; Needful, Pennsylvania; Mud Lick, Kentucky. . . .

There are stories everywhere in the USA, and the problem of the USA Storyviller is not so much to find them as to learn what they are by locating the local storyteller. Every ville has its story, but *Storyville, USA* represents our best effort at finding the most intriguing stories in Storyvilles across America. During twenty thousand miles of road travel, we loop a line across and around the United States: starting at Start, taking a break in Hot Coffee, driving safely through Accident, zigzagging at Zigzag, eating chicken soup at Chicken, and getting cold feet in Coldfoot. We stop at Nothing, and with little or no Goodluck our road finds its end at Roads End.

Storyvilles are fun, and I think of this book as, in large part, a whimsical overlook at the American landscape from a linguistic and toponymic cloud. But Storyvilles are also socially and historically distinctive. They are typically very small towns, and they were often conceived on the run by stubborn pioneers and brave eccentrics. To some degree, they are conceptual folk art. They are also ciphers or secret messages. They are minihistories, in other words, and so exploring a Storyville means digging a well in time. Some are surviving into our contemporary catastrophe quite well, thank you, but far too many are being buried and forgotten: overwhelmed by twenty-five thousand tract houses serving as many dazed commuters, or entropically shrunk into one collapsing shack and one weekender bar along a lonely road a hundred miles from not much.

Our journey is a sentimental one, in short, a search for old-fashioned America in the garage sale of the open highway, a long winding trip into the back roads of the country and a longer one into the hinterland of our own hearts.

LEG

Start

*S*tart: Our little expedition dropped out of the New Orleans airport into a stormy afternoon with dark clouds overhead, bits of rain and splinters of lightning, and then, as we stood around the National Car Rental island in a macadam sea, a sneaker-soaker deluge. We gathered our supplies, including one big teddy bear named George. There was also a white baby seal named Snowy. We had another stuffed bear, whose name I couldn't recall.

"Bayne, what's that bear's name?"

"Bear."

Bear is not a teddy bear, I'm obliged to mention, just a stuffed bear. I had left my own teddy bear back in Boston, where she was working on her book about Herman Melville. We also had three *Archie* comics. We had our own music cassette for the trip, with "Low Rider" and "Sweet Home Alabama," Simon with Garfunkel, Simon without Garfunkel, Beatles, pygmy music, and so on. We had a good skateboard. We had brought, stuffed inside a duffel bag, two tents and other camping supplies. Not to mention three other bags containing clothes, toiletries, and whatnot. And finally we had our guide and arbitrator, our map of maps, our cartographicus magnus: *The American Automobile Association Road Atlas for the United States, Canada, and Mexico.*

We located the right vehicle (dark blue Buick Regal), threw supplies and selves inside, stoked the starter, wipers, and defroster, and (laughing and joking in high spirits) took off out of the airport and over a ground of mist and swamp, an auspicious start in spite of inauspicious weather.

Britt had won the coin toss and so now sat in the front seat, wearing her black T-shirt and Levi's, with the cartographicus magnus spread out on her lap. She was navigator. Bayne lurked somewhere outside the mirror's box in the back seat, wearing his favorite Boston Red Sox baseball cap and Boston Red Sox red shirt and reading an *Archie*. "I'm not going to talk that much," he said, "and I don't want you to talk too much so I can read."

I should confess right here and now that planning is not my strong suit. We would start at Start, of course. Basic principle. But there is more than one way to skin the cat, and at the last second I had thought it might be smart to get to Start by tracing the Natchez Trace in Mississippi. The cartographicus magnus said we could do a right turn at Baton Rouge, follow the Mississippi River up to Vicksburg, and then cross back into Louisiana. From there it would be a straight shot. So I had Britt working on it. Britt was not so certain. "I don't think I'm going to make a good navigator. Wait. Where's 61?"

"You see the curly snake on the map? That's the Mississippi River. We'll reach 61 right before we cross the snake. Just the other side of Baton Rouge."

"Where's Start?"

"Follow the snake up to Vicksburg. See it over to the left? Back in Louisiana?"

Time passed, and then we were crawling in midafternoon traffic at the edge of Baton Rouge. Pretty soon we were crawling over the river, enjoying the view, what we could see — "Look at that one tow boat pushing about twenty barges!" — and then thinking that maybe we had missed 61 to Mississippi. "What's going on here? Britt, I think I may have missed the turnoff for 61!"

"Oh, my God! We're going to Lafayette!"

So much for Plan A.

Soon we were tooling along, listening to Simon and cutting through swamp forest with vines climbing up the trees. It seemed very wild, foresty, green, and swampy, with probably a lot of crocodiles. We were going on a causeway that frequently turned into a road on high stilts, giving the pleasurable sensation of sailing through the forest instead of driving through. We were sailing through the kind of place, as Britt said, where you would expect to see a dinosaur.

We hung a right at Lafayette onto 49, headed for Alexandria. This was all bayou country now, humid with the sky seeming to rise up from the humidity on the ground, struggling out of the primordial ooze at the very bottom of a continent and a continental river.

After getting pathetically lost in Alexandria a couple hours later, we wound up that night at a place called Pineville in a Best Western with cottage cheese ceilings. Next morning, we drove north through one big pine forest, avoiding Dry Prong, passing blithely through Paradise and the Paradise Catfish Kitchen to Interstate 20, where we turned east. And then, before we knew it, we were taking the magic exit marked START.

Bayne wanted to know if Start was in the Southern Hospitality area. I said I thought it was.

We drove north for a mile or two on a small country road past a convenience store gas station and the Crew Lake United Methodist Church of Start, across some railroad tracks where we arrived at a crossroads with another country road. That seemed to be the commencement of Start. I thought we should just drive through town a little and see what it looked like. It looked inauspicious.

The main drag dribbled briefly down with a very small number of businesses, including most prominently a Citgo gas station and U.S. Post Office, and (in a cinderblock building with rectangularized wooden front) Whitten's Barber Shop and Start Flowers and Gifts ("Gifts For All Occasions: We Deliver").

We also noted some kind of a farm-implement business in front of an old cotton gin: a few corrugated metal sheds and some hoppers and various tubes and things. Altogether, the main drag of town was half a block long, but there were houses and a few streets criss-crossing the main road, and so we criss-crossed a bit to check it out further. We found the Start Elementary School.

"I wonder if they have a Head-Start program here," I said. But suddenly we had dropped out of town into a field where upstood an upstart water tower with START on it right next to the Start Fire Station. The water tower had a little guard-dog house at the bottom, apparently to guard the water, but no dog. The Start Fire Station was closed. We knocked on the door, but no one answered. I guessed everyone was out stopping fires.

It was hot. In the field around the water tower and fire station, a zillion cicadas and crickets were making the usual racket, while overhead and down the way two snub-nosed yellow-jacketed crop dusters were buzzing like a couple of giant bees. And on the other side of the fire station a field of corn was quietly growing.

The water tower and fire station were just outside of town, as I said, and so now we drove back in and started back up the main drag until we stopped at Whitten's Barber Shop and Start Flowers and Gifts. We entered the barber shop and discovered it empty. But the barber, Billy Whitten, stood twenty feet away, behind the counter at Start Flowers and Gifts and ready to start serving flowers and gifts, if that was what we wanted. He answered our queries as best he could and, when his own expertise on Start stopped, picked up the phone and called someone named Dolly Sapp.

Back up the highway toward the interstate a short distance, we found Mrs. Fred "Dolly" Sapp: waving and friendly. She wore black shorts, red button earrings, and a white T-shirt with a cartoon portrait of a cow on the front. The cow had black and white spots and was wearing a red bandanna. Dolly's earrings looked to have been made from the same red bandanna. Her lightish brown hair had been recently cut and decently curled on her head. She was a retired schoolteacher, we soon learned, and, like most teachers, she was pleasant and patient. Her attractive face widened with a generous smile.

"Y'all come on in!" she said.

We soon found ourselves sitting in her kitchen in front of soft drinks and snacks and looking from there directly into the living room, which had watermelons ripening on the floor. They looked fresh and just about perfect. The tiling on the kitchen floor looked like Tostito Chips. A lot of plates had been set up on display around the top of the kitchen. There were also ceramic animals of various sorts and some religious hangings. The refrigerator had a welcome mat on the floor in front of it, and on the refrigerator door was a picture of country singer Billy Ray Cyrus with a milk mustache.

"Now, where did you say y'all was from?" she said.

"Massachusetts, near Boston," I said. "We're writing a book about place names. And so we're traveling to places with unusual names and trying to figure out what's the story behind the names."

Well, she said, most of the place names in Louisiana are derived from Indian names, Civil War generals, and things like that. Had we looked at any Louisiana history books? What she was fixing to tell us was that the Louisiana history textbook she used to use in school, when she taught, was superb. The author's last name was Davis, and his first names were — she jogged her memory here by finding the book — Edward Adams. She emphatically recommended that book.

But Start, she continued, hadn't started as Start. Before Start it was something else. It was Charlestown. And as a matter of fact her family had begun in the place long before the start of Start or even of Charlestown. Her dad's family was Robertson, and his mother was a Wynn. But this land we were sitting on was the Mill Sapp Plantation. OK, she decided, probably we needed to go all the way back to when the Illinois Central Company rigged up the railroad track out here. And that was in 1884. The railroad went between Vicksburg, Mississippi, in one direction and Monroe, Louisiana, in the other. Then, in 1898, a man named J. M. Morgan built the first house in Charlestown. He built his house right up close to the railroad track because that's where all of the business was. The old house and everything have been torn down since then, but when we came across the railroad tracks up there did we notice that vacant lot? J. M. Morgan built his store there. His home was there, and there was a store there. It was an old general store. And, she added, she could remember when she was a little kid she could go in there and take a nickel and buy a sack that big of cookies. The cookies were that big around, and it would be completely full, just for a nickel. When she was a little girl all the kids went there, and Mr. Morgan would give them what was called Uncle Sam's kisses. It was like this little banana tacky stuff that you get nowadays. That was some treat, to get those Uncle Sam's kisses.

So Mr. Morgan built a store, and it was attached to his home. And the people from the local communities and the farms would come in and trade with him. They called it a general mercantile store. In 1900 people from Wynn Island, up north of Charlestown, and people from the Robertson settlement, south of Charlestown, would come into the store.

"These were at that time just settlements?"

"Plantations was what they were. Huge, big plantations. And this area right here that we're on, right in here, was called the Mill Sapp Plantation."

"Oh, I see. So this was pre–Civil War, back when these were built?"

"Yes, um hmm."

"They were slave operated?"

"Um hmm. And my granddaddy did not have slaves. The Wynns did not have slaves, so it must have been after."

Most of them had big families to run the plantation. In her grand-daddy's family, there were four brothers. And her grand-daddy had sixteen children. And his brothers had a lot of children as well. So they did their own farming. This was during the 1900s, and their main crop was cotton. Anyhow, she continued, the actual village of Charlestown didn't officially get started until about 1908, when Mr. Charles Tick gave land for the town. Charles Tick. No one wanted to call the place Tickstown, so they called it Charlestown. The main street then is now Highway 133 in front of her house, but when it reached the crossroads near Start Flowers and Gifts there used to be another crossing, but it had an unfortunate hump on it, and eighteen-wheelers would come through and get hung up on the railroad tracks.

Now, after Mr. Morgan built his store, and after Mr. Charles Tick donated the land so that it was Charlestown, then a post office was established at Mr. Morgan's store. But the post office caused all this confusion because at that time there were about sixteen other Charlestowns in Louisiana, so people decided that they would submit some more names and see if they couldn't get it changed. Well, they sent in several names. But the postal bureaucracy would turn them down. They already had this name somewhere. They already had that one someplace else. But Mr. Morgan had a real pretty daughter, and he was so proud of his daughter, he said to her, "I'll just let you name it." And she said, "Well, we're the first people that started the post office here, and we're the first people that started a store here. All right, why don't we just name it Start?" So they sent that name down and told them why. And they accepted that. And so that was how Start got started.

Well, that was very interesting, I thought, but I wanted to know more. "What do you know about the town these days? What's the population of it, for example?"

"I have no idea. It has just grown so much since I was a kid until it's unbelievable, you know."

"Really? It doesn't look very big."

It goes way back on that side over there on the lake, she said, and up above the schoolhouse, all up through there. Well, Dolly Sapp continued, she could remember when her mom and dad first moved here. She could remember Mr. Morgan's store. And they had a post office and a library, and then they had two gins in the community. Cotton gins. They have only one gin now. And the town has two churches. There is the Baptist church on one side of the road and the Methodist church on the other side. When she was a little girl if they had revivals going on at one church, everyone would go there. And whenever they had a revival at the other, everyone would go there. But now they have four churches.

And now they still have a post office and then also two grocery stores and of course the flower shop and the barber shop. They used to have a pharmacy, and someone's about to open an antique shop. Their school now — the high school — has been consolidated out of town, and so Start currently only has kindergarten through eighth grade. But she's been in school in Start all her life. She went to elementary school, and she graduated from high school at Start. And when she graduated from college she came back and taught the third grade one year. Then she taught the seventh grade three years. And then after those four years was over with she taught the eighth grade. And she taught eighth grade for the rest of her time, which was thirty-one whole years.

"You found your niche!" I said.

Oh, she loved that grade. The kids came in the room babies, and they left grown people. They went through such a tremendous change in the eighth grade, and it was always a challenge to her. She loved them. She taught English, reading, spelling, Louisiana history. And what else? When she first started out she taught math. But thank the Lord they got her out of math. But Louisiana history was her favorite. She loved it.

"Well, that's great," I said, "because I have some historical questions." I wanted to hear more about the plantations. And I wondered who lived in the area before it was first cut up into plantations.

Tunica Indians lived in the area at one time, Dolly said. And when she and her husband first moved into this house, her father-in-law farmed the area behind the house, and they used to go out there all the time and pick up arrowheads. She couldn't say how many thousands of arrowheads they'd found over the years. Including tiny bird points. Her son came in one day with a matchbox. He came in, and he said, "Mother, guess how many arrowheads I've got in this matchbox?" She said, "Oh, probably four or five. Why?" He opened the box up and poured them out. And he had thirty-five. That's how tiny they were. And right here on the piece of property we were sitting on was the only land — did we ever read about the 1927 flood? Well, they had a flood, and the Mississippi levy broke and all that water rushed this way. Everything was under water except for this land right here. Even the railroad was under the water. The Mississippi is normally fifty-eight miles away, so that was a big flood. Now, it turns out that they have pretty severe winters in Start, with snow and ice, and so on. And they have some hot summers. They've had summers where it was so hot it cracks. You can stick your fingers down gumbo ground.

Gumbo? What's gumbo? Well, gumbo is a sorry piece of land. It's sticky. When she was a little girl they used to go out into the woods to cut Christmas trees. And her daddy would tell her, "Put your boots on. Don't mess up your shoes because you can't get that gumbo off your shoes." And you'd go into the woods being one height, and you'd come out four inches taller because the gumbo would stick to your boots and things. But in the summertime it gets so dry that that gumbo will crack open. It actually will have big, wide cracks in it. This piece of land right where we were now, she said, was kind of a sandy, clay soil. But down at the edge of her yard is where the gumbo starts. From there on up to the railroad tracks is nothing but gumbo.

"I wonder what gumbo—what causes it," I said. "Whether it's old river silt." Probably, she thought. Because all of that Delta farm area from the Mississippi River back this way is dark like that, too. It's all an old floodplain. It's called the Mississippi Delta. That's why they have such good farmland, because all the good soil is being washed down from the states up north down the Mississippi.

"You're stealing it from Illinois!" I said.

And so it went. We talked a lot more. The Research Assistants and I got very comfortable there, drinking soft drinks, eating snacks, and in general wallowing in all that Southern Hospitality. I'd like to tell you a lot more about all the things we learned while stopping in Start at the Sapp house, but we've barely begun this long journey of ours, so perhaps it's best to terminate this germination right here.

Uncertain

We stayed overnight at a Howard Johnson's just a quarter of an inch above Shreveport. And in the morning, after we checked out (and perhaps I should note en passant that it took a very big screwdriver at the end of a very patient security person to pry us out of that motel in the morning because *someone* managed to lock himself inside the room by twisting the chain lock before putting it in place on the door), our car was pointed west. So west we went into East Texas, a place with trees and lakes and a few roads that eventually took us to where we hoped would be Uncertain.

It wasn't, however, because we had gotten confused by a two-part handlettered sign on Route 43 going north that pointed in two directions at once. The first part said

TURN RIGHT 1/2 MI. *to* UNCERTAIN

THISIT $\longrightarrow$

while the second part, right below the first, said, in bigger letters

UNCERTAIN INN

$\longleftarrow$

See what I mean?

We stopped to think for a few minutes, imagining at least two possibilities. The Research Staff voted for the first. I voted for the second. My vote won, and so we turned back onto the crossroads and drove down that old country road for two miles until I was certain it wasn't Uncertain though we did shake out an alternative, a four-corners called Karnack, which had a beautiful little cafe in an ancient building, a fire department, and, behind a couple of broken-down gasoline pumps, a store that sold Elvis dolls and Bowie knives. Inside the store a friendly lady said we weren't in Uncertain, but she gave directions that took us through a piney woods to a sign that said WELCOME TO UNCERTAIN, TEXAS.

To the right of this sign stood a welcoming team of about twenty cows and a couple of horses. Just a few yards farther was the Uncertain Caddo Lake Church, which, so we could read, was a nondenominational church of love and forgiveness. A portable rental sign in front of the church added the further information that

GOD

IS   SO

GOOD.

Right down the road from the church, on the left, a brownish shed of a building was situated with a big yellow sign mounted on a post out front that declared it to be the New Rocket Club, with the word "Rocket" hitching a ride on the side of a rocket.

That seemed to be the Uncertain outskirts, and, moving into the Uncertain inskirts, we passed a few bungalow-style houses, the Uncertain Inn (a small motel made out of logs), and then came into what was probably the Uncertain center, which included a big shed called the Motor Supply Warehouse Headquarters for AC Delco Products and, at the town's single significant intersection, a smaller shed called Uncertain City Hall. No one was home at the Uncertain City Hall. Nor was anyone home at a metal fortress a little farther down the road called The Fishhook Beer Wine and Liquor. We turned down the intersecting road and arrived finally at the Bayou Landing Restaurant and the Caddo Grocery.

The Bayou Landing Restaurant drooped down toward a landing at what seemed like a very scummy little pond with a lot of frog playground equipment on it. The restaurant was closed. But the Caddo Grocery, right next door, looked open, and we pulled into the lot. The Caddo Grocery was a plywood building with big windows, a bench on a porch, and some hummingbird feeders above the bench. There was also a public thermometer out front with a color code and a needle that ran into the very red, which would explain why we were sweating and felt just about suffocated right about then.

Inside the grocery we bought some snacks and bumped into a middle-aged man with a beard who said his name was David Applebaum and offered to give us a boat tour of the pond, which he called a lake. Caddo Lake. And he told us in no uncertain terms how Uncertain got its name. Uncertain was incorporated around about the 1950s, he said, and the man who was doing all the legwork was voted in as mayor. He was going to put a liquor store in, and maybe that was why he wanted to incorporate Uncertain, so it could counteract the county, which was dry. So he did everything legally. He got together a city council, secretary, and treasurer. But then the lady filling out the paperwork came down to where they were supposed to write down the name of the town, and no one had figured out the name yet. She could have left it blank. She could have written *Don't know* or whatever, but she happened to write *Uncertain*. And so that's how Uncertain got its name. "And," David Applebaum concluded emphatically, "that's definitely a fact."

It was too hot, he went on, to take a boat out on the lake right then. Also, he was about to go home and have lunch, so we would have to wait until about 2:30 if we wanted a boat tour. Meanwhile, he had to go.

In short, we had about two hours to kill, and so we got in the car and drove farther down the road and discovered that there is more to Uncertain than first meets the eye. Several casual little roads had been tossed off the main road, and many small vacation cottages were lurking here and there, plus a couple of pretentious houses, a few marinas and lodges, and so on, all tucked away behind trees and bushes and Spanish moss. There was certainly a lot of Spanish moss.

Soon it was about time for our boat tour with David Applebaum. When we got back to Caddo Grocery, however, David had been replaced by his son, Aaron, a strong-jawed young man wearing a Miami Dolphins T-shirt, dark green shorts, and sandals, who took us down to a dock and boat at the edge of the pond called Caddo Lake.

Soon we had climbed into the boat and were putt-putting through a long thin arm of swampy water. "This is the Big Cypress Bayou right here," Aaron said, "which is the main channel that feeds Caddo Lake. It is considered Caddo Lake, but it's only about fifteen feet deep in the main channel. And this main channel is what feeds these shallow-water deltas that we're coming into now. And back here it's only about three feet deep. And the average depth of the whole lake, one hundred fifty thousand acres of it, is three feet. That's kind of what sets it apart from most other lakes."

"So it's a real bayou."

"Very much, very much so. All this was created by some earthquakes in 1811." They were called the New Madrid quakes, Aaron went on, and in fact we were right now motoring the boat across the New Madrid fault line, which runs up through St. Louis. The New Madrid quakes of 1811 were some of the largest quakes recorded in history in this country, and they created voids in this part of the country and the low lying areas. It happened in 1811—"Look over there!" he said, interrupting himself. "That's a yellow-crowned night heron. And I bet you'll see some blue herons, too."

I thought I saw one already. "Hey, kids, look at the blue heron over there!" I said.

"No, actually, that is a wood stork. You'll see when he opens his wings he'll be black and white. If you can get him flying it would be a neat picture. Because they are on the endangered species list. There he goes. See his wings?"

So we watched the wood stork flying away. We looked for blue herons, saw a lot of strange and beautiful long-legged birds that weren't blue herons, and slowly grazed a maze of waterways and twisty cypress trees draped in Spanish moss, moving deeper and deeper into a swamp or lake that seemed more a dream than a body of water.

Spanish moss, Aaron told us, is a parasitic organism that lives off the trees. To me the trees and Spanish moss looked like ghosts in the distance and closer up looked like Miss Havisham's wedding cake after the spiders had worked it over for a few years. But the Caddo Indians thought the moss represented tears from the crying of their people after the earthquake happened and the rising water level forced them out of the basin. Basically overnight, the basin got flooded with water because of land subsidence—and then about thirty years later it got even more flooded because of what people used to call the Great Raft, which was a natural log jam on the Red River. Because of the Great Raft, as a matter of fact, Jefferson, Texas, became until approximately 1872 the largest inland port in America. So, anyway, before the 1811 earthquake, Aaron summarized, the Caddo basin had been basically a low-land collection area of water and mud, but there wasn't water in there full-time. Then the earthquake came, and then the Great Raft came, backed water in there for years and years. It was navigated by the steamships. Then Shreveport blew up the Raft, and the water drained back out. And then in about 1911 somebody put in a low earth dam and spillway that now maintains the Caddo water at 168.5 feet above sea level. Without that it would just be a mudland.

"It's beautiful. It's like a little Everglades," I said.

Aaron nodded his head in agreement—and kept on driving our little expedition farther and farther into pea soup and floating salad. The green film we were seeing in the water was duckweed, Aaron said, the smallest living plant in North America. It is a simple parasite. This time of year it begins to die off and turn that auburn color, he said. Because of all the vegetation, this was oxygen-poor water, and yet Caddo has a lot of fish. But in the winter months, all the lilies and the water hyacinth and the moss all die off. They deteriorate. So in November, this water will be relatively clear compared to what it is now. It won't be navigable, because there are still a lot of stumps out here. You've got to follow the channels that the Corps of Engineers have dredged and put in here. But an interesting thing about Caddo is through the seasons it takes on so many different appearances. And these cypress trees—

"Kids, check this bird out," I said, interrupting. "That's a blue heron, right? Well, it just disappeared into the trees."

As Aaron was saying, in the fall when the temperature begins to drop, the cypress trees will turn a burnt-orange color which is really pretty. In the winter they'll completely defoliate, and the lake takes on a real gray and dismal appearance. You can take a photograph here now, and take one in November, and take one in February, and it is like three different parts of the country. But yet lately there's been an influx in the last three or four years of jet skis. More and more, every summer there seems to be more and more jet skis. Last summer they were showing a lot of people alligators on a regular basis, but now because these jet skis kept running up and down these channels and in these back waters, the alligators have gone back farther into the swamp.

Now as for how Uncertain got its name, back when there was river-boat traffic coming up the Caddo basin into Jefferson through the Big Cyprus Bayou, there was a lot of uncertainty because a lot of the channels would split and fork. And there were three or four places between Shreveport and Jefferson where the channels split into three. A lot of the water was uncharted, and in the bend in the Big Cyprus Bayou—where we got on the boat—that area was labeled Uncertain because the Big Cyprus Bayou splits really into three places there. So river pilots were sometimes uncertain which way to go: left, right or straight to Jefferson. So that got transferred on the maps. That was one theory. A second theory was that in the early '50s when the people in the community wanted to form a town, they were uncertain as to what to name the town, so they put *uncertain* on the application, and it got processed into Uncertain.

I suggested that an easy way to find out which story was true would be to find a map made before, say, 1950, and see if the name existed before then.

That was a pretty good deal, Aaron thought, but unfortunately there really is no governing agency that's collected the history and artifacts and sort of organized the history of Uncertain. But in any case probably the most accepted theory is the latter.

Aaron was born in Texas, and he lived there until he was fifteen years old. Finished his freshman year of high school and then moved to New York City and lived with his mother. His parents had divorced. She had remarried at the time and moved up there. And so from '86 to '89 he lived in Manhattan and went to school in Manhattan, always coming back down to Caddo Lake for his summers. Then he went to school down in Texas and after graduation worked for two years and then got involved in working on a congressional campaign. And after the election in November, when his candidate wins, he is going to Washington to be on the candidate's staff. But he had been down to Lake Caddo for the last twenty-five years, seen it go through all these stages, and it never ceased to amaze him how much this lake changes from month to month, from season to season.

The Applebaums were one of about three Jewish families in Marshall, Texas, Aaron went on, and his family used to be in the scrap metal business. They had a big salvage yard. His great-grandfather started the business in 1905. And his grandfather really built it into the machine and salvaging processing plant that in the late '70s made the family a real good living in East Texas. Then the early '80s came with the oil crisis, and the market went kaplooey. Basically there was so much industry around the area that thrived on the oil industry. They got a lot of salvaged scrap iron from the oil works, and basically everybody in the area had put all their eggs in the oil market. So the Applebaums went out of business in 1984. The scrap metal business did not actually go under, but his grandfather died in '81, and then with that and the bad oil prices the price of iron and steel just went phtook. It used to be that the scrap iron took care of the payroll and maintenance, but the good money was in copper. But the whole scrap metal market went berserk, and basically it was no longer a good business, and his dad was ready to get out.

"Check out the duck flying! Is that a duck? That's a nice little house over there."

We had come into an area of the swamp where a number of duck blinds had been constructed. They looked like small houses on little islands, and a lot of them, Aaron said, had heaters in them. Anyhow, he continued, before his father got involved in running boat tours on the lake, there was a lady down here. She was retired from the army, a sergeant. She was known as Sarge around the lake. And she had a barge that she took people out on for a while. And Aaron's father saw that tourism was increasingly getting better down here. Caddo was no longer a secret. And as they were getting out of the scrap business, he was looking for something else to do, to make an income from something that he enjoyed. So this is what he chose.

We came into a pretty part of the swamp. "This is a pretty part," Aaron said. "This is called Goose Prairie."

In the water all around us waved a sea of giant lily pads shaped like umbrellas, waving about a foot above the water. The water was very thick there with a cuprous oxide green and a creamy surface, but where the surface cleared a little, you could peer down into smoky water with a dark, mossy bottom.

We found a great white egret frozen in stance like a statue, hiding, half obscured by trees and moss and leaves, looking at us looking at him looking at us looking at him, scared and tentative, as still and fragile as a brushed pictograph.

Then we came into a straight part of the swamp. It was called Star Ditch, we learned, named after a riverboat captain, Captain Star, who got confused and off course en route to Jefferson. He got stuck on the wrong side of the bayou, and the water level was such that the boat couldn't double back. And history has it that the one straight channel through there, about three or four hundred yards long, was hand-dug by the slave labor on the boat in order to float it back over to something that may or may not have been Uncertain, depending upon whether or not Uncertain was there when Captain Star was.

Cut and Shoot

Route 59 pointed like a double-barreled shotgun right down to the heart of Houston, and we were blasting down one of the barrels. We were passing fields full of multicolored cows, several of them relaxing in a cow lounge beneath a low-hanging tree, and then a flea market, some peaches for sale, carpets, collectibles, gasoline, and a poor tortoise who was desperately trying to cross the highway. As far as I could see in my rearview mirror, he did. I hope he made it, but it didn't look like a safe

19

place for a tortoise to cross. Then Route 59 became a corridor through woods, and the sky overhead opened up full of gray convoluted clouds, like brains.

We found Route 105 and right at the intersection found a place called Security. Security seemed safe but boring, and so we continued west on 105. We came to a big, empty flea market and a Texaco station and Donut Palace. Birds' nests were half-dangling off the edges of convenient ledges in the E and A of TEXACO, and bars protected all the windows of the Donut Palace. A lady at the counter inside the Palace said Cut and Shoot would be about a mile and a half down. "But don't blink." About five miles later, we came to a sign that said

CUT & SHOOT
CITY LIMIT
POP 903.

"City limit" was optimistic. There wasn't really a city or, as far as I could tell, a limit either. There was not a lot to Cut and Shoot. But we did come upon a few buildings and some signs, and pretty soon we had arrived at a white metal shed with blue trim, decorated on the panel between two roll-up doors with a cartoon image of a Yosemite Sam sort of person with red hair and a red hat, cutting quite a figure and shooting water out of a hose. On top of Yosemite Sam, we saw the legend CUT-N-SHOOT. And beneath his boots: VOLUNTEER FIRE DEPARTMENT.

In front of this shed a police car was parked, and in front of the car stood a tall and handsome young man in uniform, with dark trim hair on his head and a trim dark mustache on his lip, who was also cutting quite a figure and shooting water out of a hose. The water was being shot onto the car. A star had been painted on the door of the car, and another star, we soon saw, had been pinned over this man's left chest. Just as we began turning in, he was turning off the water. He turned out to be a very friendly man who had lived in Cut and Shoot since he was four years old—and currently, as Marshall, embodied the town's entire professional police force. His name was Ivey.

We asked Marshall Ivey how Cut and Shoot got its name. He must have been asked this question before but still wasn't entirely clear on the details— except for the fact that back in the 1800s or so, two different church congregations were trying to share the same church building, and they ended up having a squabble about whose turn it was to use the place. Everybody got their guns and knives and converged on the place one Sunday morning, intending to sort the matter out. Then one of the kids from one of the congregations, supposedly, said something about *cut and shoot,* and that's essentially how the town got its name. It was actually incorporated in 1969, Marshall Ivey continued, and made a city. "That's the town hall right over there," he said, indicating a small building just down the road.

Marshall Ivey went on to tell us that Cut and Shoot used to be a pretty rough little spot. Used to be lot of beer joints there until, oh, about ten years ago, he said. There was about six at one time. Most of them closed up, various reasons. Stuff like that. It used to be a pretty wild little place.

"I see. So it lived up to its name," I said.

It lived up to its name, he confirmed. But now, he continued, there are only about two bars left. One of them's just kind of a quiet little place, where you can get something to eat and stuff. The other place, called the Longhorn Barroom, is a little different. It used to be wild. Marshall Ivey said "wild" the way it should be said, with a melting slab of butter on the vowel: "waaaalld." He could remember when he was a kid. Something he first remembers, when he was probably four five years old, the town had real beer joints. Real seedy places that were real waaaalld.

"The kind of places where you wouldn't want to say the wrong thing?" I asked.

"No, more like some of 'em you didn't even wanta *be* in."

But now, he went on, Cut and Shoot is more just your average community. Why is it quieter now? He couldn't rightly say. Maybe because they have a law now that you can't sell hard liquor inside the city. Since the city started in '69. And that helps a little. You keep the hard liquor out, people have to bring it in. Most people don't want to have to bring something in. But still, Cut and Shoot was wild up until about '82 or '83. But not real *real* wild. Bar fights, mostly. It was never bad like New York City.

Well, that was reassuring if a little disappointing, and we thanked Marshall Ivey for talking to us and then traveled on down the road to see if we could learn anything else about Cut and Shoot. Down the road we soon passed a few buildings and houses, a long shed housing the Tropical Illusions Tan and Nails—and then we came upon an L-shaped building, small and simple, made out of wood and painted red, with two porches and two entrances. One porch and entrance led, according to the signs, into Linda's Gift and Gab, where a person could buy Texas souvenirs and gifts as well as, presumably, gab with Linda, who may or may not have been represented by the plywood effigy of a tough-looking pioneer woman, hands on hips, dressed in pioneer finery, who helped hold up the Gift and Gab porch roof with her head. The other porch and entrance led, so we could read, to the Cut 'n' Shoot Texas Post Office 77303.

First we went into Linda's Gift and Gab, hoping to gab with Linda and maybe get some nice gifts at the same time. I could hear Linda's voice in the back of the shop, but the voice seemed busy so we walked out. "Baaaa!" Linda called after us as we left.

Then we walked around to the other end of the building and moseyed into the Cut 'n' Shoot Post Office. Through a double-squeak door we entered a narrow, low corridor that seemed more like a tunnel, with mail boxes on one side and missing kids' pictures on the other, and then were greeted with a "Heidi!" from the same voice that had just said "Baaaa!" at the Gift and Gab. It was Linda all over again. Linda Starkey was her full name, and she was the town postmistress, sitting in what I now realized was a neutral junction between the two businesses, from our current perspective occupying a low and confining post office window that seemed more like the entrance to a cave than an office.

Linda had the gift of gab, I'll say that much, and it was a gift possessed by one of the world's nicest people. She smiled like a pumpkin and turned out to be as genuine and open hearted as a puppy. She had a tattoo on her left wrist: broken chain and an escaping butterfly. She wore a blue T-shirt, cut off at the neck and arms for comfort, that included across the front a Girl Scout insignia and the legend *Camp Time Warp*. Every once in a while the phone would ring, and she would pick it up and answer with a musical cheer: "Cut-n-Shoot Post Office!" And then every once in a while more someone would come in, introduced by the double squeak of the door opening then closing, amble down the tunnel, and she would stop talking to us long enough to sell stamps, answer queries, and in general be as helpful and pleasant as anyone could be.

"How many stamps?" she would say.

"Couple dollars' worth."

"There you go, thank you," she would say, leafing out some green and then silver change. "I guess you want ya stamps, too!" she would add, passing over the stamps. Then: "Baaaa, Pat."

"Baaaa. You have a good'n!"

"You too, dear!"

And then the door would double squeak its finish to the transaction.

Postmistress Starkey was able to give us the town history a little more particularly than Marshall Ivey had. The place was named in 1912, she said. There used to be two churches, one Baptist and the other Methodist, and the community had one building that they all used. And then one Sunday they were going to have a service. This Sunday the Methodists thought it was their turn, and the Baptists thought it was theirs. Some of them said, "Well, this is our week," and the other ones said, "No, it's ours," and so they came into town with their guns wrapped up in their blankets and their knives—Linda Starkey said "knives" the way Marshall Ivey said "wild"—their *knaaaves* wrapped up in their blankets, and they were ready for any kinda confrontation that they might have to get their legal week in. And there was a young boy that got real upset, and he got scared, and he said, "Imo *cut* around the corner and *shoot* through the bushes!" And that's how the town got its name. There was no actual shooting or fighting. At that time. But later there used to be a lot of bars in Cut and Shoot, and there used to be fights in the bars and stuff. That reinforced the name. And then the town really got on the map by having a boxer, Roy Harris.

At this point she stopped to retrieve from one of her many nooks the autographed picture of a fierce-looking young man with bony face and heavy eyebrows, stripped down to fight in a ring: bare chested, bare knuckled, and poised to cut with one fist and shoot with the other. Mr. Harris was a heavyweight contender, she said. And as a matter of fact his nephew, to this day, fights in boxing. And as a double matter of fact, Roy Harris was one of the reasons that the Cut and Shoot Post Office was established, because they needed somewhere to send all his mail.

"All his mail!" I said, amazed.

Yes, all his mail. So he kind of put Cut and Shoot on the map as far as that goes. He still lives in Cut and Shoot, having just retired from being a lawyer. He took the money that he got from boxing and, as he said, made a much wiser choice: went to law school and became an attorney. So, in summary, the town has quite a lot of history behind it, and the postmaster—or rather, the man who owns this building and employs her as postmistress—he is usually gone during the summer, but he has elephants and camels and stuff like this for circuses, and he travels through the year. Well, he's got three elephants. He's got an African, an Asian, and she couldn't think of what the other one is. Maybe a mix, she thought.

But the significant point is that he goes around to all the little circuses and all the different type things and performs. He does the elephants, and then one of his sons works on another elephant, and then his wife helps him with the camels, and then they have llamas. It seemed like they have something else. Linda didn't think they had a giraffe any longer. But a lot of times they do the festivals, and when he comes back to Texas for the winter he'll let his elephants—because he just lives right over there—he'll let his elephants right over here out to graze. Oh, when he does that you can just hear tires just squeal when people stop, and they have to back up to see if they really saw what they had seen.

Humble

We went back down the double-barreled highway, Route 59 south, which soon added to its original four another couple of lanes on either side. The cartographicus magnus said we were driving toward Houston, and although there was still no sign of the city itself, we were certainly entering an urban outer ring of junk and commerce, all prettified and waving at our little eyes with hundreds of clotheslines full of flags and banners—advertising cars and trucks and RVs, custom houses and steak houses.

But the cartographicus had suggested we would soon stumble across Humble, and I thought it might be an excellent place to eat some pie.

But the traffic got thicker and thicker. Pretty soon we came into a Martian village, a great wilderness of bright signs and letters on big posts sticking out in front of our eyes, and I tried to keep my eyes on the highway and sneak looks at the cartographicus at the same time. Had we tumbled up to Humble yet? It never did become apparent. Meanwhile, everything was starting to look bigger and bigger. We were coming into a giant land with giant high tension lines crossing the highway, giant construction projects going on to make the highway even bigger, and giant posts with vast domes of lights of top. We passed the sign for

EAST TEX GUN RANGE.
CONCEALED LICENSE.
LICENSE PHOTOS PRINTS NOTARY $89.

And I believe by then we must have fumbled right past Humble, because Route 59 suddenly turned into something egotistical and terrifying, a whole spaghetti-way of ups and downs and ins and outs and constant highway construction, an M. C. Escher maze into which we were ingested and passed through—pretty soon sighting spread out before us a wall of giant buildings against the skyline: proud and turgid erections filled with twenty thousand big men in ten-gallon hats doing megamillion dollar deals. Houston! The road had gone from four to six to eight to who knows how many lanes, and now the drivers took advantage of every extra inch they could locate. "Yikes! Crazy driver! What was his license number? Get his license number! I'll put it in the book!"

Britt: "I didn't see. He came through on the right."

"He went too fast for us to even get his license number. I swear I'll put it in the book if I ever find it," I said, and, intending momentarily to make good my threat, I pressed down on the gas, but by then he had already disappeared. And so, with the highways crissing and crossing and me fussing and cussing, our little expedition rumbled from Humble to proud to terrifying, and old Highway 59 became like a python swallowing a very big pig.

Noodle

Four or five days later, on a Sunday morning after some major rest and relaxation in San Antonio at Aunt Bea and Cousin Leslie's house, we hit the road for Noodle. Interstate 10, the cartographicus magnus said, would take us all the way up to a junction with Route 83, which we could then climb up all the way to Abilene and from there to Noodle. The junction would be easy to locate because it was called Junction.

We found Junction junction around noon. A small restaurant was situated right there, called according to the sign on its roof Junction Restaurant, and we pulled into the parking lot of the Junction junction Junction Restaurant restaurant and went inside. It was a Truckers and Bikers Welcome place, and they had good chicken noodle soup.

With noodles in the belly, we put Noodle on the noodle, and nodded north along the old macadam fetuccinus, Route 83, turned up the burner all the way, and sizzled into a tasty pasty sauce of rock and desiccated grass, diced scrub, and chopped cactus. Every once in a while we could see a tin-bladed windmill out back in the scrub, which suggested somebody was pumping water for some purpose, and then we would see wooden posts and wire fencing along the road, which suggested that someone was demarcating land for some purpose, perhaps the same one.

On our way out of Eden, with twenty-one miles to Paint Rock, Bayne (who was sitting in the front seat that day) had an idea for a perpetual motion machine. You take a windmill and put it inside a house and wire it up to an outlet in the house, so it generates energy into the outlet, and then you take an indoor fan and hook it up to an outlet near the windmill and put it on full blast and fan it into the windmill, and so that's what makes the windmill go. It would be like electricity making electricity, and it would be going in circles.

Except, I thought, the problem with all perpetual motion machines is that in the process of the machine working you lose energy because you're creating friction, and that means that the amount of wind energy produced by the fan will not be enough to move the windmill to return same amount of electrical energy back to the fan.

Bayne: "So you grease the windmill a little."

But the land we were driving through seemed like its own perpetual motion machine. We dipped into a valley, crossed Hog Creek, which looked like a dry little gulch, and there was Paint Rock, population 227, with a few wooden houses and a few planted trees, and a beautiful stone building that looked like a bank but also looked closed. Paint Rock seemed just about as small as a town can get and still exist. We crossed Brushy Creek and Fuzzy Creek, and turned into wide-open grasslands, with some cattle grazing on the grass.

Bayne said, "I wouldn't like to be a bug."

"Why wouldn't you like to be a bug?"

"Because your whole life is based on making more bugs and just like eating and sweating and stuff."

"Sweating?"

"Splattering."

"Splattering? What made you think of that, Bayne?"

I know that these little conversations in the front seat aren't seeming to bring us any closer to our destination in this chapter, which is Noodle, but remember this: A watched pot never boils.

Well, it was a long long long drive. And if Noodle turned out to be underdone, we were thinking, we might just try going all the way to Goodnight where maybe we could find a good place to spend the night. Meanwhile, we mowed right past Lawn but did pause at an ovalish spot called Ovalo, which consisted of two small and declining buildings that may have been abandoned but in any case also served, so the hand lettering on the side of one building informed us, as a meeting place for the Cowboys for Christ Bluff Creek Chapter.

Eventually we ran into the bottom of Abilene, ran out, turned west, took the exit for Route 126, and—presto pesto—saw a sign that noted NOODLE 11.

That was a good sign, I thought, because if a place is marked at eleven miles that means it is significant. Our plan had been to eat noodles at Noodle, but that depended upon the existence of an eatery, and all the signs now (Noodle 8, Noodle 5) seemed to promise that the place might be big enough to have one. We traveled along a flat road with some oil-pumping birds in the fields on either side, and then the land opened up onto a great vista of furrowed farm field. When, according to the odometer, we were two miles from Noodle, we came to the Noodle Church of Christ: pink stucco, very small, and without a steeple. We came to several farm buildings, some farm equipment, and an old refrigerator just to one side of a crossroads.

That crossroads was Noodle center, it became apparent. Down one way we could see a cluster of modest houses, and down another we saw an old school bus, an old cotton gin, some old cotton trailers, and a beautiful old brick building that seemed absolutely abandoned. The building was a junkyard now, with broken windows, weeds growing high, grasshoppers popping up in the weeds, plus about thirty junked cars and an old motorcycle. In the brick at the arched portico of this edifice was written the sad legend: Cross Roads High School 1929. Next to the high school stood a cinderblock building that had been painted an alfredo cream. A hand-lettered sign out front said it was the Noodle Community Center.

Just down the way we found a burned-out and abandoned house with weeds in front, and to one side a tiny windmill losing its blades and a single forlorn tree. Right across the road from that we discovered a small white building with peeling paint that announced itself to be the Noodle Baptist Church.

So that, in short, was Noodle: a little stretch of road with the Noodle Church of Christ on one end, the Noodle Baptist Church on the other, and nothing much in between.

Certainly we were not going to find any noodles in Noodle, because there was no restaurant. In fact, I began to think it was a ghost town, and we stood there in front of the church, listened to the wind rattling in our ears, and saw in the distance a stretch of land going on for miles and miles until it finally ended at a gigantic wall of clouds. But a closer look at the Noodle Baptist Church revealed the following signs of life: curtains, a trash can out front, and inside (peeking past a curtain's edge) a well-furnished nursery. Plus a sign on the door that said: "Please excuse us. We are preparing to paint." So that was a good sign. But were there actually people living in Noodle?

Driving back the other direction and down the crossed road at the crossroads, we found more abandoned houses, another junkyard of cars, and a house that didn't look abandoned. It had three barking dogs out front and an old man inside who didn't know a thing about a thing. At last we found a small house with a couple of cows in the yard, a friendly dog, and someone inside who came to the door. He was wearing cowboy boots, a cowboy shirt, and he had cowboy skin. He told us to go find Harold Sloan who lived down the road just about three miles outside of town in a brick house and would know the story of Noodle. If we hurried, we might catch Mr. Sloan before he left for church.

Harold Sloan wasn't home, however. He must have already left for church. And having been disappointed by the nonappearance of Mr. Sloan, we turned our burner down to simmer and headed back toward town, feeling disappointed and thinking it was getting late. But just as we got back to the edge of town, we spied a woman standing in front of the Noodle Baptist Church. She said she was the wife of the Noodle Baptist Church preacher, and she was just opening up the building for the Sunday evening service. When I began asking her questions about the town, though, she deferred to her husband, who had walked up and whose name was Matthew Van Hook.

Pastor Van Hook looked as much poet as preacher. He was distinctly young and he wore Levi's, a forest-green shirt, and round wire-rimmed glasses. He had a trimmed mustache and goatee, an open and slightly roundish face, and a soft-spoken and pleasant manner. He was about to start the evening church service, he affirmed, and we were certainly welcome to attend, but he still had time to talk to us because people were still coming in. Indeed, as we stood in front of the little church and chatted, cars were pulling into the grass and gravel along the road, and people were getting out, saying "hello" to each other and the pastor, and filing in the front door of the church.

"The pastor that was here before me, he was a historian," Matthew Van Hook began. "He did research. And he told me that Noodle doesn't stand for, like, noodle pasta."

Well, that was disappointing—if predictable. *Who, after all,* I suddenly thought, *would name their town after a transient object of Italian gustation?*

But, he said, the way people in Noodle keep up with each other is—that old white refrigerator at the crossroads—had we seen it?—that's where the people pick up their newspapers. And so when anybody wants to deliver a message or to let people know about something going on in Noodle, they put a little sign on that refrigerator to be read when people picked up their newspapers. And so that refrigerator is the Noodle center. Well, they do have a real Community Center, but he hadn't seen anybody use it very much. So these days Noodle sort of revolves around the two churches and the refrigerator. As for the farming, other people could tell us much better than he could, since he isn't a farmer, but the crops around here are cotton, maize, and down the road some emus and ostriches. For meat and boots and eggs.

He said he was pastor of the church at the moment and there are about twenty-five members of the congregation. The Church of Christ at the other end of town was about the same size, he supposed, though he'd never been in it. He had only lived in the area a couple years, so he wouldn't know everything there was to know. In fact, he went on, a lot of the members of the church don't live in Noodle. So the congregation is kind of scattered out because in this area the farms are getting larger as people are having to farm more to make the same amount of money. But in any case, he had to go now because (after a long tall cowboy with light-sensitive glasses parked a truck and empty cattle trailer into the grass next to the church) most of the congregation had arrived. It was nice talking to us, he concluded, and if we sat through the service, which we were welcome to do or not, as we chose, we could meet some of the congregation afterwards who might be able to tell us more about Noodle.

An organ was starting up inside, wavery music was drifting outside, and so I conferred with the Research Assistants. "Want to stay for church?"

I should say right here and now that churches usually make me uncomfortable and melancholic, as do preachers. Yes, I am your typical backslider. But then Matthew Van Hook seemed a little different from your typical preacher. Well, it was seven o'clock. The sun was getting lower in the sky, making its final yellow burst before turning in for the night. It was way past pasta time, and we (having foolishly saved our appetites for a mirage) were hungry. We were tired. And where were we going to spend the night? But didn't we need to get to the bottom of Noodle?

Like its exterior, the interior of the Noodle Baptist Church was plain and simple, with four rectangular windows on either side, no stained glass, and two banks of about eight pews separated by a central aisle leading to a small pedestal holding a big Bible. Behind the Bible stood the preacher at his own podium next to a television set hooked up to a video machine.

We started out with a pledge of allegiance to the flag of the United States. The words popped up onto the video screen. Then we went on to a pledge of allegiance to the Christian flag. The words appeared on the video screen. Then after that we pledged allegiance to the Bible. Those words appeared on the screen as well.

Then we had a prayer, sang some songs, and gave out the Vacation Bible School awards, and after all that the pastor gave his little sermon. Pastor Van Hook read from the Bible about where a lot of people were bringing their little children to Jesus, but his disciples tried to turn the children away, thinking that

Jesus was tired. But Jesus saw what was going on, and he said, "Suffer the little children to come unto me." And he said, "I tell you the truth: Anyone who does not receive the Kingdom of God as a child will never enter." And he took the children in his arms and blessed them. Now, the preacher went on, to understand what was so unusual about what Jesus said, we have to remember the time that he lived in. In the first century, children were looked upon as powerless possessions of their parents and of society. And so when Jesus said that no one can enter the kingdom of heaven unless they came as a child, that would be shocking to these people. And the disciples thought that Jesus couldn't be bothered with little children. But Jesus was talking to us about children. And he was saying that God loves little children. So what was it about children? Well, the first thing we have to remember is that children are powerless. What can a child accomplish over an adult? Not very much. And so the first thing that a child learns from adults is that adults are powerful and they, the children, are powerless. And the first thing adults can learn from children is that we should be humble, because outside of God's grace we are powerless, too.

A baby started crying right about here — but Pastor Van Hook didn't miss a beat. There's another very important characteristic of children, he went on, that had to do with what Jesus was talking about. Children have a simple trust and innocence. Jesus was not saying here that we should be gullible, ignorant people. But that we should know that God loves us enough to trust Him even when it doesn't seem right. And even when we're going through pain and suffering, because God loves us. . . .

Well, in spite of being a backslider, I found the sermon compelling. And after the sermon, there was a social time of Kool-Aid and cupcakes and so on, offered to the congregation at large and any visitors. And so we three as politely as possible stuffed ourselves with cake and cookies and so on, shook hands, said hello, and in general explained to various members of the congregation the principles of Storyville and why we had come all the way to Noodle. And people were truly and genuinely nice. We had driven all day into what seemed like an alien and difficult land of cactus, rock, and windmills, and had become strangers and wanderers and outcasts, and now we were being comforted and blessed by the generosity and kindness of a community. This whole thing made me appreciate in a fundamental way the function of a little country church.

About the only person we didn't talk to was the long tall cowboy with the light-sensitive glasses, who had been sitting by himself at the back during the service. He stood around eating cookies at the social time, but while everyone else seemed relaxed and gregarious, he looked just a little unpolished and remote. After half the congregation had left and driven away, Pastor Van Hook took us aside and introduced us to the cowboy. As soon as I shook his hand, though, I realized that "cowboy" might be an inaccurate and slightly disrespectful description.

He was a rancher by the name of—the pastor had just said it, but, dazed by too many recent introductions, I instantly forgot.

He was wearing those light-sensitive glasses. He had a long face. He was very tall, though I couldn't tell exactly how tall because a pair of high-heeled cowboy boots raised him up at one end while a high-crowned Stetson hat elevated him further at the other. He wore faded Levi's and a pearl-snapped Western shirt. He seemed modest, self-contained, and full of a quiet authority, and if I were looking for someone to play the Marlboro man, the only reason I wouldn't select him would be that he seemed too authentic. Also, I don't think he smoked. Anyhow, he thought he might have some ideas about good places to go see on our Storyville trip, and so we all ambled out of the church and over to our car, laid the cartographicus magnus out onto the hood, flipped it open to Texas, and began looking over things.

"Y'all are right about here," the man said, putting his finger on Noodle — which suddenly seemed really far away from anything.

"Where are we? Ah, way down there!"

"Yeah. So, the best way to go into Oklahoma is up through Wichita Falls. It's just a hundred forty-something miles."

"See, I was thinking of going maybe to Goodnight, Texas," I said.

Well, Goodnight would still be a very long way, he said. And there was not much there. Just vacant buildings. In fact, there was not a lot of anything anywhere out in that part of Texas. Goodnight was named after Charles Goodnight, he said. And I thought: *Not even a Storyville!* So then we traced the best route out of Texas, which would be through Wichita Falls. Then we flipped through the pages of the cartographicus until we found Oklahoma, and I showed him our intended route. We spotted the town of Loco, in Oklahoma, which I was thinking could be one of our destinations.

"Why, I've got a friend that lives at Loco!" he said. "Yeah. Look up a guy named Boyd."

"OK. And what's your name?"

"Glen Sandusky," he said. It's a Polish name, he explained. The name started out Sedowski, and the family started out with a person who came over in 1672. He came to Jamestown. In Pennsylvania. And if we ever got up through there, we should take a look at the statue of Anthony Sedowski at Sedowski State Park. And anyway, so he, Glen Sandusky, was a rancher. Yep. He has about three hundred fifty head of cattle, and his son lives on a ranch about fourteen miles away. Together they have, oh, about eighty-seven hundred acres, which might be considered pretty good sized if the cow market got better.

Well, back to the cartographicus. There was Bromide, Oklahoma, where Glen's cousin Joe Bill Sandusky lives. And to find him, we should go up to Bromide where the road ends, stop at the little general store, and just ask for Joe Bill. He could tell us all about Bromide. Joe Bill might cuss a little bit, but he could tell us all about Bromide. Now, as for where we should stay for the night, we ought to drive down this road and up that road and go on over there (Glen had turned back to Texas on the cartographicus and was tracing out his ideas with a finger) until we got to the town of Albany. Right there. Where there is a hotel. Oh, also, while we were coming out of Texas, we ought to stop at the old Fort Griffin. After Albany, we should turn north and go to Fort Griffin State Park, and after we did that we should go along that road until there would be the sign for the Matthews Ranch, and we could turn in there and find an old rancher named Watt Matthews. And Watt Matthews had restored all the old, original houses just like they were when his family lived in them before he was born and when he was a baby. His ranch had the old bunkhouse there, and the cook shack. And that would be one of the most interesting deals we could take. So we should go in there. Mr. Matthews was a fine old gentleman.

And as for Noodle, he went on, there is a little creek about one or two miles away called Noodle Creek. And the creek there was where Noodle got its name. One of the theories is that it was an Indian word, and nobody knows what it means. Out around his place was a big Comanche campground. The other theory is that some people were driving cattle north, the trail drivers, and they'd always try to camp close to water. And the scouts went out ahead and found this little old creek, but it was all dried up. Nothing there. So they came back and said to the trail bosses, "It's dry as a noodle." So that was all he knew. Which story was right, he didn't know. But it was probably—he was going to say—the Indian deal because the area was a big campground for the Comanche Indians.

I thought Glen Sandusky had a lot of interesting things to say, and we talked a good deal more than I've represented in these pages. But while we were standing outside the Noodle Baptist Church and talking away, consulting the cartographicus magnus about this and that, the sun began its final descent on the western horizon, shooting out buckets of rays like big handfuls of angel hair. The sun grew big and red, like a tomato, and it drifted behind the clouds until the clouds became orange and soft, like a big bowl of thick tomato sauce. And so we said good-bye to everyone, climbed into the car, and I drove like a maniac, racing through the darkness to find the town of Albany.

Loco

We passed a long line of black cows going to a funeral, and then we headed right into a big storm, with veins of lightning popping forth, a heavy curtain of rain pulling and lifting out of the clouds, and a good deal of purplish activity. The storm took up about a quarter of the horizon, and it seemed dangerous and coming our way.

But we made it to the Hereford Motel in Albany, and after a lousy breakfast the next morning turned left onto Route 283. Glen Sandusky had told us to look into the Matthews Ranch, and as soon as we saw the sign we did. We drove into a maze of dirt roads, got lost, found a big turtle at a section of muddy creek, and passed here and there clusters of brown cows hiding in the bushes and trying to look innocent.

We crossed patches of scrubby brush with a few cacti, some grassy fields with white wildflowers, and eventually came to the center of the ranch, a collection of buildings called The Ram's Head. There were oxen yoken and long-horned skulls hung up all around, and at the center of the compound was something that looked like an original homestead building. It was called the Picket House, we learned, and it was made of old vertical logs with some kind of mud or mortar in the cracks between the logs. That's where old Mr. Matthews was. Everything was nicely kept up and painted red except for the Picket House, which wasn't painted at all. We knocked on the door there and were greeted by a nurse, who told us the old man was ninety-seven years old and still asleep.

We decided not to wait, but just as we were leaving about a half-dozen real cowboys jangled from out of a corral, where they had anchored their horses, coming in from whatever work it is that cowboys do. I say "jangled" because they were wearing spurs as well as boots and big hats. They were big, tough-looking men, with dust settled onto their gaunt faces and handlebar mustaches.

We said hello, talked about longhorn cattle for a short time, and then hit the road again until we came to Fort Griffin, another place Glen Sandusky had told us to check out. Here were the remains of an interesting outpost used to besiege the buffalo and hostile Indians, but now the fort was besieged by hostile grasshoppers.

From Fort Griffin, we followed a road through formerly bison land up 183 and 283, and over on 277 and 82 to Wichita Falls, where we lost our way. We were looking for 44, but the signs just disappeared. There had been too many signs lately anyway. We stopped for a bite to eat and learned from reading the *Wichita Falls Times Record News* that the weather we were scared by last night was the bottom half of a tornado rodeo. A man named Cletis Cummins got to see the inside of one, the newspaper noted. "Cletis Cummins saw the white twisting shape descending as he ran for the storm cellar about fifty yards away. 'I looked up and it was right up there,' he said, jabbing a finger above his head. 'I heard roaring for about two minutes.'"

I put away the newspaper, pulled out the cartographicus magnus, and tried to make plans: "We're going to take Route 44 north out of Wichita Falls and head for Loco. It's pretty straightforward. Can you remember 44, kids?"

"I'll remember 4."

"OK. Bayne can remember one 4, and Britt will remember the other 4. Which one are you going to remember, though?"

We finally fought our way out of Wichita Falls and crossed the Red River until we came to a sign that said: Welcome to Oklahoma. Discover the Excellence. But Oklahoma so far looked a lot like Texas. One of the first differences I noticed: more farmland here than in the northern part of Texas. But the land was still flat to the horizon, where there was a thick haze and a gray sky that looked unpleasantly like clam chowder. From 44 we turned onto a country road with a variety of numbers, going east and headed for Loco.

We passed a lot of small farms and a small wooded area, then a stretch of open land with a cogitating congregation of thirty milk-and-chocolate-cookie cows. Everything looked wet, as if they'd been having some good rains recently, and here and there we were surprised by a few bright orange Georgia O'Keeffe flowers, the kind that jump at your eyes.

In the town of Comanche, we saw our first sign for Loco. It said LOCO and pointed with an arrow straight ahead. We just followed that arrow down the highway right into Loco. The highway was also the main drag of town, and it drew us past a series of small houses, trailers, prefabs, a shed or two, and Fit City Aerobics in a squat cinderblock building with a little picture of a leo-tarded lady dancing around on the side.

We came to something that may have been a country store at one time or a gas station but was now slowly collapsing. And just down from that building, just a little way farther down the highway, was a combination gas station and convenience store, where we turned around. Aside from this main section along the highway, Loco seemed to consist of two roads cut out on either side and parallel to the highway, and a half dozen little criss-crossy streets.

We turned one way and found a small church with no steeple and a sign in front that said: Welcome to the Loco Methodist Church. We turned another way and found another church: the Loco First Baptist Church. This second church did have a steeple, a short pyramid with a sharp point on top, possibly to discourage helicopter landings.

We met an older man who looked quite friendly. He had roundish glasses and a nice smile, but I forgot his name. We asked him if he knew someone named Boyd. He didn't. We also asked him if he knew how Loco got its name. He said he'd lived in Loco since, oh Lord, 1935. Used to have a big place out in the country, and he still pumps a little bit in the oil field and still runs a few cows, but that was mostly all it was around here: oil field and cattle. He didn't know who or where this fellow Boyd was, but he'd heard a lot of different tales about Loco. He'd heard the name come from the loco weed. A horse or something would eat that weed and he'd go crazy. Then he heard the Indians named it. And the last he heard was a doctor named it. But basically he didn't have no idea. But he imagined we might stop at the convenience store and gas station up the road. Anne, the lady in the store, sometimes she might know some stuff.

We thanked him and went off to find Anne, the lady in the store. Anne was nice but busy right then. There were a half-dozen pickup trucks outside her store, including one with a Confederate flag and a woman in Wranglers and a sleeveless T-shirt who came into the store to buy a case of beer, and another with a boiling-over radiator and a suntanned muscular guy hosing water into the radiator to make it stop boiling. Anne thought we should go find Allene Edmondson in the house just down the road.

Allene Edmondson's house was a white one protected by a wire fence and metal gate with vines growing all along the fence. She was home but mildly suspicious when we first peered through the screen of her door — and who can blame her? She looked small and vulnerable, a little frail maybe, and it was getting to be evening by the time we got there. We could have been serial murderers or encyclopedia sellers. But once she decided I was merely the itinerant Confidence Man with his two Assistants, her face lit up, she unlatched and pushed open the door, and welcomed us in.

She was a dear, sweet lady, with curly brownish-grayish hair, big roundish glasses, and deep blue eyes. She wore navy blue pants, a blue plaid shirt that was button down, black sneakers on her feet, and a rhinestoned barrette in her hair. She invited us to sit down on her couch, and she sat in a rocking chair.

She hadn't heard of the fellow named Boyd either, Allene said, but she did know about Loco. A hundred years ago, Loco was kind of a pioneer town. The cowboys and the ranchers all used to meet here, and the Indians, too. In fact, she went on, there were still a lot of Indians, a family up here, over there, still around, living here and there, and in fact her grandmother was one quarter Indian.

She went on to say that people once told her Loco was down on the creek, and then it moved up here. Loco was small now, she added, but it used to be a big and lively place. There used to be two cotton gins. There was a bank, a drugstore. Now that was a long time ago. Because she is getting up in years. But anyway, they had a big school. They had two grocery stores, a barber shop, a painting plant, a moving picture show. There were two garages. There were two blacksmith shops. There was a hotel. Two mercantile stores. And there was a little bakery. And she guessed there might have been some more buildings. But, anyway, that was on the Main Street. And then one gin was off down one way, and one gin was off down the other way. Of course she went to school in Loco and graduated. And there was a mill—like where they fix hats?

"A millinery?" I suggested.

Right. That was there. Of course, as she said, there was a grocery store. She mentioned that, didn't she? Well, Loco was big. And even when she was going to school, of course she graduated in '33, but even when she was going to school there, Loco was a pretty good-sized town. But then, well, Allene guessed that several people began to burn their homes or businesses or something for insurance, like they used to do. And they finally lost their school. It got where there weren't as many kids as they had to have, so they lost the school. And it used to be that everyone would pick cotton or everything like that. Then they quit raising cotton. Or corn. They quit doing that. So anyone that wanted a job just kind of got up and left and went other places. And now different ones who do live in town drive to work. So it just kind of went down. They've got a big fire station, with fire trucks and all. And of course so many of the older ones died. And, Allene said, did we see the new post office on the south side? It's really nice inside. She started out in '68 working in the post office. Of course, her husband, when he was living, he worked in the oil field. They used to have lots of folks around here that worked in the oil field but now have gone off someplace. The oil is pretty much gone. Oh, there may be a few pumps around. And there was several places around here that had cattle, but of course cattle's gone. The beef has gone down.

We talked for some time about Loco, but as we did the picture got gloomier and gloomier—and soon we were both doing our best to lighten it up again. Loco is still, if not so busy a town, still a community, Allene thought. Oh, yes, it is still a community. She meant she guessed there are over two hundred people or something like that. And then they have, of course, the rural water. In other words, they don't belong to some big outfit. It is just the local little Loco Water District. And, even though Loco used to have five churches, they have still got three. "So we had a pretty good community for a long time," she concluded, laughing brightly, "and still do! I am still kind of proud of Loco!"

"Well, it looks like a pretty nice little town to me," I said.

"Well, it's little, but it used to be big," she said.

"People seem very friendly here," I said.

"I hope so," she said.

"The lady at the grocery store was really nice," I said.

"Well, she's real nice," she said. "She's kin to kinfolks to me, too. Different ones around here, we're kind of kin, you know, in a roundabout way. So, yeah, she's just real nice. And, oh, any of these men that you meet around here they'll talk your leg off."

"Oh, really? Well, that's good."

"I'm not going to leave here!" Allene Edmondson concluded firmly. And as for the exact origins of the name, well, some people have said one thing and some another. But she had an article about it somewhere, which now after a little searching she was able to find and show us.

The article was taken from a historical sketch written by Lieutenant Colonel Percy W. Newton, Secretary of the Loco Picnic Association back when there were Loco picnics. Lieutenant Colonel Newton noted that Dr. Albert G. Cranfill came to that part of Oklahoma in 1888 and was instrumental in founding and naming the town and establishing, on June 3, 1890, the Loco Post Office. Now, it seems that a brochure published by the Oklahoma Highway Department stated that Loco was named after loco weed: that crazy weed, also known as wild hemp, that cattle eat and go bonkers, wacko, cuckoo, or loco on. But he (Lieutenant Colonel Newton) had been cognizant of the Loco locality for half a century and if any loco weed ever grew there he never knew about it. Also, he once spoke to the former Ola Cranfill, recent niece of the late Dr. Albert G. Cranfill, and she said that he said that Loco referred to a Latin word that meant *place*. Dr. Cranfill liked Latin, and since Loco was a local focal point for rendezvousing ranchers, he found the lost Latin *locus* to label Loco.

Little City

I forget where we stayed that night. Somewhere OK in Oklahoma. And in the morning we took off again, shooting west along the bottom of the state. I enjoyed this part of the trip immensely.

We skated along a beautiful country road, a two-laner, past a band of elegant brown horses all walking in the same direction and flicking cascading tails.

We passed grassy fields with trees, little ponds and a beautiful little lake, and then a minor field speckled with teeny white wildflowers that looked like minuscule stars. The field looked like a small galaxy.

We came to a place called Little City, but it was a distinctly minimalist production, almost nothing: a couple of trailers.

Hogeye

Hogeye was in northwestern Arkansas, the Ozark Mountains, and I was eager to get there because a friend of mine had (if I remembered correctly) told me to look up a friend of his in Hogeye.

We broke into Arkansas by midafternoon, passing through on the interstate conveyor belt, and soon had turned north. Right about then Bayne started worrying that Hogeye might be named after a person. He had read in a book of facts about a rich lady named Ima Hog, and so he thought there might be a person named Hogeye who had been honored by the establishment of Hogeye, and that would be disappointing. I agreed that it could be a problem, but did we know anyone named Hogeye? Had we *heard* of anyone named Hogeye?

Route 71 led through a clutter of resale shops and used furniture and antique shops and who knows what else, but the clutter went away after about ten miles, at which point we emerged onto a regular country road with weeds alongside and a few houses. The road wavered back and forth into the hills and woods, past some old houses and old cars and then a warning sign that said "Very Crooked and Steep Next 17 Miles" and another warning sign that said "6 People Killed Past 3 Years Don't You Be Next." So we slowed down.

At last we came to the town of West Fork and passed a sign that said: "Junction 170. Devil's Den State Park." I didn't know anything about 170 or Devil's Den State Park, but I was beginning to think I might settle for 170, so I turned around and turned right. By then I had a headache. *This is an awful lot of effort just to go to a silly little place named Hogeye,* I thought to myself.

The road rose steeply and then turned sharply onto a crooked road with a double line in the middle. We followed that road as it rode down like a tunnel into deep, shadow-blessed countryside until we came out in a place with a big turkey house with a thousand turkeys inside and a crossroads where stood a gas station and convenience store. Three or four old guys were loafing around outside by the gas pumps watching three or four young guys working on the roof of the convenience store. I parked the car there, went inside, and asked the attractive young woman with blond hair at the counter if we were on the right track to Hogeye.

"This is it," she said. "Well, this store here is called the Hogeye Mall, and the rest is Hogeye itself."

I was disappointed. There didn't seem to be anything else to it. But I still had my good contact to find: the friend of a friend. "Well," I said, "I'm looking for someone in town named Roy Reed."

She had never heard of Roy Reed. But the woman thought she would try the phone book. No luck. She then suggested I go ask the loafers lingering outside. If there was a Roy Reed in Hogeye, one of them would likely know. And as luck would have it, one of them did. He even happened to know Roy Reed's phone number. There was a pay phone outside the entrance of the store, and so I dialed the number and pretty soon a man's voice answered.

"Roy Reed?" I said hopefully.

"Yes?" the voice at the other end said, very tentatively—and all of a sudden I was thinking: *I should have made this phone call earlier, maybe a week earlier.*

"My name is Dale Peterson," I went on. "Harry Foster told me to call you."

"Harry Foster?" the voice said, blankly. "Harry Foster? I'm sorry, but I don't know anyone by that name."

Welcome to an awkward conversation. I should have planned this one better. But Roy Reed was graceful enough to meet the challenge, and when I explained what we had come to Hogeye for, he invited us to come out to his house for a brief chat. He said he and his wife were about to leave, but we were welcome to come out for a short visit. He gave directions to get there that immediately become foggy, but the old man who had known Roy's phone number also knew where he lived and even was about to drive out that way.

The old man's name was Seth Timmons, and his hair was white and puffy on top. He was wearing a blue-and-white plaid cotton shirt and Sears overalls, a straw hat and thick glasses. He drove his ancient Ford pickup very slowly, about twenty miles an hour, with an elbow out the window and an eye in the mirror. Someone with a hyperactive thyroid roared up in a big truck behind both him and us, desperate to pass, but Seth Timmons just kept on puttering along until we came to a dirt road where he pulled over. We turned off there and drove up a dirt road until we got to the Reed house.

This was a modern house with a high, open-beamed ceiling and an open porch or deck that looked into a small shady grove and, beyond that, a serene little valley. The Reeds, Roy and Norma, turned out to be a very pleasant pair, and they offered us tea and soft drinks and talked with us in the cool shade of their deck.

Roy and Norma said they had only lived in Hogeye for sixteen or seventeen years, so they were newcomers. Ozarkers were a proud people, they said, and had a reputation for not taking to newcomers very well. But they, Roy and Norma, had always been treated very well. Until very recently, the area was quite isolated, and the road coming out used to be a one-lane gravel road with trees arching across the top of it. But now, of course, the road has been opened up. All kinds of traffic coming out here now, and people from all around the state coming out and buying up land. Until recently, the area used to be so isolated that there were pockets in the hills where the people spoke a distinctive dialect. But now, of course, with television that's all going. Most Hogeye residents don't live in Hogeye proper, but several hundred people in fact live out in the hills around Hogeye and considered themselves Hogeyeans. As for how the name came to be, well, there are a few theories. But really we ought to ask Seth Timmons, the old man who brought us out there, for the full story. He was about eighty-four years old, lived there all his life, and he would know. And while we were talking to Seth about other things, we might ask about his dowsing. "Get him to show you how he dowses for water. He really can do it," Roy said.

They gave us directions to find Seth Timmons's farm just down the way a bit, and so we rolled down the hill back onto the main road and wandered back and forth along the road until we weren't lost. We turned through a rickety gate, followed a rattley road past two or three rustic barns with rusty roofs. We came to a garden, a shed sheltering a new car and an ancient Ford pickup, and an old white house with a wooden porch, some cats and chickens in the yard, a hummingbird feeder, and a television sound filtering through a screen door.

I knocked on the door, and pretty soon Seth Timmons appeared on the other side of the screen, acting as if he had expected us.

He pushed open the screen door, came out onto his porch, and told us right off how he thought Hogeye got its name. The only place to travel to get over this mountain was down through Hogeye, Seth said. And they had a tavern down there. And people used to come from far away, as far as Cane Hill and somewhere, to get their whiskey. And they ran a stage coach up and down there. That road that's now highway 265 was once the Butterfield Trail. And so the Butterfield stage came down that way. And at that stop, there was an inn and the tavern. And there was a guy there one night was a-playin a fiddle, and they asked him what the tune was. And he said it was "Hogeye." And so they named the place "Hogeye." Now maybe "Hogeye" was the name of the song, or maybe the name of the song was something else, like "Hawkeye," which after two or three whiskies sounds like "Hogeye." And maybe the guy that was a-playin the fiddle didn't know how to play any other songs, and that's what made the one song so special. But anyhow, it was this fiddler and his fiddle that started Hogeye.

"What was the town like in those days?" I asked. "This was before your time when they got the name?" I added.

Yeah. It was before his time, Seth said.

There used to be three stores in Hogeye. And there was one big store when he was a young boy, right across from the gas station. Had a large hall above it and a general store with a lot of stuff in it there. There used to be a canning factory at Hogeye. They canned fourteen to fifteen train carloads of tomatoes a year. So people raised tomatoes, not to mention milk cows and berries. And there used to be a lot of apple orchards in the county. These days cattle and hay, mostly, is all there is left around there, and poultry. So Hogeye is not the same as it used to be back when they had a canning factory. That was back in the '20s, when the canning factory was there.

Now right now, Seth Timmons went on, he is semi-retired. He has a garden. Would we like to see it? And so the four of us wandered downhill from the house, right past the barn and shed with the car and truck inside, down to his garden, where he grew peanuts, okra, cucumbers, strawberries, corn, beans, and peas, as well as some beautiful flowers whose name he temporarily forgot but which turned out to be — after Bayne ran back to the house to ask Mrs. Timmons — gladiolas.

The garden was located in a spot where we could see a couple of falling down barns, and pretty soon Seth was apologizing for the state of his barns, which he had been trying to keep up, he explained, but now he'd gotten old. People hit him up now, they say, "I never thought I'd see you let a barn go down that way." He says to them, "That ain't mine." But you can't rent property here in this country without your dandruff getting up. People won't pay you, or they tear up stuff. When he bought this place, his dad was a-living. He, Seth, wasn't married yet then. His dad told him, he said, "Son, if you buy this place, but one thing about it: We're not gonna rent it." Well, Seth owned a bunch of cattle, too, but he had them leased out. He farmed the cattle up to about two years ago. Put up hay and fed the cattle and everything. But the cattle got in a fright and knocked him down one day, and so he came in and told the wife, "Just get somebody and haul them cattle off and sell 'em. Quit foolin with 'em and rent the pasture out." But a neighbor boy said that he'd like to make a deal. He would take care of all of them. So that was a-workin out good so far. But the boy ain't a-makin too much out of them now like he'd used to, since cattle's gotten to be about half the price that it was.

Plus, there's the road. Well, they got part of his land already, three times, and now they want to build another road. Or make this one out front bigger. About three months ago, some fellow from the state had stopped his car, and he had a book out. Seth wanted to know what was going on, so he just got in his truck and drove down there. The man said, "We're gonna have to rework this road through here to this new highway over there." And Seth let him talk a little while, and then he said, "Well, let me tell you one thing right now," he said, "I might not be a-livin when it happens, but," he said, "in my lifetime I've moved this fence back three times to give the land for the road. And built the fence back myself. But," he said, "Seth don't aim to do that any more." He said, "I think three times is enough."

So that was the road — but I changed the subject: "Roy Reed said that you know how to dowse for water," I said.

That's his hobby, Seth informed us modestly. He's done switchin for he guessed sixty-five seventy years. Started when he was a kid. He saw someone else doing it and just got fascinated with it himself.

We walked on over to his pickup, and he rummaged around in back and eventually pulled out a number of odd and interesting items. First he pulled out a stout crotch stick taken from, he informed us, a wild cherry tree. He called it a forkéd stick. "Now here is my forkéd stick," he said. "It's gettin kind of old." Next he pulled out an L-shaped iron bar that was held, loosely, inside an old plastic handle. Finally, after more rummaging around in the back of the truck, he located a cable, three strands of thick copper wire that had been twisted together to form a rough, stiff cable perhaps four feet long.

With those three tools in hand — Britt and Bayne with the forkéd stick and iron rod, Seth with the copper cable — we ventured down into a weedy, treey, hummocky field back behind the shed. Seth held the stiff copper cable in front of him in his outstretched right hand. The cable commenced to quiver. Then it started to vibrate. Then it began to whip around and around, and soon it was whipping away with a circular motion in front of Seth. And Seth was walking as if the cable were a propeller drawing him forward.

"See how that's a-circlin?" he said. "That means water's over that-a-way. See how that's a-workin? All right, you watch that."

The cable slowed down. Then it sped up again and started propelling Seth and his three observers faster across the hummocky field. Then it slowed down again, as we did.

"See that now? That indicates we're over it. See here? Now watch this."

"When it goes straight up and down?"

"Yeah. Now, get over here. See it? See how it's comin back? That says an underground stream of water. Here and I'll show you how, which way that stream is runnin. Right back here, walk toward the stream, see that?"

"Oh, yes," I said, trying to sound intelligent even though by this time I was getting confused. But then we came to a good place, and he stopped, handed me the cable, pulled an antique carpenter's plumb bob out of one of his several overall pockets, and squatted. "And here," he said, "I'll show you how to get the best of it." He held the plumb bob by the string and let it spin. "Now, here," he said, "every time this makes a circle it's ten foot down to where the water is."

We watched the plumb bob turn four slow circles before petering out. "Forty foot. And that's the only way I can tell how much water there is is the way that swings."

So that was the copper cable. We started all over again with the L-shaped iron rod. Balanced as it was in the plastic handle, it swung freely this way and that like a giant compass needle and in general seemed to work on the same principle as the copper cable, as it led the four of us this way and that across the hummocky field on our way to water.

Finally, we got to the forkéd stick, which had been my favorite device all along. Grasping both ends of the fork in both hands, Seth held that big cherry stick right up to his face, in front of his eyes, with the two forked ends near his ears and the trunk of the stick pointed before him like a big nose. The stick seemed to vibrate a little, and Seth's eyes squinted to a close. His face took on a look of deep concentration, and pretty soon, slowly at first and then faster, he began tripping along. Britt, Bayne, and I eagerly tripped after.

"I hear it a-poppin'!" he said.

I couldn't hear anything. "Maybe it's just something *you* hear," I suggested.

"Yeah, I can hear it, hear it poppin'!" he said, and then suddenly he veered sharply in another direction, wandered erratically for another half a minute, and then stopped. He lowered the stick, panting, out of breath.

"I didn't hear it," Bayne said.

"You want to try it?"

And so Bayne took the stick, held it up to his face—with guidance. "Come here, get it like this. See? Now walk straight towards her. Feel anything pullin?"

"Ah, not really."

Seth helped him adjust his arms higher. "Hold it out this a-way. Sometimes it pulls down right away. You feelin anything?"

It was the kind of thing that a person would need to study and practice, I believe. We did come to a couple of nice places in the field where, Seth assured us, it would be good to drill a well.

Seth said he uses all three dowsing tools whenever he goes to start a well. He doesn't charge for the service, either. He does it for free. Oh, if he had to take his own vehicle, he would expect some compensation, but when people come to get him, he doesn't charge. He has had some big old arguments with well drillers, but he figures he's got just as much right to find water his way as other people have to do it their ways. He likes to set a well where he's found two underground streams that cross. And he's had about an 80 percent success rate. Yes, he does miss sometimes. Anyhow, he covers a big territory. Clean over into Oklahoma sometimes. Well, he's been fooling with it for years, and the reason why he uses a big forkéd stick like that one is that it don't pull on a little stream like a little stick does and get you confused. He has had lots of enjoyment, met a lot of nice people. He doesn't do it for the money. Of course, there was the time he thought he might have figured it out for diamonds. But he hadn't. He didn't have what it took.

We stood out in that field as the shadows got longer and talked with Seth Timmons until the sun turned into a red wafer, at which time it became clear that we needed to dowse for a place to stay for the night. Seth thought we would find a hotel up in Fayetteville, but in the meanwhile, since we were interested in places with unusual names, had we heard about Bug Scuffle?

Bug Scuffle

ug Scuffle? Bug Scuffle! I never saw that one on the map," I said.

"It wouldn't be. It's not much there."

But there was a fellow down at the Hogeye Mall might could tell us, Seth said. Cooksey was his name. Cooksey might could tell us how Bug Scuffle got named. Now, if we went down there first thing in the morning tomorrow, there was a bunch of loafers down there who might could tell us a lot of things. A lot of people raise chickens down in that part of the country, and they come up to the Hogeye Mall and drink coffee. And, Seth added, he himself might be down there in the morning, too. Or he might be over at West Fork. "I never know what I'll do," he said.

Well, we stayed overnight in a generic place outside of Fayetteville and first thing next morning went back down to the Hogeye Mall to find Cooksey. Inside the store, there was indeed a group of loafers including an old man but no Cooksey. Nor had Seth Timmons shown up. The helpful blonde behind the counter said she hadn't seen Cooksey yet, though who knew when he might appear? But we might just drive out to Cooksey's house in Bug Scuffle because she thought he might just still be at home.

How would we get to Bug Scuffle? I wondered.

Well, it wasn't so hard, she began to say. But before she got any further, the loafers in the store crowded around and helped out. We should drive down that road that way for a few miles, they said, then turn right or left on another road that would be a dirt road and it would be Highway Something, and then drive and drive until we came to a very steep hill whereupon something something James Cooksey.

Back in the car, we followed those directions, driving for a few miles across some very lumpy countryside of woodsey hills and hollows and valleys sliced up and converted into farmland with green-scummed ponds. Then we turned and drove along a dirt road lined with high weeds on either side, with the occasional old house trailer and farm, past a two-year-old child pushing a stroller with a puffy dog following, past an adolescent boy driving an all-terrain vehicle, and up a steep hill.

But there was not much at the top of that hill. We did find an old house and a mailbox that said 19499 Bug Scuffle Road, so we were on the right road at least.

We flagged down a truck coming the other way, and the guy driving the truck said we still had a few miles to go before we got to Cooksey's house. We continued through forests and fields, hollows and crickets, and the occasional curlicue turnoff that looked a little mysterious. We topped another steep hill and came to a little farm with a beautiful pond surrounded by grass and wildflowers and an old wood barn so full of hay it was spilling out the windows. But the farm had a lot of antisocial signs around: KEEP OUT NO TRESPASSING NO HUNTING PRIVATE. And still no sign of Cooksey.

The road twisted and rose up to a shady dell on the right and a grassy glade on the left. In the middle of the grassy glade stood several gnarled oak trees and a little white church. The church was a gable-roofed box with three rectangular windows on one side, three on the other, and no steeple. A gentle path in the grass led from the road up to four concrete steps and a double white door at the front of the church. Above this double white door hung a light bulb, and above the light bulb hung a sign that said in black letters:

BUG SCUFFLE
COMMUNITY
CHURCH.

It was a lovely little country church, glowing in the sun and reverberating with the vibrations of a grassy field full of crickets and katydids. We walked around to the back and then wandered through streaks and shafts of sunlight and a small cloud of fluttering butterflies (black streaked with blue and fringed with rows of white spots) to a small graveyard situated to one side of the church. The graveyard was very peaceful. We shuffled around and read names for a while—Lee and Means and Coffman—and dates, and then we drifted back through the sunlight and butterflies back to the car.

We never found Cooksey. We did find his mailbox and house just past a steep hill another couple of miles or so farther up the road. His door was open, but he wasn't home. We drove another mile or so until we came to a lazy dog lying in the middle of the road marking the end of the road, where we turned around.

Back in Hogeye we stopped again at the Hogeye Mall where the helpful woman told us that Cooksey had just come in but then had gone out again.

The woman's name was Arleen Thompson. I bought three Eskimo Pies from her and asked if she happened to know where the name Bug Scuffle came from. She said she didn't. No, she did not know. Cooksey might know, but she didn't. Well, she added, the only story she knew was what the old-timers told her. That Bug Scuffle got its name because it was on the old stagecoach road, the Butterfield Road? And when the stagecoaches stopped up there, the people getting off would notice these beetles going across the road in the morning into the woods and stuff. And she guessed the beetles denned up under the stage-coach stop at night because they'd come back out of the woods in the evening? So people said that the stagecoach stopped at that one stop, at that place where all the bugs scuffled across the road, the bug-scuffle place—here she made a scuffling motion with her hands and fingers—and the name got stuck that way.

Greasy Corner

We took Interstate 40 east heading for the eastern side of Arkansas beneath a dumplings-and-gravy sky.

The highway was clear until we came to the exit for Toad Suck Park, at about twenty-seven miles before Little Rock, when it suddenly started becoming crowded. We spotted a police car hiding in the bushes just outside Little Rock, but we were going exactly the speed limit. Interstate 40 was old and beaten up, not really the sort of highway that you could speed on anyway, and so we passed right on through Little Rock without a problem and found ourselves on the other side in a nice clear stretch and barreling straight for Memphis.

I turned on the radio and listened to "My Heart Needs a Woman's Touch." The concept was simple: My heart is a little messy. I haven't picked up my dirty socks lately, and my sink is full of rotten garbage. The next song, slurred and deeply melancholic, told a tale of unrequited love. The third song was another really sad ballad: The singer left her Tennessee boy for a Hollywood Dream, which was basically a bad idea.

This was cry-in-your-beer music, and I enjoyed it — though Britt didn't. By the time we had finished crying in our beer, we were close to the end of the state. It was late in the afternoon, and the car was running out of gas. We pulled off the interstate and turned into a gas station and convenience store at a place called Shell Lake to buy gas. While paying for the gas, I asked a woman at the counter for directions to Greasy Corner. She directed me to a round-faced man wearing a hat and drinking coffee, and he said I should go back, turn left, and go for some distance until I found a brick house where there would be a man named McCollum.

We turned back, turned left, drove past a field full of one hundred and seventy-three sparrows taking off, past a collapsing barn, across a railroad tracks, and past some metallic silos and more farmer's fields. This was Mississippi Delta land now, flat and hot and damp. The smells were rich and invigorating: of grass and earth swelling and brewing and heaving in a humid late afternoon air, with lots of dazed insects swimming in the soupy air.

We came to a corner with Route 50, an old country road, and turned down that. We were still passing through farmland, but then the road turned into clusters of forest. The road crossed a bridge, the forests got thicker, and soon it seemed to me that we'd been driving for a long time. The round-faced man in Shell Lake had said to find a brick house. McCollum. We found a brick house with two horses, two tottering colts, and a vigorously barking three-legged dog. No one home.

We drove some more and came to a small cluster of small wooden houses with two or three old cars in the middle of the cluster and about eight or ten people hanging out around the cars. At first glance, this seemed to be an ex-clusively African-American community, and given the fact that it was situated at a gentle curve or possibly a corner in the road (this curved road was starting to seem all corners to me) I pulled in there, thinking that, even though there was no brick house in sight, perhaps this was one small corner of a larger cor-ner called Greasy Corner.

I got out of the car. "Is this Greasy Corner?" I asked.

An older woman in a flower-print cotton dress moved forward to handle me. I introduced myself and the Research Assistants, and explained our mission. No, this wasn't Greasy Corner, she confirmed. This place here was known as Wildwood. Greasy Corner would be down the highway a stretch. She pointed down the road, and I looked where she pointed and thought I might be able to see a brick house.

"Thanks," I said.

I drove some more, but what I had thought was the brick house wasn't. Soon we came to a corner where Route 50 intersected with Route 149. But there was nothing there except an old abandoned cinderblock building, plus about three or four small houses. It seemed like a corner all right, but there was no grease and no sign for Greasy Corner, so we spun right on through. I'm trying to think up an excuse right now as to why I missed the proper brick house that was, I later realized, only about a half mile past that intersection, but I can't think of any. In any case, I had soon driven long and far enough to realize we must have already slid past Greasy Corner and the brick house. I was about to turn around when I noticed a man messing with his car alongside the road. The hood was up. It looked like the radiator had steamed over.

I pulled up behind him and got out of the car. "Howdy," I said. I had developed the "howdy" in Texas and now accidentally fell back into it. I asked if he needed any help.

He said he didn't need any help.

"We're looking for Greasy Corner," I said.

It was steamy hot, and the man was sweating big dark patches into a ragged T-shirt. Did I mention that he was big? He was huge. His face was big and lobster red. His arms were as big as most people's legs. And beneath his T-shirt was suspended either a big belly or a very big beach ball. A mustache collected sweat on his upper lip, and a jagged dagger pierced a heaving heart on the slab of his left forearm.

We just passed Greasy Corner, he said. Who were we looking for?

"Somebody said the name McCollum. But we don't know McCollum," I said, and I introduced myself and the Research Assistants (still sitting in the car) and explained our mission.

Well, the man declared, Greasy Corner used to be right back up the road, right up there at the junction of 149 and 50, but it ain't there anymore. The cinderblock is about all that's left. It used to be a store and maybe a garage and stuff, but the place got burnt down. It used to be owned by old man McCollum, but he died. We should look for young McCollum, but the man didn't know where he was at. We should try the brick house down the road. But he didn't know whether McCollum would be at home or not.

Greasy Corner was an unusual name, the man agreed. Now, there was a woman down the road, and if she was at home she could tell us more about it. And he didn't think her dog would bother us. But, he believed, McCollum's daddy lived up at the corner till he died. And it was his grandpa, maybe, that built that old store that now is the cinderblock wreck. But it got burnt. Greasy Corner used to be called something else years ago. He didn't know what. But like he said, we might try McCollum. Or if that lady was at home, and if she was willing to talk to us, and if her dog didn't attack us, she could tell us a lot. But we ought to be careful of her dog. But the old store got burnt up. As for old man McCollum, he had two boys. One of the boys got killed by niggers. Niggers killed him with a claw hammer. Then the store burnt down. Still, the place used to be called something else, and he didn't know *why* they called it Greasy Corner.

"I see," I said.

"Maybe, like I said, she knows," he said.

Niggers killed him with a claw hammer. The ugly words drifted, rattled, and faded with a grotesque little reverberation, and I felt, suddenly, tired and disturbed. But I kept on in the usual way. "Well, thanks," I said finally, and I walked back to the car. We pulled out, turned around, and started back up the road.

Britt and Bayne had been sitting in the car with the windows half open while I was talking to the man, so they hadn't heard everything clearly.

"What did he say?" Bayne said.

"He said old McCollum had owned a store back at the junction with Route 149, which was Greasy Corner, and it got burned down," I said. I was reluctant to say the rest, but I did anyway: "And then he said one of the old man's sons was murdered, I guess. He said: 'Niggers killed him with a claw hammer.'"

Bayne said, softly and emphatically: *"That's so bad!"*

"What? What's so bad?"

"That word!"

We continued down the road now, windows still open. The slow, chewing sounds of the evening insects were emerging from the trees and fields along the road now and climbing in through the car windows, and the dark, muggy air was starting to draw around us like a curtain. The place felt suddenly isolated, and we seemed suddenly a long way away from home, floating and floating on a flat and humid landscape with a desperate history. That's what I was thinking. But while I was thinking that we found the brick house I had failed to see earlier.

It was indeed the young McCollum's house, and before long we were welcomed and treated to some warm hospitality by Mr. and Mrs. B. McCollum. Mr. McCollum seemed fit and full of vigor, and he talked with forceful gestures, throwing his arms out whenever he wanted to emphasize something. He was sixty-nine, he said, but he looked as fit as a twenty-year-old. He was wearing tan work clothes. He had neatly cut brownish hair. He wore glasses. He handed me his business card, from which I learned the correct spelling of his last name. I also soon learned that his first name had been legally economized into the initial B.

"So if you can stand a dirty house," he said, "come on in. My wife and I worked until 3:30 last night. We canned stuff and put it in the freezer. I guess you're familiar with how the poor Southern people do?"

B. McCollum went on to describe all the canning they'd done in the last three weeks — okra, somewhere between fifty and seventy-five cans of tomatoes, and so on — while ushering us into the house and introducing us to Mrs. McCollum. Jeanette McCollum looked like Barbara Bush: white-haired and handsome, a gracious hostess who, once she had finished apologizing for the state of the house and describing more about their canning ordeal, would not rest until we each had seated ourselves comfortably and gotten a cool and refreshing sodapop to drink. "Do y'all want a Coke or something?" she said. Pretty soon we were all settled down with clinking glasses in hand.

It seemed that a lot of people had been asking about Greasy Corner lately — the word "greasy" is squeezed to rhyme with "breezy" — and at first I got the impression B. McCollum was tired of telling the story. But now I don't think he was. He was just tired from canning. He said he had several newspaper clippings somewhere. Someone from the Associated Press had come knocking at his door a couple of years ago, asking the very questions we were asking now. And this boy was out of New York, Mr. McCollum said. He saw the sign, Greasy Corner, so he come up here and stopped up the road there. And the boy sent him on up. The boy. McCollum interrupted himself at this point to explain his use of that word. To him, he explained, just about everybody was "boy." He might call me a "boy." The point was that he was sixty-nine years old, so he guessed he considered all people "boys" who were younger than he was. Anyhow, this reporter did a story. But it wasn't in a local paper. But the *Jonesburg Arkansas Sun* picked it up. After that article, other reporters and journalists starting showing up, too, lured by the slippery promise of a slick name. And so I and the Research Staff were simply taking our turn in the queue.

B. McCollum went on to note that he had been Justice of the Peace in St. Francis County for about forty years, during which time he had helped tie approximately twelve hundred nuptial knots, but farming was his main business. He farmed until 1979. He farmed two-and-a-half sections. A section, he explained, was a plot of six hundred forty acres. He farmed two-and-a-half sections for about twenty-nine years. But then the man he was renting the land from, they couldn't agree. Well, the boy that — there again, McCollum apologized, he was using the term "boy." But then, he explained, that boy *was* a boy, because McCollum knew his mother and father before they ever married. So he *was* a boy. And, Mr. McCollum wasn't going to use any profanity because of my children sitting in the room, but he was a *so-and-so boy* as far as he, McCollum, was concerned. And this boy never worked a day in his life. His daddy was a multimillionaire. His daddy come into B. McCollum's house one day, and he said, "I know if I die, or something happen to me, that you and my son can't get along. And he gonna put you off the farm." He said, "I'm going to give you an eleven-year contract." How and why and what possessed him to make it eleven years remains a mystery, but anyhow McCollum went ahead and said, "OK." Well, he got the contract written up and signed, and about six years after that he died. And, sure enough, like he said, McCollum couldn't get along with his son. His son was very bred as far as education, whereas McCollum was raised up more to farm. He was born and raised here, born right behind the house here. And had been living here nearly sixty-nine years. Anyhow, this boy went to a couple of fancy colleges and got some degrees, including a degree in business. And he could tell you how to make money. But then he started telling B. McCollum how to farm. And yet he never worked a day in his life on a farm. He even told McCollum which way to run his rows. He was running his rows wrong. He needed to run them north-south, whereas he had run them east-west. And finally McCollum got to the point where he decided to quit. This was in February or March of 1980. He had already started preparing his land for the crop in 1980. He said, "I'm quitting now."

The boy said, "Oh, no. You can't quit. I won't let you quit."

McCollum said, "You ain't got to do with it. I can quit any time I want to."

And the boy said, "Well, I don't want you to make a rash decision and do something you would regret later." He said he wanted to give McCollum a week.

And McCollum said, "OK. I'll take a week."

Then about a week later the boy called up. From California! "Well, what about it?"

McCollum said, "I'm quittin. I told you the other day, I'm quittin." And the boy said, "Well, what are you going to do for a livin?" And when he asked that question, he didn't know B. McCollum. My God, *he did not know* B. McCollum, who may have thrown away a little money in his life, but who has overall been one of the most conservative, stingiest farmers in the country. This was not bragging, not patting oneself on the back. But Mr. B. McCollum had done better than a lot of these "educated derelicts," to borrow a phrase from Calvin Coolidge. Anyhow, the boy asked him what was he going to do. He said that he didn't have to do anything. He said, "I got my rent paid for, my land paid for, and my house paid for." He don't owe anybody anything. He had a little over seven hundred acres of land of his own land already paid for, which he was renting for around $30,000. And he said, "Oh, and by the way, my wife's got a job, too."

So that's when McCollum went ahead and quit farming. Now, this boy was all easy grease now. He had inherited two and a half sections of land in Arkansas and probably another couple of sections or so in Mississippi. Didn't owe a dime. Not to mention he owned part of a company that was doing a multimillion dollar a year business. Anyhow, this boy—McCollum was still calling him a boy because he was very immature—he lost everything he had within six years' time!

That was a little side track in the conversation, but I thought it was interesting. And within a few minutes we had skittered over to the subject of how Greasy Corner got its name. Back years ago, B. McCollum said, when his daddy moved to the area about 1918 or '19, this road used to come up here. It was the main road between Little Rock and Memphis. The main highway. Equivalent to what the big interstate is now. And McCollum's father put in a store. He had a store and a grist mill, and a service station and a little repair shop and a blacksmith shop. And he had a little restaurant there. And one day this fella from Hughes, Archie Pryor, drove up, and he needed some oil in his car. So the man working for McCollum's father, he put some oil in Archie Pryor's car. And he got some grease, McCollum guessed, on his hands. His hands were probably already filthy anyhow. But he went on back in the store there.

At that time, which was way back in the 1920s, the restaurant and the highway junction were named Mack's Corner. Mack after McCollum. And there was a great big sign, something like, at least four-by-eight, if not five-by-ten or -twelve, up there at the corner that said MACK'S CORNER. Well, anyhow, this Archie Pryor, after having his car worked on, went into the restaurant and ordered him something to eat. (Now, McCollum's dad told him this story years ago, when he was just a little tot.) Archie Pryor ordered something to eat. (Now whether it was a plate lunch or a sandwich, he didn't remember.) But the fella that put the oil in his car was the one that fixed his lunch. So when he served the plate there, he had his grease on his plate. So this Archie Pryor said, "Damn, this is not Mack's Corner." He said, "This is not Mack's Corner! This is *Greasy* Corner! Looka here: You got grease on my plate!" And so his dad had that great big sign: MACK'S CORNER. After two or three years they changed the sign to GREASY CORNER.

His dad was a farmer himself, who moved over from Tippaa, Mississippi. He came over to Arkansas, and he farmed, but of course he also had the restaurant and garage. And we could believe it or not, but he had the first movie theater that East Arkansas ever had. And also he had a little bottling plant. He made different types, like orange, grape or lemon or strawberry sodapop, and some kind of a cola. And he used to deliver them to the countryside. And that was back mostly when about all the roads was mud except this one kind of through here, and it had a little gravel on it. Would we like to see the newspaper pieces?

So we reviewed three newspaper articles B. McCollum had pulled out from somewhere. I read aloud, for the benefit of the Research Assistants, from a piece by a reporter for the *Commercial Appeal* that started like this:

> The wind was blowing hard off fields prepared for planting as B. McCollum Jr. lined up his Lincoln's hood ornament with the center line and accelerated into the past.

I liked that! I read further:

> Greasy Corner, whose population has dropped to under 10 with recent deaths, is like a long list of communities nearby where dilapidated buildings rise amid the purple hue of verbena weed to provide perches for redtailed hawks.

Why couldn't I write like that? What was verbena weed anyway?

> "We woke up the other morning, and the ground was covered with snow," said McCollum, a storyteller of first rank, preparing a lesson. "I went to town, to the cafe, to drink coffee and came back out and damn near every bit of snow done melted. That's just about the way it happened on these farms. People leave."

Nicely said! I continued to read the article out loud and then turned the page — only to stumble over a story so terrible it made me cringe:

> One sad tale he tells involved a brother he never met, murdered 15 days before he was born. The Commercial Appeal of December 1927 made the murder at "Greasy Corner" front-page news. "Angry Posses Seeking Slayer of 11-Year-Old Boy," it says, noting that the town had a "bonfire already laid for purposes of summary justice" for the killers of Julius McCollum. The boy had been drowned. His killers were caught; they confessed and went to prison.

I finished the article in silence before passing it along to Britt and Bayne. Another article elaborated on the subject. In 1927, the article said, two black farm workers were said to have robbed the young Julius McCollum of $35 that his father at the store had given him to carry home to his mother. After the robbery, possibly to silence the boy (the article didn't say), the two men drowned him. The father, Bunge M. McCollum, gathered a posse, found the suspects, and prepared to hang them from a high beam in his barn. However, a friend named Archie Pryor wisely prevailed on the elder McCollum, and so the accused men were brought to trial. After being convicted of murder and condemned to death, they appealed, served time on a reduced charge of second degree murder, and after some years got out on parole. Meanwhile, fifteen days after the killing of his eleven-year-old brother, the present B. McCollum was delivered from his mother: naked and bereft.

It seemed to me then that McCollum had given us those pieces to read partly because he didn't want to talk about the murder. I didn't know what to say. It was just too horrific. And so we chatted on. He wanted to know about our trip. I told him. He wondered, discreetly, about our own family situation. Where was my wife? I explained that she was back home, enjoying her peace and quiet. We looked at a photo album, at a picture of old Archie Pryor, and we talked about the nearest actual town now, Hughes, which used to have three picture shows, excellent restaurants, food as good as you could get anywhere, and it used to be on Saturday afternoon that you couldn't hardly find a parking spot in Hughes. Every building had a business. But now over half of the buildings were boarded up, glass busted, and just plywood over the windows.

Since it was by then getting pretty late, he wondered where we intended to stay for the night. I said I wasn't sure. He noted that there was a Best Western, a pretty nice motel, in Shell Lake, but if we stayed there he wouldn't advise us to get out and walk around at night because there were so many damned blacks around there we might get robbed. He didn't mean the black people staying at the hotel, but he read in the paper pretty regularly that people maybe walking across the street to the truck stop over there end up getting robbed.

Well, I wasn't sure where we would stay, I declared, but anyway it was time to get going. We said our good-byes, thanked Mr. and Mrs. McCollum for their generous hospitality, headed out the door, and got in the car.

The truth is I was upset by a picture in my mind of that little boy, eleven-year-old Julius McCollum. The murder of a child! And, in the meantime, as I drove into the deepening darkness I tried to think of something intelligent to say to the Research Staff about history and hatred.

It was completely dark outside now, and we moved slowly north across a flat black humid landscape with waves of bugs swarming and rising and turning suddenly luminous in our headlights before bursting against the windshield. . . .

Alligator

Memphis was a pleasure to drive through, all lit up and dramatic. And as an added bonus, while stopped at a blinking light and a clanging bell for a whistling train, we spotted the faded image of Elvis on a Graceland Furniture van.

It was very late by that time, so we didn't look for the real Elvis but instead just dropped out of Tennessee into Mississippi south on Interstate 55. We took the first motel we could find, a Day's Inn that provided a stinky room. It is a cause for suspicion when someone gives you a "nonsmoking room" complete with ashtrays for your noncigarettes. I don't want to hurt anyone's feelings, but as the Research Staff agreed (and they should know) our room smelled like guinea pig poop. Nevertheless, the young woman at the checkout counter next morning was nice. She asked what we were doing in Mississippi. I said that we were tourists, going out to the Delta to find a town called Alligator.

Alligator? She had never heard of it, and so we pulled out a map and, sure enough, there it was. She was from Greenville she said, a city in the middle of the Delta. I asked her if she liked it better out here in the hilly country. She said she did, and then, after we had chatted a little longer, she said, "Well, be careful." *Be careful?* I thought to myself.

We motored south on Interstate 55 under a threatening sky down a channel through pine forests and followed for a long time a truck carrying a pile of pine logs that looked like brown asparagus. It was along this Interstate 55, I believe, that we had our first vision of the future, and it did not look good. Kudzu (as you probably already know) is a scary vine imported a few years back from North Korea or somewhere because some fool in the Highway Department of probably California was looking for an effective vine to cover up mistakes along highways. But kudzu isn't merely effective. It takes over. And now we were driving past entire villages of kudzu: growing over the ground, over trees, telephone poles, barns, old houses, and with probably a few slow-moving people stuck in there too. Kudzu tosses a green blanket over everything it touches. And I don't want to go all negative on you, but as we watched kudzu take over the hills of Mississippi, we turned on the radio to hear warnings about weather taking over the lowlands. *Rainfall totals of more than six inches have been reported in some areas since yesterday. Meterologists anticipate show-*

ers, thunderstorms, and flooding in north and central areas of the state, with flash-flood warnings particularly for the low-lying areas.

About fifteen minutes after that warning, it started to rain. I turned the windshield wipers on, and they began whacking ineffectually at the water with a whack whack whack. We made a right turn off 55 and jumped onto Route 6 into Batesville — only to be confronted by yet another warning, this time written in giant letters: WHERE WILL YOU SPEND ETERNITY, SMOKING HELL OR NON-SMOKING HEAVEN? That was a Mississippi version of the Surgeon General's cautionary note, I thought, and I quite liked it. But very soon a two-laned Route 6 took us away from Batesville and into agricultural land, wheat and corn fields, and the land turned from hilly to flat, which made me think we were quickly drifting into the Delta. Then it was raining hard enough to occasion debate.

Bayne: "It's pouring."

Britt: "It's a downpour."

Bayne: "It's a torrential rain."

Britt: "It's a torrential downpour."

It was a torrential downpour, and the little streams and rivers we drove past were looking alive and slithery. We were driving into gray, and in the process we passed a barn that said PECANS and came to Clarksdale, which didn't look like much on the edge except a series of the predictable: Day's Inn, Kentucky Fried Chicken, and so on.

"Keep your eyes peeled for the Blues Museum, kids," I said.

Clarksdale, situated near the top of the Mississippi Delta, is home to the Blues Museum. The Delta is mother to the Blues, at least the Delta Blues, and the Blues is mother to a whole lot of music, including the style that made Elvis so famous his face is still miraculously appearing on clouds, cut tomatoes, pigs' ears, and moving vans. Charlie Patton was first to record the Delta Blues in the 1920s, followed notably by Tommy Johnson. Charlie Patton and Tommy Johnson were regularly hanging around the plantation of Will Dockery during the '20s, where their songs and styles were praised, imitated, and in some cases devoured by such other notables as Howlin' Wolf, Bukka White, and Robert Johnson. Robert Johnson cut twenty-nine recordings in 1936 and 1937 and became the legend of the Delta. He went from being so bad to so good so fast that people said he sold his soul to the devil one midnight at the crossroads in front of Dockery's plantation. Invited to play at Carnegie Hall in 1938, Johnson died instead, poisoned by a loving woman's hating husband, fading from this hard life in a spectacular hydrophobic paroxysm: "foaming at the mouth, crawling around on all fours, hissing and snapping at onlookers like a mad dog." That's what the book says. Then there was Muddy Waters, born at Rolling

Fork, Mississippi, in 1915, recorded as a Delta acoustic Blues artist during the early '40s. In 1943 he moved to Chicago and plugged his guitar into an electrical outlet. . . .

But why am I rambling on like this when we have a big storm to drive through? We came to an underpass passing under a railroad tracks. The tracks had a train parked on them, and the underpass had a flashing yellow light and a trooper (possibly a storm trooper) in front who was separating the traffic with his hands, sending big trucks under, the rest of us over — and unfortunately that long train made our detour very long so that by the time we had recovered we were dangling out the other end of town. That's what happened. As far as I could see, Clarksdale was a shopping mess at one end, a shopping mall at the other, with a long detour in the middle. We missed the Blues Museum, I know that much, and so in the far end mall I stopped at a music store. We dashed through the downpour, trolled through the Blues section, and hauled up "The Best of Muddy Waters," which (as we hit the road once more) was stuck into the dashboard slot. . . .

Out came a hand collapsing onto a piano keyboard with a light drop down and a hard bluesy landing!

Out came an old chain-smoking harmonica to help with the landing and make it bluesier!

Out came a finger to pluck gently on the bass: boot-de-do, boot-de-doo.

And out came a voice, a big rough slurry voice, that (as the harmonica squawked and squeezed itself into an everlasting trill across two bluesy neighbor notes) announced in a slow emphatic growl:

> I don' want you to be no slave
> I don' want you to work all day
> I don' want you to be true
> I just want to make love to you.

The harmonica bravely tried to translate an echo of the last three or four words into its own reedy tongue, but before it got very far the voice had grabbed the tune back and jumped away with it into some more growly lyrics ending at last with the same refrain: *I just want to make love to you. . . .*

As Muddy Waters and the harmonica were wrestling away inside our dashboard, stormy waters were battling away overhead and overflowing onto our windshield where the wipers bravely snapped at them with a snap snap snap. Oh, it was so rainy and hazy there on Route 61 south: just gray. But very soon we spotted a sign that appeared like magic out of the rain and haze and said, ALLIGATOR 13, which was a good sign because it meant not only that Alligator lay within striking distance but that it was also a substantial enough place to strike. Even better, the rain eased up and after about thirteen miles the road made an emergency twist to the left while a big sign to the right said

Welcome to
ALLIGATOR.

A small sign beneath that pointed with an arrow off the main highway and said helpfully

BUSINESS
RESIDENTIAL.

We turned off the tape player and Route 61, followed that arrow, and quickly found ourselves crawling down the gullet of a wiggly road that followed a wiggly river or a lake past a young cigarette-smoking girl wearing a football T-shirt with a big number 10 on it, past a very nice brick house to the left, a disintegrating wood house to the right, then an abandoned house with plywood over the windows and another house with a giant dish antenna out front, and so on, until we reached the Alligator downtown, which was dilapidated and shaped like an L. On the first side of the L were three relatively modern buildings made of wood, metal, and glass: Mary Ann's Variety Store 627-5343 (open), Mary Ann's Antiques (closed), and Town Hall of Alligator (closed).

At the corner of the L loomed (on the far side) a water tower.

Turning left and onto the second segment of the L, we found Main Street: with a '50s or '60s brick post office on the right side and on the left side two minor clusters of run-down '20s or '30s brick and wood-frame business buildings followed (after a vacant weedy couple of measures) by a five-doored and mostly boarded-up long wooden shack with a blue sign above the first door that said KING LOUNGE. The King Lounge looked closed and abandoned, but I would guess it opened at night because there was an intact Budweiser sign in the window and some relatively new signs on the door that said things like "Must be 21" and "$3.00 Charge on All Drinks Brought In."

That was downtown Alligator.

And just down Main Street a little farther, we could see out to the tail end of the place, which amounted to a collapsing house or two and then a broken-windowed boarded-up cotton gin, the Continental Gin, twisting in agony from being eaten alive by kudzu. There was not a lot to Alligator, in short. The post office was open, though, and so we went inside and waited behind one customer in order to talk to the woman on the other side of the window who was at that moment busy weighing packages. The woman at the post office seemed — how can I say this nicely? — a little short with the customer in front of us, and when our turn came she seemed a little snappy. She must have been busy. She said we ought to find somebody out at the mouth of Alligator named Bruno.

So we left the post office and wandered on across Main Street to the first of the two '20s or '30s brick buildings, half of which seemed permanently closed and the other half of which was a grocery store with no name on the front. The No Name Grocery had a couple of people inside and about three people outside sitting on an old wooden bench. The three people outside on the bench didn't seem very talkative. The two people inside (behind the counter) were certainly pleasant enough, but the man who spoke said he had only lived in the area a short time and so didn't know very much.

He said we could go over to the next set of business buildings and stop at the Whale Store, which was a dry goods store owned by a ninety-year-old Jewish man named Aaron Klein. But Mr. Klein wouldn't be in until about two o'clock in the afternoon. So, he concluded, we ought to go back out to the highway and find a fellow running the modern package store who was maybe the second oldest Alligatorian. He would be Bruno.

We got back in the car, turned around, and drove back the way we came until we arrived at Mary Ann's Variety Store 627-5343. Mary Ann was working behind the counter inside, and she was very friendly. She wanted to leave the story-telling to her husband, she said, who was the mayor but also happened to be at work right now. "But Alligator," she went on, "is supposed to have had its name from a lake. As you came in here, say from the air, it looks a lot—"

"Oh, I see," I said, "it looks like a—I thought it was a river."

"It's a lake," she said.

"Maybe I'm seeing something different. When we came in, it looked like a curvy river, but it's a lake? Do you have any alligators in the—"

She wasn't sure, but at one time someone caught a very big fish in the lake. And she also had some articles posted up by the door, including pictures of soldiers stationed near Alligator during World War II, Italian prisoners of war is what they were, and they built a bridge that used to be right down the road. But, she went on, if we really wanted to learn about Alligator we ought to go out to the highway and find Bruno. And there was an elderly Jewish man, but he never came until after lunch. His name was Mr. Klein, and he had a dry goods store on Main Street called the Whale Store. He'd taken everything out of the windows, and he came into the store every afternoon just to be somewhere.

"The Whale Store? OK, we heard about that," I said, and I went over to look at the pictures and read the articles posted near her door. In the process of doing that, though, I fell into a conversation with a man who had been hanging out in the store all this time. His name was A. V. Anderson. He had mahogany eyes and skin, a wide face, and a thin and grizzled mustache. He wore a cream-colored boating cap and a shirt that busied itself with a series of ropes, compasses, and nautical whatnot. A. V. Anderson said he had lived in Alligator all his life, and when I asked him what he thought about the place, he smiled and said, "Oh, it's pretty good! It's pretty good."

Someone came out to Alligator not so long ago making a movie, he said, and he was in it. A bit part. People said to him, "Take your hat off." He took his hat off. Then they said, "Put your hat on this young thang here." He put his hat on the young thang. And that was that. It was a movie about the Blues, but unfortunately no one in Alligator has seen it. Well, I went back to reading the articles on the wall and soon I read that there used to be a hotel in town, so I asked Mr. Anderson about the hotel, and he said something or other. I asked him about the town economy, but at this point in our conversation my hearing or comprehension must have fled altogether because what I heard was *rabbit foot*.

"A rabbit's foot?"

"Uh huh, yessir."

"And what was the main business of the town?"

"Rabbit foot. Salad green — from New Orleans."

He made *green* rhyme with *Orleans*. Or at least I thought that's what he said. Maybe he didn't say that at all. I didn't want to seem stupider than I really am, though, so I mumbled two or three careful inanities and went back to looking at the pictures. In the meanwhile, Britt had fallen into a more fruitful talk with a bright and cheerful girl who was, oh, maybe ten years old and had just come into Mary Ann's Variety. I didn't hear this conversation. I only watched it from halfway across the store, so I report it now as it was reported to me. The girl had a coffee can in her hand and asked Britt if she wanted some coffee. Britt said she didn't. The girl offered coffee again. Britt said she didn't really like coffee. But the girl insisted. She handed Britt the coffee can, and when Britt didn't open it the girl did for her. Zowie! Out popped a big cloth snake with a big spring inside.

All right. Having gotten that far, we climbed back into the car and drove back up the wiggly gullet past the cigarette-smoking girl with the football 10 T-shirt (who had made good progress since we saw her last) until we emerged back out of the mouth of Alligator right at Route 61, hoping to find Bruno.

There was a car wash at the highway called BRUNO'S CAR WASH. Then there was a Phillips 66 station with a long stucco building behind it. That building was new and clean, divided into three sections with each section announced by its own new and clean cloth awning. The awning to the far left was blue, and it said BRUNO'S COIN-OP. The awning in the middle was red, and it said BRUNO'S KWIK MART. The awning to the right, blue again, said BRUNO'S PACKAGE STORE.

We parked the car in front of the middle section and paused for a moment to notice two additional things. First, in the window of the Kwik Mart was an odd little sign that said: "Respect Yourself and Others. NO CUSSING. It's the law!" Second, this whole little area in front of Bruno's was actually very crowded. In contrast to the downtown of Alligator, Bruno's parking lot was jumping! Possibly I'm exaggerating the number of people out there, exaggerating in my own mind as I'm recalling it now. And, incidentally, all of the people hanging around Bruno's were black.

The three of us stepped out of the car and walked into Bruno's Coin-Op, which was (of course) a coin-operated laundromat. Everyone inside the place was black, too, except for the guy at the counter, who was white. I told the white guy at the counter we were looking for Bruno. He said Bruno was over in the package store. We walked out of the coin-op, passed Bruno's Kwik Mart, and went into the door of Bruno's Package Store.

Bruno sat behind a counter in front of shelves racked with wine and liquor. He was white. He was wearing big glasses and a clean, striped, short-sleeved shirt. He had dark eyes and very dark bushy eyebrows beneath a forehead capped by wispy white hair. He was seventy-six years old, if I heard him correctly, and I believe he had concluded at some point that his advanced age entitled him to say whatever was on his mind. That's my indirect way of noting that Bruno was a straight shooter with both barrels: a direct, blunt man with a wiry build, a strong nose, and a strong chin. He had two pencils in his shirt pocket and maybe a couple of pens there as well. He had his phone to the right, his address file to the left, and a telephone book placed face down and open on the counter in front of him. Well, this was a business, and Bruno was a hardworking businessman. There was not a lot of nonsense about this guy is what I'm trying to say, and so the first thing he did, after I introduced ourselves and explained our mission, was to pull out an old newspaper article that summarized the whole story of Alligator.

Alligator may have been named for the alligators that may once have swum in a twisty lake named Alligator Lake that some people say is shaped like an alligator. Other than that, fishermen used to come to the lake to fish for caviar, which they sold to the Hotel Peabody in Memphis. Someone once caught a gar the size of an alligator in that lake. At one time the town had two schools, two churches, sixteen brick stores, six wood frame stores, two smithy forges, a couple of lumberyards, same number of doctors, and about three hotels. During the early 1920s, a passenger train would stop at Alligator about eight times every day to see if anyone wanted a ride. The train used to be called the Key Lime Train for reasons the article failed to make me understand. And at 152 feet above sea level Alligator is the highest town in the county.

Alligator is also, Bruno added (after I had read aloud the last part for the benefit of the Research Assistants), probably the only town in the entire state of Mississippi that's named after a living thing. And what else did we want to know?

Well, I asked him about the name. What did he think? Were there actually alligators in the lake at one time? He said when he came to town in 1934 there weren't, but there may have been during the late eighteen hundreds. But at one time there was a big flood of the Mississippi River, and it could have been that any alligators in the lake escaped or were washed away during the flood. What else did we want to know?

I said that it really looked as if Alligator was a town in serious decline, and I wondered if Alligator was once a lot more prosperous that it looked now. He said that when he first came to Alligator, in the old days, the downtown would be so crowded with people on a Saturday night you could barely walk. Was there anything more?

I asked him why he thought Alligator had declined, and he said it was because of mechanized farming. Before mechanized farming, about all a family could farm would be maybe sixty acres, with sharecroppers or your own family. Everybody did everything by hand. They picked cotton by hand and everything. But then mechanized farming arrived, and that just put a lot of people out of work. The good people just left, he added, and so the good people are now all gone. What more could he help us with?

I said that it kind of looked as if Alligator were predominately black, and I wondered if he had any idea what the ratio was. What percentage of the town was black, what percentage white? He thought it was probably about 75 percent black. What else?

I mentioned that all the businesses I had seen in town looked to be owned by white people, and I wondered if there were any black-owned businesses in Alligator. There used to be a grocery store owned by a black man, he said, but he was gone. Well, there was the King Lounge, he added. That's a black-owned business. It's a juke joint. What else?

What is a juke joint? I wondered. He said that a juke joint, oh, that's a place where people go to act like damn fools. I asked how he would spell "juke." He wasn't sure. I asked if he knew how the word originated. He said he didn't know, but maybe it was something like a nickname. He did know, he continued, that just about everybody in the Delta has a nickname. You say something like, "I'm looking for So-and-So. Do you know where So-and-So is?" And people will say, "We don't know nobody by that name around here." But if you ask for the same person using his nickname, Bobo, they'll say, "Oh, Bobo!" And so everybody has a nickname, which makes it hard to find someone when you need to. Such as when someone owes you something. People like me, he went on, have been brainwashed into thinking that whites abuse colored people around there. The truth is just the reverse. Colored people abuse whites. What else did I want to know?

I couldn't think of much more to ask and so thanked Bruno for the information, and then we left the package store and went back out to the car parked in front of the Kwik Mart. The first thing I did, upon getting back into the car, was recall the conversation with Bruno as well as I could for the benefit of my notebook, but while I was writing in the notebook with one eye I was watching all the people lounging outside the car with the other. Why were they lounging? Why was no one *doing* anything? And, yes, there was some loud talk and drinking from bottles inside paper bags. . . .

Well! But we still hadn't met the man named Aaron Klein who inhabited the Whale Store in downtown Alligator in the middle of the afternoon, so after I finished writing in the notebook, I started the car and started up the wipers. It was still raining. Or rather it was sometimes and wasn't other times, but it was now. And we crawled back down the gullet of Alligator.

This time, however, as we wiggled along that wiggly road beside the wiggly lake, we were met by a dog. He was a big tan German Shepherd lying alongside the road, who (as we approached) elevated himself up on all fours, crouched, and (as the distance between us narrowed) opened his mouth. I thought this dog was yawning at first, but now (as we moved alongside him) he trotted and ran and lunged and tried to damage the heels of our car with a growl and a woof and a snap snap snap. (You might be thinking that a dog who chases a car is a stupid dog. A car is not good to eat. A dog could get run over. But can you believe that three days after this event, the Research Assistants and I were listening to a program on the radio called "Car Talk" and some lady phoned up from Michigan to talk about a car-chasing dog who punctured tires with his teeth? Maybe this was one of those kind of dogs, maybe not, but in any case we were faster than he was.)

Back on the Alligator Main Street we parked our car to the right of the No Name Grocery and to the left of the King Lounge. In front of the Whale Store. We waited there in the rain for Mr. Klein to show up. His store had two big windows on either side of the door, and on each window was written The Whale Store, so we knew we were in the right place. But Mr. Klein wasn't there.

For a while, a soft-spoken dignified man named Homer Lathan sat by himself on the bench in front of the No Name Grocery, and so we did talk to him for a few minutes. Mr. Lathan had brown skin, greenish eyes, and a grayish whitish mustache on his upper lip. He was neatly dressed in a blue-and-white striped shirt, blue pants held by cream suspenders, and a forest green hat on his head. I said Alligator looked like a pretty quiet town. He agreed. It sure was, he said. Everybody was gone, he added. There was nothing to do. He had moved into Alligator about ten years ago to work in the cotton gin, he said, but then about seven years ago it closed, and so now he was sitting out in front of the No Name Grocery on that bench watching the rain fall down.

There wasn't a lot else to say, but I did notice a group of people slowly accumulating beneath the Alligator water tower. Someone had a radio out of which came loud music. There was a lot of loud talking. And I imagined that this was the beginning of a party that would eventually start to jump and maybe end up at the King Lounge as soon as it got dark. Of course, the sign on the door of the King Lounge still said, "You Must Be 21," and my Research Assistants were only barely older than twenty-one if you added their ages. And so after waiting a long while for Mr. Klein to show up at the Whale Store, we gave up and drove back out of Alligator.

The off and on rain had turned off but was now turning on again, and so I unleashed the wipers and let them bite the rain with a snap snap snap. Meanwhile, that surly German Shepherd down the road was waiting for us to cross his territory once again. *There they are!* he said to himself. *There he is!* we said to ourselves. And as we approached he stalked and trotted and then exploded into a rage and a chase with a woof woof woof and a snap snap snap. I stomped on the gas, wailed on the horn, and cut right between his teeth, and before long the growly beast had turned into a panting failure with a droopy tongue, a backwards image fading fast in our rear-view mirror.

Hot Coffee

Downtown Hot Coffee consisted of a general merchandise store inside a big rectangular building with a high façade with big letters: R. J. KNIGHT, HOT COFFEE, MISS.

We walked inside and said "Hello" to a pleasant-mannered woman at the deli bar and counter. Her name was Judy Harper.

Bayne hung out at the deli counter and chatted some with Mrs. Harper, while Britt and I slowly wandered around the store, making for our own edification mental lists of things ordinary and extraordinary. Among the latter, I might include the coffin at the back and, at the front, on top of the deli counter, a big jar full of pickled pigs' feet next to the big jar full of pickled pigs' lips. The lips seemed to wallow and drift ponderously inside their jar, and they reminded me of the tonsils Tommy Blaire had brought floating in a jar to show our fifth-grade class after a doctor had snipped them out. I don't think those were *actual* lips of pigs, though. There were also dresses for sale, umbrellas, live crickets, dishes, and so on.

In the middle of the store was an old coffeepot with some old coffee inside, next to some Styrofoam cups, a can of Cremola, and some stirrers. Not very enticing, but I paid 25 cents and poured myself a Styrofoam cup of lukewarm leftovers, dumped a wad of Cremola into it, and stirred.

There was also, near the front of the store, a small cage with some kind of mean little animal inside, a weasel or ferret possibly, but I make it a point never to look that kind of animal in the eye.

Did I mention this was a big place? It had enough shelves and deer heads on the walls, an interior wall or two, that for a few minutes I imagined the background noise, a grinding and creaking and rushing sound, to be the byproduct of an inefficient air conditioner. Unobservant me. After a few minutes I looked up to see near the rear of the store a man with grayish whitish hair and beard, wearing Polaroid glasses over his eyes and a giant gun strapped to his hip, sweating hard and making a serious lack of progress on a treadmill.

So I put "treadmill" on the mental list and thought to myself, *How advanced. They even rent exercise equipment in this place, and here in fact is the Hot Coffee Sheriff taking a break from crime to get his daily workout.* But that big gun was slightly unnerving. First it made me want to be polite. Then it made me think about robbing the place. Then it made me say to myself, *Don't do it!*

I returned to the deli counter to chat with Mrs. Harper, who once every ten minutes would have to stop talking to me when a real customer appeared. In between dealing with real customers, she said that she had grown up around Hot Coffee, but then when she married her husband, he took a job up in New Jersey, so they moved up there for three years, but she never felt perfectly at home up there. For one thing, people kept commenting about her Mississippi accent. She'd open her mouth and people would say, "Where are you *from?*" and "What are you *doing* up here?" It seemed she couldn't get out of the house or go anywhere without somebody saying something about the way she talked.

After a while, all that whirring and grinding background noise stopped, and the Hot Coffee Sheriff got off the treadmill and very sweatily wandered up to the deli counter. He turned out not to be the sheriff at all. Hot Coffee doesn't have one. He was Herbert Harper, the store's co-owner and co-manager and the husband of Judy.

He had been working out on the treadmill, he said, because his doctor told him he had to lose weight and get in shape, so that was what he was doing. And today was his best day so far. "I got 2.48 miles in 30 minutes, so that's cruising," he said. His goal was 2.5 miles, he said, but he just started off too slow today.

Herbert Harper was a big man with a broad chest, big arms, and a powerful nose. He was a mesomorph, in short, and also an extrovert. He liked to talk. He and I, for example, got into a quite extended discussion at this point about exercise, high blood pressure, losing weight, good versus bad food, too many sweet things, and so on.

Also, he liked to tease — in a good-natured sort of way. In service of the second inclination, he began offering us a taste of those pigs' feet and lips in the jars atop the deli counter. I laughed and pointedly declined. So then he focused his offer on the Research Staff. Britt escaped by wandering off, but Bayne didn't. And Bayne, I began to see, wasn't sure how serious the offer was or how far his status as a quite young person would allow him to retreat from compliance. As Herbert Harper began extolling the virtues of pigs' feet and pigs' lips — tasty, surprisingly delicious, good fat, and so on — and repeating his offer, I watched the growing expression of alarm on Bayne's face. He politely declined once, twice, three times. And, as this was still going on, I started asking myself why the idea of eating lips and tongue was so off-putting to people who are not, for example, French. And then I was thinking to myself that the problem is this: *Lips and tongue are things you eat with, not up.* In the end, we were able to turn the conversation around to a more comfortable direction: the mean little animal inside that cage at the front of the store.

"You ever seen a wampus cat?" Herbert said to me.

"A wampus cat?" I said.

"Sort of like a mink."

"Never seen one," I said.

I wasn't sure I wanted to, but by this time Herbert Harper was standing at the front of that little cage, futzing with the latch and door. "Let's see if I can get him," he said. "Stand back: He's real shy." And he fiddled some more . . . until GREAT GAWD AMIGHTY a vicious furry thing catapulted out of the cage snarling and flying through the air smashing into my chest and preparing to bite me right in the jugular! After hammering that terrible THING away and beating it to the ground — only to discover a limp projectile of cloth and yarn with two glass-bead eyes — I burst out laughing. It was great! Practical jokes of that sort have to send you directly from dreamy complaisance to shock to amazed amusement within nanoseconds, or they're just irritating. This one worked perfectly.

Now that we had been initiated, Herbert and Judy told us the full story of Hot Coffee.

A hundred and some years ago, a man named L. N. Davis owned a store across the road. He sold coffee there. The coffee was hot and good enough that farmers making a haul on the road to Ellisville, a few miles south of there, would always stop at Davis's store to get some hot coffee. They would say to each other, "It won't be long until we can get us some hot coffee." And pretty soon, because farmers don't like to use more words than necessary, they shortened their sentence to "It won't be long until we get to hot coffee." And pretty soon after that, because farmers don't really care whether letters are lower- or uppercase, they began saying: "It won't be long until we get to Hot Coffee." So the whole place was called Hot Coffee.

Well, L. N. Davis in 1920 sold the store to Judy Harper's granddaddy, V. O. Knight. The original store burned down in 1929, though, and so this new store was built then, run by V. O. and eventually his son, R. J. Knight, until 1984. In 1984, she and Herbert had the opportunity to acquire the business from R. J., her daddy. They were in New Jersey then, but they came back to Hot Coffee, took over the store, and have run it ever since.

There used to be a lot of farming in the area, Herbert added, but now there's not so much work, and there's a lot of people on welfare. There are a lot of folks between the age of twenty-four and thirty that have never worked a day in their lives, he said, and of course it hurts to sit in the store eighty hours a week and pay all those withholding taxes so someone else down the road can sit and do nothing, so people can stay at home and have kids. Now you're looking at whole generations, none of them have worked. Well, it can't go on, and of course the government is now trying to get people off welfare and in jobs. It's got to change. It'll be slow and it'll be gradual, but it's got to change.

Now the reason (he continued) he had that big gun on his hip, and the reason (I concluded) they kept that big shotgun Scotch-taped right behind the counter, was that a friend and neighbor got killed by a robber about three years ago. This man had a little business. He'd sell used car parts and new car parts. And he had built that business up. He had it going for a year or two, and it was just getting to where he was making some money when somebody went in there, stuck a shotgun up to his right eye, and pulled the trigger. The day that happened, Herbert sent Mrs. Harper up to the house to get the big gun, and he strapped it to his belt. He's worn it ever since.

So that was Hot Coffee, and after chattering a few more minutes, we thanked Herbert and Judy Harper for their help and left. Bayne, still recovering from the idea of maybe having to eat those floating slimy lips, was now thinking about nothing more exciting than a big head of lettuce. "Right now I have a big craving for a huge head of iceberg lettuce," he said. Britt was just hungry and wanted to get lunch. And I was still laughing inside about being so completely fooled by a silly little practical joke, the flying wampus cat, and at the same time crying inside about the idea of good people getting a shotgun stuck into their right eye and having their brains blown out.

Equality

We spent the night on the edge of Mississippi and in the morning followed Interstate 20 and 59 into the state of Alabama, working ourselves into the proper state of mind by turning up loud our tape recording of "Sweet Home Alabama."

What first surprised me about Alabama was how much seemed to be forest and wilderness. It was quite beautiful, and we crossed the Tombigbee River, a wide deep river, and kept on going through forests. So far so good! And after we had played "Sweet Home Alabama" about a hundred times, we turned on the radio and listened to a series of Country and Western tearjerkers. Then we found a great Gospel station with some really terrific music and a singer who would pause between ecstatic outbursts to say things like: "I'm going to sing another song, and I want y'all to listen to the words of the song. And if you can be a witness, I want y'all to be a witness!" The Good Gospel music brightened us all up, and we rode that station all the way to the edge of Birmingham, where we got into a minor skirmish with major trucks, and I turned off the radio in order to concentrate.

Coming into Alabama, we had stopped at a Welcome Station where somebody gave us a tourist brochure telling about the Civil Rights Museum in Birmingham. That seemed promising, and since Bayne had been studying the Civil Rights movement in school, we decided to visit the museum.

Birmingham looked like a big industrial town. I saw a factory straight ahead that looked like a giant ship, with all kinds of smokestacks and smoke coming out and seeming very serious indeed. To the right was a field in the middle of which sat a building called Midfield Carpet. We saw a sign for the Archie and David Phillips Taxidermist Studio, complete with a big picture of a happy man holding an unhappy fish. So that was Birmingham, only with more factories and smokestacks and gas station signs sticking up and then a big traffic jam. We had been driving at seventy miles an hour behind a Buick that was going backwards because it was being towed on a tow truck. A soaped message on the windshield said "$650 Needs Motor." And suddenly the traffic went from seventy to zero, so we almost bought the Buick and soon were inching painfully at three miles an hour past the Omelette Shoppe.

I turned on the radio once again, but the Good Gospel had been replaced by a Bad Gospel, told by a disturbed little man who was saying things about devil worship and sacrificial worship and a temple. He said, "Now this temple will be there in Jerusalem. This will be the temple where the Ultimate Abomination will be committed when the Man of Sin himself sets up there claiming that he is the Christ! Claiming he is the Messiah! And of course the Abomination, the Desolation, the Desolation follows the Abomination, and let me tell you it will be a time of DESOLATION which the WO-ORLD has never seen!"

Kind of scary, if you know what I mean, and it sobered us right up. We peeled off the highway and entered the business district of Birmingham. After getting lost, we found the Civil Rights Museum. The museum was busy that day, with a few quiet grown-ups along with big platoons of noisy schoolchildren moving from exhibit to exhibit. And most of them, adults and kids, were black. I was surprised to observe that we were among just a few white people in the museum, which probably shows how naïve I am.

I love the South, and I think Alabama is about as good a state as you can find anywhere, but the story of the Civil Rights movement there (as the museum reminded us) has its yin and yang, and the yang includes big bully cops, malevolent dogs, murder, arson, bombings, and a bunch of pointy-headed cross-burning transvestites. Innocent people were killed, sometimes solely because of the color of their skin: like those four beautiful little girls who died in the bombing of the 16th Street Baptist Church, which has been rebuilt since then and happens to sit across the street from the museum.

Legal segregation started in the South once the U.S. Supreme Court, in 1896, decided that blacks and whites could be required to use "separate" public facilities — schools, restaurants, waiting rooms, rest rooms, bus seats — so long as those facilities were "equal." But separate was never equal. As the Supreme Court concluded in 1954, segregation in schools was "inherently unequal." Separating "black children solely because of their race," the Court hypothesized, "generates a feeling of inferiority as to their status in the community that may affect their hearts and minds in a way very unlikely ever to be undone." Segregation was morally and legally wrong. That's what the Supreme Court said, but in Birmingham and elsewhere, brave people had to face cops and dogs and risk their lives before the habits and structures of segregation could be dismantled.

Out of Birmingham we turned south on Route 65, drove behind a truck full of tires, and then after about one or two hours we turned left onto a two-laner called Route 22 and headed out into the boonies with just about nothing on either side of the road except trees and the occasional small wood house and rusty-roofed barn.

Finally we came to the end of 22 and, at the Golden Rule Shell Station and Food Mart, made a right turn onto Route 9, which roller-coastered us for about a dozen miles right up to a sign that said EQUALITY. There was a junction with Route 259 and then the Equality United Methodist Church: a grand old church of white-painted clapboard with a green-shingled roof, stained-glass windows, and a fish-scale-shingled bell tower.

Downtown Equality presented itself to the highway as a scattered smattering of businesses including: the Curiosity Shop on the left as well as a yard full of cement birdbaths and St. Francises, a CLOSED Antique Store, an Equality Vol. Fire Dept., a two-story white wooden building, and a Quality Food Mart with three gas pumps in front of it. That was just about it for Equality on the left (on the one hand). On the right (on the other hand), we passed a nursery and flower shop with some guy out front watering the flowers, the Equality Post Office, maybe a couple of churches, and then not much more.

The Equality Post Office was musty and antique, and it faced the road with a front porch and a door between two sets of windows. There was a small letter box and a sign that said FASTEN SEAT BELT. As we drove up, in fact, a truck driver had just fastened his seat belt and was steering a mail truck away from the mail box. But by the time we had pulled in and parked our car, that truck was gone and the post office was closed and locked.

A young man wearing a red and white UPS NEXT DAY AIR cap on his head had been chatting with the mail truck driver, and now he was just about to cross the busy Route 9 from the post office over to the Quality Food Mart on the other side, and so I asked him if he knew where the name Equality came from. He said we should go right across the road and ask at the Quality Food Mart.

The Quality Food Mart was a squeaky-screen-door kind of place with a giant inflated Budweiser Frog inside. Sitting in a chair at the counter, with a pocket calculator in front of him and a few shelves full of cold, allergy, upset-stomach, and head-ache remedies behind him, was a pleasant gentleman with rectangularized glasses named Charles Wilson. Charles was pink-faced and pink-armed. He may have been sun-sensitive or possibly suffering from a case of psoriasis. He had darkish hair, grayish eyebrows, hazelish eyes, thinnish lips, and a regular nose with a roundish end. He said that Equality used to be called Brooksville. That was a long time ago, around the middle of the last century, he said, but when people wanted to put in a post office the name had to be changed because there was already a Brooksville. When this happened, the town was situated on a major stagecoach route up from Montgomery to wherever. Montgomery was the state capital. And the first important point in the direction of wherever was called Sylacauga. Equality was equally distant between Montgomery and Sylacauga, and so someone named the town Equality in honor of its geographical relationship with those two other important places.

Now, he continued, the road out front, Route 9, was a plank road. "A plank road?" I asked, not sure I had heard that one correctly. That's right, he said. A plank road. They paved the road with lumber all the way from outside of Montgomery and up north, altogether about sixty miles of wood. This was done around 1850. They had the two sawmills in this area working, both of them, so there was lots of wood.

Well, after talking with Charles Wilson, we walked back across the road to our car, parked in front of the post office. Right down the road from our still-parked car was that nursery and flower shop with the guy out front who was still watering flowers.

His name was George Brown, and he seemed happy to stop watering and start talking. He was a solid man with pleasant if somewhat reptilian eyes and a clean-shaven face curved and lit up by an agreeable smile. His face suggested a complete absence of guile that strongly reminded me of Jimmy Carter.

George confirmed the story about Equality: halfway distant between A and B. Equality is a quiet little community, he went on, although on the other hand, what with all the traffic coming down Route 9, it isn't actually so quiet. A lot of local people live in the area, he said, which some of them have got their own businesses while some go elsewhere to work. But in fact a lot of people come there on their way down to the lake. They get a lot of the lake traffic. Lake Martin. One of the largest lakes in the state. We all hadn't seen it yet?

After talking to George Brown for some time, we crossed the highway once more and wandered down to the antique store, which was interesting but closed; past the cement lawn ornament business, which was open but not interesting; and into the Curiosity Shop, where we didn't feel curious.

So we walked out again and wandered back up past the Quality Mart until we came to a little house or cabin, possibly a business of some sort, with a CLOSED sign on the door, a small porch in front of the door, a glider hanging by chains from the ceiling of the porch, and a man sitting in the glider and casually leafing through a magazine about canoes or something.

He was wearing a red-and-white cap that said UPS NEXT DAY AIR, and indeed he was the same person we had spoken to earlier while crossing the highway from the post office to the Quality Mart.

His name was Samuel Slaughter, he said, and he was forty-six years old. He was black—to be more accurate, a warm brown—and he had a trimmed goatee and mustache, a major scar on his nose, and a soft voice and gentle manner.

Equality, he said, was just a common country town. Only thing wrong, it had lost a few of the ingredients, like the beauty parlor, drugstow, and right over there—he gestured vaguely in a northerly direction—used to be a mechanical shop. And there was the ice cream shop where you could get five different flavors: strawberry, vanilla, chocolate, walnut, and, possibly, peach.

"So, in other words," I said, "Equality has kind of gone downhill a little bit."

Well, that wasn't how he would put it. Not really. He meant, it *goes* down, but it comes back up. They did away with the old school. There was a lot of things, but really it's not the deadest town on the road, between twelve miles this way and eight miles that way. The town of Seman, down to the south, it went dead. Town of Nixburg, to the north, it went dead. And there's still a post office in Equality. Now they've got the only post office up and down the road. That's in Equality. And so Equality is still there. It's basically the same town, basically same people. You've got a few migratories, but in general everybody around there just about knows everybody. You can sleep with your windows open and your door unlocked. That's something you can't do in the city.

Samuel in fact had traveled pretty widely. But he was born in Equality, and when he finally came back home he slept for two days. Never heard a siren. Never heard a cop or nothing. And his Mama say, "I thought you were dead." He woke up, he said, "I think I'll get ready. I think I'll go to the club." She said, "Do you know what day it is?" He said, "It's Sunday evenin." She said, "No, it's not. It's Monday."

When you hear a siren around Equality, it's serious. That's right. And you can hear the whippoorwills. Late in the evening. At night: owl. Turkeys gobblin early in the morning. Coyotes howlin at night. It's nice. He wouldn't trade it for the world. Yep. If he had to trade Equality for any other place in the world, no dice.

It did sound nice, I concurred, and then, still trying to get a handle on the size of the place, I asked him about the churches. I thought I had seen three churches in town. "There are three churches. Right?" I said.

Four, he said. And he named them. Then he corrected himself. That was white churches. Four white churches. And, he added, they also have one black church in Equality. What happened, it was two black churches, and they combined both churches. The old original building was first a schoolhouse, and if we went out there we'd see the old original building still down there now, but what they did they turned around and built a church on the side of the old building. And if we wanted to see that old church, we could go see it. We could just open the door in the old church, walk in, old pews, and everything. Original pews. Cemetery and everything.

So we followed Samuel's directions out the other side of town until we came to a quiet little grove of trees and a spread-out blanket of grass with a little shady graveyard over to the left and the two churches. There was the new cinderblock church, and there was the old wooden church.

The old church was an architectural representation of the straight-and-narrow, and the new church was not so fancy either. It was a box-shaped building with a low-pitched roof. Four walls made of cinderblocks, a front door at the front, a back door at the back, and about three rectangular windows on each of the two sides.

While we were looking at the churches, a man and woman pulled up in a small truck and now were busy fixing up the graveyard: trimming weeds and tending flowers. I asked them about the history of the church. The man said nothing, and the woman said she thought we ought to try asking one of the deacons. Maybe Adolphus Murphy, she thought. He was a church deacon and also had lived all his life in Equality.

The Murphy house, a white bungalow with green trim and green shutters decorated with big white half-moons, was set back from the road about twenty or thirty feet on a broad tree-studded lawn, and the lawn was decorated with windmills and birds and flowers and beaucoup objets d'art made of welded this and welded that. The front porch was wonderfully dripping with about a hundred wind chimes, and since it was windy that day, after we parked our car next to the house and climbed the blue stairs onto the porch, we were enveloped by a pleasant rainfall of chinging dinging and tinging.

The front door was open, the screen door shut, and I knocked. Mrs. Murphy came out, sat down, and chatted with us until her husband eventually emerged.

Adolphus Murphy was handsome and self-possessed, with a young man's physique and an older man's white hair—along with white inverted **V** eyebrows, extended white sideburns, white mustache, and a thin vertical line of white hair at his chin. He wore a plaid short-sleeved shirt, dark salmon-colored pants, and sandals. He was, it soon became apparent, an advocate of the Gospel of the Good Kind, a man guided by the best of the Christian virtues. He seemed open and generous, gentle and trustworthy. And yet the sharp arch of his eyebrows, the vertical line at his chin, and the athletic vigor of his posture suggested a latent angularity of character, qualities beyond blessed meekness: such as tempered righteousness. Anyhow, we sat down in the cushiony chairs on his porch, listened to the musical racket of the wind chimes, and gazed relaxedly and lazily over the spread of his yard.

I said I thought it was a pretty stretch of land. I mentioned that Mrs. Murphy had just mentioned that they used to farm on their property, and I asked him what kind of crops they grew.

And so soon we learned that they grew corn and peas and stuff like that. They had an acre of cotton one year. Well, they rented the place for forty years until they got the chance to buy it. The owner, after she inherited it one day when her daddy died, offered to sell to them. She said, "We don't want you to leave." She said, "Y'all have took care of that place so well, we want you to have it." She even financed it herself. Of course, when they moved there nobody didn't want it. It was in a mess. Adolphus and his wife spent a lot of hard days around there trying to make it look like somebody live there. But farming was not his steady occupation. He drove a truck for the county until he retired about four years ago.

I described our interest in Equality and also in the history of his church. And Adolphus said that the Goodgrove Missionary Baptist Church had just a long history, of which he could tell us some. The church was first organized back in the 1800s, and the church used to meet in a log cabin. Well, that was in the woods now. Then later they took the old school. That building beside the new church was the old school. They had service in there for a number of years, and Goodgrove church was established in 1965. There was a church down below Equality called Good Hope. The church in Equality was Oak Grove. So when they decided to consolidate the two churches, they came up with the name Goodgrove. He said the name of the present pastor—and then he listed about a dozen of the previous pastors. Active members, the church has just about maybe twenty-five. But the Lord has blessed them to build that new church now, and it is paid for. They've been in it about two years, and they've carpeted the floor, put in air conditioning, bought a new piano and organ. And that was about the history of the church, he concluded, good as he knew.

"Is it a hundred percent black?" I asked.

Yes, he responded, it's predominantly black. They have some whites come every once in a while, but it's predominantly black. Of course, their congregation has been invited down to the Methodist Church. They always invite, but it's hard to visit morning service when you're full-time and have your own morning service. They have been in white churches. The white churches invite them. And they have one or two whites at Goodgrove sometimes. They welcome them anytime, he said.

Having just stopped at the Civil Rights Museum a few hours earlier made me wonder now about the situation in a small town like Equality in the old days, thirty and forty years ago, before the Civil Rights movement. So I asked, "Was there segregation in Equality?"

"Yeah, yeah," he said.

"They had white and colored drinking fountains?" I asked.

Yeah, he said. They had water fountains for the whites and water for the black, and of course black had to go to the side door of restaurants and things like that, had to ride on the back of the bus. That was what the boycott was all about in Montgomery. Rosa Parks wouldn't get up, and that was what started that boycott. In fact, he saw it all reviewed on TV this morning. And he and his wife were just talking about it this morning. He was reared on a farm, and he and his daddy used to have a lot of white people round, on the farm. And he could just name just a few whites that would sit down to the table and eat with them. Most of the time you had to walk back out to the well, and they'd fix your food on another table.

So when the law changed, I said, after the boycotts and everything and the law changed, did things change fast around Equality?

Well, it was a slow change, Adolphus Murphy began, because they *still* have some prejudiced people. And yet the Bible tells us it's not but one church, one Lord, one faith, one baptism, and if they're teaching something different in another church, well that he didn't know about, because his Bible says there ain't no difference.

I wondered about the economic situation in Equality, if there were any black-owned businesses. I had noticed about five or six businesses, I said, but it looked as if they were all owned by white people.

"Mighty little business in Equality anyway," Adolphus responded. Now up in Alexander City, about fourteen mile northeast of Equality, it's one or two little black-owned businesses. Ain't no big business. But in any case, Equality, yes, it has gone downhill economically, he thought. Because he could remember when it was four stores at one time was operating. That was back in the 1950s, he would say, late '40s and '50s. It was a bunch of stave mills in there.

There were lot of people in there, blacks. The Dallas Cooper Company came from south Alabama, and they had five stave mills in the county. They made staves for nail kegs. They'd cut timber and cut staves out of it, to make those nail kegs. They would make them, haul them to the railroad tracks, and ship them out. Because there was good wood around there, lot of timber in the country at that time. And so it used to be a pretty big place, Equality did. It used to be a calaboose there, like a jail, back in those days, and they had a big cattle barn sold mules. But they tore down all that barn and calaboose and all that. That was before his time, though. He was born in '32 and that was a little before then. Anyway, there was a lot of money circulating through there in those days, because they worked about forty men to the mill, and there were, like he said, five or six mills in the county. So there was good work. The stave mills left in the '60s, and he didn't even know whether they were still in operation now because people don't use nail kegs now. They use cartons or boxes.

But Alabama is still a pretty state, Adolphus continued, and he still reckoned it was about as good a state as he knew of in the South. They didn't actually have a lot of problems. He himself ain't never had no problems, because he has always tried to be a man who would tend to his business. He never had time to mess with nobody else. Like he said, he's been used to white people. He grew up with 'em, played with 'em, ate with 'em. He never had no problem. They worked the fields together. They all got water from the same spring. And he helped a lot of them. Fed a lot of them. His daddy did, too, back in what they call Hoover's Day. The Research Staff and I might have heard talk of President Hoover. That was back in the '30s. And there was a lot of what they called "tramps" on the road. They were white, but everybody called them "tramps." There wasn't no jobs then, and if you wasn't a farmer you couldn't hardly live. Those tramps would just get out walking and hitchhiking and finding something to do, and they would stop in at his daddy's place.

He remembered one couple in particular. They had two kids with them, and they stayed at the house about three days. His daddy had a pile of sawmill slabs, and the man said he'd cut them up for a quarter. But that was to stay there and eat. So his daddy let him do it, and so they stayed there about three days. He cut them up, too, in the three days, and then they said, "Well, we got to move on further, see if we can find something else to do." They had a little dog, and they said that before they came up to the house they had gotten so hungry, back down from the house about maybe a mile and a half, they said they had stopped and built a fire, fixin to eat that dog. And the poor little dog jumped out of their hands, and they said that's what saved him.

So, yeah, anyhow, things are better than they were. Yeah, they are better. He could see some change, some difference. Better than they used to be, but it was not a hundred percent. Not a hundred percent. Probably won't be in his day, but maybe before the end of time it will. Most of the old heads has died out, and whatever you are taught you believe in that. And these people were taught to dislike black folk, and well, you can't fault them for it. They were taught that. And of course like he said most all those has died out, and the young generation knows different.

As for the Ku Klux Klan, they never had no problem with them in Equality. He'd seen them parade through, but they never stopped. Yeah, they'd parade, they'd come right through, right on down the highway we had driven on and were looking at now from our seats on his front porch, like they be going to parades or whatever. That was back in the '60s. Well, that was the time Dr. King was fighting for equal rights and equal justice and all, and the Klan didn't like it, but Dr. King just kept fighting for equality. And equality will come. It will. It's going to come a day when it won't be no difference between the races: Black and white, we're all going to heaven before the end of time, because that's the only way the Lord is going to have it.

"That's right," I agreed—and then I asked some more questions. I asked questions until he was all answered out, at which point we both fell into a wordless reverie and listened to the windchimes go ching ding and ting. The Research Staff, who had been not saying much, also listened to the windchimes.

Bayne later told me he watched a bee sit on my arm for about ten hours straight without moving at all.

Between

Between Equality and our next major destination (my brother's house in South Carolina) stretched hundreds of miles of concrete, at the halfway point of which besat Between. After a thunderstormy night and a sleepy morning, we pointed our ornament north and east in the appropriate direction. But before the beginning of Between began began the Atlantis of Atlanta, through which, a few hours later, we bestrode lickety-split on a six-lane corridor known as Interstate 20.

Between listening to the Supremes and designing (in our minds) motorized skateboards, we bemused ourselves enough that, although it was already midafternoon, it didn't seem so by the time we passed out the other end of Atlanta and turned left onto a two-lane Route 11. We beamed ourselves north through a couple of old Southern towns before betaking a left onto Route 78, four lanes bringing us to an intersection where we beheld the sign: WELCOME TO BETWEEN.

We bent right.

But between the Between Grocery on the left and an older lady on her front porch on the right, there didn't seem to be a lot *to* Between, just (riding down the street) a closed City of Between City Hall, the New Hope United Methodist Church (Welcome Food for the Soul 11 AM Sunday), a few houses, and one busted barn bedeviled by vines of the beastly sort. Between seemed more concept than community, in other words, and we drove back to the place between the Between Grocery and the lady on the porch. The lady on the porch was Miss Frances Thompson. Miss Frances sat in a plastic chair with a fluffy white pillow at her back, a cane propped against the door to her left, and, at her feet, a glass with watermelons painted on it and a flyswatter. She was petite, white-haired, and wearing a modest cotton nightdress and slippers. She may have been temporarily up from bedridden. She bemoaned the fact that she didn't know the story of Between and had never heard it because she had only been in Between since 1950, but the woman across the street inside the Between Grocery would be sure to know whatever it behooved one to know.

The Between Grocery was a convenience store in a modern building with aluminum-framed plate glass windows between decorative flagstone walls. Taped onto one of the double glass doors a sign said *Please notice. We DO NOT have a public telephone! No beer either. We are a Christian establishment in both word and deed. However we will be glad to pray with you, give directions if we can, and send you on your way with a blessing and a smile. Lois Stowe, proprietor.*

Between the doors we went, and, since we wanted neither telephone nor beer, I thought we had come to the right place. The proprietor, Lois Stowe, was standing behind the counter between the cash register and a stack of Nestle's White Crunch. She had dark hair and light eyes, a full nose and thin lips. She was bespectacled and benign.

"Between, I have been told," she began, "got its name from the mail carrier. When he got here he was halfway between his route. And that's where it got its name. It was halfway between Monroe and Loganville, and it's halfway between Athens and Atlanta. And it's halfway between heaven and hell. Where are you from?" "Massachusetts," I said, and I explained our mission. Then I said that Between looked pretty small. She said that about a hundred people live there, more or less, and the town was originally founded in 1908. But the grocery isn't the only business in town. A heating and air business was on the other side of that big house we could see way over there out the window.

Between seemed like it was in a pretty part of the country, I said, and I noted my surprise at seeing how rural the area was while on the cartographicus magnus it looked awfully close to Atlanta sprawl. "Not yet, not yet," she said. "We're working on it." She said that was bound to happen real quick. She herself had been in Between since 1968, and even since then the place has changed quite a bit, quite a bit. It has been growing on the outskirts, she said, and subdivisions were beginning to appear all around Between.

We might have talked longer with Lois Stowe in Between, but right then a bunch of customers began bursting through the doors in a bustle that, I believed, could have become bedlam. At the same time, I perceived, we had to hustle to reach bedland at my brother Dwight's house (actually his wife's house) in South Carolina. So we bought some things, betokened our gratitude, and betook ourselves out of Between.

It seemed as if we drove for a long long long time between one thing and another all the way down to the bottom of South Carolina where my brother Dwight's wife's house (actually on temporary loan from the U.S. government) was sitting in the middle of a big Air Force base. We were stopped between gates at the base, then finally passed on through until, after an ultimate twist and turn (boxed betwixt the benighted bungalows of a sleeping major and an insomniac colonel), we in bedraggled befuddlement belatedly beheld our bemused beloveds and were bewelcomed with hugs and mugs and three soft beds with six fresh sheets doubled and opened (like envelopes), into which we (as into a cloud or a dream) besettled ourselves gently down between and between and between.

Harmony

Life on the Air Force base was satisfying as well as exciting. We got a lot of VIP treatment including an exclusive tour of the inside of a C-17 so significant I'm not allowed for security reasons to say any more, except to note that it looked like the inside of a giant silver whale.

We had such a relaxing time at the base that when we did finally pull out, waving good-bye, on a hazy Tuesday or Wednesday morning—I forget which—we all felt homesick and tired. We were tired of traveling and tired of being in the car and tired in general. Another problem: Britt was tired of the music I liked, and I was tired of the music she liked. For security reasons I won't say any more. In short, by the time we were humming northbound for North Carolina, a lot of disharmony had started floating around inside our car. In a desperate effort to improve the situation, at the first gas station we ran into I rummaged through the musical tapes rack and found three possibly agreeable ones: classic favorites by Johnny Cash, Chuck Berry, and Bob Dylan. What they don't tell you about those tapes in the gas stations is that the songs are there because they were never good enough to appear on actual records. Johnny Cash was so bad—especially "Ring of Fire"—that we finally got into the habit of playing it whenever we needed a complete howl.

After about two or three hours of fiddling along into North Carolina, we saw a sign for the Harmony Chiropractic Center, and then we passed some brick suburban houses and dish antennae, Dawn's Clip Joint, some wood barns with rusted roofs, worms and crawlers for sale, and, at last:

WELCOME TO HARMONY
PLEASE DRIVE CAREFULLY.

At that point, the highway became the main street of town, and we followed it past the Harmony Galaxy Food Center, the Mission Hispana de Harmony offering Estudio Bíblico on Domingo 7:00 PM, and a somewhat grand Baptist Church at town center, as well as a cafeteria, a bank, funeral home and chapel, a video store, the Harmony Church of God, a flower shop, and so on. It seemed like a pretty tuneful little place with lots of active businesses, and the road came to a four corners with Route 901 in the middle of things around the Square Deal Garage.

We drove for a few measures, rested a few more, and then decided to improvise. Seeking a few good notes, a tune, or even a major melody, we turned onto 901 and dropped into the suburbs and out again, past Soft Serve Ice Cream for eighty-nine cents and into fields of dark tobacco. Tobacco is really an attractive plant. It looks like a giant cabbage. But we picked up the tempo and became lost, wandering aimlessly along Fox Hunter Road past houses and barns, plants and animals, until finally, as the morning turned into noon and increasingly hot, the curtain rose on lazy flies buzzing around farm buildings and a hawk circling over a farmhouse built ten years before the Civil War.

The house was simple but satisfying, and it consisted of a gabled second floor above a first floor and a wraparound porch. Vinyl clapboard had lately been placed over the original wood siding. Furniture and other objects from the inside of the house were spilling outside onto the porch, while a flag with a cow picture dangled in the humid half-breeze from a flagpole attached to the center front-porch post.

A chorus of actual cows chomped and mooed just beyond the right side of the house. To the left of the house, in a dirt parking area shaded by a big tree, sat, on two white plastic chairs, a pair who introduced themselves as Lonnie and Edna Harris. Once we described our mission, additional plastic chairs were brought out and arranged. Approximately four sleepy dogs, after ushering us into our places, curled up in the dirt around the five plastic chairs, groaned, and became even more sleepy.

Lonnie and Edna Harris were tobacco farmers. Lonnie was at the moment recovering from pancreatitis and gall bladder surgery that required six weeks in the hospital. He wore slippers. He had a full mustache and big eyebrows and a rectangular face, and, although his heroic baritone occasionally rang out a phrase or two, mostly he played a backup role punctuated by his own steady percussion. A cigarette butt lay in the dirt next to his chair, and, while Edna took center stage, Lonnie chewed and unchewed tobacco, coughed occasionally, and steadily drummed the cigarette butt with the end of his cane. He hit that cigarette butt with his cane about two million times.

Edna had shoulder-length hair and a forceful chin. She wore a black T-shirt that said D.A.R.E. to Keep Kids Off Drugs, lavender shorts, a blue hat, and Keds without socks. She was a wiry but powerful protagonist, a feisty contralto who delivered her stirring aria on the theme of harmony in Harmony with a sure cock of the head and a steady fix of the eye.

She and Lonnie grow mostly tobacco but also hay for dairy cows, she declared. It's a good area, good climate for farming, she added. Sure, they have droughts once in a while, but they still have a good growing season. But people have been growing tobacco in that area forever. Well, we were in the tobacco belt. She knew, Edna continued, that a lot of people don't believe in growing tobacco. They say that it's a health hazard. But everything is a health hazard if you don't use a little common sense with it. You can drink a gallon of milk a day and just sit down and set there. That's a health hazard. But tobacco generates so much taxes, and these people that vote in Congress maybe they'll talk how they want to see the tobacco go out, but yet and still when it comes down to voting on paper, in secrecy, they vote for it. If they didn't, tobacco wouldn't really be here. Of course, right to the north of Harmony about forty or fifty miles used to be the moonshine capital of the world. Brooks County. And Junior Johnson, the big race car driver, that's where he got his start. That was where he learnt to drive a car was running moonshine. That was how he learnt, and there's just lots of those race car drivers back in there that was born and raised.

Now, as for the Harris farm, Edna generally goes to the field and helps do all the work in the field. There's nothing that she don't do. She drives the tractor. She mows the hay. She can plant the corn or bale the hay, plow the tobacco. But this year she had to have surgery on her eye, an aneurysm, and Lonnie was sick. The first of May, he was real sick. He stayed in intensive care about six days. And so two Mexican migrant workers came along a-hunting work, and they are really good. They just go on with it. And when she came home with the patch over her eye, they shaked their finger at her and told her to walk back to the house. They don't speak English.

Now, tobacco used to involve lots of work, Edna continued, but these days it's pretty much mechanized. It used to be one man and his wife and three to five children could only work about three or four acres of tobacco. And then they had to work constantly. But now she and Lonnie have got thirty-two acres of tobacco.

Well, they used to sow the seeds along in January or February. Back years ago, before plastic, they sowed them under canvas. And every day, you had to take that canvas off, if the weather was permitting, and let the sun through. And then you had to put it back at night. But now, they've got a greenhouse, so that's a lot easier now. Then when the plants were big enough to set, they used to go through the fields and plow with their horses or their tractors and make a row, and then they'd go back and put that fertilizer in the row. And then they would set the tobacco. And most of it was set by hand. You dropped your plant in. But now that is mechanized, too. Then toward the end of summer comes harvest time. Well, they don't harvest the plant all at once. They harvest the lower leaves first, when the leaves get slightly yellow. They take off about six or eight leaves at a time and then later come back and take off the rest, when it's ready. And then once they harvest the tobacco, it has to be dried. They have to put it in the barns, and it used to be they put the plants into stick barns. You racked that tobacco on a stick with a string, and you placed it on the poles in that barn. And you hung it. It took a long time to dry. But these days it takes about a week to dry the tobacco in barns fired by propane.

So things are maybe getting a little easier, but yet and still they have had some hard times, and not so long ago there was a lot of foreclosures. Edna and Lonnie themselves almost lost their farm. She was going to have to give up. But she has been in this community since 19 and 39. And Lonnie was born and raised here. And so they just hung on by the hair of their teeth and stayed in there. And when people seen that they survived, then they started going: "Well, how did you do it?"

They just fought it out and done without and done the best they could do. Well, the lending agency made it easy for farmers to get in this hole. They go to a farmer's home, and they'd say, "Oh, if you need $10,000, let's build you another building over here. Let's buy you another tractor." And sometimes farmers would be gone in debt maybe $50,000 or $60,000 that they didn't even need. It wasn't essential. And then the prices and their equity dropped. And so then people had to start selling it off.

So anyway, after they saved their farm Edna went to mediation classes and became a certified mediator. And a lot of people did, so they could go with the farmer to the banker that was fixed to foreclose, and tell him, "Well, if you're going to foreclose on him, the next one that comes and fills his shoes is not going to be any better off. And just give him a little longer." They saved several farms like that. She just begged farmers not to give up.

And then the farming community in that part of North Carolina was almost completely wiped out from the drought in 1986. But people rallied behind one another. At that time there was a lot of them that did lose their farms and everything, but people rallied behind one another and tried to help one another, and she was one of the people that had a big hand in that hay deal that they brought in there. They didn't have rain from March to September, not a bit, and in July that year they had about thirty days that it was over ninety degrees. But they just got behind one another and united, and there was people all over the country that helped out one way or another. There was a lot of church groups from Massachusetts that sent down bales of hay so their cattle wouldn't starve. There was a whole bunch of people that were sitting in a bar in Ohio. And someone in Ohio says, "Looka there, it says Tarheels are in trouble," and so in about three days they had about eight or ten loads of hay coming in from Ohio, and it was a help. And they even brought a helicopter that come and landed in the crossroads. That was the only place they had to land. They came and landed up there, and they brought church people and different groups that come to help out.

As for how Harmony got its name, well, the mayor of town, John Ray Campbell could tell us more about it than she could. It must have been way back around 1850 or so. And the farmers, they set aside one week a year. And they all gathered at a campground. They called it Harmony Campground. And they'd go and spend the whole week with the neighbors all the way around from everywhere. It was a Christian camp where they sang those old Christian harmonies. And the farmers tried to work their crops to get them harmonized to where this was a time of lay by, where there didn't have to be a harvest in it, and they were really just waiting for the crop to cure. So that's where Harmony got its name. But if we wanted to know any more about the camp meetings, we really had to go see John Ray Campbell, the mayor, who was working down at the Galaxy. His great-grandparents were part of the ones that helped to organize this Harmony singing.

We talked a lot more until it was time for Act Two and a change of scenery, at which point Edna and the three of us piled into the car and drove *allegro con vivissimo* into town, where we found Mayor John Ray Campbell bagging groceries at the Galaxy. Mayor John Ray was tall and lean, bespectacled and positive, wearing a white shirt and a blue-and-yellow Galaxy Food Center cap. He took time out from bagging long enough to stand in front of a wall of Coca Cola two-liter bottles on special for eighty-nine cents and provide his own distinctive variation on the theme we had just enjoyed.

There were camp meetings, he began, and after the camp meetings they started with a school, a farm school, which was the oldest school in North Carolina. Well, now, this year they are celebrating the 150th year of the camp meeting coming up in October, second week in October. And this part of the country, they are sitting on a hill here. And so what they did, they named it Harmony because of the camp meeting and singing. And because of the hill, they named it Harmony Hill. And so that continued as Harmony Hill until probably some time in the early '20s. Then it went just to Harmony. And then the village was there until 19 and 27. In 19 and 27, they wanted to get electricity, and so then they formally incorporated it as a town so they could get money.

As mayor of Harmony, since there is no town manager, John Ray continued, it falls on him to see after the solid waste, lights, the police, and everything. It's a one-man police force, really, is what it amounts to. But Harmony is actually real quiet. It's mainly a farming community. And then they have about seven or eight industries close by. Only one inside the city limits but real close. Lowe's Hardware has one of their biggest distribution warehouses within four miles of there, and Harmony also has a big rendering plant where useless chicken parts are rendered into useful items such as lipstick and body oils. After World War II, these men came back from the service, and they would pick up the livestock and sell the hide and cook the livestock for a byproduct. And then gradually the livestock turned into poultry so that now, any waste from a chicken, they cook it and then render it. There are a lot of tobacco farmers in the area, too, and the main buyers for the tobacco would be all of them. R. J. Reynolds. Phillip Morris. All of them.

Well, that was interesting, I thought, and after we quietly applauded Mayor Campbell for his contribution, he exited stage left and went back to bagging groceries.

Next came Intermission, during which we drove *poco con meditativo* around Harmony here and there, until we arrived at the very spot where the original meetings used to take place at the far edge of town. There was a historical plaque there, a gazebo, and a school. Then we drove around town some more while Edna returned to the central theme. Mayor John Ray Campbell and his family were born and raised in this area, she said. She wasn't. She was born in West Virginia.

Now, her husband's grandpa on his mother's side was the only one that was surviving from the Civil War in that family. They were all killed in the Civil War except his grandfather. And so they gave him a land grant or something after the war. And he brought his bride and settled and took that land grant in a quiet little spot just south of Harmony. But during the Civil War, Harmony was turned upside down and shaken until it turned into a place of great disharmony. The Yankees had what they called the foot soldiers, and then they had the ones that rode the horses, that went through. And some of them were decent, but some were not. There were several battles and a lot of destruction of property as the army came through. There was a lot of hatred.

Of course, that's all demised now and gone, Edna went on. But her grandmother was living up in Wilkes County, and *her* mother was about fifteen years old when the Yankees came through. They killed her daddy. Her daddy was an older man, and he was an invalid, and they killed him. The soldiers did. And her great-grandmother run and hid. And she got away. There was the soldiers that ravaged a lot of women, but she got out and got away and lived in the woods about two years. And Edna's grandmother didn't ever tell how, but she would slip back to the homestead. The Yankees, when they came in and run you off, they just held onto the land. And they had a lot of dried fruit, apples and peaches and stuff that they dried in the sun. The Yankees fixed it in the sun and dried it to take care of their needs through the winter. And her great grandmother slipped back and got one sack of those apples, one bag. They generally put them in a cloth bag or a hand-spun bag. And she got that one. And that was all the food that she had. She would always tell her grandchildren to just be thankful when you went to the table if you just had one biscuit or one piece of bread, or one bite of one kind of food to eat.

Now Edna didn't think you could say that there was really anybody that kept slaves around Harmony in the way that, like some people on farther down

South, where they beat them and it was all that way. These people through there, plum on back into the early 1800s, there had been blacks and whites together. And when they desegregated the schools, they didn't have no trouble in Harmony. Maybe there was trouble in North Carolina, but around her part of the state at least if there was trouble it was because somebody from the outside came in.

And there are enough people to work the farms if social services and welfare hadn't ruint a lot of people in this area. Are you going to get out here and work in the fields if you can set there in the shade and draw a check? If you can go to the doctor and get your doctor bills paid, are you going to make any effort to do anything different? And now there was young black people that were getting away from it now, but there was young black people in this area that wouldn't hit a lick at a snake. And there was a lot of white ones, too. They say, "Well, I'm going to stay at home with Mama, and we're going to draw our check. We're not going to work." When Lonnie and Edna first bought the farm, there was a family living in the renter house. The woman's husband had died, and she had four boys that was about the same age as Edna's boys. Edna's children worked, and they worked hard. They done anything there was to do. Well, the woman that was their renter set up there. She had the four boys and three girls. And the welfare was furnishing her wood. They were hauling her wood up there. But Edna and Lonnie had plenty of wood, too. Edna told her that if she'd let her boys go out and help the Harris boys cut wood, they would furnish her wood in return. And she said, "No." She said that if she let those boys go cut a load of wood, her welfare check would be cut. Well, now, was that learning those children to take care of themselves?

So it just becomes a cycle, where people never get off it. Of course, there are those people that need it, too, for one reason or another, but there's been enough abuse to make it bad for everybody.

Soon we were back out in the countryside, and soon after that we came upon James Smyre, one of Edna's longtime colleagues in the tobacco-farming business, and we talked to him in what might be considered Act Four. I noticed that when Edna started talking about tobacco with Mr. Jim, as she called him, what had been *tobacco* for our benefit became a cozier *baccer* for theirs.

Mr. Jim was a velvet tenor with a full, handsome face, who wore a brown plaid work shirt, a comfortable set of bib overalls, and a dark-blue tractor cap over white hair. One of the few African-American tobacco farmers in the Harmony region, Mr. Jim is actually now retired from farming. But he worked hard all his life, and so now, he explained, he has earned the right to set. When we got there, he was setting in a chair out in his carport next to a python in a box that had been his son's pet, got loose, then was caught again. Mr. Jim was very quiet and spare with words.

Lord, he didn't know exactly how many acres his tobacco farm used to be, he said. He just didn't know exactly. He used to farm with the help of his children and grandchildren, but they're not farming any longer. They have all begun to sail out. One of them went to work in a factory somewhere, and another one is now in Virginia. Mr. Jim started out farming after the Second World War. And in the winter time, when they couldn't farm, they was sawmilling or doing something like that. They didn't lay down. They kept a-goin: cuttin wood or doin something. As for Harmony proper, he hadn't ever really paid too much attention to it, one way or the other.

Well, Mr. Jim and Edna hadn't seen each other for a while, what with all the recent medical problems, and so it wasn't very long before Mr. Jim's solo merged into a recitative duet with Edna, a duet on the subject of catching up with each other.

"Henry got home, Mr. Jim."

"He did?"

"He's been in the hospital six weeks."

"What was it for?"

"He had pancreatitis. They operated on him and went into his pancreas and split part of it open. And they took out his gall bladder."

"I declare."

"I thought maybe you knowed he'd been sick. And you know, he's been sick for a year now, off and on, you know, when he'd take them spells. So it just got so bad we took him to the hospital, and they told him if he didn't have that surgery, he was going to die."

"I declare. Is he big as he used to be?"

"No. He weighs 126 pounds."

"Oh, boy. He *has* come off."

On went the duo in their catching-up duet on an increasingly hot afternoon. Edna said she hadn't seen Mr. Dobson. Or Robert and them either. Mr. Jim said he had seen Robert the other day. Edna wanted to know if Robert's baccer was doing any good. Mr. Jim said he was working it. He was talkin about it. That last rain, if something didn't grow then, it just wasn't no count. Well, Edna thought, tobacco is like a weed. It can stand there dormant for two or three or four weeks and not move. And then it will just come right out. Edna had been sick herself, she went on, with the eye problem. And she hoped they were going to let her go back to driving next week. She would be going back to the doctor next week, and the doctor had told her she better not drive any more until her eyes got fixed. The doctor said if she did and she was to have a wreck, her insurance probably wouldn't honor it. Well, Mr. Jim hadn't done any driving either, he said. He hadn't even drove a tractor. Oh, he might have moved it, but not driving.

Time passed, the sun moved, the day got hotter still, until at last we shook hands with Mr. Jim and excused ourselves. We drove around some more while Edna showed us more Harmony sights and then invited us to go see the Harmony rendering plant. We decided against the rendering plant, and so made a final change of scene *andante perspirante* back to the house, where we found Lonnie still sitting in the plastic chair in the shade and beating down the cigarette butt with the end of his cane.

By this time the afternoon was growing to a hot close, and the audience returned to their original plastic chairs in the shade and allowed themselves to melt a little. We listened to a mooing brew of cows from the other side of the house, a winged woodwind of insects inside the tall grass beyond, and the distant drumming of farm machinery in a field. The hazy morning and hot afternoon now had turned into a sleepy late-in-the-day finale, and for a long while we just set in the shade back by the Harris house and tested the breeze.

This was a lazy time, a quiet dénouement where themes once powerfully expressed and expanded were recalled and restated but with rests in between and a humbly mumbly subtlety: *sotto voce*. The quiet breeze, the soft and gentle notes of nature on a hot afternoon in the North Carolina countryside, drew us into our own dreamy quietude.

We listened to the birds.

We listened to the cows.

We listened to the tobacco.

"I don't know what about you," Edna said at last, "but lots of people come to my house, and they say, 'How in the world do you stand it? I couldn't stand to stay here. Since it's so quiet and still.' That's what we like! You can hear the birds. You can hear the wind. A girl from Charlotte was on the phone the other day, and her husband was settin there, and he was a-talkin, and she told him to be quiet a minute. He says, 'What's the matter?' She says, 'I want you to listen at the wind.' Says, 'It's running through the trees. The leaves are running together.' And he says, 'You can't do such as that in Charlotte.' Well, I'm glad I'm where I'm at. I'd much rather be where I'm at as to be in some city."

The audience would have liked to pass the rest of the day, maybe the rest of their lives, right out there on the plastic chairs, chatting desultorily with Edna and Lonnie, listening languidly to the harmony of nature and considering seriously the harmony of Harmony. But the final curtain rolled down at last, and so they applauded most gratefully and appreciatively, gathered themselves out of their seats, and departed.

Toast

We stayed in a cheap motel near Mocksville that night and in the morning forwent breakfast, intending to order eggs and toast at a nice little eating spot in Toast.

The trail to Toast, up from Mocksville and through Mt. Airy, took us at first into some hilly farm country with fields of corn, tobacco, and whatnot spread into the hills. And, along the road, tanning salons. Hard to imagine, I know—to be in farm country and people paying for tans—but that's the way it was.

Somewhere along that route, we came upon an old graveyard filled with ancient tombstones, often half legible, sometimes half illegible, and many cracked and broken. And trees and weeds. There we found the tombstones of Daniel Boone's parents, Squire and Sarah Morgan Boone. A little farther over, a plaque said that Daniel Boone had been born to Squire and Sarah Boone in 1734 and after about twenty-four years married Rebecca Ryan, had some children, and lived in that part of North Carolina where he farmed and hunted and trapped and killed deer. There were a lot of deer to begin with in that part of North Carolina, fewer after Daniel got through, so then in 1779 he and Rebecca and their children (minus a son who had already been killed by Shawnee Indians) hacked a trail through the wilderness and led a large group of settlers and real estate agents into Kentucky. But it was in North Carolina that Daniel Boone developed the true grit that enabled him to become the pioneer and hero he became.

I liked that, and Britt and I spent some time looking over all the rest of the tombstones. Bayne was too hungry to look. But it was a peaceful little place, an ancient graveyard settled in a green minigrove of trees and weeds. A lovely little nook of nature. And directly outside, close enough for convenience, not so far away that old Squire Boone couldn't have climbed out of his grave and filled it full of holes in a trifle with his trusty rusty rifle: the Squire Boone Plaza

89

and Wal-Mart and Video Odyssey, as well as a rumbling roar, a clackety racket, a big parking lot, and Ronald McDonald's infantile colors and moronic smile. Gr-r-r-r-r-r!

But enough crusty crankiness.

Our goal was to eat toast at Toast, and so after a brief gnashing of teeth we hopped back in the car and mounted Mount Airy.

Soon we were moving down the far edge of Mt. Airy, about where Toast ought to have popped up if it was ever going to, a region of suburban houses, country houses, mini-malls, stores, day care centers, and tanning salons offering free three-month tans with twelve-month memberships. And then we dipped into a small traffic jam and from there just about hit our heads on the overpass for Interstate 77. In other words, we found the jam but missed the Toast, and so we pulled into a minimall at the edge of 77 and compared two restaurants, at last choosing the one that offered Breakfast Any Time Day and Night.

"Everybody has to eat toast, OK?"

"No."

Pinch

We turned right onto Interstate 77 and soon entered Virginia. Moving into a series of forested mountains, acquiring elevation, we wiggled through giant blasted gaps in rock on a six-lane highway. Every once in a while a big view would open up and we would see gray mountains and gray forests, just a great vista swimming in a gray haze. The mountains represented various body parts, such as knees and elbows, noses and ears, covered with trees, and they were the Blue Ridge Mountains. Everything looked very gray in the haze, but you could imagine the gray as blue. The view was glorious except for an ugly Day's Inn sign right in the middle of it all. At times it was almost like riding through clouds.

We turned through another gap and then came to a giant tunnel. The tunnel dropped us into West Virginia, but we just kept tooling along the interstate, slipping between a convolution of mountains and an involution of woods.

The Virginias were cooler than the Carolinas had been. The Research Staff had wanted to camp out ever since we started this trip, and now that we were moving into a cooler part of the world, camping out made sense. We came to a sign indicating Camp Creek, where there would be, further signs suggested, a place to camp. So we exited and drove down into a little hollow filled with cows and warmed by a late afternoon sun. Soon we had located a state park and a ranger who rented us a little campsite down by a creek. The creek was probably the Camp Creek creek, and the camp may have been the Camp Creek camp.

We drove to our campsite and parked the car. There was a picnic table, a fire ring, trees, and two flat, cleared areas that would do nicely for our two tents. And as a former Eagle Scout, I had come well prepared for a good camping experience. We had been carrying in the trunk a red duffel bag with two tents, three sleeping bags, and plenty of outdoor cooking equipment in case we needed to cook. I opened the trunk and started pulling things out of the red duffel bag. We had two tents, all right, but, as I soon noticed, one of the tents was missing a pole.

No problem. We had to buy some food for dinner anyway, and so we got in the car and drove up the road to a convenient roadside store. The store was well stocked with relevant merchandise, including hotdogs, rolls, ketchup, mustard, plastic utensils, paper towels, marshmallows, matches, things to drink—and a broom and duct tape. Back in camp, the tent was repaired in no time. We now had, in addition to a solid tent pole, a broom that would come in handy at some future moment.

We had three sleeping bags, all right, but, as I soon discovered, someone had forgotten to pack one of them, so only two were available.

No problem. Being an experienced traveler, I always carry my own Space Blanket, one of those little red and silver sheets made of recycled aluminum that the astronauts carry in case they go camping. The Research Assistants in the good tent could use the two sleeping bags, and I in the broom tent would wrap myself in the Space Blanket.

Meanwhile, the Research Assistants were excited about camping and in high spirits. We bought some firewood at the park headquarters and built a fire. One of the logs had a hole in it, and, as the fire started up, a small twist of smoke began pouring out of that hole. Bayne was very pleased. "Isn't it cool the way the smoke is coming out of that hole?" he said. I looked, and it *was* cool! And I thought to myself that Research Assistants are basically great to have around. They teach you to appreciate things that you ought to appreciate. They keep you young.

The creek next to our campsite consisted of olive water rattling slowly across rocks, and, what with the crackle of the fire and the rattle of the creek, I thought we had a nice little camp there.

We cooked hot dogs. Britt and I had made a vegetarian oath twenty-four hours earlier, but the hot dogs were steaming and smoking and taking on such a wonderful crust and starting to smell so rich, we forgot our oath. After dinner, we roasted marshmallows and sang campfire songs, including Bayne's song: *Sardines on my plate, don't want a steak. Sardines, hey, hey, and pork and beans.*

It had been warm when we started dinner, but now it started to cool off. It even started to get chilly, and so after some time we decided it was time to call it a night. We went to our respective tents, unzipped the hatches, and said good-night. And for all I know, after a little talking and rustling and some flashlight activity, the Research Staff fell into a deep and restful sleep for the rest of the night.

I had a different experience.

I kept my clothes on and wrapped myself snugly in the Space Blanket and a sweater or two, and closed my eyes. I was tired. I listened to the frogs and insects. I listened to the creek. I listened to the frogs and insects again. As I closed my eyes and gradually started to drift, the forest outside my tent turned a little spooky. I lay half asleep and turned half awake, tossed by a dreary energy, a dizzy fatigue, a vertiginous feeling, and was left quaffing a dream of the dark, slurping with a snore and start the sylvan syllabub, sipping with snort and fart Yggdrasil's peglegged punch, eggnogg for the eggnoggin, becoming with boar and hart a winsome lose some lonesome woofer of the woods. Did I say "dream"? More like filmy hallucination — and I popped wide awake.

I was cold. I rearranged my spare clothes, put something extra around my feet, snuggled back down, and tried again. This time I tried counting sheep — well, girls kissed. The first girl I kissed was Eldefonz Rutz (I just made that name up to avoid lawsuits), who had soft and eager lips coated with lipstick that tasted like delicious candy. We kissed secretly and passionately in a dark slot beside a garage one hot August evening. The second girl I kissed was Hildegard Wussenbender. She wore white lipstick on petite and willing lips, which touched my own around 9:47 one October evening in the shadow of a giant elm tree on Third Street. After reviewing girls kissed in youthful ardor I found other things to consider, and soon my mind had expanded into a great cave of remarkable detail. It was like when the eye doctor shines that sharp little light into your eye and the inside of your eyeball looks like a veiny cave. That was what my mind was like, a veiny cave, and so now I was pulling out memories and reviewing them as if they were Seven-Eleven security video-tapes. For some reason, however, the memories began to lose their initial positive buoyancy. Soon I was thinking about the twelve guppies who died as a result of my incompetence in tropical aquarium management when I was eleven. Then I was remembering the time in tenth grade when Cherie Nichols made a probably ironic comment about my favorite red sweater. Now I was counting my nine most embarrassing moments. Eight cases of unwarranted meanness to dogs. Seven worst typographic errors.

I never did sleep, and, although I had forgotten how cold it can get in the mountains at night, I spent most of that night remembering it. No amount of scrap clothing wrapped around any part of my body seemed to make any difference. As bad as the cold, though, was the lumpiness of the ground. By the time the night was over, I had developed a really severe crick or cramp in my lower back, so I was shivering from cold and trembling from pain as well. I was determined not to ruin the sleep of the Research Staff, however, and so bore up stoically until after dawn's first light, at which point I crawled out of the tent and dragged myself into a semireclining position on the picnic table bench.

Slowly it became lighter. It didn't become warmer. Nor did my lower back become more comfortable. My feet were cold now, and I thought I might be more comfortable with my shoes on. My shoes had been left on top of the picnic table overnight, and so now I reached over and loosened the laces, but my back was so cricked and cramped I couldn't bend over far enough to guide my shoes onto my feet. I dropped the shoes to the ground, kept myself in that semi-reclining semiseated position on the bench of the picnic table, and waited some more, hoping the Research Staff would wake up soon, now that it was definitely morning.

They didn't, and so I was reduced to waking them up. "Kids," I said, softly, hoping they were already half awake.

I waited three minutes.

"Kids," I said, more loudly.

I waited another three minutes.

"Kids!" I said even more loudly. "Wake up! Time to get up!"

"Yeah? What?" came voices from inside their tent.

"Kids!" I said, laying my cards on the table now: "I need your help."

"What?"

"Come on! Get up! I need your help! Quickly! I need help getting my shoes on."

They climbed out of their tent, helped me put my shoes on — one Research Assistant per foot — and then tied them, got my toothpaste and toothbrush for me, and so on, and got me all cleaned up and arranged to start the day. And I just semisat in great pain and thought gloomily: *This is exactly what it'll be like when I'm ninety-six and they're coming to visit me in the nursing home.*

Meanwhile, I couldn't move, so the two of them, one on each arm, pulled me up into a standing position, guided me over to the car, helped me pull the car keys out of my pocket, unlocked the door, and then helped me lower myself into the driver's seat. The seat had an electro-mechanical adjuster to one side, so, once settled in, I adjusted my position into the most comfortable I could find and waited. The Research Assistants did everything else. They took down the tents and broom, packed the car, and then at about eight o'clock that morning, when the sun was actually starting to penetrate between the trees and warm things up a little, I started the car.

I drove slowly slowly slowly out of Camp Creek, grinding gears and my teeth from the pain of a Camp Creek camp crick cramp. It was definitely morning now, and the cows in the hollow were already up and eating breakfast, feeding on fodder with a fiddle-de-dee even though they had been out late last night.

Back on Interstate 77, we plowed through a dense and swirly fog until we found a hot breakfast and hot water, which helped a little, and then continued north until 77 turned into 64, going through woodsy forest with a fog that turned into a haze that made the mountains in front of us disappear into a series of receding ridges. After a while the mountains started looking like giant lion paws, and we were going between the toes. It was beautiful country, but of course when we came to the most beautiful part of all, we got hit over the head with a giant billboard: McDONALD'S SUPER PLAYLAND 11 MILES.

After another hour or two, we came to West Virginia's capital, Charleston. It looked like an ordinary big city in many ways but was superbly transformed by the landscape, which included a couple of major rivers and some mountains, and we allowed ourselves to be swept across the rivers along with a lot of other traffic until we were headed on 79 going north and east, at which point we located the exit for Big Chimney, which we took.

I don't like to complain, but I was still experiencing that lower back pain. Sitting in the car seat and driving was tolerable. Standing bolt upright (even walking for about ten paces) was semitolerable. But getting from one to the other or back again was generally intolerable, and so I had to rely on the Research Assistants to help me slowly slowly slowly up out of the car, for example, and then help me down slowly slowly slowly back into it again, whenever either seemed necessary.

We paused in Big Chimney to look for the chimney (which we failed to find) and continued out the other side. We crossed a river and came upon a sign that said PINCH with a small arrow pointing to the left. The road to the left was a tight little thing with a double center line, and we followed it to the outer limits of Pinch, where a sign said WELCOME TO PINCH. Pinch began in a narrow hollow with a series of small brick houses and then some larger brick houses. Next came the Elk Pinch Family Dental Care, and that was all there was to Pinch. So I thought.

"Ah, we've already gone out of Pinch. I can't believe it!"

"How do you know we've gone out of Pinch?"

"I don't know, but if we have gone out we'll have to stop at the dentist. Oh, wait a minute. Is this more of Pinch? This could be more of Pinch."

There were more residential houses and at last a squeezed little row of bricked businesses, including a convenience store, gas station, and Husson's Pizza, in front of which we stopped. Britt and Bayne pulled me slowly slowly slowly out of the car. Together we lumbered gingerly into the place to ask directions of a pizza guy at the counter.

"What are you looking for?" the pizza guy asked.

"Well, we're actually looking for somebody who will tell us where the name Pinch came from."

"Where the name came from? Hey, Sean!"

Sean called out from the back: "What?"

"Come here. He wants to know where the name Pinch came from."

"Where did the name Pinch came from?" Sean said, coming up to confer. It turned out that he didn't know either, but he thought we should go ask Bill Rogers at the Rogers IGA store over in Pinch proper, and he gave us directions. Sean had blue eyes and a fashionably cut helmet of hair. He wore a tasteful choker necklace with some tiny alphabet blocks on it that said METALLICA. At least I think that was Sean. It could have been the first pizza guy. I got so distracted trying to read the tiny blocks I forgot who was who. Anyway, Sean or the other one said that we were standing in front of a fork in the road. If we went to the fork's right, we would soon hit Quick. Going to the fork's left would take us into Pinch.

We should bop up that little hill on the left, he said, bop down the other side, and there would be a school and after that something something Bill Rogers IGA. And, both the pizza guys agreed, once we found Mr. Rogers and found out how Pinch got its name, we should come back and tell them, because *now they were curious.*

We lumbered gingerly back to the car. Britt and Bayne lowered me slowly slowly slowly back into the driver's seat. I turned on the ignition, and we pulled back into the road and onto the left tine of the fork, past the Church of the Nazarene of Pinch, Pinch Park, Pinch Elementary, Buddy's Double Bubble Maytag Laundry, Raceway Video and Tanning, Encore Hair and Nail, until we came at last to a long warehouse-like cinderblock building with a mural painted on its side. The mural showed a long wooden building and yellow gas pump and the sign IGA ROGERS GROCERY on the wooden building, which was exactly what we were looking for, only now it was a cinderblock building with a wooden building painted onto it.

Inside was a grocery store with people buying and selling groceries, of course, but inside that was an office the size of a good aquarium where Bill Rogers sat in a chair and managed things, surrounded by some useful and some decorative items: safe, desk, family pictures, baby pictures, cheesecake calendar, Coca-Cola memorabilia, antique cash register, plaques, old post-office rubber stamps, and so on. Bill Rogers had freshly barbered, gray-and-white-streaked hair, and dark-brown eyes behind light-sensitive glasses. He had a handsome, hawkish, Hopperian face: long and thoughtful, open yet possibly inclined to meditative melancholy. It was possible to imagine him wearing a dark suit and fedora and sitting in a trance inside a lonesome late-night diner. Instead, however, he was wearing Levi's and a black T-shirt, and on his black T-shirt appeared the picture of a pink motorcycle being ridden by an enthusiastic giant eagle and the words "Harley Davidson" above the eagle.

There was a second chair in that office, luckily, and the Research Assistants soon had lowered me slowly slowly slowly into it, from where I proceeded to probe the problem of Pinch.

The first thing I found out was that Bill Rogers's dad, Dennis Rogers, had been the postmaster of Pinch for like thirty-seven years. His mother was from Widen Ridge and his father was originally from back Clay County. But Bill's grandfather and father came down to Pinch in 1936, and there is a little building down the road — Bill showed us an artist's drawing of it — that was the original store that they bought in 1936. And that's when his dad first got the post office, the Pinch Post Office. A fellow by the name of George Summers was owner of the store and postmaster at that time. And Bill's dad took the store in '35 or '36. March of '36 he came down. And then the war broke out in the early '40s, and so his dad thought he was going to have to go to war and therefore sold or lent his store and the post office back to George Summers. And for nine months he worked at a rubber plant. After nine months he didn't get drafted, so he came back and took over the store and post office again and stayed in Pinch for the rest of his life.

Bill Rogers was born in that store, and he grew up there with a sister, just one sister, who was now married to a man down in Huntington. And the original store in Pinch had a little wareroom on the side, and that was where his mom and dad lived when they first moved there. That was downstairs, because the upstairs was rented out to the Odd Fellows.

So that was the story of the store.

Now, Pinch is a tight little community, Bill went on to explain, but it's also outgoing and prosperous. They have a nice school and a real nice fire department, water, sewer, his grocery store, a hardware store, and so on. They have three fabricating places in the area, a painting contractor who works out of his home, heating and plumbing, a Shop and Go gas station, and a Pizza Hut and several churches. Back in 1950 there was only the Upper Pinch Baptist and the Lower Pinch Methodist, but now it's hard to count how many churches they have. Seems like somebody gets aggravated, they go out and start up a church. So there's probably nine churches in the area now.

There used to be a big coal mine in the Pinch area, but that has since closed. But people in Kentucky, it seems, has bought that land out. And they are just sitting on it really. But Pinch is still pretty prosperous. Most of the people around there are working-class people. There are a few on welfare, but most everybody, man and woman, works. Of course if we were to drive around through the community and see some of the houses, we would understand that they almost have to work.

Now Pinch was originally established as Dial. And that was in 18 and 98, and it stayed that way until 19 and 12, when they changed it to Pinchton. OK, it stayed that way until 19 and 21, and then they changed it from Pinchton to Pinch, and Pinch has been just Pinch since November the 4th, 1921.

Why all of this happened as it did was actually a little hazy, but eventually we figured out (if I remember correctly) that, first, the name Pinchton came from Pinch Creek, which was once called Pinch Gut, with "gut" being an archaic word for a small stream. And the small stream was called Pinch because some white men who came down into the area in pioneer times got held up by the Indians for so long that they almost starved to death. So, in honor of being almost starved—being in a really *pinched* condition—they called the creek Pinch Gut. Somehow Pinch Gut became Pinchton, a name used for both the creek and the village growing up at the creek. Then along came an assertive Methodist minister named Dial, so Pinchton was called Dial Pinchton or possibly (this part was not quite clear to me) just Dial. But then they dropped the Dial because of postal confusion with another place called Dale. And later on they dropped the ton from the end of Pinchton because of postal confusion with Princeton. So that just about tightened the name down until what was left but Pinch?

As it turned out, Bill Rogers happened to have some T-shirts in the store that said "Pinch, West Virginia." He gave us the best one of those shirts for a souvenir. He was the only one that sold them, he said, and he sold them because he liked Pinch. He'd been there all his life. And he had a hand in putting the signs up on both ends of the road. They got a sign, "Welcome to Pinch," down there.

"We saw that!"

"I try to keep that grass cut there all the time."

So that was the story of Pinch, and as we were lumbering gingerly out of the store, Bill Rogers told us how to find the old Pinch schoolhouse down the way that they were trying to restore — and also the original store that his father and grandfather bought in '36. I said I figured we would go check them out, but between the time the Research Staff had pulled me slowly slowly slowly out of the chair in Bill Rogers's office and had lowered me slowly slowly slowly back into the car seat, I concluded that we should instead go back to Husson's Pizza and have lunch.

We got back to Husson's Pizza while the lunch hour was still going on, but only a few people were getting or eating pizzas. The Pinch dentist was there, dressed in his dental fatigues and waiting for a pizza to go. A couple of other Pinch denizens were hanging out as well. But in any case, the place seemed pretty sedate. We ordered a thin-crust pizza, some narrow noodles, and three tight Cokes. We told Sean or the other guy what we had learned about how Pinch became Pinch. Then the Research Assistants slowly slowly slowly lowered me into the pizza booth where we waited for our food and drink.

While waiting, we considered where to go next. Quick was right down the other stretch of road. Should we go to Quick after lunch? Nah, we concluded, Quick would take too long.

Left Hand

Getting to Left Hand was not as straightforward as one would have hoped. The cartographicus magnus was imperfectly clear about this. Or if it was perfectly clear the lines were so tiny I couldn't follow. But as a general fact, Left Hand was represented as a speck on the left-hand side of arterial Interstate 79 with some twisty veins and capillaries leading up to it, and so when we arrived at what looked to be the right turnoff from 79 for Left Hand we left 79 and turned left right onto the left-hand road.

Wrong move.

The left-hand road veered sharply left and took us right to a sign that said we were headed for a place called Clio. Uh-oh. We turned and returned to the right of passage over Interstate 79, and tried again. Left Hand still looked to be on the left hand according to the cartographicus magnus, but we went right to the right-hand road, which took us right down past an Exxon station and a telephone booth on the right. Then this so-called right-hand road left the right side of the Interstate and drew us into a right of passage under 79 and over to the left-hand side.

Right move.

But now the once right-handed now left-handed road split three ways: right-wing, left-wing, and middle-of-the-road road. Which was the right road to Left Hand? The left wing turned out wrong. We found a sign that said Little Left Hand. The right wing turned out wrong. We found a sign that said Community Church Big Sandy Creek. So we tried the middle-of-the-road road, and it was just right. It was a crooked country road, and it more or less followed a crooked country creek on the right, which I suspected might be the Big Sandy Creek, which could have been sandy but didn't seem big.

We came into a little valley with wildflowers and brush and then a dithering cluster of houses, some old, some new, including one contemporary bungalow on the right-hand side in front of which sat an old man with a cane in his right hand who looked as if he were enjoying the day. We stopped to see if he knew anything about Left Hand.

The old man wore thick glasses, and he had a long chin. His brown pants were being held up by a pair of suspenders. He tended to mumble, I think. Either that or my hearing was disintegrating along with my back. His name was Carper, if I heard correctly.

He said we were in Left Hand, or just about. There was more down the road.

Left Hand, he went on, originally referred to a fork: the left fork of Sandy Creek, which was the crooked country creek out in back of his house. There are actually two Left Hands around, a big one and a little one, he said, but possibly he was referring to forks rather than places.

Left Hand is generally a pleasant place to be, Mr. Carper said. Though on the other hand, he went on offhandedly, there are times when it is and times when it isn't. But when he moved there thirty or forty years ago, the whole area was being farmed. Then there were no woods on the hill across the way from his house. Now of course it's just a big forest as we could see. But then it was all farms. Older people used to farm a lot in Left Hand, but the younger people don't now. They ain't got time because they're too busy watching TV. In the old days, furthermore, people didn't care about rock. They plowed with mules, and they'd just take a mule and pull the rock out.

Mr. Carper told us we would have to go down the road a few miles before we got to the Left Hand Post Office. We would have to go through that one bridge, right to the left of that curve there, and then about a mile or so. They built a new bridge there right in front of where the post office is. But there's a place down the road a stretch beyond that, he said, called Looneyville, and if we were interested in crazy names we might want to go out there after we were finished with Left Hand. To get to Looneyville we should follow the road out of Left Hand until we hit 36 and then turn left.

"Left on 36. All right," I said, and then I added, "Do you happen to know where Looneyville, where that name came from?"

"It comes from balooneys."

"*Balooneys*? What's a *balooney*?"

"The Looneys."

"Looneys?"

"They lived there."

"Oh, the Looneys. It's a family name!"

We ran out of words soon after that. The Research Assistants and I clucked with him about raising chickens for a while. He used to have seventeen chickens, but after the dogs had their day he was left with three roosters and no hens. And then we thanked Mr. Carper most sincerely for helping us out and left right after.

We drove down the road a few miles and turned to the left to the Left Hand Post Office and talked to the lady in the window, who was the right-handed postmistress of Left Hand but didn't know too much more than we had already heard, and so we turned around and turned right and drove right back up the road until we had left Left Hand behind. I was never sure how much of that piece of road was Left Hand and how much wasn't, but it was still a pleasant little stretch of houses and barns, gardens and corn patches, lawns and satellite dishes.

Accident

*S*omewhere near Lost Creek on Interstate 79, a couple of inches before the northeastern end of West Virginia, we stopped at one of those generic motels and felt much better in the morning. Unfortunately, thunder, lightning, and rain were coming down when we woke up, and so, not wanting to test the roads under such circumstances, we sat around the motel room, watched cats and mice beat each other up on television, and had the following conversation.

"So are we going to get to Accident this morning or not?"

"Yeah. Even though there's a thunderstorm and the driving may not be —"

"If we have an accident that would be cool."

"Well, an accident is never cool. What if we had a serious accident and got hurt?"

"It would be better if we had a little dent in the fender."

"I'm afraid we're going to be infinitely careful *not* to have an accident."

"If we get hurt that would be bad. We'd have to like write down in the book and say, 'Well, then we had an accident and we died. The end.'"

Life is an accident in progress, it's possible to imagine, and one might present as primary evidence the fact that all babies and most children are perfect and beautiful, whereas a lot of adults (with the clear exceptions of you and me) are not. What happened to all the beautiful babies and children? That's the accident of life happening, a slow entropy from ecstatic perfection at one end to saggy randomization at the other, and, really, you can only try your level best not to accelerate the process unnaturally. Children are the opposite of accidents, in other words, and the job of parents is to protect children from entropy of the fast and traumatic kind. Hence, the three of us were sitting around in a motel room somewhere near Lost Creek, watching cats and mice beat each other up on television, and waiting patiently for a storm to abate because I didn't want to drive into a place called Accident on a slippery road.

We spent half the morning that way, but finally the morning started getting away from us, and so we took off, driving in a steady rain, going about ten miles below the speed limit and being passed by everyone in sight including all those giant trucks that carry along their own intense little swirling shower-steamclouds that they spray onto your windshield, thus producing cataracts outside and glaucoma inside. Nevertheless, what we *could* see out the window looked spectacularly beautiful. This was what a lot of places must have looked like before they were spoiled, I thought: miles of pristine woodsy hills and a white haze that made everything smoky and a little bluish, especially as we proceeded down this or that valley and looked ahead to the distant ridges. We passed an old brown wooden barn with white writing on the side that said in bold ecstatic print I LOVE MISSY!

After an hour or so the rain stopped. At Morgantown, we made a right turn onto Interstate 48 and into a low cloud that wrapped itself around us. The cloud sprinkled for a while, and then it misted. Interstate 48 drew us east into Maryland, but the road still seemed slick, and I wasn't enjoying the drive very much.

We left the interstate at a spot called Friendsville and dropped south into a very deep valley: a farming valley, more or less. The mist petered out about then, and the cloud finally started to coagulate and go somewhere else. The road became a narrow winding passage up and down with trees on either side in which a lot of tent caterpillars were camping, and then it bumped into another road onto which we turned left into a bee-kissed land of goldenrod and Queen Anne's lace, corn patches, little houses, and the occasional Rorschach cow. We drove past bales of hay and a simple, handlettered sign: Sweet Corn For Sale. A stone house here, a tanning and styling salon there, and just beyond a lovely country church with an ornate, four-gabled bell tower and a cross on top.

Momentarily distracted by a Chelsea Clinton look-alike walking along the road, we collided into a minor mess of Commercial Office Space, Miniature Golf, as well as A & A Realty Office Ahead Two Miles (Check Out Our Lake Front Homesites!). We had hit Vacationland, I guessed, but pretty soon we stopped hitting it and fell into another little stretch of splendid countryside, with goldenrod and Queen Anne's lace sprinkled across a green field looking like a painter's dropcloth. Then suddenly:

WELCOME
TO
ACCIDENT.

Accident didn't look like much at first, a few brick bungalows and a small aggregation of plastic-signed businesses splattered along the road next to one of the world's best barns: a red, four-cupola affair, sagging slightly with a cobwebbed nod in the direction of some old farm equipment lying out in the weeds. Down the road a bit more, dripping along randomly like the final dregs of a garage sale: real estate, tans, tuxedos, wedding accoutrements, car wash, and the Family Dentistry of Doctor Ted Reader.

But that was just the edge of Accident I'm pleased to report, and the road made a quick twist to the left, the speed limit dropped to twenty-five, and we rolled past a wonderful Victorian with gingerbread, some other nice old houses, and soon were cruising along Accident Main Street where people were trying to sell cars, wines and liquors, beds and breakfasts, and thrift items and more. We bumped past the Flour Shoppe Bakery, the Accident History House, Matthews Grocery, the American Trust Bank, and, finally, at the very end of Main Street, a grand church called the Zion Lutheran Church, around which several dressed-up people were swarming, a few of them looking teary eyed either because of a wedding or (more likely, I thought) a funeral.

So far Accident may seem like your typical sleepy little place anywhere, but I haven't yet made clear the setting. Accident had been thrown down there as a small collection of houses and businesses in the middle of a long and broad

Maryland farming valley. There was an extended gentle rise and ridge far away to one side, another rise and ridge far away to the other, and along both those rises and ridges great farms and fields were settled in for the duration, prosperous and gleaming brightly (now that the clouds were broken into drifting pillows) under blue sky and warming sun.

Accident was basically a three-streeter: Main down the middle, North running parallel to one side, South to the other. North Street, short to begin with, was divided into North North and South North, whereas South Street was North South and then South South. The town had a post office, a fire department, a log cabin soon to be historicized, and an Accident Community Park with its own picnic area and pond. ("No Boating, No Swimming, No Ice Skating. Not Responsible for Any Accidents.")

So Accident was a real town, not just a highway happenstance, and we finally stopped at the Thrift Store and More to learn what we could learn. The Thrift Store and More sold clothes, toys, mirrors, and painted cow skulls from Mexico. The woman working the counter there, with bouffant red hair, freckles, and hazel eyes, wearing a sleeveless red sweater and overalls cut into overall shorts, said she didn't know much about how the town was named. She had only lived there about thirty-one years. She did know, however, that seven to ten years ago the town had like 357 people, five cats, and one bird. But if we really wanted to know about Accident, we should go down to the oldest store in town, Matthews Grocery, down Main Street across from the bank, and talk to Rosie, who was like the Queen of Accident.

Matthews Grocery was part of a large, green-shingled, white-trimmed, two-story house. We pulled into a small parking area next to it. The grocery and house combination opened onto Main Street with a long front porch and a flag-waving porch roof supported by seven or eight round wood pillars. Inside, the place seemed like a combination candy store, hardware store, and pharmacy—with groceries thrown in as an afterthought. It was your old-fashioned everything store, in short, with a stamped tin ceiling and flyswatters hanging on the walls. A bell rang as we passed through the creaky door, and, in Pavlovian fashion, Rosie Smith Moon appeared from behind a curtain immediately after.

Now the lady at the Thrift Store and More had called Rosie the Queen of Accident, but I think of Rosie more as the Grandmother of Accident. Rosie, we eventually found out, didn't actually have any grandchildren of her own, but she was still as grandmotherly as they come. She was small and short, and she smiled with great warmth and a natural benevolence. She had blue eyes, rosy lips, and a soft face with cheeks that swelled up like bread dough when she smiled. She had full, dark-gray hair that surrounded her face with the shape of a heart. Rosie seemed as sharp, as clear-voiced and clear-minded, as a twenty-year-old (depending, of course, on which twenty-year-old we're talking about), and she was wearing white sneakers, dark-blue pants, and, over a pink and white short-sleeved blouse, a full apron with tiny red and white flowers.

"Hello," I said. "Are you Rosie?"

"Yes, I am," she said.

"Your neighbor at the Thrift Store up the way said we should talk to you," I went on. "We're writing a book about towns with unusual—"

"Accident is about as unusual as—"

"We saw Accident on the map, and we thought it was—"

"Oh, did you ever wonder how it got its name?"

Accident began, she began, because around 1751 King George II of England gave a land grant of six hundred acres to someone named Deacon. George Deacon. So Mr. Deacon, intending to get the maximum benefit out of this deal, sent not one but two teams of surveyors into that part of Maryland with the simple instruction that they ought to find the best six hundred acres they could find. Neither team knew about the other. After they had finished their respective surveys, the two teams, not knowing of each other's existence or mission, returned to Mr. Deacon and showed him that they had claimed the very same piece of land, bounded by the very same landmarks. Mr. Deacon followed his surveyors' double advice, took the land, and called his tract the Accident Tract. And that was the story.

That was pretty much how Rosie told the story. But, slow me, I was having trouble already. "OK. I'm sure I understood it. There were two different surveyors. . . ."

"Two different surveyors, and they met at the same place," she said. "By accident. See, if you are to send up two surveyors, and they are both told, 'Go ahead and find the best section you can find,' and they both selected the same one patch, then that was it."

"They were told to go find the best section," I repeated, slowly. "But. But that wouldn't have been an accident then, would it? It was more like an agreement on what the best section was."

"And I'll tell you something," she continued (ignoring my immature quibble), "they couldn't have found a prettier plot." Rosie had lived in Accident all her life, she said, which would soon be seventy-seven years. Born and raised there. Her grandparents emigrated from Germany. And they just settled in Maryland and just came here to Accident. They owned a little farm out west in the country, which was still owned by members of the Smith family. Her grandparents just chose the area, as they always said, by accident. And her family—she had eleven brothers and one sister. There were thirteen of them

altogether, enough in the family to make nine for a baseball team and two um-
pires and two cheerleaders. That made the thirteen kids. And they did have a
baseball family. A big baseball family.

And one thing around here: People don't forget to vote. And they don't forget to fly the flag. That is one of their great things there, the Fourth of July picnic, and they make sure that nobody tramples on the flag. And then they also
have a Memorial Day celebration, where they go down to the plaque com-
memorating their boys who were killed in the service. In fact, Rosie lost a
brother in the service. She had five brothers in the wars, and so, anyhow, they
have that. They have a very nice band there in Accident. It's a town band, and
the drum they play goes back a hundred years. Accident is a proud town, strong
on tradition, and it is a strong Lutheran community.

Now Matthews Grocery was opened in 1839. Someone named Richard Far-
rell did that. The Joe Matthews who put his name on it bought the place October 18, 1945. One reason Rosie could possibly remember that date was that she
started work in the store just a couple of months before Joe Matthews bought
it. She started there in August of 1945. Accident's first phone service operated
out of Matthews, run by Samuel Masser, who also had a radio and (after a few
years) TV-repair business on the second floor. Well, Matthews is a grocery
store, but it might be best known among the children of Accident as a candy
store, and every Halloween ever since Joe Matthews bought the store in 1945,
they've given out free Halloween treats for all the Accident children.

A couple of years back they had a fiftieth anniversary celebration of Matthews Grocery, and that was nice. They had the band out, and people all came
out. And it was terrific.

And this area right here was always considered the beauty spot of the state
of Maryland. They've got a lot of dairy farmers in Accident, but their biggest
thing was schoolteachers. They had the Greater Maryland Tool Works, and
they had the state and road men. But she would say there was more dairy farming than any other kind of farming. Of course, there was a lot of farms that
have corn and potatoes and what have you. Not so much potatoes, but corn
certainly. And that beautiful red barn with the four cupolas right on the outskirts of town, the man that owned that was the Mayor of Accident until about
a year ago, and he passed away just this summer.

But Accident isn't as quiet as it used to be. Matthews Grocery porch, in fact,
was situated precariously at the very edge of Main Street, hardly more than a
half an inch higher than highway level — and, as Rosie and I talked, I began to
notice how many cars were going past with a swoosh and a swoosh and a
swoosh.

I commented on the traffic.

Well, Rosie explained, people are driving their cars from the rest of Maryland out to Deep Creek Lake. And the lake has changed, she said. The lake has changed, she repeated. When Rosie was a kid—had we been out there? It's crowded now. It's not the same as she remembered it, when she and her siblings were kids. And then there was all this traffic passing through Accident, and one of the things people were thinking about was bypassing Accident. No, they don't have too many accidents in Accident. It's pretty safe. But they just don't like the traffic, the way it is now. She, in fact, could remember when the road was first paved out there. That went back a lot of years, and, of course, in her family she had five brothers that worked on the state roads, so she was always kind of interested in roads. So she was just waiting for the bypass. And not long ago she had a good conversation with two of the state men that was inquiring. They went from place to place and wanted to find out what people thought. And she said, "You can bypass us any time." The traffic don't bring nothing, no business or anything, and they are just wearing the roads out, because there is no business brought here by that traffic.

But Accident, Rosie concluded, it's a nice town. It's got a nice feeling about it. "I've got an awful lot of love for it, and you better believe it," she said. "I have collected more friends than anybody has a right to. Got a tremendous amount."

After we had finished talking about Accident, Rosie directed the Research Assistants to the candy shelves. They had already been observing the sweets section, as a matter of fact, and I had actually been thinking to buy them a bonus for a job well done, but Rosie wouldn't hear of me spending a cent. "Now what do you want?" she said to the Research Staff. "You go get your candy. You don't need any money. Go get what you want over there. Go get it. Pick it off, and then come over here and get your pop. It's all right. If you like, you can all go and get yourself a can of pop. I hope it's good and cold."

And when they had both carefully but politely selected an item or two each, she sent them right back for more. "Go get some more, get whatever you want. There's suckers over there. Go ahead. You better take something with you. You may never get back to see me again. This can be Halloween for us, for you guys," she said. "Get something else, you haven't had anything yet. Go get some more. Go on. Get what you want, and then get yourself some pop. Right down here in the big case."

"Thanks. Thanks for the candy."

"Thanks for the candy."

"Well, you're welcome, I'm sure. And, if you ever get back my way, I'll be here. Just don't make it too long. Now, go get yourselves each a can of cold pop out of the fridge."

So that was Rosie Smith Moon: a five-foot-two concentration of positive ions wearing a flowered apron and dispensing sweets at the heart of Matthews

Grocery in the heart of Accident. We said our final thank-yous and good-byes and took the bags of candy and cans of pop out to the car. Amid contented chewing and some minor slurping and burping, I started the car and then turned from the parking area back onto Main Street, past the American Trust and from there right on out of Accident, noticing just as we left town that an entire congregation was now swarming outside the Zion Lutheran Church and nobody seemed to be crying any more.

Maybe it wasn't a funeral after all.

Everyone seemed to be smiling and laughing, in fact, and then I caught a fleeting glimpse of that happy happy happy couple fleeing down the church steps in a hail of rice and a shower of flowers.

Detour

Detour, a little town in the top-central part of Maryland, was our next destination. But first we took a brief excursion down to the bottom eastern part of the state, where we rested and relaxed for a few days with Aunt Deb and Uncle Milan and Cousin Katie and Cousin Robbie before jumping into the car and heading back north toward Detour, which might have been a nice diversion except we were diverted at the last minute onto an alternate route that dropped us across the Mason-Dixon line into Pennsylvania.

Bird-in-Hand

In Pennsylvania, the Research Staff and I spent the best part of the day at Gettysburg and finally stepped east onto Route 30 before stopping overnight at a Holiday Inn in Lancaster.

The roads east out of Lancaster the next morning were simply harrowing, and, as we tentatively headed along Route 30 east, we found ourselves grinding in the wrong direction against an interminable assembly line of big cars with big people inside and New Jersey plates on the front. The crowds and traffic were all the more surprising because we had suddenly landed right in the middle of Amish territory. Where people live the simple life.

We had barely started the day, but already I was tired of fighting the traffic on Route 30, so when a sign suddenly appeared that said BIRD-IN-HAND, I instantly completed the thought: IS WORTH TWO ON THIS ROAD. And when, very soon after, I saw a sign that said

ABE'S BUGGY RIDES
2 MILE TOUR THRU AMISH COUNTRY

I slammed on the brakes.

The Research Assistants had their doubts, but I didn't. I've always wanted to be Amish, at least theoretically, and I thought it would be terrific to have a buggy ride. I followed the driveway around the back of Abe's house and parked the car next to a couple of bored horses grinding hay. We walked around the front to take our place in the queue at Abe's front steps.

It was hardly midmorning, and yet already a dozen people were locked ahead of us in the queue. Still, I was glad to stop battling traffic for a while. I was feeling pretty calm and patient right then, as a matter of fact, and so the three of us stood in front of Abe's, waited for the buggy to show up, and in the meanwhile listened to garbage trucks, vans, pickups, and cars roaring past, and looked across the road at a semiindustrial-commerical building harboring AUTOMATIC SCREW MACHINES. I didn't think to ask anyone what an automatic screw machine was partly because I had gotten distracted by the people standing in front of us.

First in line was a trio: mom, dad, and a giant baby on mom's knee. The baby was huge. I think he may have been stealing nourishment from the mom when she wasn't looking, because she was ectomorphic to an extreme. The giant baby was squirming on his skinny mom's knee, crying and saying, "I want to go with daddy! I want to go with daddy!" Daddy, having walked down from Abe's front steps to the road, was leaning over and looking for Abe and the horse and buggy to show up. The giant baby wanted to go down to the road and lean over and look for Abe and the horse and buggy, too. But the skinny mom, grimacing from behind sunglasses at her oversized offspring, was crying back, "OK. You're not going at all!" And to the father, still leaning over and looking down the road for Abe and the horse and buggy, she shouted, "He's not coming! He's too fresh!"

At that, the giant baby launched himself into a thousand violent squirms, slithers, and howls, which led the mom to nail the lid on her box of threats: "That's it! You're not going! Sorry! Sorrrrrry! You can't go now!" Her face became a sneer. Her voice took on a taunting, teasing tone, which of course catapulted the giant baby into even more squirms, slithers, and howls.

Meanwhile, the second family in line was carrying on its own little battle. Mom and dad were wearing Chicago Bulls T-shirts and holding a place in line, but the three kids, in Orlando Magic T-shirts, kept shuffling and getting out of line, thereby causing mom and dad to fire out from between clenched teeth a full barrage of ineffectual negations and corrections: "No! No! No! Don't do that!" "Walter, get down! Get over there!" "Jamis!" "Walter!" "Stop!" "Up! Up! Up! Off the driveway! Off. The. Driveway!"

There are times when children, at least other people's children, don't seem like any fun at all, and you wonder what madness induces people to have them. But pretty soon sane Abe showed up with horse and buggy and hauled away mom, dad, and the giant baby. Not so much longer after that Abe's young assistant with a second horse and buggy showed up and hauled off the three unruly children, leaving their parents to fight each other. And about a half hour later, at last, it was our turn to climb into the buggy with Abe.

The Research Staff took the cozy back seat, and I took the cozy front seat right next to Abe and right behind Abe's brown horse, whose name was Star. Abe was a calm, likeable man with roundish glasses and a full bushy beard looking more like a waterfall than a bush, who wore a straw hat on his head, a purple work shirt, and black pants held up by black suspenders. "Looks like you're under a lot of pressure today with these long lines," I said as I attempted to fit my big self inside the small buggy. No seatbelts!

"It's normal for this time of year," Abe said, as he skedaddled Star.

"Oh, it is, huh? You're probably used to it," I said.

"Wait'll 2:00 on Labor Day afternoon."

After those introductory exchanges, Abe began his historical tour. The road we were traveling on right now was originally known as the King's Highway, then the Old Philadelphia Pike, he said. It ran from Philadelphia to Lancaster. It was built in the colonial days by King George II in 1733. *So this big ugly Route 30 with its eternal parade of belching garbage trucks, vans, and pickups is actually historical, huh,* I was thinking cynically—when suddenly Star hung a right and clip-clopped right off Route 30 away from the noise and fumes and into the peaceful countryside.

"What a relief," I said.

Star sailed down that quiet road into the quiet country and then proceeded through a wonderful series of corn fields and quiet farmhouses, as I questioned Abe about the Amish and a thousand other things. Well, the first thing I learned was that Abe wasn't Abe. He was David, last name of Fidler, who had bought the buggy-ride business from the actual Abe some time ago and just decided to keep the *nom de commerce*. The second thing I learned was that David wasn't Amish. He was a River Brother.

The River Brethren are another old-order branch of the Mennonites, David explained. Well, the only difference doctrinally between them and the Amish is the River Brethren baptize by immersion and the Amish baptize by pouring. River Brethren, that's a geographic name because the church group started up along the Susquehanna River. But when the Civil War began each church had to establish a proper name, so his church became the Old Order of River Brethren. They are Christians, he said. They believe in salvation through Christ, and they believe in separation from the world. They try. They try self-denial. And self-denial would characterize a lot of the Mennonite groups. The Amish, for example, don't use self-propelled machines. For machines that move they use horse power. OK, a lot of them might have engines to power things that are not moving vehicles, but for moving vehicles they would rely on animals for power rather than make them self-propelled with an engine. The distinction between self-propelled machines and other machines is just a way of keeping them back, keeping them into the old ways more.

"They just want the simplicity?" I suggested, thinking after all the fumes and vibrations of Route 30 what a brilliant idea simplicity was.

Yeah, he said, simplicity and just not getting — the further you go in life, with the modern, seem like there's no limit. It's on, and it's on, and it's on. But they like the simple. Their order, now they have electricity, but they don't have radios or TVs. And everybody tells him they're not missing anything. There are good things on TV he was sure, but anyhow they didn't have it. Now, he went on (as Star clip-clopped past a field of tobacco), there are a lot of tobacco farms in the area, but there again, since the River Brethren are opposed to tobacco, they don't farm it. They're pacifist as well. Plain People. That was a blanket term. That covered the whole outfit. And if I wanted to learn more, he said, up the road in Intercourse he had a friend, Stephen Scott, who goes to their same church, who would probably talk to us.

Theirs is much smaller than the Amish, probably a little over three hundred people maybe. The Amish, you're talking between eighteen and twenty thousand. But it's not numbers. Numbers don't mean a thing. And like the Amish, the River Brethren wear simple, utilitarian clothes, and so on. This is the practice of outward nonconformity, the insistence on an outward separation from the world. As a matter of fact, David once took his family up to Massachusetts for a vacation. They visited the Plymouth Plantation at Plymouth Rock, where they sort of blended right in. Some of the other visitors thought he and his family were part of the exhibit, which he thought was pretty amusing.

"Well, I find the simple life attractive," I said, "but I'm not sure I could go all the way with it. Do you have people who leave the order?"

"Oh, yes. Yes. People do leave," he said. "People always see greener grass. Some people are always bucking the system."

I could see his point, all right, but then the idea of bucking the system made me think about Star, patiently moving along and keeping his thoughts to himself. By the time I had stopped thinking about Star, he had clip-clopped us right back around to that crazy Route 30 and then sidled up to the curb in front of Abe's Buggy Rides. We climbed down, said thank-you to David and Star, and started walking back to the car.

Now it was time to — but wait!

I had enjoyed myself so much, I actually missed the big opportunity to ask David Fidler where the name Bird-in-Hand came from. And I realized that fact just as we turned around at the top of the driveway to watch Star pull away with another load of customers. It was a lost chance! Oh, we had the bird of opportunity right in hand — and we left it fly away. Yes, we could have inserted ourselves back in the queue and waited behind more giant babies, but the Staff and I decided instead to eat lunch at a place back down the road.

After lunch, we hauled ourselves back up the road until, just before Abe's Buggy Rides, we happened to see a likely looking older man wearing black sneakers with a hole in the top of one, who was sweeping detritus from beneath a chestnut tree beside a bed and breakfast place. His name was Frank Weaver, and I believe he owned the bed and breakfast.

Bird-in-Hand, Mr. Weaver told us, used to be a fairly quiet little town, but then tourism changed that. There was a play in New York about the Amish life, called *Plain and Fancy*, and from that time all the tourists started coming in. That was quite a few years ago, and it's built up ever since. Now it's gotten to be a little too much. Now they've built these tremendous big shopping centers around. And a big Wal-Mart is coming in, a tremendous Wal-Mart.

Bird-in-Hand used to be the name of an inn along the road, the old Philadelphia Turnpike, that crazy Route 30 with its belching garbage trucks, vans, and pickups that we started out on. And that old inn kept an old wooden sign with the carved picture of a bird in a hand for all the travelers to see. That was the first turnpike in the United States, and people used it to haul supplies or raw materials back and forth. In those days, they had Conestoga wagons, the ones with a canopy over, running along that road, but there were pretty big hills between Philadelphia and Pittsburgh, and the loads could shift and cause trouble. The teams running these wagons would have to stop and sleep and be supplied at inns or hotels and barns along the way, so one of those places was the Bird-in-Hand.

And, he wondered, did we wonder how the old inn got such a name in the first place? One story says that two of the original turnpike surveyors had an argument at the point where the inn was built about whether to stay there for the night or proceed into Lancaster. The surveyor who won the argument appealed to the power of a well-known aphorism, arguing that they should seize the present opportunity rather than take a chance with future potentiality.

Intercourse

We said good-bye and thank-you to Mr. Frank Weaver, got back in the car, and headed up the road three or four more miles until we reached the outer limits of Intercourse.

Twice or thrice during the short drive from Bird-in-Hand to Intercourse we came upon horses hitched to black buggies and trotting casually down the road or waiting patiently to turn a corner. Inside these vehicles, we saw but tried not to gawk at sober people in sober clothes thinking sober thoughts. But then we entered Intercourse, and Intercourse looked already wise to the ways of the world: a little jaded and more than a little touristified, offering ice cream, candy, antiques, souvenirs, genuine this and genuine that, mass-produced fake symbols of the simple life for more-than-simple prices.

The best part of Intercourse was the People's Place book and information center, providing books and information on the lives of the Mennonites, and, across the street, a People's Place quilt store and quilt museum. At the entrance to the quilt museum I eventually found David's friend, a very pleasant man named Stephen Scott. He was selling tickets to the museum as well as a few small gifts on a Mennonite theme.

Stephen looked a lot like David, at least superficially. They wore the same clothes and had the same beard, only Stephen's was slightly longer and more ethereal at the peripheries. Stephen also had a balder head and a wider face; and it was from Stephen that I learned a lot of the deeper aspects of the River Brethren, things about clothes, beards, beliefs, and so on.

From him I also learned how Intercourse got its name. In the beginning, there was on that very spot a village named after a stage-coach tavern, the Cross Keys. Then somebody bought some land, plotted it off, and started a larger village called Intercourse in about 1814. And Stephen didn't really feel the name required any further explanation. For over a hundred years after the village was founded, people didn't really consider the name Intercourse unusual. The word didn't have the association it does now. If I were to read Henry David Thoreau, for example, I would see that he uses the word frequently. As in "social intercourse." Where people just meet and converse. So it wasn't considered off-color or whatever for a long time.

Stephen and I talked for a long time. But the Research Assistants just didn't seem very interested, a fact I found mildly disconcerting. Myself, I was fascinated by the pious people dressed in black and trotting around on horses. I thought it would be great to be a plain farmer with a stone barn, horses, and . . . a beautiful wife. But here's the truth, pleasant or not: The Research Assistants during the last couple of days had been slacking off a little. And now they were wandering aimlessly around looking bored until before I knew it they had started behaving like ordinary American kids. Not Research Assistants at all. What could I do? I turned into an ordinary American dad, gave them some money, and sent them across the street to get ice cream.

I did enjoy talking to Stephen Scott. But after I finished learning about the River Brethren and looking at quilts from the plain life, I rushed over to the ice cream parlor to join Britt and Bayne in the sweet and sticky life. Then the three of us wandered casually into an Intercourse art gallery and pondered art for four minutes and thirty-six seconds. Well, the quilts and the River Brethren were excellent and fascinating, but the rest of Intercourse was starting to seem overrated. We didn't linger longer. We drove back and forth for a while until we got lost in the country behind a buggied horse with dancing feet. Then we slipped back inside the city limits and drove back and forth again until finally we just shot out of Intercourse altogether and headed north to Climax.

Climax

Getting from Intercourse to Climax took longer than I expected, and we wound up in a hotel at midstate before, next morning, climbing out of the top of Pennsylvania and pushing into the bottom of New York. From there we tripped across the fringes of the noble Catskills, pulled into the valley of the majestic Hudson River, hitched ourselves onto a line of traffic shooting up the New York State Thruway, and quivered thus at top speed to our exit at Coxsackie.

We barely touched Coxsackie before slipping on a pleasant little road past a beautiful stone house, across the New York State Thruway, and from there directly into a sleepy little hollow of trees and fields, bees and blossoms, farms and houses, the Quarry Steak House, Trudy's Lounge, and at the side of the road the following statement or command: CLIMAX.

Trudy's Lounge was open, but Trudy was busy doing a private banquet right then. She said she couldn't tell us the meaning of Climax, but we should go up the road and ask at the post office.

So we drove a few dozen yards and pulled into the customer parking lot of a small clapboard building consisting of a rectangle with a triangle on top. A pair of antique multipaned windows, one on either side of the front entrance, were softened from the outside by red and white petunias in window boxes and from the inside by white lace curtains. The place, in other words, looked more like a small Dutch cottage than a post office, but a sign above the door made things clear: U.S. POST OFFICE CLIMAX, NY 12042.

We walked inside and said "hello" to a young woman administering postal duties on the other side of a counter and open window. She had brown hair, brown eyes, and red lipstick, and she wore dark-blue slacks and shirt as well as a set of silver half-glasses. Her name was Anne Foster, as we could read on the little tag at her breast, and she was the Climax Postmistress.

Ms. Foster patiently explained that Climax used to be Guinea Hill, because of a hill, then it was Limerock, because of a rock. But when the first local post office arrived in 1892, New York State already had a Limerock. The area also already had a village called Surprise and another called Result. And so George H. Scott, the Coxsackie Postmaster at the time, declared in a spasm of inspiration, "We've got a Surprise and a Result. How about a Climax?"

That's how Climax got its name.

And were we wondering about the post office? Anne Foster wondered. Had we noticed the old blackboard on the wall behind her? Or the raised platform in front of it? The Climax Post Office, the current one inside of which we stood now, used to be the Climax School. That was a while back. The schoolhouse had an octagonal clock on one wall, coat hooks near the entrance, and thirty desks situated around a wood-burning stove and a water cooler in the very center of the room. The teacher and teacher's desk would have been situated on the raised platform in front of the blackboard. The floorboards on which we stood now were the original floorboards. We should notice how they were laid diagonally, which is how they did it back then for some reason or other. And as a matter of fact, where Bayne right that moment was standing, that very spot was almost precisely where William Vincent stood as a boy in September of 1901 when he heard the news that President McKinley had been shot.

Climax, Ms. Foster went on, had recently celebrated its centennial, and the county historical society had just published a little book with photographs and some pieces written by old-time Climaxeans. That's how she herself learned the things she had been telling us. So were we interested in seeing it?

In the old days, the little book said, before the New York State Thruway blasted its way through this part of the country, Climax was the social and commercial expression of life in a drowsy valley of fruit and dairy and honey farms. It was a summer resort, too, with several country boarding houses rescuing hot people from New York City and transporting them to a place that promised cool breezes and home cooking, fresh eggs and vegetables, fresh fried chicken, hot country pies — also cards and croquet, an evening drive into the town of Earlton for a dance, and a casual afternoon stroll down to Spickerman's Spring for a dip and drink.

There had been an old toll house. Anne Foster leafed through the illustrated section of the book until she found the relevant photo. And it charged a few cents for passage along Route 67 into the Catskills, although nuzzling newlyweds hurrying to honeymoon in the mountains could slip through for free.

And there had been a small and ramshackle hotel next to a big old elm tree.

In 1925, however, Mr. James Jerry Zavatone came up to Climax from New York City, bought that hotel, rebuilt it, added some extra buildings, and turned it into the hottest little spot in the whole county: Jerry's Climax Hotel. Jerry put in a big dance hall, and he imported class acts and name bands up from the City, including Dusty Miller and the Colorado Wranglers. Sitting on a stool at the mahogany bar of Jerry's Climax Hotel, you could rest your foot on a brass foot rail, spit into a brass spittoon, munch on free pretzels, and order a beer for five cents. And when the live band was taking a break, you might drop a coin in the player piano or, later on, the juke box, and enjoy such pleasant tunes as "It's a Sin to Tell a Lie" and "I'll Never Smile Again."

Legs Diamond, the Prohibition gangster, used to turn up at Jerry's Climax Hotel from time to time. One day somebody turned up dead beneath the elm next to Jerry's Climax Hotel. Hit and run. Then the hotel burned down. Someone broke into the kitchen and set the place on fire early one morning. Jerry and his daughter, who slept on the second and third floors, woke up when the building was already full of smoke and, since their front door had gotten wedged shut from the outside, barely escaped with their lives. Jerry rebuilt the hotel and bar but not his heart. He closed down for good in 1945 and died four years later. A few years after that, the State of New York bought half of Jerry's original land as part of the Thruway's right-of-way. However, Anne Foster told us, it was still possible to drive down there and find what was left of the hotel. It wasn't far, she said, just right or left down the road and over something down a something just before the something.

We thanked Anne Foster for the information and headed out to find the remainder of Jerry's Climax Hotel. The day, meanwhile, had settled warmly into late afternoon, rich enough that I didn't mind getting lost but just drove in a minor trance on a sleepy scramble down a road that advertised trees and bees, apples and honey, until we came upon a small farm that included a big red barn, a smaller white barn, a rambling old red brick house, and a pond and some beehives way out back. A sign on the white barn said TWIN SPRUCE APIARIES est. 1941.

At the back door to the house, we met a bright and energetic woman by the name of Jessie Bauer. She had honey-brown hair, dark eyes, and an open cheeky smile. She wore a turquoise dress.

Jessie said she was pretty busy right then because she was getting things ready for a Glee Club barbecue, and so she and her husband, Wolf, were kind of cleaning up and doing things, but in the meanwhile she would be glad to take a few minutes and chat. And if we were interested in bees—as I said we were!—we also ought to talk to her husband, Wolf, who had started their bee business in 1941. Wolf, her husband, was eighty-four years old, and he came over to Climax from Germany when he was twelve years old, so he could tell us a lot about Climax. Their son Walter, he might talk to us about bees, too, since he now ran the business, but in fact he was just now getting together a truck to drive down to the market. They have nine hundred hives, and her son and his wife take a truckload of honey to Manhattan every Saturday, so he was getting ready now. Would we like to come inside and try some cookies and tea with honey?

In that manner we were invited into the Bauers's house, seated at their kitchen table (overlooking the pond out back), and treated very well. Meanwhile, Jessie's husband, Wolfgang Bauer, showed up. Eighty-four years old, huh? He was an extraordinary man, square-built with a thick neck and forceful chin (dimpled at the leading edge), thick bushy eyebrows, a grizzled mustache, and one powerful right arm. His left arm was missing as was his left shoulder, and over that trauma the left sleeve of his gray T-shirt had been neatly folde 1. When he laughed, his eyebrows arched ecstatically while his eyes closed in pleasure. And when he expressed displeasure or serious impatience, he chopped the air and shouted or pounded the table to emphasize the energy of his feeling. Maybe it was the bees. Maybe it was the beekeeping.

Whatever the reason, Wolfgang Bauer talked with the energy and passion of a child or a very young man. He laughed, he frowned and grimaced, he imitated other people saying foolish things, he pounded the table, he shouted.

Meanwhile, I was gingerly blowing and sipping on my hot tea and sweet honey, watching the Research Assistants bite into a couple of giant honey oatmeal cookies, and trying to think arithmetically all at the same time. If they had nine hundred hives, I wondered, how many bees would that be altogether?

Wolfgang thought he knew. It isn't so easy to figure. First, they have to have a certain number of bees in a hive to produce a surplus. In other words, the bees do not work for us or for him. They bring in the honey for their own purposes! To survive! For the apiary to make a surplus, you need at the very least about sixty thousand bees per hive. And he's already got swarms you couldn't put in a bushel basket. There's about five thousand bees to the pound, and so if you've got nine hundred hives full of bees, well, you're talking in big figures. So, we can imagine. He figured out one time, he figured they must have had in the neighborhood of twenty-two to twenty-three million workers.

I tried to go over the figures more methodically: "You said that there are how many per hive? Sixty thousand or—"

"Sixty thousand. That's twelve pounds of bees."

"That's a lot of bees," I said. "If you have sixty thousand per hive, then you've got, according to my thinking here, you've got . . . fifty-four million bees altogether."

"Oh yeah, you got quite a few!"

I asked Wolfgang how he got started in the bee business, and he said, "Well, you know, this bee business, you've got to have it in your blood!" His grandfather had bees in Germany. And Wolfgang came over to the United States when he was twelve. His father was in the Great World War, and he lost two brothers, and one brother came home half. Wolfgang used to listen to them as a youngster when he was nine ten years old. And they all said the same thing: "We haven't done anything. We have this war here with all this killing and stuff. Nothing was established. We are going to have another war in twenty-five years." And his father said, "Well, we are going to move. We are leaving Germany." The man was an engineer, but he came over here on a farm and brought his whole family with him to be on the farm in Climax. Wolfgang's brother, Herman, he liked it better. But Wolfgang never liked cows. Oh, no. He didn't like farming, because to farm you had to like cows. He would go and milk cows in the morning. Hey, listen, you go with the cows, you got to change your underwear! You got to take a bath after your work! Otherwise, everybody calls you a *damn farmer*, we know that! You smell! No, he hated it! No, *he didn't like it!* Wolfgang concluded, pounding the table for emphasis.

So they came over to the States in 1925. He was twelve years old at the time. He didn't know any English. His sister knew a little bit. But yet he could never forget bees because his grandfather used to take him to a bee house. It gets into your system. He in fact is the only one in the family, with his son Walter, who likes bees. All the rest of them. His brother, "Yuh!" His father, "Yuh, bees!" But his grandfather, he got his love of bees from his grandfather, Wolfgang guessed.

His grandfather was a schoolteacher, and so bees was a sideline. A schoolteacher, and the most he ever had was fifty-four colonies. But there were times that he had a bigger income from his bees than he had teaching school. So, anyway, that's how Wolfgang Bauer got started, and he came over to the United States when he was twelve and saved his pennies and had his first colony when he was fourteen years old. Then of course, when he lost his arm, oh God, that was devastating. No compensation. When he lost his arm, he had in the neighborhood—how many colonies? He would bet no more than about thirty. When he lost his arm, compensation said, "You can't take care of bees any more." And they wouldn't give him anything. And they had regular— could we imagine? They had regular set laws. The loss of an arm was 312 weeks times two-thirds your salary. But you had to go to court to get it. And the wages those days. He was making forty-five cents an hour. He had taken an ICS course from Scranton, Pennsylvania, and he was a foundry man. In fact, at one time, he was the boss of fourteen women and five men, and he was twenty-one twenty-two years old. But he got his arm on the conveyor belt, yep, when he was twenty-seven years old. It pulled the arm right out and took the shoulder blade with it. The doctor said, "The trouble with you, you were too muscular." Boxing and doing things, he was very muscular in the shoulder and upper arm, so the conveyor took his arm off and the shoulder with it. So, he has been living since 1939, he has been living with one arm.

Now, to start a bee colony you usually begin by buying bees. Right now the Bauers get their bees from somewhere in Georgia. When they order, they usually order a two-pound package with a queen. It's important that you get a good cluster, and also get them early when you still have cool nights. They're shipped by parcel post. They come in a screen cage: wood frame, screen cage.

The queen herself is in a little bit of a cage. A queen cage. And she has an entourage. Oh, yeah, hey, she's a queen! Very attractive! There's three compartments in a queen cage, and one compartment is semisolid sugar. Her worker bees chew that out completely. Those bees then meet the queen, and the queen makes out. And in the meantime, she adopts the odor of the hive. Otherwise she would be a perfect stranger. Let's face it, the queen is raised separately. Oh, sure, they have people that raise nothing but queens down there. They raise the queens by themselves. And the queen hatches, she goes out to a mating flight where she mates in the air! And they give the queen so many days for her to mate because when you order queen bees, you can pay as much as $7 or $8, as much as $10 for a queen. And sometimes you get them, they're not mated. They're still virgins. And some, most of the times the virgins are killed by the bees. They know she is no good. Because *she can't lay any eggs!* She can't propagate, she can't propagate the species!

Bees! Oh, bees! The life of a bee is only thirty to forty days. Bees divide like bacteria do. That's to propagate the species, to enlarge the species, because it has such a short life span. So you make sure that you have a young queen, good laying queen, and plenty of room for the bees to work, and it's very important. Because you're working against nature. The queen, you recognize the queen because she is bigger. Especially the abdomen. The thorax is a little bit larger. Of course the abdomen, because she's an egg layer. She can lay up to two thousand, twenty-five hundred eggs a day!

"Wouldn't you like to have a chicken like that?" Jessie broke in.

Wolfgang continued: Could we imagine that she has to thrust her abdomen into a honeycomb cell, and she puts the egg right in the center, and the egg sticks up. Meanwhile she has her entourage that follow her around all the comb. And they go around, feed her and groom her and make a big fuss over her. And yet if she falters in her production, her days are numbered. They raise more queen cells from her eggs. Usually there's a young queen hatching, and it's always the old queen that goes out in the swarm, the early swarm.

Her followers: That's what a swarm is. It's the old queen and her followers. Now he, Wolfgang, is sometimes called out to catch a swarm, and he'll do it, all right. *He loves to catch swarms!* But, of course, he'd never put them back in the same hive that they came from, always in another. You leave the new young queen alone, let her build up her own brood of all young bees. So a swarm does divide the hive. If you have, say, a swarm, and you have most of your bees swarming, you're cutting your honey production in half because your working force is hanging up in the tree. And there again when you catch them, they usually have an old queen. So that's not good, especially when it's toward the end of the season, because the old queen may not have time to build up a new hive.

Jessie cut in here: "It's an old saying, 'A swarm in May is worth a load of hay. A swarm in June is worth a silver spoon. A swarm in July isn't worth a fly!' Because you've got to build them up. You've got to feed them. And in July it's already late."

Winter coming on, Wolfgang added, and they can't build up strong enough to survive the winter. So you see the swarm out there, he continued, and you just shake them down, and there's a queen in there, and if you get the queen, she's usually in the middle and you always get her. But you don't look for the queen at all. You just shake those bees, shake them down into the box. Sometimes Wolfgang will put a swarm in a box and drive them right on home in the box. Then he will dump the swarm in front of an empty hive, and the bees spread out like a blanket, and it looks like somebody gives a command, and they all go one direction and walk into the hive. And the queen sometimes walks right on top of them. There are times you see the queen, she walks right on top, because —

Here I interrupted: "Do they *walk* into the hive or do they *fly* in?"

Jessie: "Walk."

Wolfgang: "They walk in. They walk in."

Me: "Oh, now I see why you're interested in bees. Because they're really interesting!"

And you never learn enough, Wolfgang went on, repeating himself and pounding the table for emphasis: *You never learn enough!* And can we imagine this cell, the comb that they've built, every cell is an exact hexagon? *Who taught them how to do this? Why do they use hexagons?* For a very simple reason! If you take anything round and you put it in two clusters like that, you have a triangle, this empty space, it shoves together, and that space is used up. And it's exact! *He is telling us*, Wolfgang said, *he is telling us it's an ex-act hexagon!* Six sides! *And they do it in the dark!* A hive is dark inside, there's no light! They don't fool around! It's so organized! They have their guards in the front of the hive, they have their nurse bees, that's all they do is take care of the larvae as it matures and hatches. You've got your eggs, got your pupae, and you got your adults, right, and so on and so forth. And he is telling us, yeah! And he can tell, he can tell if the queen is good if she lays a nice solid pattern! And when everything is going well inside the hive, you can tell because there's a *contented hum.* Oh, he loves to hear that sound! But if there's a different sound in the hive, you know it. You've been around bees long enough, you know when they're out of the queen. You know exactly when there's something wrong! Different sound! Isn't that contented hum in there! Kind of a frustrated hum!

The pleasure of raising bees, you can't explain it, Wolfgang said. *You can't explain it!* He's retired, but he still loves it. He still wants to get out into the bee yard. He gets a thrill just catching a swarm! And he has such a respect for that little insect! Such a respect. And it can sting him all it wants. He takes it. He just protects himself. He puts something heavier on. He got to a hive one time that was knocked over by a deer, and it had snowed that night. The hive was tipped over, and there was snow in all four corners clustered in there. When he picked it up he had to put on his leather coat and go down there because they were stinging him. It wasn't below zero, but it was around snow time.

Temperature must have been thirty degrees, and they got underneath his coat. And he does believe if he had $5 every time he got stung, he could compete with the Rockefellers maybe.

A hive of bees, you just can't beat it, that's it! You can't explain it. It's in your blood, and there's no getting away from it. The ancient Egyptians believed in life after death, right? When the Pharaoh was buried or put in his tomb, there was usually everything there that he owned or he would need for further life. They took *honey* out of King Tut's Tomb. That was buried over thirty-three hundred years. That honey was *edible!* Yep. Honey. Everything else that was taken out of King Tut's tomb fell apart as soon as it hit air. Meat? It disintegrated. *But not the honey! Honey lasts forever!*

And so we talked about bees at the Bauers's kitchen table.

We talked a good deal more than I've indicated here. I thought bees were the most fascinating creatures alive by the time our conversation started its gradual decline, and it wasn't until then that I shook my head and remembered I'd forgotten to ask about Climax. Especially Jerry's Climax Hotel, which we were still hoping to find. "There's one thing I wanted to ask you," I said. "Were you around when Jerry's Hotel was around? Do you remember Jerry's Climax Hotel?"

Jessie: "Sure."

Wolfgang: "Oh, sure."

It was a dance hall, Jessie said. The young people used to go there. Sure. Yeah, she'd been there. Sure.

The only thing is, Wolfgang continued, he was not one to dance. He was not much of a bar fly. So, you go in there, say on a Friday night, and buy a beer. And have maybe two glasses of beer and play some pool. Now, Jerry was a decent sort of man. He was an Italian. He had four or five sons. People said that they were kind of mixed up with the law. One son did get shot by a gangster. Yeah, sure they were involved. Down in the city, they were involved. But he, Wolfgang, never wanted to delve too much into that stuff.

And, Jessie added, there was the *still* over on Jordan's farm. Oh, yeah, Wolfgang said. That was a big thing. You go down through the woods. It was a winding place you go down in. They used to see lights go down there at night. Twelve, one o'clock in the morning. There was something going on. Because they could see from their bedroom window the cars going out there and lights down there. That's the way it was in those days. Well, if the farmer can further his income, let him do it. That was the way it was. And Mr. Jordan, yeah, he didn't care any more whether his cows gave milk or not. Well, the police, or whatever, what do you call them? They smashed everything. Oh, they found out. Oh, there were several police raids. The police coming out in the cars and so on, they'd yell, "Eliot Ness!"

After thanking the Bauers sincerely for their hospitality and the information (not to mention that jar of honey pressed into my hand), we followed the road back down past the post office and down a little farther. We made a right turn and drove down to a small hollow at the edge of a minor jungly woods and a few wooden buildings.

The bigger building looked half burned, though possibly the wood had just blackened with age. I couldn't figure out the building's former function. It had a two-story, house-like structure on one end and, on the other, a one-story kitchen-like structure that stretched along for a while before terminating with a pink door. The pink paint on the door was disappearing. A couple of windows were broken. And when I looked through the broken windows, I saw a dreamy gray light pour through a break in the ceiling and settle through a cloud of floating dust onto decaying wood, a heap of rat turds, and a pile of garbage. It was memory in the process of amnesia, abandoned and boarded up and being overgrown by vines and falling into a final dissolution.

"Oh, there it is!" Bayne said suddenly. Bayne had discovered part of a sign above part of an old garage.

A tin roof was half peeled away from a disintegrating shed of ghostly gray wood, open at the front with some minor junk on a dirt floor. Across the top of the open front, we could just discern the word JERRY'S in faded paint. After pulling away a few branches and bushes, we could make out the next word, CLIMAX. But the third word, where was it? It was nowhere to be found, and so we were left with only the melancholic memory of JERRY'S CLIMAX. And that wilted little construction, that old gray garage, looked small enough to be a kid's clubhouse. It must have been, I thought, a small erection to begin with. And where, come to think of it, was the main building of the hotel? I couldn't quite reconstruct the thing in my mind, and while I was trying to, we heard the long rolling peals of approaching thunder and so climbed back into the sanctuary of our car and left.

LEG²

Sunshine

After a major interlude of rest and relaxation in our very own home just north of Boston, after sunny days followed by damp and drizzly ones, after a wallow in middle-aged domesticity followed by a shallow impatience with it, after a dozen serious dog walks and a thousand gentle strokes on the grateful canine cranium, at last we put down our collective foot and raised Storyville's second leg.

Soon we were sailing north out of the Boston area on Route 95. It was a warm and clear day, the sky silky blue, the wind stern and steady, and I shinnied up the mizzenmast and hoisted the topsails. We enjoyed the first couple of hours, listening to Bob Dylan and the Beatles, keeping the windows wide open, and discussing such important issues as the Pythagorean injunction on beans and why feet sometimes smell.

Route 95 took us out of Massachusetts through a corner of New Hampshire and across a bridge into Maine, where we briefly stopped at Bald Head, intending to get a cheap haircut. There wasn't much there, however, other than a spectacular view blocked by an ugly hotel, so we kept on going. It was completely dark by the time we ricocheted off Augusta, careened all the way out to the coast, and then got lost and even a little concerned at a place called Blue Hill. I happened to have a nephew in the area who was already ready to feed us a spaghetti dinner. Andrew Peterson is his name, and I phoned him anxiously from Blue Hill. Distances had begun to seem much greater than I had imagined they should be. But my nephew patiently clarified the directions over the telephone, and finally at about nine o'clock that evening we pulled into the mud alongside his house.

Andrew's house was built 160 years ago, but it still needed work. It had pine-plank floors, low ceilings collapsing in places, a couple of missing chimneys, and one good piano in the living room. Andrew, who welcomed us eagerly and generously, looked like himself: a bearded, broad-shouldered, twenty-five-year-old boatbuilder, quick of mind and steady of speech, with suspenders holding up his pants and muscular arms sticking out the arms of a short-sleeved shirt. He was cooking spaghetti on a wood-fired stove in the kitchen and listening to a radio tuned to some terrific station with actual music on it.

We drank beer and sat down to a late dinner. Our goal was to reach Sunshine and Sunset, which were, said the cartographicus magnus, located on the island of Deer Island off the coast. Andrew had a much more detailed representation of the area, though, which he now unfolded so that we could study it while slurping on our steaming spaghetti.

Me: "So where is Deer Island?"

Andrew placed a finger on it: a Rorschach splatter right off the coast. Then he put his finger on top of his house. "Deer Isle is down that way about five miles," he said. He traced the road. Then he said, "The island is hooked to the mainland by a suspension bridge here." He pointed to it. "That is a sister bridge to the Tacoma Narrows Bridge, which if you were in high school physics you'll remember seeing the black and white film of the Tacoma Narrows Bridge collapsing."

"Yeah! I did see that! Very dramatic. In a storm, and the bridge starts flapping up and down like laundry and then flies apart."

Since that episode, he continued, the authorities have taken steps to correct this bridge, and it has aerodynamic things glued to the side of it. They have anemometers all over the thing, and if it starts to blow they close the bridge down. But Deer Isle's a weird place in and of itself, regardless of anything else. Kind of strange. Well, because for ages and ages it was an island, and even after they built the bridge, all the islandness of the place didn't evaporate. It's introverted. Stonington, which is the principal community of Deer Isle, at the far southern tip of the island, down as far as you can get, and as close as you can get to the open sea—Stonington drove out its police force. The state designated two police officers to take care of Stonington. The Stonington Police Department. And the fishermen of the town antagonized the guys so badly that they couldn't stand it any more and packed up and left. The state's now in the process of trying to find people that are willing to be police officers in Stonington, and there are no candidates, which is fine by the people of Stonington because they believe that problems in Deer Isle are the business of the people of Deer Isle and not the business of people from the outside. They've got their own way of doing things. Andrew ate several forksful of spaghetti and then summarized: "Yeah, they ran the cops off and nobody wants to go back."

"That's pretty funny, don't you think?" I said. "How'd they run the cops off?"

"They just antagonized the guys so badly," he said. There was a less dramatic example of the way that kind of thing works on Cranberry Island: that island just down the way where the abstract expressionist William Kienbusch used to spend his summers. Cranberry has got a constable. But the constable is a middle-aged widow on a mountain bike, and she doesn't really do much except enforce the leash law against summer people. She's in no position to enforce the law against any other members of the community. Socially it wouldn't be acceptable. If somebody's misbehaving on Cranberry Island, or Deer Isle, or some of these other islands, then the community at large deals with it. Kind of like a benign form of vigilante justice. If you go out and drink a bottle of whiskey and drive your car at full speed up and down the road, you'll find by and by that somebody's stolen your distributor cap and thrown it off the end of the pier. And that's the way people like to do it out there on the islands.

"What else can you tell me about Deer Island?"

"That it's called Deer Isle. People will be very adamant about that. If you ask for directions for Deer Island, they will probably deliberately give you directions for Buckport just to joke on you," he said, and then, as I dug away at the salad bowl: "There are tomatoes and such like on the bottom of that thing. You'll have to dredge for them."

The next morning Andrew went off to his boatbuilding job near Penobscot, and the rest of us drove out to Deer Isle, looking for Sunshine and Sunset. The day turned out to be overcast with a forecast of clouds, clouds, and possibly rain, so we decided to look for Sunshine first. An arm of deep blue water known as Eggemoggin Reach separated the mainland of Maine from the island of Deer Isle, and we reached the Reach that morning and overcame it with some help from the bridge.

Deer Isle was big enough that you couldn't tell you were on an island while driving through — until you came to the causeway connecting Little Deer to Big Deer. The island was a pine-pricked puzzle of nooks and crannies, which the road, Route 15, solved with loops and scoops. We twisted past some old houses, a church, a graveyard, and after half an hour turned away from 15 to wind up a smaller road until we came to a cluster of white buildings, including one that resembled a church and declared itself the Sunshine Advent Christian Church. Sunshine! We stopped right there because two people were walking across the road, carrying in their arms several objects that looked like video equipment. They were wearing Levi's and in their mid-forties, and they looked serene and pastoral in a gentle, teddy-bearish sort of way. I thought maybe they had just emerged from the church.

I stopped and rolled down the window. "Excuse me," I said.

"Morning," the man said.

"We're looking for Sunshine."

"You're here. This road is actually what they term 'Sunshine.' Any specific area?"

"We saw it on the map. We thought it was kind of an overcast day. We thought we'd see if we could find Sunshine."

That was the best I could come up with, and it wasn't good enough. A sudden and severe case of shadestroke, moreover, prevented me from pursuing the conversation much further, so the pastoral couple soon assessed us as tourists on a lark and looking for a good view: "Oh, where's a pretty place? This road right here, if you turn around, right here, goes down to a boatyard, and it's wide open down there, very pretty overlook."

They had walked away before I realized I hadn't asked them where the name came from. But what would they know? And wasn't it obvious? The road was lined with trees, but I could imagine the trees parting at any minute and allowing a flood of sunshine to pour down. It was the eastern end of the island, and if it hadn't been so dark and dreary, we surely would have gotten the full effect.

OK, so we drove back onto Route 15, and since that single highway makes a loop all the way around Deer Isle, no sophisticated navigation was required to find the main town, Stonington, which was draped across some rocks and around a harbor.

There was an old factory at one end of town, and next to the factory, with a view of the bay, we found an old restaurant called Bayview. The Bayview was an unpretentious place put together a long time ago, with red white and blue tiles on the floor and ornate tin topography on the ceiling and walls. Paintings of old ships hung on the walls, and so did a huge sampler of a patriotic eagle holding onto a liberty bell in front of a red white and blue flag. There were no other customers in the place, and the absence of customers and only one waiter-cook meant it was quiet. The waiter-cook, an agreeable man with the dazed look and shuffling manner of someone surprised before the end of hibernation, said we could sit anywhere, so we sat near a window overlooking the factory and the bay.

What I liked best about this restaurant was the quiet. Adding to the effect, some wonderful piano inventions by J. S. Bach were being drawn gently out of a radio somewhere. I never did figure out where the radio was. We ordered lunches, and after the waiter disappeared in the back to become the cook, it was so melodiously quiet in there we couldn't help talking in hushed tones. But the Research Assistants were hungry, and I could detect a dark contentiousness creeping into their subdued banter.

Bayne said he was hungry and started talking about food, and Britt, probably out of sheer hunger herself, called him a heathen. "You're such a heathen!" she whispered nastily. Her tone was aggressive. It made him defensive: "Me? No, I'm not. I just like food. Everybody loves food." She pressed: "What about anorexics?" He qualified: "I mean anybody who's happy."

But I just sat back and listened to a steady procession of notes on the disembodied piano from the hidden radio, an elaborate and divine architecture of tone and harmony, memory and desire, and as a matter of fact when the lemonade was brought out the Research Assistants' voices soon were transformed into a satisfied patter. Looking out the window, I could see the bay rolling in triangles, with several fishing boats anchored and turned to face the same direction.

Then their voices began edging toward disharmony again. "Stop playing with your utensils." "Get your elbows off the lady, young table!" "Oh, Bayne, that's not funny! Stop it!" Then the food arrived, and we began eating.

But my attention remained fixed out the window on the view of the bay, with its hidden sunshine falling and filtering through clouds and rising and reflecting back through seawater, soft and bright at the same time and cast in shafts and slabs and planes over this boiled rock of an island. The waiter-cook came over to check our progress: "Howya doin? All right?" And a pristine gray light passed through the window like a bright painting on the wall and became an intelligence, illuminating faces and turning them blissful and beatific. It was a deeply pleasing moment, and I can only assume the Research Assistants shared it, because the food, which by the dull glow of strict rationality was ordinary, still seemed near perfection. Bayne loved his hamburger. Britt loved her grilled chicken. "That was the best chicken I've ever had, I think," she said, after swallowing her last bite. "It was soft, chewy, tender. It had taste. It was a little burned on the outside, which is always good because it makes the inside seem better. It wasn't at all stringy. It was juicy."

And when raspberry pie with vanilla ice cream arrived for dessert, we all were persuaded to give Stonington's Bayview Restaurant ten stars on a scale of five. "Arrgh! This be good!" Bayne said.

The waiter-cook said that the factory next door used to process lobsters and then sardines, but now it's just closed down because the times have changed. He said they didn't get many tourists on the island. He's lived on Deer Isle all his life, he said, but he still could never remember which place was Sunshine and which was Sunset. He knew they were named after sunshine and sunset, though, and he knew how to get to them when necessary, and wasn't that the important thing?

Sunset

We drove up and down a couple of roads through town, past some shops and a man loading lobster traps from a truck onto a boat, and then just followed Route 15 around the western side of the island, looking now for Sunset. There were absolutely no signs for the place, though, and finally I stopped at a small U.S. Postal Service building to ask directions. Inside the building was a small man with a wide mustache, dressed like a postman and acting like one, who, when I asked him how to get to Sunset, said, "This is it. You're here."

"This is it?"

"This is it."

I said, "Why is it called Sunset?"

And he said, pointing out a window, "Well, go out that way and turn down that road over there. Go down about a mile, and you'll come to the ocean. If you do that at eight o'clock in the evening, you'll see why it's called Sunset."

When I left the postal building, I noticed lettering on the front that said SUNSET, ME 04681, and we bounced down the road about a mile until we came to its end right at the edge of the open sea. A couple of waterfowl slipped through the water there, and a couple of whitish cottages had settled along the shore. But the sky was dark and misty, starting to rain, and the time was early afternoon. We looked at the triangulating water for a while and then decided to leave and come back before sunset if there was any sun. There wasn't, we didn't, and that's all I have to say about Sunset.

Feeding Hills

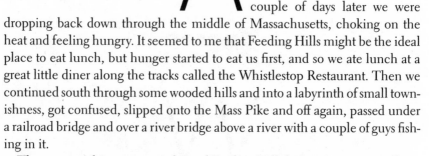

A couple of days later we were dropping back down through the middle of Massachusetts, choking on the heat and feeling hungry. It seemed to me that Feeding Hills might be the ideal place to eat lunch, but hunger started to eat us first, and so we ate lunch at a great little diner along the tracks called the Whistlestop Restaurant. Then we continued south through some wooded hills and into a labyrinth of small town-ishness, got confused, slipped onto the Mass Pike and off again, passed under a railroad bridge and over a river bridge above a river with a couple of guys fishing in it.

The cartographicus magnus showed Feeding Hills before Agawam, so when, a half-hour later, we sighted the Agawam Polish Club, I figured we had over-shot the mark and stopped to ask directions. The Polish Club was a beer fort with a sign that said "Bingo Every Tuesday. Doors Open 6:00 PM. Early Bird

Specials 6:45." I parked the car in the gravel lot, got out, and looked around. The land was basically flat there, semirural, surrounded with trees and a little farm. Inside the Club was—no surprise—a television set, a pool table, and a bar with people swallowing beer and nuts. I spoke to the bartender, a pleasant white-haired woman with a rather wide nose.

"Hi," I said. "I'm trying to find Feeding Hills."

"You're in Feeding Hills."

"There's no sign on the road that says Feeding Hills."

"Well, you're in Feeding Hills right here," she said and, after I asked her where the name came from, declared: "The Indians used to come up here to feed their horses. They used to graze their horses. Indians were up in the hills, feeding their horses. Used to come up here to feed their horses on the hill."

"Do you know when this was?"

"Before my time. It was before my time. I was born here, but I wasn't born that long ago."

So Feeding Hills was a spot, an appendix, an addendum to the duodenum on the way to Agawam. I thanked her, got back into the car, and we pulled out and continued down the road, which gulped and swallowed us into a pulsating canal of traffic. We passed the Agawam Junior High School, saw a sign for the Feeding Hills Animal Hospital, found a building housing Mr. Shower Door of Agawam with an American flag waving out front. And right next to Mr. Shower Door, we discovered the Feeding Hills Public Market, a modest place with brick front and light-blue shingle sides, with specials posted in the windows in bright letters. OK. That looked promising. So I stepped on the brakes at the Feeding Hills Public Market, and we went in. The woman behind the counter, very friendly, said she had no idea why the area was called Feeding Hills, but she did know why Agawam had the lowest Zip Code in the country. It's 01001.

"Why does it have the lowest Zip Code?"

"Because the man who invented it lived here. He did a favor to his home town by giving it the lowest number."

A man inside the market, buying Cheezwhiz and Coke, said, "It's called Feeding Hills because people used to bring their cows over from Springfield to feed in this area."

"Really? How long ago was that?"

"No idea. Some time."

To be polite we bought a few things in the store and then returned to the car. We continued driving, and the road swept us past the Soft Serve softy ice-cream center, the Paradise Grooming Salon, Dale's Grooming, The Clip Shop, Parade of Pets, Golden Dream Coiffures, The Kid's Place (Leader in

Quality Child Care), and then a Stop and Shop Super Store monolith with big signs selling everything. The bolus of traffic turned thicker and more insistent, and soon we had passed right into and through the very guts of Agawam, which processed, as far as I could figure, an amorphous mass of commercial activity: bright signs and squalid enticements to consume everything. Even the voice on the radio turned crass: *It is absolutely unbelievable! And to help us celebrate we've got a gazillion specials in there!! But the biggest one is twenty pounds of Pro-plant at four dollars off! It's the lowest price in the history of the whole world! And this is going on in all our stores!!! So come on in, take a look at our new store on Allen and Cooley Street, and you will love it! I promise!!!!*

I was hoping to find somewhere in the heart of Agawam a library or historian who could tell me the truth about Feeding Hills, but I never found the heart. I must have made a wrong turn somewhere, but the car kept going around in circles, and the place I saw seemed without center or soul, a lost hollow stripped of presence and lacking past, a fatuous flatulous fata morgana dedicated to inflating appetite and then deflating it back again. For a price.

But I wanted to get a newspaper, and so on the way out of there we stopped at a place called Colonial News. When I asked the lady who sold me a newspaper where the name Feeding Hills came from, she said, "Well, this is where the Indians fed."

I said, "They fed — or their horses fed?"

She smiled at my mental vagueness and said, in a friendly sort of way, "I don't know. I don't care. I just live here."

Index

After spending the night at the house of our friends Phil and Carol in Northampton, Massachusetts, we got lost and found ourselves in southeastern New York State looking for Surprise. We found the sign SURPRISE but not the story, so we turned north and followed Route 81 past woods and children riding their bikes.

Before long we had turned right into Cooksburg and were drifting through

beautiful farm land and alongside a meandering inviting river, which reminded me that we had forgotten to bring fishing gear.

Could we imagine wild bears there? I wondered. Certainly there were wild
deer, and I thought we were passing through some really wild and unspoiled
land. Right up to the Hubcap Heaven sign: HUBCAP HEAVEN. ONE-
QUARTER MILE. OVER 10,000 HUBCAPS!!!! We paused in the parking
patch at Hubcap Heaven, which seemed closer to Hubcap Hell.

Dallying near small towns and around small mountains, we crossed a river
into historic Middleburgh, settled 1712, tucked ourselves under Interstate 88
and out the other side into an inviting valley of old Dutch names, caves, and
the occasional total ugliness sitting alongside the road like a giant block of shit
from outer space: SUPER CENTER OPEN 24 HOURS. The road wound
underneath a steel railroad bridge and right into Cobleskill, where we stayed
overnight at a bed and breakfast operation more attractive outside than in.

Eagerly the next morning, we set our sights and fingers for Index. Index was
on the road to Cooperstown, home of the Baseball Hall of Fame, and from
Oneonta we just allowed ourselves to be sucked up north on Route 28, observing all the signs to the Baseball Hall of Fame as we ascended. This was not a
bad drive, and we plowed through some wide-open farm country, with an orphanage and farms, but as we got closer and closer to Index on the cartographicus magnus, still we could find no indication that the place existed in real life.

From a reflex of the solar plex, we stopped at a joint called the Hamburger
Hall of Fame, where I inquired of Index from the waitress, who said, "I've lived
here all my life, and I'm not sure I remember where the sign is. It's more like
a place on the highway. There's a spot down by the river—and there's an old
house. Maybe that has something to do with it." But the cartographicus magnus showed Index at the inmix of 28 and 11, so after lunch we continued on
past JJ State Liquor and Lollipop Farm Petting Zoo until we came to the junction with 11 and a sign that said INDEX.

Good! But there was nothing else except a cornfield and a low building that
identified itself as Cooperstown Glass and Mirror and, across the road, a couple
of houses. We stopped at the Cooperstown Glass and Mirror and located out
back a friendly guy with short brown hair, glasses, and a walrus mustache,
dressed in gray, who, while working on a shattered rear window of a Ford Taurus, answered the telephone to find out that someone had just robbed a bank
in Cooperstown.

He told us about the robbery, and then he told us to try Mrs. Dodge across
the road. "She ought to know." Mrs. Dodge's house across the road was a white
house with an American flag unfurled out front. A roofer was roofing the roof

out back, and he suggested we knock on the side door. No one answered, so we returned to the Cooperstown Glass and Mirror to ask the man working on the Ford Taurus out back if he had any other suggestions. Go try the restaurant back up the road, he suggested.

I wanted to make sure: "The Hamburger Hall of Fame?"

"Just go out here and then go up the hill," he replied. "It's called The 1819 House. Ah, they might know. You got me curious now. I'm embarrassed to say, 'No, I don't know what it means.'"

Keys into the ignition, we started the car and a domestic goose chase that took us into the kitchen of The 1819 House, where we spoke to a big friendly cook with a round face and trimmed beard, who was working on an impressive spread of onions and steak and who said he'd lived in Index all his life but had no idea. He suggested we continue on into the village of Hartwick where there might be an historically inclined person in the public library.

Libraries like that, though, are sometimes open on the wrong days. This library was open only on Mondays, Wednesdays, and Fridays, not today, and so we went back down to the sign for Index next to the Cooperstown Glass and Mirror again. It seemed to us that Mrs. Dodge held the key to this mystery, and so, thinking to try her door again, we parked our car and walked once again across the road.

Mr. Dodge came to the door, not Mrs., wearing blue shoes, blue pants, a white shirt, and white sticking-out hair. He had been working in the garden, and so there was some garden dirt on his pants. Understanding exactly what we wanted, however, he instantly invited us in, as if he had been waiting to be asked the question for a long time. Inside, we met Mrs. Dodge, a pleasant woman wearing teardrop earrings. And we sat down in their living room. Their living room had pictures of grandchildren in it, a red ceramic cat sculpture, and a couple of Raggedy Ann dolls under glass.

"Now: Index," Mr. Dodge began. First of all, he said, he wanted to tell a little anecdote.

Oh, it was about thirty years ago, when he first got out there, that he went to a football game, local high school. It was deadly boring. The team wasn't the greatest team in the world. Never has been. Now there was an old gentleman sitting beside him. They got into a conversation. The old gentleman's hobby after he'd retired was to go over all of New York State and find out why a post office was called what it was called.

Post offices! That was a strange one. He told Mr. Dodge he had found the answer for every single post office that existed in New York State with the exception of Index.

Quite a short distance, well, just over there across the street, used to be a thing called the Hope Factory. And if we thought about that, we might get an idea of the age of Index. At the Hope Factory, they manufactured canvas for the Union Army, and all the tents were manufactured over there. And at that time little Index up here was a thriving little community — had a grocery store, pharmacy, everything. Post office, too.

Rationally, the old gentleman explained to Mr. Dodge, the only reason that he could see why it might have been called Index was that someone in the very early days was going through the county clerk's office and registering deeds. At the top of every deed: *Index* so-and-so and *Liber* so-and-on, with *Liber* meaning *Book*.

Someone must have seen that on a deed of property somewhere, got confused for a second, and said, "Oh, it must be Index."

That was the only reason the old gentleman could think of, and that was the only reason he, Mr. Dodge, could think of as well. The old gentleman could not find any other reason to call it Index. And he was an expert.

Used to be, Mr. Dodge continued, that they had in that area a railroad line, a trolley line, electric trolley, ran up behind the house here, came up from Oneonta. And they had four junction points up there in Index, and one of the junction points they called "The Index Finger." It looked like four fingers pointing one way, and one was the other way. The "Index Finger" was pointing the other, people said. And now the majority of the people around that area, Mr. Dodge went on, they say that Index is called Index because of that. "Well it was called Index long before —" he said, pausing long enough for me to finish the thought, "— the railroad line."

"Very good! You've got it. So that's my theory," Mr. Dodge concluded. And he continued: Now there was a story about Nome, Alaska, he said. Why is it called Nome? he asked rhetorically. There's no reason for it being called Nome, except a second lieutenant, an engineer, was sent up there right after the Russian purchase. After the purchase from Russia. He was sent up there to rename and to survey the coastline. Because it was all Russian. They didn't want Russian names. So he named most of them, except he found this little fishing village with an unpronounceable Russian name. And he decided to let the Secretary of the Interior name it, as a sort of gesture. So he wrote across the place on the map: "Name." Only he didn't write too well. And down in Washington they thought it read: "Nome." And that's why Nome is called Nome. It was a mistake.

"Well, that's a good one!" I said. I liked that. "So you think it's the same with Index!"

Xactly, he said. He did. And after a good deal more chitchat about this and that, we thanked Mr. Dodge for the information, said good-bye to both Mr. and

Mrs. Dodge, and dutifully took the story back across the road to the Cooperstown Glass and Mirror.

Yes, we passed that story along to the man with the mustache working on the back window of the Ford Taurus, who in turn thanked us, and then. . . .

Zip! We hit the road.

Painted Post

The highway followed the river, and inside the river whiskered carp raised ribbons of mud from the bottom. Not far from the whiskered carp and the ribbons of mud, two fishermen fished and talked, and their words drifted clearly across the calm surface of the water.

We followed the road that followed the river, and it took us through the town of Corning and into the village of Painted Post, where we landed in a parking lot in front of several low, interconnected brown wooden buildings — jaunty '70s-style architecture in fluted plywood — and found a door with a sign above it that said: Buds N Blossoms.

We passed through the door and entered a minijungle of potted plants and vased flowers and a permeating perfumy sweetness, a ceiling of acoustic tile and recessed fluorescent lights, and more racks than you could shake a stick at full of such tokens of esteem as stuffed white gorillas with red hearts saying "Make Me Wild." The workers at Buds N Blossoms eyed us suspiciously, in between answering the phone and wrapping cut flowers into paper, but they said their boss would be there soon. "He's out on a delivery."

A thunderstorm appeared suddenly, and it crackled and boomed and splashed at the windows and on the other side of the door. We sat there waiting for the proprietor of the shop, Ray Underwood. He did eventually show up, wet but in good humor, gray-eyed, brown-haired, wearing blue slacks and a lemon-yellow polo shirt with a picture of a horse embroidered on it, and ready to talk to us about the origins of Painted Post.

Well, as he understood, Ray began, the first settlers came into this area. There was a post, which had been erected by the Indians. It was all carved and

136

ornate and so forth. And that's how the name was derived. And then some time in the late 1800s they erected a monument to the post, an Indian standing next to it, and that originally sat out in the street, in the center of town. During a storm the Indian blew over and it was destroyed, and so they ended up replacing that, and after the flood of '72, when they built this complex, they moved the new Indian out of the street over into the corner of the square.

"Why did they move it out of the street?" I wondered.

Well, the traffic was starting to become — the congestion, crowding, and so on and so forth. That was kind of one of the reasons they wanted to build this complex. So that was, in brief, the story.

One thing I haven't mentioned yet. I already knew the story of Painted Post. I was born next door to Painted Post, as a matter of fact, and I grew up in the same river valley, a stone's throw downstream, in Corning, New York. My father worked for Corning Glass as a civil engineer, and after he retired, he and my mother moved to a small house in Painted Post. I was in college by that time, but I regularly mowed the lawn and spent my summers there, lifeguarding at the local pool one summer, then working on construction jobs — building houses, a factory, and then laying down topsoil onto the lawns of all the new houses in one section of Painted Post. So I knew the story of Painted Post. But the Research Assistants didn't.

Another thing I haven't mentioned yet. I already knew Ray Underwood, proprietor of Buds N Blossoms. Matter of fact, Ray and I are contemporaries, and we both grew up on Corning's Northside — Corning is divided in half by the river — which meant we went to the same schools: elementary, junior high, and high. Never close friends, true, but friendly acquaintances since first grade. To my mind, Ray hadn't changed a bit. Still the same old calm personality, the same crew cut and casual good looks, the same rectangular head and chiseled jaw. He even seemed to be wearing the same clothes.

"So how's business?"

"Not bad. We're still pluggin away. The years continue to show up. We're twenty years here."

"I can't believe it!"

"Yep. I have been right here twenty. I have been in the business one way shape or manner since part-time in college, twenty years ago. Time flies!"

"Sure does," I agreed. Then, enthusing for the benefit of the two Research Assistants, I declared, "I tell you, Ray hasn't changed a bit. This is exactly how he looked when he was your age, Bayne!"

Ray tried to inject a note of realism here: "Maybe not quite that, ah —"

But I ignored it. "Bayne's going to be in sixth grade this year," I said, "and Britt's going into her first year of high school. Do you remember your first year of high school? Who was your home room teacher? I had Mr. Yawdes, I think."

"Ninth grade. Gosh! I think I may have had Mrs. Richards. Do you remember her? She was an English teacher."

"English teacher, right," I said. (I remembered her well: She scolded me in front of the entire class and said I had a chip on my shoulder. "Which shoulder?" I asked.)

We chatted a good deal more, until finally I sprang the question most directly on my mind: "So what's life like in a small town?" Was he happy and liberated, or bored and miserable? I really wanted to know the answer; and I scrutinized his voice and tone for all possible eddies and undercurrents, for the telltale tic or illuminating hemidemisemiquaver—but can't say I detected any: "Ah, it's not much different from what it was back when you lived here."

Our words drifted out the door of Buds N Blossoms. It would be nice to imagine they continued drifting along the valley through low, woodsy mountains. Or hills: green, then blue, then gray in the distant haze. Sounds, in Painted Post, travel farther than you might expect. Standing at the top of one of the hills, you can listen to the noise of traffic below, the bang of coupling railroad cars, sometimes the vibration of a diesel engine transversing the valley, sometimes a long train whistle. The valley is an echo chamber, and along its edges a summer heat forces out the smells of goldenrod.

Two rivers, the Tioga and the Cohocton, join forces at Painted Post. They move into an area of small brush-covered islands, gravel deltas, deep swirling pools and rushing channels, and in the process become the Chemung River, which curls southeast through the valley broadly and gently with a smooth, green-glass surface, in places reflecting the gray of sky, with small eddies and ripples scratched in white.

My brother David used to fish in that river.

I grew up with three brothers and a sister next to the river just a stone's throw downstream from Painted Post, as I said a few paragraphs back, in Corning, a modest town with an immodest glass factory humped over the southern side of the riverbank. The glass factory was a byzantine complex of twisted pipes and chemical storage tanks and smoke stacks (eight of them, all sizes and heights) and cat walks and scorpion vents and power lines and conveyor belts, emitting a constant low rumbling and the occasional bump and clank in the night. Trains went into the factory, and trains went out.

In Corning, as in the rest of the universe, social and geographic elevation were closely related. We lived in the lowest part, the bottoms of the old river valley, during those first years, on a street close to our town's version of Baltic and Mediterranean on the Monopoly board. One good thing about where we lived was that my father had to make only a short walk down the street and across the bridge to his office at the glass factory. And when he came back from the factory, late in the day, my brother Dwight and I would be out there on the sidewalk in front of our house, waiting eagerly and shouting gleefully: "Here comes Meatball, here comes Paul." My father was bald. His first name was Paul.

Then he, a gentle, generous man with big hands and big mustache, would take us both out for a walk onto the dike along the river. This was before they built the Benjamin Patterson bridge and fired Route 17 across the river there, and so the bank on the wet side of the dike was a wild place then, with trees and an approximation of wilderness. High in a big nest in a crooked tree sat a kingfisher, who, when not snatching fish, regally surveyed his kingdom of the river. We would sit down in the grass and watch the kingfisher.

An old railroad trestle crossed the river just about there, maybe a hundred yards before the kingfisher's nest, already abandoned and collapsing by the time I became aware of it. Once my father walked with just me out onto the trestle, way out (so it seemed) over the water. I looked down through wide gaps in the structure to the water and stones far below, and experienced the first anxiety I can remember. It looked like a long way down. The trestle seemed a high way up and not very substantial.

"What would you do if I fell into the river?" I asked my father.

"I'd jump in after you."

The answer was perfectly satisfying.

But time passed. One day we moved away—to Michigan and then Kentucky—where my father helped build new glass factories. A couple of years later we moved back. Back in Corning, then, I went to church every Sunday, took violin lessons from torpedo-chested Miss T, fought off the snowball-pitching Lando boys next door, became a Boy Scout, delivered morning newspapers, watched Annette Funicello's breasts grow on the *Mickey Mouse Club* show, graduated and went away to college. By the time I came back once more, for my first summer vacation, my father had retired. And my now aging parents had moved to a new house, smaller but more elevated, at the edge of Painted Post.

The new house had a new lawn, which I mowed whenever I came back to visit. When I mowed the lawn, every once in a while I would look down and see an unusual shape: *dark triangle*. I would pick it up, examine it most carefully, and then hold onto it. I knew what it was.

The land that my parent's new house was situated on used to be hilly farmland. It was being converted into segmented residential land. In other words, theirs was part of a development of houses, stretching away from Painted Post like a tiny suburb away from a small urb. This development was ongoing during those years, and one summer I took a job there as a carpenter's apprentice, employment that as my talents became clearer changed its focus from wood to dirt, so that my task became hauling and spreading and combing dark topsoil onto the yellow clay that surrounded all those newly built houses. A truck would appear on the road in the morning, drive up to the house I was currently attached to, and drop a small mountain of dirt. With wheelbarrow, shovel, and rake, it was my job to make a meadow out of the mountain. I did, and while doing that, every once in a while, I would look down and see an unusual shape: *dark circle with two notches.*

What were these things? I picked them up. They were small, flat, rounded stones. No sharp edges. Not very big or heavy. Too small, too light to serve as hammers or crude axes. They didn't even appear to be worked or shaped or marked — other than the two notches. One time I showed a couple of the stones to my boss, an old grouch who correctly deduced that no one could gather stones and rake topsoil simultaneously. Impatiently, he said they were just worthless stones. Nothing. He thought I should toss them away.

Finally one day I went down to the Painted Post museum, located on the third floor of an old stone building right next to the river, and there, amid cases of stone axes and knives and arrowheads, I found a heap of stones with the same shape as mine — and the answer. These were sinkers, fashioned by the Indians, lashed to their seines stretched across the river, and then, in the rushing water, dropped and washed away and buried in the loam at river's edge where they slept for five hundred or a thousand years until one day their dream was cracked open with a power shovel, light and air poured in, and they were scooped up and dumped into the back of a truck, then hauled away from the river and up the road to me: with my wheelbarrow, rake, and shovel.

I learned more at the museum. Woolly mammoths and mastodons used to amble through the Tioga and Cohocton and Chemung valleys, I found out, eating whatever it was they ate, cooling down in the river, and in general dropping gigantic piles of mammoth and mastodon manure while they were alive and big heaps of bones and tusks after they were dead. Chemung is a Delaware word meaning "Big Horn," which was the name of the home of the legendary Quis Quis, the great monster who died and left all those giant bones.

Around nine thousand years ago, it seems, people of the Clovis culture moved through this part of New York, pursuing big game. The Clovis hunters may have gotten frustrated, though, because the mammoths and mastodons had already gone extinct by then. Seminomadic people of the Lamoka culture arrived next, followed by the Susquehanna people from the south and then the pottery-making Algonkian people. Around two thousand years ago, from what is now Illinois and Ohio came the Hopewellian Moundbuilders, a cultural group trading with flints and promoting a funeral practice that required elaborate burial mounds. By perhaps one thousand years ago, the Owasco culture had appeared in our little valley. These people lived in pole-framed, bark-covered, rectangular houses. They fished, farmed, and gathered, and they hunted with arrows tipped with unnotched triangles.

Something happened to the Owasco. They either disappeared or maybe they changed into the Iroquois when no one was looking. By the time the Europeans showed up, the Iroquois were there. From the south, a tribe of Iroquois known as the Andaste came as far north as the Chemung Valley, while, from the north, five confederated Iroquois tribes eventually pressed down into the area. They built semipermanent villages on high and level patches of land overlooking water. And they lived together, sometimes as many as a thousand people in a village, within communal longhouses: pole-framed, bark-covered, and up to 150 feet long. The longhouses had no windows but doors at either end, and smoke from fires along the lengthwise corridor rose up and went out smokeholes in the roof. The Iroquois planted and harvested maize, beans, and squash, as well as tobacco, sunflowers, and pumpkins. They gathered nuts and berries, roots and fruits, mushrooms and maple sugar. They wove baskets; fashioned pottery and effigy clay pipes; and carved wooden bowls, cups, and spoons. They hunted in the woods, fished in the river, and in their spare time, in the fashion of human societies around the world, made occasional war upon their neighbors. Thus, their villages were fortified with strategic ditches and palisades.

This Painted Post, this very spot, included an Iroquois village of several houses and a good deal of cultivated farmland, and it was called Te-car-nase-teo-ah, meaning something like Hewn Sign Post.

Yes, there really was a painted post. General Freegift Pachen, who was taken through the region during the harsh winter of 1780 as a captive of the Mohawks, arrived at the Cohocton River to find the remains of a dead horse: enough meat to stave off starvation. And then in a clearing at the edge of the river he looked up and sighted the post, which, he was told, commemorated an old and mostly forgotten Indian victory against the whites. The post was a piece of oak ten or twelve feet high, ten to fourteen inches in width, hewn rectangularly at the base and octagonally toward the top, painted red. And the details of that ancient victory had been etched in black with twenty-eight headless figures, for the dead, and thirty other figures with heads to represent those captured.

Not even a decade after General Pachen stumbled through, Colonel Arthur Erwin drove a herd of cattle into this region from Pennsylvania along the old Indian trail, and when he came to an elevated spot above the old village, where he could see in a single vista the valleys of the Tioga, Cohocton, and Chemung Rivers, he liked what he saw so much that he hurried on down to the land office in Canadaigua and bought the entire passel: Township 2 of the Second Range, for which he traded his cattle and some extra change. This was 1789, after the American Revolution, when, with the Indians extirpated from this part of New York and Pennsylvania, land suddenly ownerless was being parceled and sold. So Colonel Erwin bought an entire valley, and where the Tioga met the Cohocton and became the Chemung, where the major Indian trails converged, just about where the old village and old post had been, he built with logs a tavern. As for the post, well, Colonel Erwin stored it inside the tavern until, old, rotted, chipped to death by curio hunters, he declared it to be a worthless stick — nothing — and tossed it into the Cohocton River.

Sentimental settlers replaced it with a new painted post. Also chipped to death by curio hunters. And then by a metal post with a rough, sheet-iron Indian on top. And then, in 1893, by a large stone monument with a cast bronze post and Indian on top. This original statue was said to represent the Mohawk Chief Montour.

He was a robust, imposing presence, protecting with his spirit the site of the original post and village. But in the early morning of November 20, 1948 — I hadn't yet woken up to celebrate my fourth birthday — a meteorological demon came out of the sky, picked Chief Montour up off his pedestal and threw him down to the pavement below, whereupon he shattered into a thousand pieces. And so he was replaced, a couple of years later, by the current guardian: this time a kinder, gentler Indian, holding a bow in his left hand, his right raised in a peaceful salute.

So I grew up downstream from the bronze Indian and the Indian post and the Indian artifacts — in a place I loved, a small town beside a peaceful river. Indians not cowboys were my childhood heroes, and Indians were why I became a Boy Scout the instant I turned eleven. I saw that warbonneted ghost standing silently in back of the smoke from a campfire around which sat three Boy Scouts in uniform on the cover of the *Handbook for Boys*, a book that told you everything. I bought the *Handbook* for sixty-five cents, a bargain, and began my ascent to the rank of Eagle Scout and Order of the Arrow camper.

In fact, my brother Dwight and our entire gang (Denny Miller and Ronnie Lewis and David Johnson and Tim Sorensen) joined the Scouts, Troop 11 of Corning Northside, and formed our own patrol, the Flaming Arrow Patrol. We learned about nature. We camped and hiked in the woods, built our own lean-to in the woods, and held our weekly patrol meetings in Tim Sorensen's mom's basement, which she allowed us to use after we painted the walls white with big red flaming arrows.

The flaming arrows took on new significance after we learned how to make gunpowder from the powdered charcoal, saltpeter, and sulfur you could buy in cans at Lamb's Pharmacy, and our weekly patrol meetings started to include, following the minutes and the usual patrol business, bomb assembly projects. Our motives were pure. We just liked a good FLASHBANG! And we started out small and experimental, making tulip-bulb packets of gunpowder wrapped tight with white hospital tape, set off by a paper clip attached to two wires attached to an old electric train transformer. When you turned on the juice, the paper clip inside the bomb turned red hot and lit the powder: FLASHBANG!

To make things more realistic, we put those early bombs inside little Erector Set houses on top of little Erector Set towers, just like the real above-ground A-bomb tests in Nevada you could see in *Life* magazine. Then we built a wooden box and a plunger and put the train transformer inside that, so you could set off the bomb using a plunger, just like dynamite. Then it was FLASH-BANG and — wow! — run over and pick up the pieces.

The Flaming Arrow patrol got more sophisticated. Someone located a length of real dynamite fuse. My brother Dwight read chemistry books and discovered you could make bigger, hotter, more exciting explosions with a mixture of powdered aluminum and other arcane ingredients, set off with a gunpowder primer. Now our bombs went: FLASH-KABOOM! And they melted things.

This was practical chemistry at work. We knew it was basically a good thing, since it was science. And since the Russians had just launched Sputnik about then, we made rockets, too, an activity my brother Dwight got particularly skilled at. A few years later he was launching real rockets and bombs for the Air Force. I am the anarchist of the family, however, and for me the whole operation might conceivably have taken a darker turn, had I moved to, say, Montana and gotten even more grouchy than I am already. I didn't. Not much damage was done, other than the small hole Yours Truly blew into the side of our house. And the Flaming Arrow patrol bomb and rocket assembly project in Tim Sorensen's mom's basement lost its main base of operations the day someone accidentally caused a spark that lit an open can of gun powder, which hissed and burned and sent a spark over to an adjacent can of sulfur, which began burning and foaming and smoking like a little volcano. Soon a noxious cloud of billowing, black stink had filled the entire basement, and a bunch of Boy Scouts were running up the stairs and out the side door only to meet Tim

Sorensen's mom, big, red-headed, and hostile, who said in an ominous voice: "*What's going on?*"

So that was great. But every utopia has its cockroach, and this brightly idyllic time was darkened by twin curses: church and violin. Our church was a box with a steeple and a neon sign out front, the latter proclaiming in faintly buzzing green and red letters the name Soldiers of Christian Misery and simultaneously suggesting its own brave antithesis to all the neon signs of all the town bars up and down Market Street. Church was a warm place near the river to which I was transported every Sunday morning and most Sunday nights, sometimes Wednesday nights as well, and if that didn't suffice to save my soul, during the summer I might be subjected to Church School and, for two weeks, Church Camp. Church was a suffocating place where I sat in uncomfortable clothes on uncomfortable benches, looked up at an uncomfortable bulletin-board-material ceiling, and was made more uncomfortable by the WORD as declared by God's agents on Earth. I got suspicious when I was ten years old and my Sunday School teacher told me there would be no dogs in heaven, since dogs don't have souls. No dogs in heaven? What about Rex?

And every Thursday afternoon after school, I would walk to the house of torpedo-chested Miss T carrying a black machine-gun case: the kind that, when hit directly with a snowball thrown by one of the Lando brothers, pops open and tosses a violin onto the sidewalk. Miss T lived in an ordinary house with her sister, who was also Miss T but gave piano rather than violin lessons. On Thursday afternoons after school, I came into the room with the piano and the plaster bust of Beethoven and the wood and cast-iron music rack, and for fifty minutes yanked horse hair over cat gut. I was never very good at this, but Miss T was. And when my efforts lagged, she would take out her own arched box of wood, tuck it under her chin, tighten her bow, and pull forth the most sonorous rondos and arpeggios, pizzas and pizzicatos you could imagine. It was hard to believe that anyone could draw such magic from a mere box, but the box itself was a work of wonder, with its graceful f-holes and elegant scroll, its nobly ivoried pegs, its finely inlaid purling.

Corning was a small town, a place like the family dog: curled nose to tail and dozing more than is proper, needing a bath, harrowed by fleas, ragged at the ears. It was a place you could comfortably walk across. The kind of place where you could stand in the middle and see the edge.

It was a place where my brother Dwight and I could bang out the back door on a Saturday morning, cut across Mrs. Mallett's back yard, run down the alley and out the other end, and go find Denny and the rest of the gang: Ronnie Lewis and David Johnson and Tim Sorensen. Where we played backyard kick-the-can after school until it got dark, and where we woke up in December to a snow that, like a quiet miracle, had stopped the whole world dead in its tracks. Where, when my brother and I sat on a stool at the counter of Lamb's Pharmacy, some willing fool gave root beers in a giant glass vase for only five cents. Where summer melted the air. Where the barber shop turned its door open and became the number one museum of Egyptian perfumes, Persian lotions, and eternal baseball on the radio. A place where you could never get completely lost and would never be a perfect stranger. But where you could still be alone if you wanted to, knowing the secret spots by the river and the birch lean-to out in the woods. It was a sleepy little town beside a sleeping river.

If you define, as the census bureau does, that a small town is any nonsuburban town with a population below ten thousand, then America has 11,897 of them, with around sixteen million people living there. According to one recent opinion poll, small towners declare themselves "very happy" more frequently than the average American, but they more often consider their marriages unhappy and their lives boring. Small towners are more likely than average to feel safe walking their neighborhood streets at night, but also more likely to have been threatened by someone with a gun. They are more traditionally religious than the average American. Sixty-nine percent believe in the existence of a personal God (compared to 62 percent for the United States in general), but they are least likely to turn the other cheek: 88 percent would flick the switch on murderers. They are more likely to espouse traditional sexual values. Overwhelmingly, small-town folk stand against adultery and pornography, yet they are more likely than anyone else to commit an act of prostitution, buying or selling.

Yes, there is social class in a small town, and, as I said earlier, social follows geographical elevation. The river curved at this place, left a wide, flat floodplain on the northern side, and on the southern side hugged the slope of a rounded hill. The main owners of the glass factory—the Houghton family—lived in a mansion terraced onto the slope of the Southside hill, as did the rest of Corning's real aristocracy. People like high places perhaps because back in the darkest bowels of time our furry ancestors lived in trees. But on the morning of June 23, 1972, another reason became apparent. I wasn't there. By then I had flown the coop. But on that morning, my parents woke up in their new house on a rise at the edge of the valley in Painted Post and noticed that everything had gotten very quiet. When they looked out their living room window, they could see why. The river had grown, overnight, and overwhelmed its banks and the dikes, and was now spread out swollen and sullen all the way across the valley.

The river had always flooded, once every two or three or five years maybe, depending on what you call a flood. An inundation in 1946 was bad enough to have been declared the once-in-a-century act of God, and in fact all the dikes raised during the century along the low banks of the Chemung and Cohocton had been intended to mitigate divine whimsy. But in 1972, tropical storm Agnes came up from Florida along the coast and at the last minute swerved west into New York and then collided with another storm going in the opposite direction. By June 22, almost a foot of rain had fallen, and it was collecting in puddles and trickling into gullies and drains and flowing into creeks and streams, down, down into the valley and the river.

Why Miss T left her precious violin in her house, I don't expect anyone knows, other than that things happened quickly. When the headlights and searchlights, the banging on doors, shouts, and the town's moaning horn all arrived at three thirty in the morning of June 23, the two Miss Ts must have thrown on overcoats and dashed into the pounding rain away from their house, leaving behind one good piano and one valuable violin.

The river, rising, churning, brown and demonic now, tore through the Post dikes at four o'clock in the morning and swept into the town of Painted Post and down to Corning, soon breaching the Northside dikes. The river rose still, and the steel-truss railroad bridge crossing over to the factory right in the middle of town (weighted down according to someone's wise instructions with a trainload of coal-filled cars) had toppled by five o'clock. By six o'clock, the river had raced across the southern dikes in Corning and flooded the factory and all the businesses lined up along the two or three low streets of the Southside. Eighteen people drowned. Hundreds more climbed to their second floors, their attics and roofs, to the upper balconies of the Lodge on the Green in Painted Post, to the roof of St. Vincent's school in Corning. And the water poured through the town, tore up houses and cars, power and phone lines, and brought this community back to the nineteenth century.

The water rose, and once the flood raged over the southern dike, it covered the floor of the glass factory with twenty-five feet of moving water. At the same time, it was pressing like the devil against the fragile box of the Soldiers of Christian Misery, and then it was bursting in the doors and windows. Within a few minutes the water was five blocks farther north and licking up the side of Miss T's house, piling against the shingles and then sliding off, flickering, gathering into thick muddy bands against the house, melting and reappearing at the start of a sluice into a broken window or a burst door, carrying calm and wavering, finny points of intelligence down a chute and a spiraled staircase of foam. It sprockled and rumbled into Miss T's living room, reached up, and took the violin.

The water passed in and out the f-holes of that lovely instrument and drifted with it in that room in a rushing, swirling, bubbling embrace with the eternal ménage à trois, two parts hydrogen one part oxygen, and made music.

When the two Miss Ts returned to their house after the flood waters receded, examining the streaks of mud up to the second story, prying open their front door, entering the living room, aghast by the ghastly stench and the mud on the floor, in the walls, inside the dripping piano, they discovered to their great surprise and heart-thumping delight that precious violin, which having danced with the water was now resting polished and clean right in the middle of the floor. Miss T reached down, gently grasped the instrument, so carefully lifted it up, and — sprong! — it sagged and sogged open, mud plopped out followed by a slither of slime, and the box collapsed into a cacophonous crumple of wood and gut.

It's all a dream now.

I left when I was eighteen. And now I can only look inside my mind and remember. The old church is gone, carried to eternity by the flood of '72. Miss T and her sister have gone as well. Denny is dead now, so I hear, killed in an accident on an icy road somewhere in the Midwest. David Johnson stayed and is still there, married, kids I think, and making his mark at the glass factory. Ronnie Lewis? I don't know. Tim Sorensen? I don't know. I miss my small town, and I grieve for those small-town times and friends.

Big Shanty

Pennsylvania seemed at first a mere continuation of New York: a complex geography of soft hills and valleys with our road a black ribbon wrapping together red barns, big silos, trees, and the occasional flashing river. But the towns seemed poorer, a little more run-down than they did in New York. Or maybe I'm just thinking here about a gray place called Knoxville, with its two ramshackle hotels and several wrecked houses. But it was getting dark and had started to rain by the time we got to Knoxville, so maybe the weather biased my perceptions there.

First it rained. Then it poured. And when we stopped for dinner at the Wagon Wheel, we had to dodge both rain and lightning as we dashed from car to restaurant, which was smoky, filled with a lot of people who seemed to know each other, decorated with hanging wagon-wheel chandeliers, and operated by waitresses in tasseled cowgirl outfits. Still, it was dry inside, and since all the diners knew each other we were kept cheerful with the regular pitterpatter of cross-table chitterchatter as — CACKLE CRACKLE BOOM! — the thunder and lightning did their catalytic calisthenics outside. We ordered dinner and, when it came at last, began eating. Suddenly, a bolt of Zeus lit up the outside and shook the building. All conversation stopped. An ominous alarm bell began to ring. Diners looked up, jaws frozen into place at mid-chew, knives steady at the steak in mid-saw. Cowgirls scurried in and out the round-windowed swinging doors to the kitchen. Finally, one cowgirl waitress rushed out of the kitchen, waved her hands, and announced, "It's all right, everybody! It's the alarm!" And the talking and chewing and sawing began again.

By the time we had finished our meal and left the Wagon Wheel, Pennsylvania no longer looked like New York State. We dodged rain and lightning in the parking lot, frantically unlocked car doors, and, with water pouring across the glass of our mobilized integument and the wipers whacking that water with a swish swish swish, we entered the great dark tunnel of Penn's Woods. There was nothing else now, no farms, no commerce, just the road burrowing through a forest vaguely aboriginal and surreal (hubcapped barn suddenly appearing), and then it was darkness and a low cloud between mountains, a ghostly strip with a still steady rain and the whipping of wipers and flash of lightning.

A final gray light shrank into pinpoints and then disappeared, and we passed through woods and mountains before hitting Route 6 west, at which point I was very tired.

We pulled up at a neon sign alongside the road. DOC'S MOTEL had NO VACANCY, but Mrs. Doc was very kind. In an office filled with animal parts nailed to the walls (was Doc a reverse veterinarian?), she picked up the phone and got us a room at the Nine Mile Motel, which, she said, was ten miles past the next town. Judging from the taxidermic testimony in Doc's office, this was bear country. And as we slid down the road toward the Nine Mile Motel, I emphasized that concept to the Research Assistants. "We're in bear country, kids! There are bears in these woods!"

There was a vein of lightning overhead, a mist rising out of the forest, and before we knew it we saw the flashing lightbulb arrow of the Nine Mile Motel, run by Ralph and Mae Wentz. Ralph told us we were lucky to get a place. He said there were ten thousand people in the hills right then because of a Lumberjack Festival at Cherry Springs State Park. And then he rented us our own little red shanty in front of a small river or swollen stream, with a fat lake in front and hysterical laughter leaking out of the shanty next door.

We made a slow start the next morning, buckling up in the rain and proceeding with appropriate caution through a white cloud until we came to a big white ship with a sign that said Potato City Motor Inn Restaurant and Lodge, where we stopped and had a potato breakfast. On the way to breakfast, we had passed something called the Pennsylvania Logging Museum, and after breakfast I overruled other peoples' objections and returned to the Logging Museum, where we mused about lumber and related subjects.

We watched a slide show that told the story of Pennsylvania logging. During the first half of the nineteenth century, Pennsylvania forests supplied white pine that became spars and structural timbers for American sailing ships, and so on. And for a century the great Pennsylvania forests produced hundreds of millions of board feet of lumber to supply the needs of the great American nation, and as a consequence the great forests we could see today in Pennsylvania were only a faint, fading memory of the vast wilderness that once grew there. How, exactly, did the vast wilderness become a faint, fading memory?

First the land and the trees on top of it were owned by an owner (the slide-show voice said). Then the owner leased out his land and trees for the job to a jobber. The jobber hired loggers to log, teamsters to team horses, a cook to cook, and a tote team to tote supplies from town to camp. Then they went to work. But wait. Most of them didn't go to work until the fall. During the muddy spring and summer not much happened, except that an improvement crew went out, cleared new roads and built new camps. The camps consisted of rough shanties made from logs or (after 1880 or so) wastewood from local sawmills, sometimes two stories high, and a single camp might include not only bunkhouse, cookhouse, and mess, but blacksmith shop and stable, office and store.

That was summer. When fall fell the chips flew. But the loggers left the logs where they lay. Then came winter, when cold turned the ground hard so the logs could be skidded out and deposited near a river. Spring sprang, the river ran, and the logs, lashed into gargantuan rafts, rafted down the river to meet at last their noisy nemesis. "Gone are the great stands of virgin timber and the rough-and-tumble logging camps," the slide-show voice concluded a little sadly, "but the heritage of the lumber industry with its reckless spirit is preserved and presented here in the Pennsylvania Logging Museum."

The best thing about the museum was that it included (parked in big barns out back) several steam train engines. And beyond the engines someone had reconstructed an old loggers' cabin, a *shanty* as it was called (derived from the Canadian French *chantier*, a workshop, related possibly to *chantey*, a sailor's work song, derived from the French *chantez*, imperative of *chanter*, itself descended from the Latin *chantus*, a song, suggesting that back in the days when most work was hard, working people sang to salve pain and banish boredom), with a rough-boarded exterior, a great woodsy smell inside, all the old bunks and artifacts from those days, and even some loggers themselves, frozen in time.

So that was the Logging Museum, and you don't need to tell me that it seems like one big digression from the point of this chapter. But if *you* know the point, you're way ahead of where we were. The problem is or was that I had no real idea where we were going. I kept pausing to look at the cartographicus magnus, hoping that if I looked often and hard enough the perfect destination would appear. Indeed, the cartographicus showed several possible Storyvilles ahead — but they all seemed chancy or iffy: Roulette, Cyclone, Torpedo, Burning Wells, Challenge. Then a place called Tally Ho beckoned from, oh, maybe an hour ahead or so, and so after the Logging Museum we pointed the hood ornament west toward Tally Ho.

Route 49 picked us up, Route 44 dropped us down, and Route 6 took us directly onto Route 59 where the rain ended and our drive turned pleasant, just tripping through an old woodsy part of the world with the Beatles on the tape player. "How can you laugh when you know I'm down?" the Beatles sang. We were still looking for a left turn when a sign with a right-turn arrow popped up: BIG SHANTY 5.

"Wait a minute! This is not on the map!"

But reality is better than representation, isn't it, and this was reality. So instead of turning left for Tally Ho, we turned right for Big Shanty — and came immediately upon a huge shanty nightmare: a gigantic fortress with wire fences and mean walls edged all around by coils of razor wire. A sign said: Federal Correction Institute. It must have been a home for wayward copyeditors, I figured, and I think we might could use one but we kept on going anyway. Now that there was a point to the chapter, I didn't want to get distracted. We kept driving down a twisty narrow road that took us past dish antennae with houses next to them until after a few miles we came to a slight curve and dip, a dozen houses, a petroleum pump or two bobbing up and down in a backyard or two, and one visible business: a used appliance and household goods operation with a man standing out front with thick glasses and a small mustache, wearing a blue baseball cap, who said that this was indeed Big Shanty. And if we wanted to know more we should go down that dirt road over there, called Lineman Road, walk all the way down to a shop called Lineman Electrical, and ask for a man called Lineman. "You ever heard of the Pennzoil company? Well he practically *was* the Pennzoil company."

Russ Lineman looked like a compact version of Paul Bunyan. He was a big man with big hands and a hearty shake, wearing blue pants suspended by suspenders and a belt, and a red and white horizontally striped polo shirt. He came out of the one-story house next door to his electrical shop and sat down on the metal glider on his front porch. The porch looked over the dirt road and a rising piece of woods on the other side, and on the porch were wooden flowers and a wooden squirrel.

Russ said he had lived in Big Shanty ever since sixth grade, when he was twelve years old. All the land in this area, or most of it, he said, is owned by oil companies. All divided leases. But timber is still being harvested off the top of the land, selectively and occasionally, he said. They take the logs off, and they haul them to different mills by truck. But you wouldn't say it's a real lumber operation going on like it was years ago.

"You're still getting good petroleum out of the ground here?" I said.

"No."

"No?"

"It's all abandoned."

"All abandoned!"

There was only a few wells left, he declared, down the road there. Well, they might get three barrel oil a day. But Pennzoil was the biggest producer in the field, and they're pullin out now, and they don't have anything producing in the field. They're pullin out first of the year. There won't be no more Pennzoil. And Quaker State's already pulled out. They're pulled out and plugged. And now the other companies, they're starting to plug all theirs too. They've got a lot standing that wasn't plugged. They have to be plugged. And Pennzoil's just about done with their pluggin. This area in here was all very rich in oil, had about forty-four feet of sand—payin sand—and it's been going since the '60s. Payin sand, that's the one you get your oil out of. You have anywhere from one to five kinds of good sand, down a well, and this particular area here is called the Bradford Sand. It produces—gas and oil—pretty good wells.

Did we realize that's sand you get the oil out of? Did we know what it looks like? We'd think it was a rock if we had a hunk of it in our hand. It's just like a hard rock. Oh, yeah, but it's sand, Russ said. If we could imagine sand compressed a thousand times, he continued, hard, real hard but there's soft streaks in it, that's where your water and oil goes through. And the average well lasts twenty-one years. Oil is still there, of course. There's a lot of oil still there. But now it costs too much to get that oil out of the sand. It's no longer feasible to flood it with water. It costs too much.

"Flood it with water?" I asked.

Did we know how oil stays on top of water? Well, water pushes the oil through. They pump the water in and pump the oil out. The oil'll only go where the soft streaks in the sand are, and that's how your flood works. You push it through the soft stuff. So actually most of that stuff's still got about

80 percent of its oil left in the ground. Oh, yeah, you *could* get it out. But it costs too much. You have to use all chemicals, and then the government, the EPA, is so hard on you.

Now his company, Pennzoil, had a lot of employees, and so now they're out of work. But there's still a lot of people producing yet, independents, and some of the old Pennzoil guys are now workin for independents. And then you have Zippo and Case down there. That's two employers. Zippo the lighter manufacturer. And Case: knives. They're just a subsidiary of Zippo. As for farming, kind of hard to get a farm with all this timber and stuff.

As to where the name Big Shanty came from, Russ Lineman didn't know exactly. He had a good theory, though. Years ago there used to be a big camp down there on the road, and it burned down, and they built another one. That's about all he knew about it. It was a big camp. And then they built another one, people tell him. Then later on the gas company had a big camp down there, and then when they was done puttin the gas lines through then they moved up to Lafayette. And that's about all he could tell us about it. They just had a big camp, there, and called it Big Shanty. Did we know how they used to build them? Just throw up boards and stuff, sort of like a haphazardly constructed chapter in a book, maybe, where the author isn't entirely sure what he's getting at or where he and his Research Assistants are driving to next. So, anyway, that's what people tell him it was.

Echo

We went in the wrong direction, fell off the charts, and tumbled into a warren of back roads and rough tracks tunneling through a little woods and out again and along a winding road. Rode into a work crew working, toured a detour, tracked a track across a stream streaming through someone's fields with Queen Anne's lace until the road terminated with a capital T. Turned onto a carriage trail long and winding through valleys and hills with horse bouquets before us tossed, lost now with only a field of corn, a pond of geese and a sign for Plumville five miles left and Trade City three miles right.

Right, so now we weren't so lost and so, found, rattled through back roads with forest edge and tree bank and fields weedy and wild with sibilant nonsense, a crackled conversation of cricket and cicada and jungle-jumper June bug. Buggy and horse trot-trot-trotting our way, we slowed down and minded our manners, not to gawk at the upright man with the peaked straw hat and Abe Lincoln beard, garbed, he and his child, in sober black. Acknowledging us, our impatiently humming machine, with the merest shiver and nod, the horse and masters clopped fast and faster past.

Stop shuffling the cards, kids (I had to say), and put them away. Wait until later, because this is something excellent and unusual: to be in Amish country. Try to keep your eyes and ears open (I said), and I'll drive carefully not to spook the horse. See, the modern world is not always so great.

At least parts of it are (Britt insisted hopefully), or maybe very nice: ice cream and sodas out of a can. *And* the fact that you're eleven years old (Bayne added) and having fun.

Funneling sunnily down the day thus we dropped into Dayton, a town of homemade soups and soft ice cream, an abandoned train station, and the Stockdale Restaurant where we fested rested restroomed and resumed our adventure to find at last (past a stand of willow trees, leaves lifting blown blueygreen in the rising breeze) the sign: ECHO 5 MILES. Less than four on the odometer, I remember now, the road knifed then forked, and we took a toss on the right tine and came to a turn and a house with trickybricky siding and also, walking four children, a young woman who, after we asked, *This is Echo?* declared, *Oh, this is Echo.*

Echo! Hoping to hear ourselves ourselves we parked the car not far along a shallow hollow, rushing green and trash and rusty wrecks between. Enclosed our voices, encupped our hands, we said (at first uncertain) to ourselves: Will it work today with the gusty breeze and the noisy trees in the way? Aye, we bellowed: *Hello! Lo,* and yes it celloed: *Hello! Lo.* Loud enough, perhaps, though not so sharp or clear as one might hope to hear but a sound more susurrant around the ear. Earnestly, we bawled: *Boo! Ooh,* and yes it called: *Boo! Ooh!* Oh, how delightful an Echo's echoing echo can be.

Behind us arrived just then those children, that woman, joined with (she explained) her grandmother-in-law, Mrs. Nellie Cogley, in a hurry late — doctor's date — but Echo was Echo, oh, as long as she could say, and today was her birthday seventy-eighth. They used to have a post office and a railroad station over there. Here they put freight on the train, there was a store and — what do you call it, they came on their horse and buggy and got on the train? Indians named it Echo, and so it was Echo long ago even before 1875 when her dear father was alive.

A livery was where, I sustained, the horses met the train. No, she said, it was something other. Her doctor was waiting, what a bother, so she had to go. Good luck, she said, then finished her tale. Let me just say, she said, there's no store now and no station. One day a train jumped the track, actually ran right into the station with a great SMASH and a SMACK followed by a *Smash Ash* and a *Smack Ack*, and that was that was that.

Twinsburg

Interstate 80 drew us on like a conveyor belt out of Pennsylvania and into Ohio. At about a half-mile from Youngstown, the land was already flatter, as if somebody had taken an iron and flattened out all the wrinkles that we had heretofore been dealing with. But 80 turned into 76 there, the land became even flatter, and we rocketed straight west into a growing darkness now with no place to stay. Finally, after fatigue had given birth to anxiety and then alarm, we found a Best Western at the edge of Akron. And when I looked at the cartographicus magnus in the morning, I realized we were exactly where we wanted to be. We could just take Route 91 straight up the map to Twinsburg.

On the recommendation of someone at the hotel desk we located a breakfast place up the road. Duffy's was your standard beer fortress: no windows, gloomy inside, with the stench of industrial deodorant used to encapsulate the old cigarette smoke from last night's bar patrons. The place was decorated in browns and yellows, with movie-star posters on the walls. But you got used to the smell, and the coffee was good. Our waitress was a friendly sort with slurred speech ("Didjafiguridout? Whajahavin?") who, when she wasn't serving us, paused to engage in chitchat with the couple seated in the booth next to ours, regulars who had just enthusiastically ordered blueberry pancakes. The morning newspapers were saying that during recent Congressional hearings someone had asserted that cigarette manufacturers knew what good customers nicotine addicts can be. And so the waitress commented to the regulars: "Pretty soon they're gonna say we're puttin somethin addictive in our blueberry pancakes, just like they're sayin they put something extra in cigarettes to get people addicted."

This comment signalled the start of a short paranoid fantasy, one that in my own paranoid state I began to imagine presented a fair sample of Ohio folk wisdom. One of the regulars responded: "I smoked for thirty years, and I'm still alive. Hey, it wasn't like it was a drug to me. I was addicted, sure, but it wasn't like an *addiction*."

The second regular added: "It's just like they don't want to do anything about cocaine and marijuana and like that. So they just go onto this. Isn't that how it is? They just *got* to get down on something!"

The waitress chimed in with: "If it was that addictive I don't see how somebody could quit. That's just the latest thing for someone to get on the bally-hoo about."

And the first regular concluded with an angry rasp: "They got their priorities all screwed up. The whole damned bunch! I tell you, they better get their act together!"

All right, we finished our breakfast and headed up Route 91 northbound for Twinsburg. Pretty soon we were enveloped in traffic and an endless twitching stretch of commerce. It seemed to me then, as we drove north, that in the hills of Pennsylvania people get stuck, but at least they nestle in. In Pennsylvania, in New York, too, there's a geological reason to keep towns together, like an ionic attraction, whereas in the flatlands of the Midwest, people scatter out like marbles across a table. That would explain Route 91, maybe, where driving felt like being a bug half-crushed inside the Yellow Pages and unable to crawl out, permanently crippled inside a painful blur of flashing symbols and bright signs, of bad spelling and false friendliness, of professional enthusiasm and a grinning vacuous greed, of the reek and ring of a million winning spinning cash registers: Roadrunner Video Club, Alliance Brothers Big Boy, McDonald's, Buster's Bustin' Steaks, Cheeza Pizza, Burger King, Sleepware Queen, Ye Olde Gift and Floral Shoppe, Victorian Whispers, Ye Garden Shoppe, Minit Lube, Fran's Frames, Hank's Hairport, Gertie's Dirtie Doggie, Care 4 U Counseling Center, Toys R Us, Tot's Landing, Richie's Dancin' Turkey, Sam's Upright Chick'n, Clips N Nips, Chips N Dips, Ships N Trips, Lips N Slips—and so on! I'm out of breath. The depressing thing about all our Yellow Pages crawling was a lingering sense that this entire area was recently farmland. Out of the smoke would appear an old barn, a little stretch of open field, weeds and crickets, and then a sign proudly announcing that this field too was about to become a shopping mall.

"I bet we're near Twinsburg now. I'm rather hoping Twinsburg will be especially nice," I said, doing my best to keep things positive. And indeed just about then we sighted the Twinsburg Post Office. I parked, went inside to find a long line of Ohioans waiting for postal purposes—and to my delight at least two people in the line were eager to help me locate the center of town and the best place to get historical information about it. The best place, so their dual consensus concluded, would be the Twinsburg Public Library.

We turned off 91, drove past some American flags, a fire signal, and the sign: Twinsburg Fire Department. Right across the road was a second sign: Twinsburg Public Library.

We strolled into the modern, expensive-looking Twinsburg Public Library and asked at the Reference Desk. But neither of the pair of reference librarians knew the story behind the name of Twinsburg. One said, "Well, I've only lived here for a year and a half." The other said, "I don't really live here." They had a conference with three other librarians. None of them knew. The five librarians finally decided we should try the Twinsburg Fire Department across the street.

We walked across the road up to the fire station and located inside the front door a pair of men dressed in a pair of firefighter uniforms. After we explained what we were looking for, the younger of the two said, "You've come to the right person," and then he walked away, leaving us with the older one, who said, "Well, I don't have a lot of time. I'm about to go out, but I think I could tell you a little bit about Twinsburg."

His name was Daniel J. Simecek. He had wavy white hair, a high forehead and cleft chin, and a strong jaw and nose. He wore thick, tinted glasses, and on the chest of his short-sleeved white shirt was pinned a badge that said "Chief." Chief Simecek took us down a hallway into his Fire Chief office that included a messy desk, tall filing cabinets, photographs of fire people and fire trucks, and a teddy bear dressed up as a fire fighter.

Chief Simecek explained how Twinsburg got started. It seems that the first settlers came from Connecticut on foot. They used part of Lake Erie in the winter to walk on the ice and so forth. That was actually a long time ago, but Twinsburg wasn't founded until the early eighteen hundreds, when the Wilcox twins, Moses and Aaron Wilcox, offered to donate five acres of land which is the town square. Which is exactly in the center of town. They would donate that and a few other things if the people in town would name the town Twinsburg. And the twins only lived there a few years, but the town did change its name to Twinsburg at that time, in 1817. So the pair kind of bought their immortality. They married sisters and lived in the same house. They held all their property in common, and they both died not really on the same day but within twenty-four hours of each other, of the same illness. More or less. They caught a cold, or something. Their grave is in the cemetery up the road.

Chief Simecek showed us where the cemetery was on his map, and he told us how to find the Wilcox twin tombstones.

He said there was a museum, open only on certain Sundays. And then Lea

Bissel, who lived right down the road from the fire house, was Secretary of the Historical Society. She loves to sit and talk to people, he said. He himself had lived in Twinsburg since 1939. Came when he was three years old. When he graduated from Twinsburg High School in 1954, there were 554 students, something like that, in the entire system. Now there's some four thousand. And they have five schools. The population now is about—well, first of all, we had to remember that the Twinsburg Township was started in 1817. But in 1955 the center part of it, more or less, was incorporated into the city of Twinsburg. So there was actually a pair of Twinsburgs, in a sense, a Township of Twinsburg and a City of Twinsburg. The city has probably fourteen thousand people and the township probably two thousand.

"What kind of place is it to live? Do you enjoy it?"

"Oh, yeah. I've often said if I won the lottery, I'd spend 80 percent of it here."

"People are friendly?"

Yes they are, he insisted, most of them. A lot of people want to keep Twinsburg like it was in the old days, but the developers bought a lot of the land some thirty years ago, and twenty years ago they started building. There's no way you can stop them. The city keeps changing its rules, upgrading them for building on bigger lots and so forth. Trying to control it. As for the Fire Department, it started in 1919. It was always a volunteer department. Had as many as forty-five members in the '50s and so forth like that. In 1988 he became the first full-time fire fighter. With the understanding they would hire four other people in 1989, as they did. But now the Fire Department has eighteen full-time and twenty-seven part-time employees. They cover twenty-two square miles, city and township, and the place just keeps growing. Almost too fast to imagine.

"So it must be losing a lot of its old character and old style?"

Yeah. They have a historical ordinance here in the city. They can't tear down a house that's over fifty or a hundred years old. But the township doesn't have that ordinance. It sort of worries him. The oldest building is in the township right now. And there's only one, really, farmer left in Twinsburg. That's the Corbet Farm. It's a very picturesque farm. He rents most of the land he uses, but there's a threat of someone building on the land each year. The fellow just down the road here farms his piece across the street, behind the library. They were all set to put ninety-two homes in there, and the only way to stop them: City bought it.

The city wants to put a school there. They need another high school, and they bought the land for that purpose. But what else could he tell us? The roads have really changed, from about ten roads when he went to school to there's a list of about eighty of them out there now. But, as he said, Twinsburg keeps growing, and it has a good tax base. And the funds are there. You have to fight, but you usually get them. They have three ambulance rescue squads and one heavy rescue. Three engines, aerial ladder, grass-fire truck and other equipment, and so forth. And the Twinsburg Police Department, he'd be guessing there's about twenty-five patrolmen, full-time. He's been there in the Fire Department starting his thirty-eighth year.

Well, we talked quite a bit more. Chief Simecek showed us the photographs of his antique fire engine and a 1919 fire extinguisher on wheels, hand drawn. And then, thanking him, we took our leave. "Okey-dokey," he said. "I'm glad I could help you."

Next we tried to track down Lea Bissell, secretary of the Historical Society, but she wasn't home. So we drove around a little, past the Christ the King Lutheran Church, which had a sign out front saying: "Hi, Twins, come in. We're prayer conditioned!" We drove out past Mattress City, Whitewood Apartments, Saint Cosmos, the Twin Haven Community Center, and various brand-new housing developments: mile after mile of the sort of thing you might get if you gave a colony of giant insects a barrel of nails, a stack of boards, some foam-core doors, some tar shingles, and a truckload of hothouse bushes — and then sent the insects to architectural school for two weeks, just long enough to memorize the names they would finally tack on: Heritage Hills, Birchwood Estates, Stone Creek Commons. Twinsburg looked like one big housing and condo development, with a couple of shopping malls thrown in and maybe a landing field or two for the occasional flying saucer. Everything was built last week. Nothing actually old that I could see. When we did sight a piece of open space, it was already on the market: "For Sale 3 Acres."

Did I miss something here? Was there a parallel town in a parallel universe?

Yes, there was a Twinsburg town square of sorts, right back at the corner of Routes 91 and 82, including a bit of a town green, a little piece of park with a small bandstand in the middle of that. And in the middle of this day standing on the bandstand four old men played with five instruments — clarinet, sax, accordion, bass, and the occasional tambourine — sentimental tunes to an audience of twelve retired people. The four old men played numbers like "Thanks for the Memories," and the twelve retired people ate modest picnics and brown-bag lunches and at the end of each song clapped tepidly. Meanwhile, a huge torrent of traffic poured by on all four sides. And on the outside of that little square, Twinsburg's downtown businesses eagerly hung out American flags and sought to snatch customers: Hair in the Square, bank, dog and cat grooming, more haircuts, a hardware store, a pharmacy, dry cleaning, and Bobka's Liquor.

We found the road to the Locust Grove Cemetery, where Chief Simecek told us the twins were buried. Chief Simecek had given us rather precise instructions for finding that grave, but I had forgotten them, and so the three of us spent a long time wandering and reading names buried in moss and lichen or worn down to a mere shadow in stone.

After looking everywhere else but where they were, we found the twins, Moses and Aaron Wilcox, buried under a new stone. The stone noted that they died on September 24 and 25 of 1827, aged fifty-five. Moses was born seven minutes before Aaron, and survived him by nineteen hours and thirty-five minutes. They married sisters, and for the last twenty-five years of their lives both were members of the Congregational Church. It was a nice graveyard, but I found it sad that this old Ohio town was being developed and tax-based to death while even the reference librarians couldn't say where its name came from. Chief Simecek was terrific, a real hero in my book. As for Twinsburg the City or Twinsburg the Township, well, I'm trying hard to think positive thoughts right now, but I don't believe I would live there or there.

Crooked Tree

We shot straight down until we came to a junction and Taco Bell, then fell through a merry-go-round, jigged south, jagged west, then hit 77 going straight down south to the southern part of the state.

We came to Canton: a piece of earth scraped clean by bulldozers, a bare pit full of a dozen or so plastic motels and food operations, with big bright signs held up on high plungerposts. Then we emerged into open country again. Southern Ohio seemed a lot nicer and softer than the northern part, I was thinking, and pretty soon we found ourselves traveling through a valley of Ohio farms, with the sun low in the sky, barns with bales of hay stacked behind, and large fields of goldenrod. Then we came to the New Philadelphia intersection and another hellish pit scraped into the earth, with huge signs held up on fifty-foot high plungerposts: the usual suspects.

Now it was getting dark, so I flicked on the headlights, and we started actively thinking about a place to stay for the night. I wanted something comfortable and restful, but pretty soon it was dark indeed and we were all tired, so we gave up being fussy and stopped at a pit located just off the town of Cambridge. The cartographicus magnus was necessary here to reassure ourselves that we were still on planet Earth, though, since this place had been cleared of any irregular green stuff and then injected with concrete, eerie bluish halogen lights on posts, and gigantic steel plungerposts advertising with crushingly massive signs the standard dozen junk eating places and the standard half-dozen junk sleeping places. Cars and trucks and motorcycles and everything else rumbled and screamed past from about eight directions, while down where our little trio sat pausing in our vehicle in a Holiday Inn parking lot, we could see no serious indications that nature actually existed or that the atmosphere was a regular mix of oxygen-hydrogen-nitrogen.

It was unnerving, but then hadn't most of Ohio so far been unnerving? I was getting used to it, I thought, and then I thought that perhaps the Holiday Inn had rooms on the quiet side, away from all the traffic noise. And if it didn't, we could just go somewhere else in this pit and locate another hotel. I had only to look up and read the lighted signs in the sky. A Best Western, for example, sat on its own little hill that looked, oh, another hundred yards away.

The Holiday Inn didn't have any rooms away from the traffic side of the building, said the girl or young woman at the desk and furthermore, she said, she could not recommend Best Western.

But why should she say anything nice about a competitor anyhow?

So we politely declined the Holiday Inn and tried the Best Western, a transfer that required only a drive up a small hill and there it was. And, yes, our room looked perfectly normal: two double beds, a cot, two lights exactly like the two lights in every other motel in the universe, two pictures on two of the walls, one big TV, one big mirror, a couple of chests, a sink in the corner, and the usual plumbing in the bathroom. Everything was too fastened down to steal, and so much for that.

Except, as we discovered during the next hour, the air conditioner stank. It would be impossible to know exactly why, but I can guess that some unhappy animal had recently crawled up inside the machine and died. It rotted, and then a room cleaning person had decided that the best way to get rid of the death smell was to pour a half-gallon of industrial cleaning fluid into the air conditioner. During an ordinary olfactory fit, someone else tossed in an ashtray full of cigarette ashes and two smoldering cigar butts, cheap ones with soggy ends. Another person, eight years old and celebrating his least-favorite sibling's tenth birthday, vomited vanilla ice cream and chocolate birthday cake with lime frosting in there when no one else was looking, as well as maybe a stomach full of peas and carrots and creamed corn, and then the room was kept vacant for twenty-one days in order to incubate a small colony of Legionnaire's Ebola.

We didn't sleep very well, and the next morning were further discouraged by a heavy rain pounding against the little box that constituted our hotel. In fact, I was so discouraged by what I had seen of Ohio so far, I was about ready to hop in the car and drop directly out of the state.

When, after a very long delay including a short side trip and lunch, we finally did hop in the car, the radio began predicting more rain: cloudbursts and thunderstorms and so on. As soon as we got on the highway, a torrential rain struck and trucks began barreling past us trailing huge slobbers behind them. But after an hour or two, we were dribbling soberly and soggily into southern Ohio down Interstate 77 south, coming into a part of the highway that was not heavily traveled and had a lazy curve in it. Not straight, as in northern Ohio. Curved roads are better, a little more refreshing and pleasant than straight ones, and driving on them feels like going down a very long playground slide. And every once in a while, I was hearing an *Ooh, ooh, ooh!* from the back seat. I couldn't turn to look, but I could sometimes get a good glimpse in the mirror: Bayne saying in universal protolanguage to look at the size of the bubblegum bubble he'd just blown.

It was already well into the day, by that time, and I wanted to keep on schedule, which meant getting to Getaway and if possible tucking into Kentucky — so perhaps it would be better just to slide down this curved super 77 to the bottom of the state and then turn right, rather than trusting our destiny to that crooked little line I could see on the cartographicus magnus that might or might not really take us to Crooked Tree, which after all was a little straightforward anyway. Crooked Tree? Well, crooked tree. That was the issue, and we debated and discussed it, then filibustered until the bill passed both houses, but in a surprise move it was blocked at the executive level by special fiat, and so we made a quick spin off the solid 77 and onto the more tenuous 821 leading to 339. Straight for Crooked Tree.

Good move. We came to Stritz Auto Parts with an old barn and wrecked cars and "Jesus Loves You, Phone 732-4359." We tasted Olive and slipped right through Dexter City, then turned at 339 and ducked and creaked over Duck Creek. "What are these flowers here?" I asked myself, looking at some flowers. "They look like purple goldenrod. There's a whole field of them. They're really beautiful."

The road quickly went from classic to baroque to downright rococo: a country concatenation of tiny villages and old barns, the occasional antique shop and the Johnny Appleseed Center. We turned right at a corner marked impressively by the ruins of a burned two-story brick house. There were lots of enticing rural smells in the air now, and the road snaked past a graveyard with a church and over the crest of a hill until we saw the sign: CROOKED TREE. And that was just about it. Oh, and also a second sign that gave the phone number for Ron's Excavating.

Next to the road, though, was a yellow house and a camouflaged van. Working on the van was a robust, bearded young man in a white T-shirt, Jackson Pollack pants, and sunglasses. His name was Herb Linger, he said, and he introduced us briefly to his blonde wife and some children so skittish and shy I never did figure out whether there were two or three. The wife was sitting on the porch next to some kittens and trimming the ends of a half-woven nylon hammock with a small blowtorch.

I could tell we were getting nearer to Kentucky now, because Herb was friendly in that Southern relaxed way, and he spoke with a pleasing Southern drawl — maybe a Southern Ohio drawl — as he pointed out where the crooked tree used to be. The crooked tree stood right over there where the truck was at, right across the road, and he went into the house and came out again with a postcard picture of it.

"Oh, there it is," I said. "Ah, it was a crooked tree."

"Uh-huh."

"How long ago did it — what did it do? Burn down or get hit by lightning?"

He didn't know. They moved to Crooked Tree in '64, and the tree was gone quite a while before that. Herb said there used to be an old blacksmith shop in town, a post office down the way, and a grange. It was a farming town. His house used to be a general store. His mother and father ran the store for about fifteen years. Then some time during the 1970s, their own house burned down, so they remodeled the store and moved into it. Well, Crooked Tree now was not much more than a collection of houses at a bend in the road, but it was a nice bend, a quiet road, and a peaceful place. And there was more to it than one saw at first glance. Herb's brother lived in the town, for instance. He did excavating. Then Herb worked the stone quarry. Then there were some retired people living in town, some people on welfare, and a guy who did electrical work. The church and graveyard, too, were part of Crooked Tree.

"It's nice to have that postcard," I said. "How do you suppose the tree got crooked?"

Herb didn't know. But next to the crooked tree, he noted, there had been a big rock with a hole in the center, where the Indians ground their cornmeal. Then a shopping center in Beverly bought the rock, and straightaway they put it out in front of the shopping center on Route 60.

Getaway

Getaway was next, but from what? We were escaping something along a four-laned divided highway west, following the Ohio River. Route 50 turned into two-laned Route 7, and we drove past poodles for sale and pretty soon got into an enduring rural landscape by Thomas Cole: with a house, a tin-roofed barn, and three horses and a colt flicking their tails beside the road.

Pretty soon we were getting away from the landscape by Cole and colliding into a factoryscape by Sheeler. First we spied three large smokestacks and some huge columns of white smoke rising and disappearing, blending into the white sky. Next alongside the road appeared a long long long long freight train slowly pulling coal along beside us. We saw the Ohio River down to our left after that and smelled industry dead ahead. Finally we arrived at a massive mesh of power lines, conveyor belts lifting coal, and four long, high smokestacks, two of them belching out fast, high-rising columns of white smoke; and down at the river, a really neat device was sucking coal out of tug boats and spitting it out again onto a huge conveyor belt, which ran the coal up into a silo.

It got dark. We pulled into a Holiday Inn just outside Gallipolis, Ohio, where we were kept awake half the night by a tremendous thunderstorm and emerged sleepily the next morning. We followed the road that followed the river out past Gallipolis, looking for 243, which we eventually found at the Buella Baptist church. We continued along a very twisty road and finally stopped at a little store. A sign in the front said: "Welcome. We are here to serve you."

Here a very friendly guy with a heavy beard said that Getaway was a real small community, but it was nice. He said that there might be a grocery store there and also a vocational school or something. And he gave directions.

We continued on that crooked and narrow road, past a sign that said "Buckle up with Jesus," past the Freedom Independent Baptist Church and some houses and the Union Missionary Baptist Church and some houses and the Mount Hope Missionary Baptist Church and houses and the Pomeranian Baptist Church or something like that. There were a lot of Baptist churches around.

One of the Research Staff said, from the back seat, "This is part of the Bible Belt, isn't it?"

"Yes," I said, and then added on a positive note, "We're coming into an area where people are extremely friendly, I will tell you. I think we're going to discover that people are unusually friendly. Southern Hospitality. I saw it in the store. That man was just friendly."

A sign said there was a bump in the road, but the whole road was a bump. Another sign said we were following Bent Creek, but I didn't see any specific bend, though the creek as a whole seemed bent, as did the road.

Then a sign along the road said GETAWAY. Not very friendly, but we kept right on driving. Then we came to the Getaway Methodist Church, as well as a rotting barn, a two-story brick house, and two country stores. One of them, with a gas pump disintegrating out front, was closed up and done in. The other, painted blue and white with a metal awning over the front entrance, with a tin roof and green asphalt fish-scale shingles at the gable, was open and done up. We parked the car and went inside.

The woman behind the counter inside — in her thirties, with black coiffed hair, smiling blue eyes, red lipstick, and gold hoop earrings — confirmed that we had gotten all the way to Getaway, but she was too busy right then with customers to talk. There was an old lady in the red brick house right next door, she said, who knew more about the history of Getaway than anybody. We should just go over there on the other side of the white fence, and go up to the door in back and ask her. She would tell us everything.

So we went on the other side of the white fence, walked up a path to the back of the red brick house, knocked on the screen door, and gradually an old lady in a pale housedress with curlers in her hair floated up to the other side of the screen and stood, limbs akimbo. "Well? What do you want?" When we told her, she declared that, no, she didn't know anything about Getaway. And, no, she didn't know who in town might. And, no, she didn't want to talk any further. She glared at us with frosty suspicion and then drifted away from the screen and disappeared somewhere back inside the house.

We stumbled back down to the store and again asked the woman at the counter there if she could now tell us a little about Getaway. Her name was Beth Day, the woman soon explained, and she still did have a couple of customers in the store. But once they went away she opened up.

There was an old man building a fence, she said, and some boys were coming through and they said, "Hey, mister, where we at?" And he said, "Get away!" And they said, "Well, where we at?" And he said, "Get away." So they went and told their parents, "Some old man building a fence told us it was Getaway." That's the first story. The second story is that the area used to be a part of the underground railway. When the runaway slaves were coming through there, coming across the Ohio River from Kentucky and West Virginia and the rest of the South, they used that area as part of their getaway route. They called it Getaway because it was part of the way to get away.

I thought that was interesting—and in my mind I had a little vision of how close we were to the Ohio River there, with Kentucky and West Virginia on the other side, of slaves escaping, of a quiet moonlit path or dirt road rising north up the bent valley. It made sense. "Sounds like the second story's probably truer, maybe," I said.

That's the one she would think, too, Beth Day agreed. But, yeah, she's heard two different versions all her life. And she has lived in Getaway all her life. She thought that the old lady in the brick house could give us, maybe, a longer version of it, and she was sorry the old lady couldn't help us more.

As for the village, lately there has been a subdivision built over there, and they started a second subdivision. But the homes in Getaway mostly are older homes. Everyone mostly owns their own home. Very quiet community. Everyone knows everybody, except for the subdivision. Different people do move in. But all of the village right through there, from one Getaway sign to the other Getaway sign, everybody knows everybody, and it is just a very nice community. And the lady we talked to in the brick house, she had the first store, and before that her father had it, and before that his father had it. There used to be a funeral home across the way. There was a grist mill across the road. There used to be another grocery store across the way. There used to be, before her store was ever there, there was a little grocery store right there underneath the tree over there.

Her store was originally Humphrey's Grocery, she told us. Her father and mother opened it up in 1943. Then, when they retired, she and her husband took it over. And so they call it Day's Market now. That's their last name. Day. Originally, her dad kept stacks of hundred-pound bags of feed all along the wall. It was more of a country store, more for farmers. Getaway was more of a farming community then. And there are a few farmers left, but not too many. At the store, they used to sell floral cloth like you put on kitchen tables, and shoes, farmers' boots, and stove pipe. They heat the store now with gas heat, Beth explained, but they have kept the old coal stove that her dad used. The pipe used to get red hot clear back to the wall, as she could remember, but she and her husband went to gas heat when her dad retired.

Still, basically, they've kept the store the same. They like it that way. She showed us a mop hanger: a wire device hanging from the ceiling and shaped like a lampshade, with wire loops around its circumference. That was a mop hanger when her father had the store. Someone came in recently, said it was a valuable antique, and offered her $400 for it. She wouldn't sell, though. And did we see the big old refrigerator back there? she said, indicating with a nod a big old refrigerator back there. OK. When her dad brought that in the store back in the '40s they had to take out the big window there because it would not come through the door. And a farmer up the road and her dad brought the refrigerator through the window. So they don't use the refrigerator any more, but they can't get it out of there, because they can't take the window out. They just leave it there. And that's originally where it was put. And the candy case was, they say that candy case was back in the '30s. So everything's basically the same except for they have pop now where they used to have hundred-pound bags of feed. But most everything tries to remain the same. They like it that way because it goes back years ago.

Her father is now one of the oldest people still in the community, but he had a stroke. He's still alive, but he can't talk now. So it was a shame, she insisted, that we couldn't meet him and get him to talk. And the lady in the brick house, well, she is the oldest person around. That's why Beth wanted her to talk to us.

"She saw these strangers at the door. I can understand it," I said.

"Older people are like that," she said.

"I was telling my kids that people here are very friendly," I said. "Southern Ohio and getting into Kentucky. Because I lived in Kentucky for a year when I was a kid. I just remember people being very friendly."

We agreed that that was true. And on that friendly note, and after I had bought some candy and gum and a few other necessaries at the store, we said good-bye to Mrs. Beth Day, thanked her for talking with us, climbed into the machine, and got away.

Subtle

Within a couple of days we had taken a short dip into Kentucky and down to Dog Walk—nice place, but no dogs—and then to Chicken Bristle—no chickens. And then we tried our luck with Goodluck. But Goodluck, as bad luck would have it, had somewhere along the line flipped wrong side up and ceased to exist. We never even found a sign for it.

Luckily, though, where Goodluck wasn't was right on the way to Marrowbone, a juicy little place that was itself, according to the cartographicus magnus, just down the road from a quiet little dot called Subtle. Up the road we went, therefore, past a gorgeous old clapboard house, empty it seemed but not falling down, then some old barns that were collapsing and an unfortunate cow standing in the shade of one of the barns, who looked like she was about to be collapsed upon. It was definitely farm country.

"Look at this bridge, kids!"

It was a handmade cable suspension bridge, held upright with wooden uprights at both ends, planked with planks in the middle, and leading to a house that happened to be located on the other side of a creek. It must be that the creek sometimes floods, because the bridge spanned thirty feet, which right then was about twenty-five wider than the creek.

The road made a sharp turn about there, took us past a small tornado of circling vultures, another creek with a flat shale bottom to it, a small cornfield, a tiny little cabin of a church labeled the Church of Christ, an old log barn, and then the end of the road: a T junction where according to the cartographicus Subtle actually would be but actually wasn't.

Not sure what to do, I turned left, roller-coastered for a while past tiny farms and run-down barns, bungalows and a couple of shacks, some patches of corn and tobacco, and then we stopped at a couple of houses and knocked on doors. No one had even heard of Subtle. We turned around and tracked back until we saw a small house trailer with a very big tractor trailer in front of it. It looked like a logging rig, and it had a confederate flag attached as well as the words "One Day at a Time." The owner of the house trailer and the tractor-trailer rig, a young guy with long, stringy hair and a mustache, came out and talked to us, but he had no idea what we were talking about.

"Subtle? Subtle? I cain't say. It ain't here," he said. Then a light came on, and he said: "Oh, you mean *Sub*-tle!"

All this while I had been thinking that Subtle rhymed with muddle or fuddle, in which we were, rather than tub-full, in which we weren't.

There would be a country store, the young man told us, a little old country store at a crook and holler just beyond the junction where we had been originally at. That would be Subtle. So we climbed back into the car and headed back. We came to a cattle crossing and shed that we had passed before, and a sign with the picture of a cow on it we had seen before. And then the junction again. As we continued through the road's crook, we came to a pond and what looked like a modest white house but upon further examination turned into a small country store with no signs on it.

It *was* an old store, with corrugated tin sides and a corrugated tin roof, pounded iron bars in front of the windows, and raw log posts holding up the porch overhang. There were no bright promotional signs out front, no advertising, no markings, nothing — only two very small signs attached to one of the porch posts. One sign said Post Office. The second, right below, said: Subtle, Kentucky.

It was a store (or at least post office), all right. But it didn't look open. It looked closed. Well, maybe it was open.

It was, and we parked out front and went up to the screen door, where we were met by the store proprietor, Dorothy Garmon, who had been standing inside ready to wait on any customers who might appear, including us if we should happen to become customers.

"Well, hi there," she said. "Come on in."

We went inside. It was dark and hot inside, and a couple of fat flies were busy buzzing and butting at the windows, trying to escape the heat or maybe the daytime blues. Spread out for sale were a few universal fundamentals — candy, gum, paper towels, newspapers, and so on — and it looked like we might be able to buy a sandwich or two if we wanted. But we just bought a newspaper, some candy, and then explained our mission.

Dorothy Garmon had a broad face, a kind smile and friendly manners, rectangular glasses, blue eyes, and a crown of curly white hair. She wore a faded purplish housedress with small white polka dots. Her ankles looked swollen. As for how Subtle got its name, well, she couldn't tell us just how it got its name because she wasn't quite sure. "My uncle, he sent in a list of names," she said, "and they sent back a note that that was too long. Had to have a shorter name."

Her great-grandfather came from Virginia and established a farm. He was a homesteader, she guessed. He bought or got a patent they called it back then, on this farm and place in below where we were. And then when her grandmother married, she bought about three and a half acres of the site where the store is now. And her grandmother and grandfather in 1905 got the little old post office established, and that's how far back the name Subtle goes. Her grandfather didn't live to be too old, though, he got cancer of the eyesight, and so her grandmother became postmistress, and when she retired, her oldest son took over — she had two sons — and then the youngest son, Dorothy's father. And then after her father quit, the post office people said, "Well, people live way back in the woods and all. And, you know, it's kind of hard to put boxes down through the road because some people live three miles." They wanted someone to continue with the Subtle Post Office, in other words, and so they stopped to see her, Dorothy Garmon. She wasn't too interested, but in '61, she did take it over. And she's still here. She takes care of the post office and store, just kind of as a hobby, and lives in the house across the road, her mother's house. Dorothy's mother's only been deceased three year. She lived to be ninety-two, and she was real active, and stayed in there on up until just a few months before she passed away.

I had already asked this question, of course, but I thought I'd try it a second time, just in case a new answer appeared: "And where did the name Subtle come from?"

"Well, I don't really know," she said. "I know everybody — except the people from around here — they pronounce it *Suttle*. And around here we all say *Sub-tle*."

Subtle may look sparsely populated, she went on, but there are quite a few people who have slid back in the creeks and back places, where they build back. It's kind of a pretty, quiet spot, though, and the men mostly work at farming and logging, while the ladies tend to work in the garment factories, such as those in Edmonton and Marrowbone. About three people on the road work at trucking, including not only fellas but two ladies as well. The store started years ago, but not so long ago as the post office. She was a little girl — she can remember when her uncle, he went to Chicago for a while and had a store and decided he enjoyed running this kind of business. Of course, it used to be it was the only thing back then. They sold work shoes, work clothes, and what have you that a farmer needed. But only about two months after her mother passed away there was a break-in. That's right. The thieves got some of her antiques, cases and things, so she had an auction, and she sold off all that stuff. And now Dorothy has people that come in for knickknacks. And she makes baloney and cheese sandwiches. Stuff like that.

She had been advised by the auctioneer at that time to take down all her old signs because thieves would steal those, too, since they are now valuable antiques. And so that was why there were no signs out front and why it was so hard to tell where the store was. She said there weren't any Subtle markers along the road either, because people did tend to steal them. And that's why Subtle was so hard to find unless you knew pretty much what you were looking for.

Monkeys Eyebrow

A couple of days later we ran into the end of Kentucky, passing west on Route 60 until we hit Route 358, which pulled us north through the middle of La Center and then past Bandana. We sneezed and missed Bandana, a little cluster of houses along the left side of the road, and then came onto land that was almost completely level. This was

169

Ohio River floodplain, and the soil looked dark and loamy. We were looking for Monkeys Eyebrow, and in fact we never did find any signs indicating Monkeys Eyebrow, the place — but we soon came across a sign indicating Monkey's Eyebrow Road. "We're on the right road, kids! Pay attention!"

The road curved into a woodsy area with a few houses, a few trailers, a business identified only as Monkeys Eyebrow Duck and Goose Processing, a high-reaching radio or TV broadcasting antenna painted white and red and anchored out in its own field. And then maybe a couple more houses and a couple of squat, metal corn cribs.

We followed that curving road until at last there appeared a compact brick house, the New Hope Missionary Baptist Church, Pastor Troy Deweese, where we stopped and knocked on the door. Was it a church or a house? Or both? I don't know, but Pastor Troy came to the door and said that we had already passed through Monkeys Eyebrow. Monkeys Eyebrow used to be a few stores and a few houses, he added, but it's not there anymore. "There's nothing there any more," he said. He didn't know where the name came from either. The only person he could think who might be able to tell us anything about it would be Melvin Redfurn, whom we could find by going back around the curve just a little ways and following the first little country road to the left, which would lead up to his driveway.

The house of Melvin Redfurn was a small old house, painted white and peeling, with a car parked out front, an old tractor parked out back, and decorated with a little decorative windmill.

Nobody home.

So we got back in the car and drove back onto the Monkey's Eyebrow Road east some more along the curve, and just before we got to the radio or TV transmitter antenna, sighted a truck along the road with a sign advertising contractual well drilling. Next to the truck, in front of a small prefab building, a young man — with brown hair, wearing cream-colored painters' pants and circular protective goggles over his eyes — was bending over some steel I-beams on the ground and slowly torturing them to pieces with the bright flame of an oxy-acetylene torch.

It was already getting very sunny and hot. He was already looking very sweaty, and as we pulled up into his yard and got out of the car, he straightened up, pulled his goggles off, and began swiping at the sweat on his face. But he didn't know a thing about it. There's a tower — he pronounced it *tire* — right up the road, he said. We could see it right over here. The radio tower. That tower is the monkey's eyebrow. And this place right where we stood is what people called Monkeys Eyebrow.

"You know how long it's had that name?"

"No, not really, I moved here in '74, and you know, and ever since I remember it's been here. So, I don't know the background, or nothin.'"

Farther along the road east, we came to a big farmhouse that looked like there might be someone inside. When we walked onto the porch, we heard a television going. After we knocked, we heard the sounds of kids running around. But no one came to the door.

So we crossed the road, where there was a modest house trailer just on the other side of some greenery, and we knocked on the door of the trailer. An old man, maybe in his seventies or more, wearing overalls, came to the door. He said he had just moved to the area and therefore had no idea where the name Monkeys Eyebrow came from. But right alongside the trailer another old man had just climbed into the cab of his pickup truck—and the first old man told us to go talk to the second.

"That boy yonder might know," the first said. "I bet he could tell ya."

So we asked the second old man, but he didn't know either. He said, "Lord, I used to know, but I cain't think of it." But, he said, we should go down the curve thataways to find Mr. Melvin Redfurn. He would know.

"Somebody else told us to try Melvin Redfurn," I said. "But he wasn't home."

"He wasn't? Well, I just don't know right now." Oh, on second thought, he added, maybe we should try that big old white house just on the other side of those trees there, on the left. James Alexander lives there. He has lived in Monkeys Eyebrow as long as anyone. "Yeah. He's as old as I am," testified the old man in the truck, getting more positive now. "He'll know."

We turned back onto the curved road a short distance west until we stopped at the big, well-kept-up white house and barn of James Alexander. There was a Cadillac parked in Mr. Alexander's barn, and a couple of tractors parked near that in a large tin shed. A number of beautiful flowers were blooming in his tree-shaded front yard, and an American flag had been painted on his mail box. James Alexander had longish brown and white hair combed neatly back, and he came out onto the porch. We discussed how hot it was. He said that he had gone out to work in the field, but then he took one look at his tractor and decided to go inside and lie down. He spent some time with us, explaining that he didn't really know where the name Monkeys Eyebrow came from either.

"Gosh, no. I really, I really cain't tell you," he said, thoughtfully. "I think I don't know."

"And you lived here all your life?"

"Lived here all my life: seventy-five year. There was a little store and a grist mill, all there was," he explained. "One or two houses, well, actually there was three houses, no two houses. Then they made a house out of one of the other ones. And they had a grist mill. Made flour for people and meal, but then the town just kind of died away. Mostly, it just kind of died. But they still carry the name. They say the TV tower's the monkey's eyebrow."

"That's not it, is it?"

"There's not even any Monkeys Eyebrow here no more."

"And were there a lot of farms around this area at that time?"

"Yeah. Just like it is now. Yep. Still farming, but the town is gone. Yeah, the little town is gone."

"What crops do you grow in this area?"

"Well, corn, milo and tobacco is about it."

"Milo? What's milo?" I asked—and he answered me very thoroughly, but I didn't really understand his explanation, and I still don't know what milo is. Finally, after an extended chat on his front porch, he said we should go up the curve past the tower and the brick house, then go in and turn to the left, and find Billy Pippin. "Seem to me like I heard him say that he, somebody said to him, 'Well, how'd it get its name?' He said, 'I don't remember. But I believe I got something.' But you might ask him. I would like to know myself."

We turned east again, looking for Billy Pippin. I think I must have missed the correct turn, however, because soon we had come to the end of the curve at the location of the Monkeys Eyebrow Duck and Goose Processing.

This was a very small duck and goose processing operation of some sort going on in a building near the back of a series of wood buildings, and the person I spoke with near the front said he didn't know a thing about Monkeys Eyebrow. But a small road edged by a few houses turned north away from the Duck and Goose Processing, and so we ducked and processed up that road until we came to a house with a car out front, where we stopped.

The man in that house, Frank Howell, was very friendly and eager to help, but he didn't know either. There used to be a grocery store, he said, and a feed mill. But it's been a long time. But he thought that if we went back up the road, made a right onto the curved stretch, and, second house on the left, right on the curve, brick house on the left, that would be the house of Ella Mae Russell. "She's eighty years old," he said, "so she ought to know."

"Thank you," we said.

"You betcha," he said.

We drove back west on the curved road until we came to the house of Ella Mae Russell. We were invited inside by her daughter or daughter-in-law (I never got that one straight), and then we introduced and explained ourselves to Ella Mae, who was sitting, bundled up in a blue blanket, in a wheelchair.

"Well, now," she said, "the woman that you need to talk to has gone to the doctor. Could you come back tomorrow?"

"I'm afraid we couldn't."

"Well," she said, "I don't know, and I've heard Ruth and them tell that story a million times. I don't know, but she does. And I'm a lot older than she is. And she's got the history on everything. She's got the history on everything, but she's gone to the doctor's today. Where you from?"

"Massachusetts."

"You're a long way from home."

"That's right."

Well, she continued, we might try Melvin Redfurn. He was gone to the doctor, too, but he ought to be back in the middle of the afternoon, by 2:30 about. Or we might try Katherine Fondaw. To get to her house, we should go back east on the curve about two and a half three miles, past a church, the Providence Baptist Church. And her house would be the next house past that church, same side of the road, on the right, set back aways. She's got a long driveway. But she also has a dog, and if she isn't there out front, we should stay in the car until she came out, in order that the dog wouldn't get us.

We located Katherine Fondaw in her garage, dogless and cleaning up an insecticide spray pump. Monkeys Eyebrow is a real place, she said, but they couldn't put a sign up for the place because every time they did it was gone in about two days. People want that sign. And, she said, people on top of people are trying to find out where the name came from, and she really didn't know herself. But we might try Walt Kinsey. He would be out that road, turn right, that road before the church, then on up the rattleroad, come to a sharp curve, and there would be a trailer, inside of which ought to be Walt Kinsey. He was way more than ninety years old, and he would know.

I followed her directions to the rattleroad but got lost or distracted and had to ask directions of a friendly old man with blue eyes and puffy eyebrows, wearing bib overalls and a cap with a couple of confederate flags on it that said "Alive and Doing Well," who was sweating and pushing a power mower at some grass beside the road. He said Monkeys Eyebrow got named a long time before his time, and he just didn't know. A year ago someone told him what it was, and so he knew it then, but he couldn't say now. He just couldn't remember. But, he said, I could try Walt Kinsey. He was the oldest man around, ninety-some year, and lived in the trailer just down the road. His wife was sick and in the hospital, but he might be there.

He would know. He definitely would know.

We finally found the Kinsey trailer and rapped on the door. Pretty soon, after some shouting and shuffling from inside, Walt Kinsey appeared. He wore a blue cap, a clean white T-shirt, baggy brown pants, and Velcroed black shoes. He was tremulous, unshaven, and his skin had a sun-battered quality. He looked as if he had recently had a stroke. The left side of his body seemed a little lower than the right, and his mouth hung open.

In a very soft voice he said that the Ohio River was just over there, about a mile from where we were standing outside his trailer. He said this is what they call the swamp lands. This is the hottest weather, he said, these last two weeks have been about the hottest weather. It's goofy and sticky, and you can't cut tobacco now. If you put it in the barn, it'll just rot. "Well," he continued, "I've been batchin it, because my woman's in the hospital. She has pneumonia. She went in last Thursday. She come up with pneumonia." And then, as an afterthought: "I'm too tough to get pneumonia."

As for where the name Monkeys Eyebrow came from, he rightly didn't know. Nope. Didn't know.

And so after a few minutes more chitchatting, we thanked Mr. Kinsey and headed back down the rattleroad once again. It was getting hotter and hotter, now, and we were thinking to ourselves that it was getting far too hot for any more of this backing and forthing. We still had a long drive ahead of us — and so it was time to wink ironically at Monkeys Eyebrow and admit defeat. Maybe we could stop and get ice cream in Bandana, if there was such a thing in such a place, and if not, then surely in La Center. We had given up, in short, but in the meanwhile had also become disoriented and lost once again on the rattleroad.

So we stopped to ask directions of a man in a blue cap and plaid, short-sleeved shirt running a small tractor mower across a lawn about the size of a throw rug thrown in front of a new trailer and a car that had Arizona license plates on the back.

His name was Frank Oliver, he told us, and he was from Arizona, not Kentucky, but he had recently retired from the Air Force and just moved up here a short while ago thinking that this would be about perfect for hunting and fishing, two things he liked to do. But now he was thinking he might be regretting the move, because he lived in the mountains there in Arizona, and it was nice and cool when he left.

"Oh, it was cool there?" I said, "It's hot this summer!"

"Oh, let me tell ya," he agreed.

After he had given us enough directions, I thought to ask him if he knew the origin of the name Monkeys Eyebrow.

If we took a look at the map, Frank Oliver said, and where Ballard County is and McCracken and everything? It looks like a monkey's face there right at the end of Kentucky, the end of the state. It looks just like a monkey's face, facing west. It takes in a couple counties. And the eyebrow of the monkey's face is right in this area. The shape of the eyebrow is. The curve of the road and the curve of the Ohio River. And that's what it is: That's the monkey's eyebrow. He laughed.

"That's interesting," I said. "You know what? We've spoken to maybe ten people. A lot of old timers, and nobody could tell us. You're the first one who's told us."

"Oh, is that right?" He laughed again.

Muddy

We worked our way around to Illinois Interstate 57 north and clambered up that until Route 13, where we hung a right. Route 13 drew us through a city, and then we rambled across farmland, fields, and forests cast over a wrinkled land with a few gullies and a little river or two. We stopped briefly to look in the window of a lonely little roadside shop, Barb's Boutique, specializing in frogskin purses and accessories.

We turned left and came into the town of Harrisburg, Home of Barbara Allen Teacher of the Year. Western Harrisburg looked ramshackle, I'd say, though the downtown part included a couple of promising blocks of old brick buildings and the Osmond Real Estate Company reaching out with its upbeat slogan of the day: AVOID NEGATIVE PEOPLE. That referred to me. I was suddenly feeling very negative as we dribbled out the eastern end of Harrisburg into one of the ugliest shopping malls and Wal-Marts ("We Sell For Less") I'd seen in a long time. Ugly but typical: latched like a giant parasite onto the edge of town and sucking all of the business out of the center.

We escaped Harrisburg and soon saw an indicator of seven miles to El Dorado. The cartographicus magnus said we would wallow into Muddy before reaching El Dorado, so I told the Research Assistants to keep their eyes peeled. But before long we had rolled into the edge of El Dorado, which meant we had missed Muddy. Well, there was a big cinderblock building at the edge of El Dorado called Books 'N Things. The man inside sold us a book and told us we had simply failed to see the sign for Muddy, but it would be right the other side of a Day's Inn, and if we just stuck right on the road we came out on, we couldn't miss it. We thanked him for the information and retraced our route until, sure enough, right past the Day's Inn we spied the sign:

MUDDY
100.

Some houses and at least two small businesses along the highway there appeared to adhere to Muddy: the New Players Club ("Monday Nite All Can Beer $1") and the Budget Nook Consignment Shop ("Now Taking Baby Furniture"). Neither was open, however, and so we turned down a little road directly west of the New Players Club and bounced deep into Muddy, which seemed to be a series of sheds and shacks and small bungalows and a small white church known as the First Baptist Church of Muddy. The road continued past some trailers and finally terminated at a stop sign and a cross street.

A dirty dog crossed the cross street.

In front of us, on the other side of that street and just beyond a stretch of weeds and trees, loomed a gigantic edifice: either an abandoned alien artifact or an abandoned coal mine entrance and elevator. We turned left and parked the car right in front of a building that seemed to be an empty and abandoned grocery store.

So far Muddy looked deserted. I perked down. But I perked up again the second I noticed just past the empty grocery store the following sign of life: a tiny white shed with a green roof and a red-shingled gable. It had a small side window, a small front door, and a small white metal awning over the door. An American flag snapped happily above the roof of this tiny shed, while a sign hung confidently out from the red gable above the awning. The sign said US POST OFFICE, Muddy, IL 62965. There was also a dark blue mail box outside next to the post office building, but it was hard to tell which was bigger, post office or mail box. What I mean is: That post office was tiny!

We tried the door. Nobody home. A sign on the door indicated we had come during the post office siesta, so we got back in the car and drove around some more, and eventually concluded that Muddy had about five streets hither and thither and maybe fifty to eighty houses, including some nifty contemporary houses made of real brick and a larger number of shifty cubical bungalows sided with fake brick. The cubical bungalows seemed to have been stamped from a single pattern, and the pattern looked like an old one, suggesting that they had been built in the 1930s or so by a town industry for its workers, probably the very industry responsible for the concrete edifice at the far end of town.

We explored that edifice more thoroughly, driving as close as we could get and walking the rest of the way until we came right up to the thing: disintegrating concrete, rusting steel, a huge asymmetrical structure about three or four or five stories high with a tower at one end that must have once suspended a giant wheel or pulley somehow associated with a big elevator. On the far side of this structure was the embossed date 1923, while lettering on the town side indicated MINE 12.

A gravel and dirt road pocked with mud holes ran out beyond the edifice, and we drove along that, soon arriving at some old trailers, junk cars, and an old house with somebody coming out of it, getting into an old pickup truck, and driving in our direction. I pulled over and when the truck reached us talked to the man at the wheel who had stopped and leaned out his window.

"Hi," I said. "We're trying to see if we can find somebody who can tell us where the name Muddy came from."

The man said: "It's muddy."

Then, since I couldn't think of anything else to say and neither could he, the man nodded politely and drove off.

Driving to the very end of that road now, we came to a nice surprise. There was a little lake and a charming church and parish house. The parish house looked empty, and the church was closed — but attractive, with a three-tiered Greek Orthodox cross stuck onto a big white bell tower. The road, terminating with a loop and flourish in front of this church, parish house, and lake, had been degenerating for some time now, and right about there it turned into a shallow lake with a muddy bottom. I executed some fancy twists and bold slides, enabling us to avoid getting stuck in the muddy middle of a mud puddle, but weren't we in danger of getting stuck in the ruddy riddle of a Muddy muddle? The day was half gone, the two or three businesses in town were closed, the post office was napping, and so far we had only managed to address one barely polysyllabic man in a pick-up truck who was bound in the other direction. Not very promising.

As luck would have it, though, once we got back to Muddy's main drag — the road going past the deserted grocery store and the tiny post office — we sighted an old man who turned out to be friendly. He was walking down the middle of the road with a handful of mail, on his way to the post office. He was wearing dirty Levi's, glasses, a new brown tractor hat that said "Tractor Supply" on it, and a white undershirt under a red, white, and black plaid overshirt. He had a feisty manner, a jutting chin to go with it, and a gray or white stubble on the chin. When he talked, he regularly emphasized his words with the peculiar habit of stretching out his arms like wings.

He said his name was Horsefly. His legal name was Robert Bean, but everybody always called him Horsefly, and he got that name because he was the littlest kid ever went to Muddy School. As a matter of fact, he was born in 1926, when they built the school. He's seventy-one now, but he was the littlest kid ever went to school there. And when he was born, people come over and looked, and they could see right through him, see his blood. He didn't weigh over a half a pound. They didn't have no generator, no whadayacallit to put a baby in. So they had to take care of him, put him on a pillow and give him goat's milk with an eyedropper. Then, when he went to school, one day there was a horsefly on the window, and he was trying to think how he was going to get that horsefly, but he was so damn little he couldn't reach up to it. He could only reach up about so far. He tried to think how he was going to get that horsefly, and while he was thinking the teacher called him "Horsefly." The name stuck.

Well, now, he continued after some minor prodding, Muddy was a mining town. The church was built first. And then they come from whadayacallit, and they built the mine. That was in about 1923, or something like that. The church was Orthodox, and it come from Chicago. He stood on the front porch, sat there, and watched them. And they had Model T Fords. Every one of them. Boy, and you could listen to the putt putt putt putt. Now the mines were run by Sahara. Sahara Coal Mines. They're near Harrisburg, and they had a big deal there in Harrisburg, but now they're closing all the mines over there. Now they only got about one, and it's ready to go. So pretty soon Illinois will be out of coal. But you could still come in here and get more coal, if you knew where it's at. You could make yourself rich after a while.

His dad was a coal miner, worked in the mines. And he had a brother, too, a coal miner. And he, Horsefly, went down into the mine once, and a bunch of coal went and killed a couple of men right in front of him, and he said, "That's it. Forget it." But his dad worked down there all his life. He's dead now. The mine closed in '48, and he was going to tell us something else, too. A lot of people might not know it, but there's more coal in them mines. There is more coal in there. If they need more coal all they have to do is go out there and just dig it up.

So anyway, he went up north to get a job. And he got a job up there. This was in the Depression, and people said there was no work. But if there ain't work, all you have to do is look around. You can get a job if you want to work.

But a lot of guys went up north, and they was mama's boys and stuff like that. Well, they didn't like the work so they come back here.

Now one of the things about Muddy that we should know is that it used to be known as the place with the smallest post office in the entire United States. And it was, until somebody in Florida built a post office that's about an inch shorter in one direction. Now it's only the second smallest post office, he said. And, he added, the man who used to be the post officer, named Jess Moore, weighed seven hundred pounds.

I said, "I think if you put a seven-hundred-pound guy in there, you wouldn't be able to get him out."

Horsefly said, "By God, you'd be so damn surprised." Jess Moore was strong was what it was. And by God, he could take two barrels of oil like that, Horsefly said—and he demonstrated the posture of holding a big barrel under each arm. Nobody messed with Jess Moore. And, as a matter of fact, nobody messed with anybody in Muddy. Muddy used to be a very tough place. It had a reputation. Guys got horsewhipped around here. Some guy would get somebody mad at him, and boy, he'd get a horsewhipping, boy, he'd be running down like that through here, naked as a jaybird and hollerin. Now, there are a lot of people right now, a lot of people here who don't know too much about Muddy. Because most of the old people are about dead around here, and the ones that are here, a lot of them can't tell you too much. He was down here all the time. But you couldn't get a person, a lot of them, to go down here. A lot of them was afraid to go down here because they might get knocked in the head. When he was a little kid, he paid no attention to those guys, the tough ones. He'd walk up and down this street and everything else. Oh, heck, they was rough around here, fighting all the time here. If we were to talk to people in Harrisburg, Harrisburg people would come out to Muddy, and come out to the joints here, but there wasn't ever a Muddy guy in Muddy that ever got shot or anything. It was always somebody from somewhere else. And it's funny how people, you'd think there'd be a lot of old people here, but there ain't no old people. Not anymore. All the old people are gone.

Anyhow, Muddy was called Muddy because it was muddy, but it was muddy for a reason. Before the Sahara coal company decided to put a mine in, it wasn't called anything at all. Maybe because it wasn't really a place yet. But then, when the coal company decided to dig a mine, they first dug a pond, an artificial pond or lake. That was the lake we saw out by the church. So the place was muddy because the coal mining company put in a pond there for pumping water to make steam to generate electric to run the mine works.

And then in turn the electric ran a big wheel at the top of the concrete tower, a big wheel up there, and then it went across to another wheel and pulled the coal out in little cars. The miners underground would put about ten ton of coal in them cars and away they went. They had rails, and they would just run them darn things out there, and before you know it, that was it. They'd haul them up out of the mine.

Horsefly himself wasn't so clear about how it all worked, but as a result of the electric generation there was a spray of warm water coming out. And there was a guy named Moody who had something to do with the spray. Moody had a place down there near the spray where all the kids used to go fishing and swimming. And because the water was heated, they could go swimming in the winter time, which they used to do. They'd take their clothes off and run through the snow, and he never knew what Moody's first name was, it might have been Carl or something, but he was called Muddy Moody. Well, they called the place Muddy Moody's. Horses would come down there, into the blue mud and blue clay, up to their bellies, and people said, "Boy, this is the right name for it: Muddy." And Moody put up a big sign that said MUDDY MOODY'S. It could be that Moody's sign saying MUDDY MOODY'S had something to do with the naming of the place, or it could be that the place had already gotten its sticky reputation and tacky toponym before Moody put up the sign. But whether it was one or the other, that was it. That's how Muddy got its name.

Goofy Ridge

The road to Goofy Ridge took us, next morning, north and west into a puckered portion of Illinois, with some woods and a few houses tucked away in the woods. We came to a pig farm, consisting of a series of pig villages with little wooden pig houses, and then a car part farm, and then we came to Chandlerville, with its own tanning salon. We took a quick dip through Bath, which consisted of prefabs, a Shell station, about three bars, and a metal eagle perched on top of an uptilted piece of cast iron sewer pipe with the following information: "In this spot Abraham Lincoln spoke to the citizens of Bath as he campaigned for the United States Senate. Taking a Bible from his pocket, he read: 'A house divided against itself cannot stand.'" We stepped out of Bath, toweled ourselves off, and emerged clean and dry and doing fifty-five.

We entered the major town of Havana, nice but nothing fancy, and slipped north onto a winding highway through a woodsy area along the river. Now the navigation became a little more taxing, since there appeared no signs whatever for Goofy Ridge, but we just followed the road all the way out to the headquarters for the Chatauqua National Wildlife Refuge, where a wildlife consultant confirmed that we were on the right road. Every time we came to a Y, she said, we should turn left. And those directions brought us into an area of plastic lawn deer and cows and then the Hialeah Club. Soon after we came to a big arrow on a post at a minor junction of roads. This arrow had broken loose from one of its two hinges and so pointed straight down, but we could still make out the legend: GOOFY RIDGE CAFE.

We turned left and came upon a man with a round face and white hair who was gathering mail and said that the guy who could have told us about Goofy Ridge died a couple of weeks ago, so we should speak to John Ebert, who lived just down and across the road on the other side of that ditch.

John Ebert's place was a green cottage with a couple of fat squirrels out front eating corn off corn cobs that had been left out for them. They looked like happy squirrels. There was also a very large bird house out in the yard, and a yappy dog yapping from inside the cottage. But no John Ebert. So we continued on down the road past a number of cottages and trailers and so on until we came to a white, cinderblock building with a small sign out front that said Goofy Ridge Cafe. Above the lettering was a nice picture of Goofy—Walt Disney's Goofy—catching a fish and, so the Research Staff were able to imagine, laughing goofily: *Ahyuk! Ahyuk! Ahyuk!*

Inside the Goofy Ridge Cafe were chairs and tables and a counter with spin stools upon which we sat and from where we gazed upon a collection of Goofy memorabilia on the wall: a Goofy hat, a Goofy key chain, and three different Goofy portraits. A sign on the door said "Children Must Remain Seated At All Times," but the two waitresses behind the counter, once we explained our mission, were friendly and helpful. No, they didn't exactly know where the name came from, but they did know to whom we should speak: John Ebert. And someone was sent away to find him. Goofy Ridge, one of the waitresses confided in the meantime, had an undeservedly bad reputation. "Everyone thinks Goofy Ridge is this real bad area, you know," she said, "but it isn't."

We waited, had some coffee and soft drinks, and soon enough John Ebert came in the door. He was a big guy, friendly and kind of roundish, with big powerful hands and a red cap on his head, with brown eyes and big glasses in front of them.

After sitting down next to us on a whirly stool, John Ebert said he had worked at Caterpillar for thirty-six and a half years as a tool-and-die maker, and then he retired.

He was about sixteen years old when he first come down here, John continued, and some kids had a duck club back up in the forest. And he come down here then on a motorcycle and, boy, if that wasn't something. It was a Henderson four-cylinder. And if you didn't have your feet on the ground when you give it gas, it would just flop you right over. But they used to have a lot of fun. Then he bought his Goofy Ridge property in '49 but kept it as a vacation home until '76, when, after he retired, he moved all his furniture out here and moved in.

He's tried to keep busy ever since he left Caterpillar. He went and bought a backhoe. He's got two front-end loaders. When he retired, John continued, he figured he'd be down here with a bunch of old guys. But the old guys are gone.

Now the Goofy Ridge Cafe, Mary Smith built that about twelve or fifteen years ago. John took the dirt out of the hillside for her. And before that there wasn't any decent place to get something to eat. At the taverns, you could get cold cuts, sandwiches, but nothing else.

John lost his wife in '83. She had colon cancer. And then his mother and dad and sister all died in one year. And in '94 he had lung trouble. Had pneumonia twice in one month. Lost about thirty percent of his lungs. All that kind of knocked the heck out of him.

Now this area was a pretty popular area for hunting and fishing. And, oh, they had a lot of guys come into Goofy Ridge from the strip mines and stuff on weekends. They'd come for drinking down at the tavern, the Mallard Club, and the old Goofy Ridge Tavern. Al Capone, as a matter of fact, used to come down to hunt and fish. "I seen him down here," John said. Yes, that was Al Capone fishing up at Clear Lake. And there was old Sis Koles. And Bill Martin. He was another old-timer. He retired from Caterpillar way back. And Hank Van Hoosier. He owned the Mallard Club. They had a big hog roast coming up for anyone, coming up on a Friday, and Hank got out of work, and he got hit-and-runned. Nobody ever did find out who killed him.

And old Frog Harley had a still in Goofy Ridge, which he had hidden inside his cabin. Frog was an old coal miner. His wife used to come down there to the still at the old cabin. She had a big, old Cadillac, one of them big, old jobs. Well, they sent her to town to get something. There was a guy behind her in a ditch, laying behind her. He was drunk. Passed out. She backed over him. After that she would never come back down.

And the way that John found out about Frog's still was that he, John, bought Frog's old cabin. John started to clean it out and fell into a big hole that had been all boarded up. So he went back to Peoria where he asked old Frog, he says, "What was that big hole underneath there for?" Frog said that part of it was for ice. That's where they had sawdust, and they would pack ice off the lake and keep it. And the other part was where he had his still. But the old guys, none of them are left any more. Then some guy came down to Goofy Ridge and bought up some parcels of land and then split an acre up into eight lots, so that's too small. It kind of messed up the whole works, and now they've got a bunch of potheads in town.

Now Al Capone probably came down in the early '60s. He was short, kind of heavy. But John had met Al Capone a lot earlier than that. He met him over in East Peoria. Capone used to stop at an old oil station over there, an eating joint. Jap Davis's place. Jap had a gambling boat down on the river, and Al Capone would come in through there. And then he hunted on some of the area farms, too. He'd come with like six guys with him, and some farm lady sets a table out, and once she does the dishes, there's a $20 bill under each plate. That was worth something. So Capone wasn't such a bad guy. In fact, when John was a kid, Al Capone gave him a silver dollar. Now Capone, he drove big Lincolns. The glass was about that thick on them old cars, and there were holes in the glass so they could stick a shot gun through.

Some people thought Al Capone was an awful nice guy. He stole from the rich and fed the poor out there in Chicago. He had soup kitchens during the Depression. He died in prison. Alcatraz. But up there in Chicago he lined fourteen guys up and shot them with machine guns. Some of them were outlaws. That was over a whiskey run and stuff like that.

But, yes (John continued after some prodding on my part), Al Capone gave him a silver dollar once. John's dad was working coal at that time, and after work he would stop at this old place, Jap Davis's, in East Peoria. He would stop there on the way home. And John was out of school on vacation time, so he went down with his dad to work while he was off that week. His dad worked in a coal mine. This was a shaft mine, went straight down, and there was a steam engine that ran a cable down into the shaft, and the cable would raise cars out of the mine. One car would go down empty, and another would come up full of coal. And in the mornings they put the men down there and the ponies, and at night they would pull them back out again. This was about a hundred and sixty or eighty feet deep, and John's dad somehow ran the steam-driven cable that lowered and raised the cars, the miners, and the ponies. Anyway, after work, he and his dad went out to Jap Davis's for a bite to eat. And Al Capone was in there. John and his dad were sitting there eating chili, and Al Capone come over and threw a silver dollar on the table. John's still got that silver dollar.

Jap Davis's was a gas station and a restaurant. He had a couple black bears out in back, and they used to put the boxing gloves on the bears and get in there with them. And, oh, the bears would really get you. With the gloves on, they couldn't scratch, but they sure could smack. They had muzzles on them. And then he had a couple turtles out there that weighed about five hundred pounds, too. He was quite a character, Jap Davis was.

Now all this happened when John was still in grade school. East Peoria. Jap Davis owned a lot of stuff over there, and Al Capone would stop in every Friday night whenever he was around. So Al Capone could have been just a buddy of Jap's, or they could have been in business together, bootlegging and hauling. But, as a matter of fact, John's dad bootlegged, too, though on a comparatively small scale. This was during the Depression. They lived out in the country, and his dad had a twenty-gallon still. John used to haul for him on a pony and a cart. His dad would give him fifty cents, and so with that fifty cents he could see a show for a nickel and get some pop corn and have a little extra left over. Some old lady down there, she ran a joint, and so she bought his dad's whiskey.

Making good whiskey is not so easy. You've got to know how to start your own brand and stuff, your variety. John's dad made rye whiskey, and then he colored it with apricot. He'd take apricots and put them in a pie pan, and then put them in the oven to brown them just a little. Then he put the apricot in that whiskey, and when they started turning a little amber color he'd pull them out. And he would tell John to go out and feed the rest to the hogs. But, well, John just wrapped the apricots up in wax paper and put them in his shirt pockets. They tasted pretty good to chew on, John concluded.

And as for the naming of Goofy Ridge, well, it's been so long ago, John said, but he can remember things that happened long ago while he's sitting over there in the house by himself. The story behind the name was pretty simple. Back a few years ago, in the '40s, there were some guys by the name of Slim Bouchet, Benny Haven, Frog Harley, and John Darling. Slim Bouchet lived on an old barge. Benny Haven only had one leg. Frog Harley was the coal miner who used to run that still beneath his cabin. And Johnny Darling, he got cancer, and it got so bad they operated on him and then they put a hole in his stomach and fed him baby food. But he'd have to go to the doctor about fifteen or twenty times a year to get new plastic put in because he poured whiskey and stuff down in there, which eats all the pipes up. Then he shot himself one day up in the Club House.

Slim Bouchet and Benny Haven, Frog Harley and Johnny Darling, they were sitting up on the ridge above the river one day, and for some reason — maybe they had been drinking too much beer and whiskey — they piled walnuts on top of each others' heads and then took their guns out and started shooting the walnuts off.

It was kind of a goofy thing to do, and after that, everybody called the place Goofy Ridge. That's it. That's how Goofy Ridge got its name.

Normal

The waitress in the Goofy Ridge Cafe had suggested we could eat lunch there, but when she listed the items available—meat, meat, and meat—I as politely as possible declined. I didn't want meat for lunch, especially after having watched on television at the motel that very morning an interview with the author of a book about Mad Cow Disease.

Mad Cow Disease, the author said, is a type of bovine brain disease with a human corollary originally noticed in New Guinea. New Guinean cannibals were eating each other's brains but unwittingly passing around brains that had been left out too long in the sun. The problem is not a virus but a protein crystal, if that makes any sense, with a long latency. You can't detect it for a long time, and when it does appear, it's too late. Your brain has already started melting. Furthermore, the author on television explained, the bovine version of the malady is transmitted from cow to cow possibly because some cow owners have been making their cows cannibals. In other words, used cattle waste, brains and so on, is ground into cattle feed and recycled back into cows. Now, it was never clear if eating a Mad Cow could give me, a sane human, the melting brain problem, but in any case I wanted a tuna fish sandwich for lunch.

So after Goofy Ridge we drove back down to Havana where a little restaurant in the middle of town offered one with all the trimmings along with a Coke, a salad, and a side of fries, and then we got back in the car and pointed ourselves in the general direction of Normal. Getting to Normal required going sideways for an hour or two and upwards for another hour or two. Normal is on the far side of Bloomington, and so we slid right into Bloomington, came out the other end at the Risqués Adult Entertainment Center Open 24 Hours 7 Days, and from there passed directly into Normal.

Normal, the sign explained, holds forty thousand people including the University High 1995 Class A Boys State Basketball Champs. Also, as we saw,

Normal houses a number of normal businesses: Wendy's, Gibson's Lawn Boy, Steak 'n Shake, Norma's Beauty Corner, Preston Golf Club Repairs, and McDonald's. We wanted to find someone normal to ask about Normal, and, we asked ourselves, where is your normal Normalite more likely to be found than pressing burgers at McDonald's?

We stopped, but, as I soon realized, it would look strange talking to people without going through the usual rituals, so we walked up to the counter and ordered Big Macs, fries, apple pies, and Cokes. And then I tried to speak to the young man at the counter who filled our request. He was sixteen years old, with slicked-down dark hair parted in the middle, a regular face, pointed chin, and blue eyes. I couldn't read his name, written on a pin on his shirt, but after he passed over the order and then pushed across the change, I said, "Do you know where the name Normal came from?"

He chuckled, shook his head. "Nope. Don't have any idea," he said. "Why?" he added. "Just passing through?"

And I, reluctant to go through the longer explanation under those circumstances, said, "Yup, just passing through."

That was it. After eating our Big Macs (by this time I had forgotten about Mad Cow Disease), we got back in the car and continued along Business 51 to see if we could find any more normal Normal businesses, passing up a Baskin Robbins and an Italian Restaurant in favor of a Burger King.

We parked in the Burger King lot, went inside, and ordered some Whoppers, fries, and Cokes. And here we did luck out. First of all, we were the only customers in the place, since it was by now midway between lunch and dinner, a very quiet time. Second, two very normal-looking guys were working there, and both were willing to talk.

The first normal-looking guy was dressed in a Burger King uniform with a Whopper logo sewn over his left pectoral. He had a normal if regular face and a normal if broad smile. He looked athletic and outgoing, with neatly combed brown hair and a space-age combination earphone mouthpiece on top of the hair. Through the earphones came the occasional squawk and hiss from a take-out intercom, and through the mouthpiece passed his mediating response. His name, he said, was Clayton, and when he wasn't rapping with the cooks at Burger King, he was cracking the books at Illinois State. "Here's your Whopper," he said.

I asked him if he could tell us how Normal became Normal, and he explained that he had heard the story from an elderly gentleman in town last summer. They were talking, and the gentleman said, "Would you like to know how we got the name Normal?" Clayton said he would, and so the man told him. The town of Normal actually comes from the University, and it used to be called Illinois State Normal University, and by that it was meant that it was a "normal" education college, and all it taught was the "normal" education courses, and you learned how to be a teacher there, and there was no deviance. Normal University. And the town sprang up around it, and hence the town became Normal.

"Right," I said, still a little confused. "So, by 'no deviance,' you mean it was all Education?"

"It was pure Education. There wasn't any Industrial Arts or anything like that. There wasn't any Industrial Arts. There was only—it was a teachers' college."

"And who was this old guy who told you? Just some old guy?"

"Just some old man I was talking to. I think I was trying to sell him a paint job."

"And, so, have you lived in Normal?"

"Actually, I'm from a town that's about half an hour away from here, but I do attend school here, and I'm familiar with the area."

"What kind of a town is it?"

"It's a normal town," he said (unable to resist the pun). "It's a very conservative town, very nice people. It's mainly middle- and upper-middle-class America with well-to-do neighborhoods, a lot of well-to-do neighborhoods."

I wondered what he meant by "very conservative." But while we were discussing Normal politics, the second normal-looking guy in Burger King chimed in and starting giving his impressions, which were a little more radical. This second guy had been on break during our conversation with Clayton. He was younger than Clayton by two or three years I guessed. He wore the same uniform with the same Whopper logo on the left pectoral, but he had red hair, round glasses, and a shy, intense cast to his lean and handsome face. He was an existential, red-haired version of the young James Dean, to summarize, and his name, he said, was Ed. Ed had gone outside briefly to take a cigarette break, and then he came inside again and sat down at one of the tables, from where he now joined in the conversation.

He wanted to know why I was asking about Normal, and when I explained, he wanted to know if I was a writer. Then he wondered what subjects I wrote about. And then he wanted to know my feelings about politics. He explained that he wanted to know because he was a socialist. "The reason I was asking you about politics," he said, "is because I'm a socialist, and generally there are a lot more writers that are socialist. I'm always apt to find people like myself." Ed agreed with Clayton that Normal was a conservative town, but, he added, it was *very* conservative. The conservatives control the media, and that's why you see a lot of antisocialist stories in the papers. As a socialist, he continued, sometimes being in Normal felt like being behind the enemy lines.

He had been attending night school but dropped out, but Ed did plan to go to college to get his degree. He had lived in Normal for about six or eight months now, having moved from Virginia, which is also a conservative place. He dropped out of high school, Ed went on, because he didn't feel that the education system was a good environment. It left a lot to be desired. He dropped out in his senior year of high school in Normal, because when he transferred from his previous school in Virginia, they gypped him for some credits. At his old school, they said if you had a credit for milking cows that you got in the fifth grade, they had to count that, but Ed had like math credits that he had got in eighth grade, and they said they wouldn't count middle-school credits. So Ed thought that there were a lot of problems with the high school system in Normal. That's one of the things that socialists like himself intend to change, along with raising minimum wage, providing more social programs, redistribution of wealth. Even things out a little bit.

I thought that was interesting, even though talk of *evening things out* makes me nervous. Still, it did seem as if he had gotten a bad deal. I felt sympathetic, and I asked him if there were other socialists in Normal, or if it was a case of being just an inspired socialist in isolation. He said it was mostly in isolation. A socialist anywhere in America is kind of rare, he said. He knows people who claim to be socialists, but they're saying that just for attention. It was a way for them to rebel against popular standards. He didn't like that kind of thing. Nevertheless, he concluded, you can find socialist-minded people even in Normal if you look hard enough, but in the meantime, his break was over, and so he should probably get back to shoveling all those Mad Cow patties onto the griddle.

That last turn of phrase was mine. He didn't say that. I was thinking it, as I insanely wolfed down the last big bite of my big Whopper and started feeling inordinately in need of a salubrious eructation. It was only my third lunch of the day — counting the tuna sandwich in Havana and the Big Mac at McDonald's — but it felt like the fifth, and so I waved weakly to Clayton and Ed, waddled sluggishly out of the Burger King, and then nodded north on Business 51 into Regular 51.

That was Normal. But before long Regular 51 had merged with Interstate 39 and spread out under an open sky. It was really flat out there, and soon we were swimming across a sea of tasseled corn that went on almost forever, only occasionally interrupted in the distance by a grain elevator in one place and the spire of a church in the other, a few trees and a few barns and farm houses, and then a hazy, pale gray in the far distance. Before too much longer, all the cars in front of us were pulling extended shadows to the right, and the sun was turning the corn fields gold. Now big trucks started appearing out of the horizon, growing bigger and bigger into huge rectangular things, with cabs like foreheads and headlights like eyes.

Caravans of trucks started coming out of the horizon, and then the sun went down, leaving us with only a few cloud silhouettes in the sky and a little bit of pink and pale yellow. But we just kept on shooting straight like a bullet, headed for Rockford, Illinois, passing all those great caravans of trucks going the other way. Now a caravan of six trucks clustered together appeared on the horizon and plowed in our direction, looking, with its long row of lights along the sides, like a big benthic beast and moving at a terrific speed — about 150 miles per hour if you considered the contrary speed of the observer.

The sky turned into a gray wall with a couple of smears of paint to the right and some bluish marbling, and we just headed for it. It felt as if we were going to fly right into it and puncture a hole right through it. And now lightning started fracturing deep inside the clouds, and once in a while a piece of lightning turned on inside the clouds and lit them up like a light bulb behind a thick lampshade.

With the velvet of full darkness on us, we began driving through a tunnel of our own light into humid fecund farm air, dashing north on nothing but gasoline and faith, with insects veering up in front of us and then smashing against our windshield. We were the Grim Reaper of Bugs plowing through the State of Illinois and headed for Rockford, where my father was born and grew up and where about a million of my relatives still live.

We finally reached Rockford, but by the time we did, it had gotten too late and I was pretty far gone. I had been to Rockford six years earlier, but now it was unrecognizable. Once a quiet little place of furniture factories and bumbling cops, Rockford had when I wasn't looking metastasized like a Mad Cow into a million K-Marts, Wal-Marts, Everything-Marts, and just one grand shopping mall forever. I had to stop at a pay phone somewhere and telephone my niece Kris to come and find us.

Embarrass

We spent a few days in Rockford, staying at my brother David's house, being treated to big dinners in big restaurants, being subjected to giant plumbing at the Midwest's Biggest Water Park, and visiting with him and his five children and many other good and generous relatives. Hi, Cousin Richard. Then we drove through Wisconsin and into

Minneapolis, Minnesota, where we stayed overnight at the home of our friends Mark and Alison.

Mark and I used to be college roommates a long time ago, back when he already knew he wanted to argue but hadn't yet figured what about. Now he argues about the law for a living. Back then he and I argued about everything. So now after dinner, the three grownups sat on the roof of Mark's garage to argue about life, while the cicadas around us argued about the humidity and a few stars overhead twinkled merrily in spite of everything.

Next morning the Research Staff and I took 35 north into farm country with lots of blue silos. By the time we said good-bye to 35 and hello to 33, the farms had started giving way to forests. There were lakes everywhere, as well as ponds, puddles, pools, and every other possible body of water. And it seemed as if we were sneaking up on wilderness, real wilderness, where you could imagine all kinds of animals peeking out from behind the trees. We also began to overtake quite a few cars with vacation appurtenances sticking out: dirt bikes, suitcases, boats, and so on.

We drove north on 33 until it turned into 53, and then we came upon (in the middle of nowhere) a series of old busses, crude cabins and other buildings back from the road and situated behind a split-rail fence and a swastika, hammer-and-sickle, and barbed-wire decorated opinion piece at highway's edge that said, among other things, IN VIOLATION OF FREEDOM OF SPEECH MINNESOTA HAS ORDERED THESE SIGNS EXPOSING CRIME AND CORRUPTION REMOVED—OR *ELSE*. MINNESOTA: I'LL GO TO JAIL—YOU GO TO HELL—I WILL NOT SURRENDER CONSTITUTIONAL RIGHTS OR BOW TO YOUR TYRANNY. But mostly we drove past trees, trees, and trees, in that order, until eventually we came upon mines, mines, and mines. These were strip mines, which amounted to many holes and their reverse, and then a giant complex of buildings with conveyor belts going hither and yon.

We peeked under the outskirts of Virginia and saw there only the usual— Toyota, Chevrolet, Thunderbird Mall—and a sign advertising sixteen pieces of Kentucky Fried Chicken for $149, which seemed expensive. There was a big jungle gym for electricity, several great heaps of rust-red dirt, and then we hung a right past another heap of red earth and through a birch forest until we came to a junction with 21, which we accepted.

So now we were going across a flat forest and a watery land with lots of rivers around. It looked as if a glacier had passed by recently and crushed and scrubbed things down a little, but there seemed to be a lot of wilderness left over. We saw a few buildings, a school bus stop, a cabin. But altogether not much. Let me put it this way: If you were a wild animal, you might choose this place to call home. But soon a sign along the road said, WELCOME TO EM-

BARRASS. After that a couple of cabins, a couple of cars. A small suburban-style house, a couple of trailers, a welding garage, and then a crossroads with a sign that said Embarrass Town Hall and Picnic Area.

We turned down that road and drove until we came to a small basketball court and playground, and then a big modern shed that turned out to be the Embarrass Town Hall. A sign suggested the Town Hall was having a rummage sale right then, so we drove around to the back.

The rummage sale was just ending as we pulled up, and a guy named Cliff, who was loading the remaining rummage into the back of his truck, told us we should go find someone named Roland Fowler. He gave directions: up the road, turn left, something something something crossroads something Roland Fowler. Tell him Cliff sent us.

I asked Cliff to draw a map, and with the help of the map we only got lost once before locating the Embarrass center, which wasn't exactly a center, but the map was a little vague about what to do next, so we wandered around for another half-hour before zeroing in on a house with a man coming out the back door towards his truck. That was Roland Fowler. Or, as he is less formally known, Charlie.

Charlie was the Supervisor of Labor for the Town of Embarrass. He had a weather-beaten face and big glasses with solid black frames. Practical glasses. He was a practical man, a working man with one finger wrapped in an almost clean white bandage and the other fingers wrapped with grease, which after we showed up he began wiping off. He wore thick-heeled working boots, practical work jeans, a blue plaid work shirt, untucked, and a dark blue work cap with a yellow embossed medallion on it that I couldn't read but probably said something about work-related technology. Charlie had a slow and careful way of talking, but he was one of those people you want to listen to thoroughly. He was seasoned. He was smart. And he knew a lot.

A lot of what he knew we didn't know at all, but when we first showed up he didn't know some of what we didn't, so there was some confusion as we sat around his round kitchen table and he began to talk about thermometers. "I have a digital thermometer, and my thermometer broke," he said. "When mine broke, I had fifty-three below. Although I had two outside. But the one outside, the mercury was set. Then, this here one, the fifty-three cut out the—"

I don't want to get too obscure here so I'll explain right away what we didn't know. Embarrass, it turns out, is famous in certain circles for being the coldest spot in Minnesota. And since Minnesota is the coldest state in the Milky Way, that makes Embarrass a very cold spot indeed. And Charlie, whose town duties included running the official weather monitoring station, where thermometers and other measuring devices were kept, had apparently thought we were drawn there by a reasonable urge to learn more about the unreasonable cold Embarrassites endure. So now he was explaining why they were unfairly scratched out of the *Guinness Book of Records* by a bitter local rival in the Cold Wars.

I didn't know a thing about any of this. Embarrass is *really* the coldest spot, we soon learned. It has an average yearly temperature of about thirty-four degrees, which is certainly the lowest average yearly in the state. And they have an extremely short growing season. They have had killer frosts recorded for every month of the year, but usually the last frosts happen around June 10th or the 12th, and then they start up again around the 20th of August. And that's why, Charlie went on, the Finnish farmers who settled this area around the turn of the century specialized in crops that grow under the ground. Potatoes is the big one. And anything that grows under the ground grows extremely well. But raspberries do well. You can raise corn and some strains of tomatoes, but you've got to be careful how you pick your seed. And as for that fateful coldest night of all, the official digital thermometer at the weather station got down to (as Charlie had earlier said) fifty-three degrees below zero Fahrenheit and then broke. Something happened. It quit at only fifty-three below. So a neighboring town (whose name will never appear in these pages) claimed to have the record then at fifty-four below, which is what *their* official thermometer said. Charlie, however, did the very intelligent thing of taking photographs of other thermometers in Embarrass, and these (unofficially unhappily) were going down to minus sixty degrees. Once he had the photographs, Charlie then sent the thermometers back to their maker to have them tested and their accuracy certified, which did happen. And so you know and I know and all of Embarrass knows that Embarrass won the Cold War. Cold is very important up there.

As for how Embarrass got its name, Embarrass the town was named after Embarrass the river, and Embarrass the river was named after *embarras* the word. *Embarras* the word is of French origin, and it means *Zis-damn-canoe-eez-stuck-in-a-damn-tight-spot-here-so-Pierre-you-want-some-zeeze-extra-beaver-pelts-eh?* The French are uncanny in their ability to compress a lot of information into a single word, but the point is that Embarrass the River at that place narrowed down to an embarrassing squeeze for the French voyageurs and trappers. In other words, an *embarras* is a narrows and a rapids, just as the word looks: with water rippling gently over the "m" before bursting explosively onto the "b" and breaking into dangerous standing waves across the double "r" and the final "s." But possibly because the French voyageurs and trappers were getting stuck in their canoes at Embarrass, today there are still a lot of wild animals left. A lot of deer come into Charlie's backyard, and they have a lot of bear around. And timber wolves. In fact, two years ago, at two o'clock in the afternoon, one of them got his dog. Well, the wolf came up and killed the dog. Ate it. He saw the tracks. It was in the winter. It was a cocker spaniel. But that's not uncommon either, like in one of the neighboring towns a couple of weeks ago someone took pictures of a wolf that killed a deer right at the edge of town. Well, a lot of folks come in to hunt deer, ducks, and partridges, but not timber wolves because they're an endangered species.

But anyway Embarrass is a pretty quiet community with about twelve hundred people where everybody knows everybody else. Charlie guessed he would know at least two-thirds of the people in the community by their first name, though a lot of people you don't see because the town tends to be very spread out. But it's a real, pretty close-knit community. And a progressive community. They're doing a lot of different things. They have a fair every year, the Embarrass Regional Fair, that will draw about fifteen thousand people for the weekend, and they have a log building in their fairgrounds that is one of the biggest log structures in the United States. And they didn't hire an architect or a contractor to build it, they just went ahead and built it themselves. It's a good community to live in, because there are a lot of neighbors. People work well together for the most part.

When Charlie first came there, Embarrass was predominantly mostly Finn. Finns started coming around 1892 when the Duluth and Iron Range Railroad put down a depot there, and at first the Finns worked in the mines, mostly, but they also took up logging, farming, and what have you. Now, of course as other folks moved in to work in the local strip mines, for example, then their children intermarried. So they do have a lot of folks in Embarrass now that, either the man or the wife are Finnish, but the other one could be German and Scandinavian or a lot of other different nationalities. But still and all Embarrass has probably the highest concentration of Finnish log buildings in the New World. And did we want to see their Finnish sauna?

The way he said "sauna"—not the amateur's flat *sawna* but the expertly curved *sa-ow-na*—meant that he meant business, so we said yes. Thus, we spent about the rest of the afternoon driving around in Charlie's truck and checking out some of the amazing Finnish log structures in Embarrass. I can see that we're rapidly approaching the narrows of this chapter, so I'll make my comments short. The Finns had been making log buildings for two thousand years in the Old Country, and they had it more or less figured out by the time they got to Embarrass. These people didn't just throw a heap of logs together in the manner of, say, Abe Lincoln's dad, who though certainly skilled in other respects was not exactly a professional when it came to log structures. In very cold places such as Finland and Embarrass, though, you can't afford to live in a crudely built log building because of all the holes through which all the weather will creep. So the Finns built very tight structures. They scribed and hewed the timbers to match snugly, grooved them inside the seams and stuffed the grooves with moss insulation, beautifully cornered their buildings with dovetails, teeth, saddles, tongues, cheeks, any number of nifty notch styles, and at last planed the whole edifice inside and out with a broadax.

Charlie took us around Embarrass to look at long barns, tall barns, short barns, skinny barns, sheds, outhouses, smoke houses, complete houses (sometimes with the logs hidden behind clapboard on the outside and plaster on the inside), not to mention the community sauna (preserved just as it was when the Finns sweated there), and (my favorite of all) the Finnish bachelor cabin.

The reason the bachelor cabin was my favorite, possibly, was that the Embarrass preservation people had carted the whole thing out of the woods from ten to twelve miles up the road to its present more accessible resting spot on the very second after the old bachelor had died and was carted away himself. In other words, this cabin seemed to be exactly as it had been when the old bachelor took his last breath, which happened in 1965 according to the calendar nailed to the wall. Not so long ago. And by exactly, I mean: towels still dirty, coffee can full of old letters still resting on a shelf above the wood burner stove, clothes still hanging on the wall, Bible still place-marked and resting beside the bed, lunch pail still ready for an insertion of lunch.

There used to be a lot of Finnish bachelors around, Charlie said, and they tended to live in this kind of little cabin out in the woods.

It was a ghostly kind of place, that little cabin.

Sleepy Eye

*S*lipping out of Minneapolis on a languid afternoon and needing a nodding, we set our somnolent sights on Sleepy Eye: going past lakes, swamps and ponds, and then across a high-grassed prairie spotted with farms and the occasional church spire. And, for some mysterious reason I suppose having to do with time, light, heat, and biology, as the day moved along I grew increasingly irritable and sensitive. Bayne had been sitting scrunched up with his bare feet on the dashboard for some time now, but suddenly I found it irritating.

194

"Feet down, feet down, feet down, OK? It's distracting for the driver."

I was the only irritable person in the car, however. Everyone else was either outright sleepy or actually asleep.

The land dipped and swelled, gently rolled, and the sky, so hot and brightly blue in the early part of the day, turned gray. Now we were tossed back into infinite corn field, and the land became flatter: fields with little oases of trees and farm buildings in the middle taking advantage of the shade. Then we dropped into prairie grassland, and a breeze ruffled the grass into gray with patches of green where the sun shone patchily into it, swaying and waving in the breeze with here and there a little stream meandering through.

And soon enough I had stopped being irritable and started really enjoying driving on that road: straight, level, with beautiful scenery and the prairie. Or at least what I could imagine was the prairie.

Prairie! The word has a special sad sound for me, because I used to hear my mother say it, and say it in what seems now an unconsciously plaintive way, as if a prairie were the most lonesome place on earth. Prairie! Which means to me wild forever grasslands.

My mother was born on the prairie of northern Montana to a Swedish immigrant father and a Swedish-Polish-Canadian mother. They homesteaded land near the Canadian border. Her father built the house, cut through the sod, and raised wheat and children. But her mother died during childbirth on an October day when my mother was three years and eleven months old. My mother remembered standing outside the door of the house, running around to peer into the windows, hearing the cries from inside, and the next day seeing blood on the bedding. And then her father had four little children to think about: Evelyn, May, my mother, and Nels. Since Pa was a better carpenter than farmer, he had to be away from home a lot — building — and he farmed out the girls over that first winter. Evelyn to one neighbor. May to another. My mother to the Frisks, a childless couple who lived on the homestead a mile away. And Nels, the little brother, was adopted by some people named Knutson but after a couple of years died.

So now there were only the three girls left. After that first winter, Evelyn and May came back home and were taken care of by housekeepers, but my mother stayed with the Frisks (she called them Aunty and Uncle), who were desperate to keep this child. My mother was desperate to be back home with her father and beloved sisters. Sometimes, she told me, she felt as though she were the forgotten one. The Frisks spoke Swedish not English in their house, so once she was left at their house — and she never returned to her father's house — my mother began speaking Swedish. She spoke it almost exclusively for the next three years, until she started going to school.

"I can still remember watching Pa drive away in the buckboard," my mother told me, recalling the moment she was first left at the Frisks. "I cried and cried. I had never been separated from my sisters or my mother before. Aunty said I just cried for the first two or three days."

Uncle Frisk worked very hard, but he was slow and methodical and remote. Aunty Frisk would sometimes ask him if he liked a meal she had cooked. "Oh, it will do," he would say, slowly.

So my mother grew up on the prairie without siblings or playmates, just Aunty and Uncle and a farmload of animals. Her only toys were made of nails and blocks of wood. She learned to milk a cow, ride a horse, shoot a rifle, throw a lasso, and bulldog a calf. In the morning, the roosters crowed, the calves bawled, the horses neighed, and as my mother milked the cows there was the swish swish swish of the milk into the pail, the chewing of the cows, and the mewing of all the cats hoping to steal some fresh milk. Sometimes my mother would squirt milk right into their mouths. Before she started school, in fact, my mother's best friends were cats. The Frisks had plenty, including two calico cats who were her favorites, and always a dog. Once she had a fight with the dog over a wad of gum that she had stuck on the door. The dog, in a gum frenzy I guess, bit her on the left eye.

In the summer, at night, the Milky Way would seem so near and clear, she told me, and in the winter she loved to watch the Northern Lights.

But she and the Frisks froze in the winter, boiled during the summer. They had wind storms that would just cross the prairie in a clean sweep, and then after all the homesteaders came and tilled so much of the land, the soil started to blow away. During the drought years, they had dust storms, and the day would be almost like night. Aunty and Uncle would stand on the back porch, look at the sky, and say, in Swedish, "If only it would rain!" Then my mother would get knots in her stomach, and maybe, she told me a few months before she died, that was the start of her stomach cancer. It seemed to her so very vital that they get rain. She would see the sky being all dark and heavy with clouds for a day. But a drop or two of rain would come and then no more. Of course, the crops were ruined. The seeds blew away. Then there were the years when the cutworms ate everything. There were other years when the grasshoppers flew in as a black cloud and ate everything green in sight. But my mother and the Frisks talked Swedish to each other and survived—with the creak of the windmill in their hearts and the lonesome print of the prairie on their souls.

So prairie, for me, is a place where you climb into the cupola of the barn on a buzzingly hot summer day, and you look out and see nothing and nothing and nothing but a sea of grass wavering out forever to the horizon.

After a few hours of driving west, we drove south. Just about everywhere now, we passed huge grain elevators, which came in several sizes and shapes. We drove until we came to a lake, houses and buildings and intersections, and the sign: SLEEPY EYE WELCOMES YOU.

Sleepy Eye was a comparatively big town, we discovered, with its own ring of residential neighborhoods and a double-spired Catholic Church that looked almost big enough to qualify as a cathedral. It had a huge old grain elevator in the middle — gray, cereal-box shaped, and advertising in black letters over white on the side: FARMERS ELEVATOR CO. SLEEPY EYE. There was a big factory of some sort and a very long freight train rumbling and clanking slowly through the middle of town. And along Main Street, the town suddenly looked like something out of a Western movie, with two- and three-story brick buildings fronted by high, squared façades. In fact, we saw two men with cowboy hats and cowboy boots walk across the street, and then we saw a sign indicating the Western Wear Corral, which explained where the men got their outfits. Other signs indicated a bank, a movie theater, and then the Birch Hotel, which seemed ratty and closed.

Another sign referred to the Sleepy Eye Chamber of Commerce, and we parked the car on Main Street and went looking for information at the Chamber. It was closed, as a matter of fact, but just outside the closed door we met a young woman with light-brown hair in a pageboy cut, who was standing there and smoking a cigarette. Her name was Connie Apton, if I got it right, and she said she worked selling radio ads out of the radio station office next door.

But she had keys to the chamber of the Chamber of Commerce and so let us in and gave us some information about Sleepy Eye and also about the two viable hotels in town. "Seven Gables. I'll get you a brochure, really nice," she said. "Um, there actually are two hotels. Where is the Seven Gables? Ha. I know they have a brochure. But I don't see it. Here it is. And this is it. It's very nice inside."

Connie likes Sleepy Eye, she said, but anyway if we wanted to know more about the place, she could take us around to the town Historical Society, which was located in back of the Chamber of Commerce and ought to be open until five o'clock, which was almost what time it was now, or maybe five-thirty.

The Sleepy Eye Historical Society and Museum was located in the old Sleepy Eye Railroad Depot, a handsome building made out of solid oak just about, nicely restored, with many glass cases full of Indian artifacts and historical exhibits as well as a resident historian named Sally Timm, a pleasant woman with roundish glasses and hair done in a coppery bob.

We were the only visitors in the museum, and so we had her full attention. "Ah, what do you want to know? Do you want to know about the town?"

Sleepy Eye is the English translation of the Dakota name Ish Tak Ha Ba, Ms. Timm said. And that name literally translated means "Old Sleepy Eye" or "Droopy Eyes." That was the name of a chief of a tribe of the Dakota nation, she said. And then she pointed out the portrait of Ish Tak Ha Ba hanging up on the wall. That picture was the actual Chief Sleepy Eye. It was a picture painted when the chief was down in Washington DC. It is actual. The picture is cloth. The picture looks like paper, but it's cloth.

"I see," I said. And I did see. I saw Chief Sleepy Eye wrapped in a robe with two eagle feathers in his hair and looking solemnly away to his right, at the same time seeming a little distracted—as if he didn't like being cheated, which was what he was being while his portrait was being painted. Yes, his eye was droopy in the picture.

The historian continued. Sleepy Eye was the chief of the Sisseton, which is one branch of the Sioux. Dakota are really Sioux. Actually, if I wanted to look in the book she had? And so I half read over her shoulder as she explained the Indian history, which, to be truthful, I'm not sure I entirely grasped. But the gist was that before the whites came and cheated the Indians out of their land the entire state of Minnesota was covered with settlements and communities of various names and complex alliances. During the middle of the nineteenth century, most of the Indians were pushed out, many were killed, and the descendants of the people who survived in Minnesota now belong to a nation forty thousand strong governed by seven tribes—including the Sisseton, which was Chief Sleepy Eye's group. And the name Sleepy Eye for the town came from the Sisseton chief, Chief Sleepy Eye. And what he had, there is a big long technical term for it, he had "sleepy eyes" or drooping eyes. When you close your eyes at night and one opens up and the other one doesn't. And you take your finger and you have to literally lift it. It was a muscular thing.

The only tribe left in the state of Minnesota now are the Mdewakantonwan—and here I made Sally Timm stop talking while I carefully wrote down in my notebook the correct spelling. Then she continued. And they are the actual ones that went on the war path. The rest of them were all peacemakers and they got—

"OK, so Chief Sleepy Eye was a Sisseton," I interrupted, trying to get things straight in my own mind.

He was an appointed chief, not a hereditary chief. He signed a couple of important treaties in 1851 that in essence gave up most of the remaining Indian land in Minnesota. Chief Sleepy Eye didn't like the terms of the treaties, Ms. Timm explained. And, we wouldn't either if we sold our land for 6¢ an acre. Ha! We wouldn't like it either. Sleepy Eye didn't think that that was enough money. And he thought they were getting cheated. So he walked out, but the next day he came back and he said, "I don't like it. But I have to go along with it because the handwriting is on the wall." It was either sign or get kicked off the land.

So the Indians were driven out. And then in 1872 the town was created. Sleepy Eye's Sisseton people, who liked to eat fish, used to camp beside the lake outside of town, and in 1872, the new town was named Sleepy Eye Lake. Then there was an Indian uprising. The Indians were starving because they were being cheated by an Indian agent, so they uprose and were massacred. After that, in a fit of anti-Indian sentiment, the people of Sleepy Eye Lake named the place Loreno. But after a year they realized what a dumb name that was, so they changed the town back to just plain Sleepy Eye.

And the reason Sleepy Eye became a town in the first place had to do with the railroad. Railroads were being strung across the state during the 1870s, and the St. Peter and Winona railroad was planning its tracks about then. But the railroad management was intending to run them a few miles outside Sleepy Eye Lake. However, a man named Thomas Allison had already come out to the Sleepy Eye Lake area during the 1860s and bought a lot of land, and when he learned about the St. Peter and Winona plans, he visited a lawyer for the railroad named Walter Brackenridge. The lawyer Brackenridge was persuaded to buy from the landowner Allison, for cheap, about 240 acres of land around Sleepy Eye Lake, and in turn St. Peter railroad was persuaded to run its pearly tracks out to Sleepy Eye. That was that. And so (I was thinking here) the name Thomas Allison literally translated into plain English means "Slimy Real Estate Conniver," while the name Walter Brackenridge, also literally translated, turns out to mean "Crooked Greedy Bastard."

There used to be a Sleepy Eye–brand flour, Sally Timm continued, which was one of the big businesses in town but isn't any more. Currently, the principal business in town is the manufacture of calendars and church bulletins. And then, of course, there is the California Packing Corporation, which cans peas and corn. Right now, in fact, we could go out and just look at the canning factory on the west end of town. And that factory keeps going like there's no tomorrow. And that's the way it is every Monday night for several weeks. They run into September, sometimes even into October. We go in the store, and we buy a can of corn. We get the Del Monte brand, and Sleepy Eye is where it comes from.

And there's farming all around. It is a big farming area. There's grain elevators all over the place. There's one right across the way over there. And then out on the west end of town there's several. Corn and peas are probably the main crops. Soybeans. Not very much wheat, though. You need a big big area for wheat. Sally would call Sleepy Eye the beginning of the prairie. And lots of times when they have grain that's being harvested out in South Dakota the trains will run almost steady through town on their way east. There's a lot of mills up in Minneapolis and St. Paul. Usually right around the fourth of July is the time for the grain harvest. For the peas and the corn: The peas usually run in June, and then the corn starts as soon as pea pack is done and runs almost until October. A lot of Spanish people come up that work in the factory in Sleepy Eye, and, basically, it's small-town America.

"Well, it looks like a great place," I said.

"It is. It's a good place to raise children. *They* may not think so," Sally Timm said, referring with a quick nod to the Research Staff.

"Yeah, well, one problem, I suppose, is when they get older, they want to —"

"They want to spread their wings. Yeah, and you can't blame them. They have to learn. They have to fly."

The last comment seemed particularly pointed to me just then, since the Research Assistants for the last twenty minutes had been randomly wandering through the museum and acting increasingly as if they wanted to stretch their wings and fly that instant.

We bought some souvenirs from the museum shop — a spike from the old St. Peter railroad and a refrigerator magnet portrait of Chief Ish Tak Ha Ba — thanked Sally Timm for her help, and then drove out to the lake. There was a small park beside the lake, where a dozen overweight guys with tractor hats were drinking beer and talking in loud voices. The sun was setting and lighting up the haze there, and the lake took on a wrinkly silvery quality like wrinkled aluminum foil. Here is how we spent the evening: throwing stones into the lake. Then, after the sun set, we went back into Sleepy Eye and got some sleepy eye ourselves at the Seven Gables Motel.

Winner

Tooling out of Sleepy Eye the next morning we passed an old steam locomotive and then we drove until we just popped right into South Dakota. A sign said WELCOME TO SOUTH DAKOTA. I knew we were in the Wild West now because a million signs told me so: Happy Chief, Ghost Town, World Famous Cowboy Town, Cowboy Breakfast, Cowboy Coffee Shop, Gas Fun Food, Cupids Curios Fireworks Exit Now.

200

Some cattle were grazing along the highway, too, and we exited and grazed the edge of the tourist trap called Buffalo Ridge. After a bit of wandering around, getting lost and exploring a few country roads, we met a three-colored cat named Patches, who spent a lot of time rolling on the ground in front of a barn owned by Adrian E. Dalen, a grandfatherly man with a kind smile. Since it was then starting to get dark and a storm was brewing, Mr. Dalen advised us to look for hotel accommodations. He recommended Mitchell, a city west on Interstate 90 about an hour, where incidentally we could see something called The Corn Palace.

"That's all decorated with field corn," he explained.

"Corn Palace. OK."

"You should maybe go out and see that, anyway."

"All right."

"I recommend that."

"All right."

"You come to a sign up there, and you go to the right. But the Corn Palace, every year they've had big Corn Palace Days out there. They used to have Lawrence Welk out there quite often, and Jack Benny. You name the big shot."

Back on Interstate 90, we pointed our three selves west once more — and began to notice the sky, which was getting agitated by the approaching storm and had become a swirling, manic mass of mythological beasts. And now there was no longer any doubt: We were prairie pioneers rolling along the long and rolling trail in our little Conestoga wagon clattering due west at about sixty-five miles an hour. "Yar! Yar! Yar! Whip! Whip! Whip!" I said, as I rallied the oxen and whipped them into shape. And the little Conestoga wagon was in turn being whipped by all those important informational markers along the road:

CORN PALACE DEAD AHEAD
WALL DRUG ONLY 603 MORE MILES
THE WORLD'S BIGGEST AND ONLY
PALACE MADE OF CORN
GOOD MORNING, AMERICA! WALL DRUG
WALL DRUG ONLY 590 MORE MILES
WHERE THE HECK IS WALL DRUG?
WALL DRUG ONLY 582 MORE MILES.

But a mother storm was coming our way, and I just wanted to tuck our wagon into the arms of Mitchell. Nihilistic winds were sweeping in, as we could see from looking at the patches of tall grass alongside the road, frantic now with the blowing. I could even feel the winds pressing formidably against the noble brows of our noble oxen, who shuddered in response. Just in time we made it to Mitchell, pulled into a busy sprawl of motels and restaurants, and checked in at the Thunderbird Motel.

After breakfast the next morning, we followed a million signs to the Corn Palace, built in 1892 by an eccentric entrepreneur who had beaucoup extra corn cobs on hand and not much else to do except string them all together. We parked our wagon, went into the Corn Palace, and returned to our wagon again in thirty-seven minutes, which I thought was pretty good time. Then we turned the team back onto the main trail west, Interstate 90, and just enjoyed the bleak and grand vistas, the great sweeping sky and endless horizon, and a trail marked well enough that even the most distracted pioneer couldn't go astray:

WALL DRUG AIR-CONDITIONED BATHROOMS
WALL DRUG THE WORLD'S BIGGEST DRUGSTORE
WALL DRUG ONLY 534 MILES DEAD AHEAD
WALL DRUG ONLY 523 MILES DEAD AHEAD.

Once in a while a magnificent vista would open up between the signs, so that we could see for ourselves the real Wild West, with gulches and gullies and bumpy grasslands dotted with a few green trees, a rolling land mostly brown, sometimes barren and sometimes covered with the stubble of olive and pale yellow grass.

Our plan had been to drive due west on Interstate 90 all the way to some interesting-looking dots at the far end of the state, but I was getting SO FED UP with all those SIGNS for WALL DRUG blocking the view that when I saw another sign pointing AWAY from Interstate 90 to something called WINNER, I peeled off at the EXIT.

We stopped in a gas station parking lot for a lot of discussion at this point because one of the Research Assistants thought Winner would be a loser. She figured Winner was not a story at all, merely pop-button boosterism, but I didn't even care. I just wanted to stop reading about WALL DRUG, and so we took a vote. With Bayne abstaining, the contest turned into a tie — and ties are always won by the most adamant (me) or the driver (also me), and so we turned the team south and dropped down a two-lane Route 47, winding our winsome way to Winner.

It was a good decision. The idiotic litter and semiotic junk quickly disappeared, and now I could see how grand and beautiful South Dakota really is, or ought to be. There were rich grasslands, farmlands, herds of domino cattle grazing on tops of hills and down into gulches, and a lot of the land seemed completely open, with no fences. We came to a slow moving, curving river, and a valley with a flat ochre and green surface below, dotted with cattle. And then everything became really spread out and scarce, with no houses, no farms, no signs of farm houses, no signs of human enterprise other than a few farmers' fields and some baled hay, and no signs of signs either.

The road forked. We took 49 down and then turned right onto 44, passing fields of corn and great combed fields of golden wheat. There was a sign for IDEAL 12 MILES, which was tempting, but not enough, and we kept ourselves straight and narrow all the way into the leading edge of Winner.

We soon found Winner's Main Street, a little tatty with some businesses boarded up but reassuringly old-fashioned and lined with the kind of enterprise I always root for: the Pheasant Bar and Lounge, Ben Franklin Five-and-Dime, the Peacock Bar, the Elks, the Pix Cinema (closed), the Ritz Cinema (closed), J. C. Penney, the Sewing Bee, and so on. Main Street was about three or four blocks long, and it ran uphill if you drove in one direction and downhill if you drove in the other.

If you stood at the low end of Main and looked uphill, you saw at the end a small grassy hill with grasshoppers in the grass and a water tower on top. Not far from the water tower was the town swimming pool, a baseball diamond, and a playground. If you stood at the high end of Main and looked downhill, you saw at the far end a freight train, a high gray grain elevator, and then a receding vision of rolling grassland and farmland. Men in farmers' overalls and straw hats walked along Main Street, both up and down, and there was a promising café right in the middle called Sergeant's, with a neon arrow that went up and down and around and pointed to the door of the building.

We parked the car and followed the arrow through that door into an interior decorated with plastic flowers and a huge doll collection. It was lunch time. The place was very busy. About five waitresses dressed in blue were working hard and looking frazzled. We sat in a booth, ordered some pie and ice cream, and I asked our waitress where the name of the town came from. She shrugged. But she asked another waitress and soon got into a complete confabulation with all four other waitresses, one of whom eventually was elected to come over and talk to us. Her name was Sandra Schmidt, and she was only able to speak between a frantic sort of waitressing activity. She said today was her birthday, and so I think she was not only frazzled but eager to get off her shift and home to celebrate, but she did tell us what she knew.

"Well, I don't know just exactly," she said. "This is all I know: There was a place at Lamro, which is off of Winner. And the railway was coming, and they had a fight to see who got the railroad, and Winner's the one that got it. So they called it Winner. That's all I know," she said, and then she ran off to take an order and deliver some big piles of food on plates. Then she came back again, and I asked her, "What was it called before it was Winner, then?"

"This I don't have any idea," she said, and took off again. When she sailed past four minutes later, having just hauled a record-breaking tray of dishes, I said, "Would you know about when this happened?"

"Not exactly. This is, as I said, this is all I know," she said, and then, "Let me speak to my mother." She wiped her hands on her apron and picked up a telephone near the doors to the restaurant kitchen, not so far away that I couldn't hear her side of the conversation: "Mom, there's a guy here that wants to know how Winner got their name. Do you know about what time, when Winner won the battle for the railroad? This phone is terrible. Nineteen three? Between nineteen three and nineteen five?"

That was all she knew, and I wasn't sure I quite understood the logic of it all. The waitresses had another confab on our behalf and finally one of them suggested we go down to past the bottom of Main Street and locate Walter Schramm of Schramm's Furniture. He would tell us the full story.

Schramm's Furniture was a barnlike building full of recliners and beds and chairs and couches. The lady at the desk in the middle of all that furniture said Mr. Schramm had a golf tournament and wouldn't be back until 3:15 to 3:30, so we left and drove around town. Unfortunately, when we returned to Schramm Furniture at 3:10, Mr. Schramm had come and gone, and now, the lady explained, he was outside of town along Route 18 fixing his sign. We might drive out there and find him.

We passed an automobile graveyard and then were out of town. Just a short while later we spied the Schramm sign, a van and a pickup parked on the grass beside the sign, and Walter Schramm supervising a couple of workers. The sign was a large wooden billboard. A section had fallen off so the men were nailing it back, and Mr. Schramm was making sure they got it right. One man had climbed to the very top and was dangling down and nailing, while the second man had positioned himself on a stepladder at the bottom, and was dangling up and nailing. The sign said

SCHRAMM
FURNITURE
INC.
HWY 18   WINNER.

Walt Schramm was big, friendly, and positive. He was wearing golf clothes that included dark blue pants and a red, white, and blue shirt with a label on it that said Billy Wallace Memorial Golf Tournament. He had white hair and glasses, and he wore black loafers and white socks on his feet.

"The town originally began," he began—and then he stopped and began over again. "Lamro was the town out here in the country, about five miles. And when the railroad was going to come through the north, it was coming from Omaha out this way, and it was going to come to an area. But they picked their track where they wanted to go. So the question was, where should the town be? So they had a big election and a big fight, much argument and stuff. And when they decided to move the town over to here from Lamro, they decided to call it Winner. Because they won the election. The people who wanted to move were winners. And that's why they called it Winner."

"So it was the town of Lamro, and they actually moved the town, did they?"

Everybody moved out, he said. There was a bank in old Lamro, and they had to seal up all the accounts and money and move them. Everything else was moved. People just moved to Winner, and they moved all the buildings on Main Street and everywhere else, and the entire town of Lamro.

Now to get to old Lamro, he continued, we would have to go about two miles south then out through the crick. He didn't know. People live on this side of the crick, Dog Ear Crick it's called. The town of Lamro was actually on the other side of the crick. He'd been there. They had picnics out there, years ago when he was a kid, many years ago. So it's a real ghost town, basically. There's nothing there except a cement structure, the old bank vault, where they had their money. But that town was called, he thought initially it came from a people's name Lamoreaux, who were part Indian. But the town was Lamro. And then this election, the people all got involved in shall-we-move-over-to-get-on-the-railroad? And the faction that were trying to move it said, "What shall we name the town?" They called it Winner. And the date, if he were to tell me 1909, that's when he thought. That's how Winner got its name.

Walt Schramm told us all this as we stood in the field beneath the Schramm Furniture sign, but after a while we decided to go back to the furniture store to talk some more. Meanwhile, the Research Assistants had talked their way into riding in the back of his pick-up, which was a great treat for them, and I followed along behind, inappropriately anxious that they might fall out the back and I would have to pick up the pieces.

Back at the furniture store, Mr. Schramm generously gave us all some soft drinks, located the very best couch in the entire store, and he and I sat down with our drinks and talked a good deal more.

He was born just outside of Winner in 1916, he said, and at the time maybe there was one doctor in the town, but it was normal practice to be delivered by what they called a midwife. He was one of eleven children, he said, eight boys and three girls, who were all born and raised on a farm and went through what might be called tough times, but they always had enough to eat. They had hand-me-down clothes from friends and neighbors but survived — and, finally, maybe it was a good thing. They turned out to be, well, generally, good people. They didn't get in a lot of trouble, didn't break the law too much, and stuff like that. But, he continued, they lived through what they called the Dirty Thirties. Had what they called the dust storms when the ground was so dry the wind blew, and actually, some days, it was like a snow storm. You couldn't see the road if you had been out in the road. They had grasshopper days when grasshoppers came in and ate the corn right off the stalks. They just got the juice out of it and ruined all the crops. There were days when the grasshoppers were flying that actually they would blot out the sun. You could see the sun was shining, but it wasn't bright because of grasshoppers. It really was quite the thing. Then it seemed like things improved as time went on. More recently, they've had good rains to make crops grow, and so on. And prosperous people raise a lot of livestock, lots of wheat, corn, some barley and oats, but now sunflowers and soybeans are moving into the area.

He spent, Walt Schramm continued, almost five years in the Marine Corps as a pilot during World War II. Other than that, he's been in Winner, South Dakota all those years, just about from the time it originated — and he's been in the furniture business for fifty years. Him personally, he said, people think he's kind of goofy. He's still working six days a week. But it's not really working. He's enjoying it. He comes down to work every morning at eight, and he leaves at six. Except when his wife gives him heck for not being home. Then he goes home. And he just likes it. He'll be seventy-nine years old in September. Well, he just kind of enjoys what he's doing. And a couple of years ago he broke his hip, fell on the ice. Last year he had a stroke in the arm. They got everything working perfect except the hand. Two fingers are not perfect. But everything else is all right. So he plays golf.

Mr. Walter Schramm, to summarize, was your average American hero, a man who endured hardship and triumphed, a positive thinker and a force for progress, a good citizen and a community booster: a winner in a town that he believed was a winner, too. He said he expected that Winner would remain a first-class town for a long time. It is a good business town, he said, a good climate for business. Not exactly trouble free, but they have very little in the way of murders and that type of thing. Occasionally somebody kind of gets out of line. But Winner is a pretty good place to raise children and a good place to live.

Endeavoring to inject an ounce of outsider's skepticism, I said, "The downtown area on Main Street looks like there are a lot a closed businesses. Is the town economically depressed?"

"At the moment," he said, shifting his weight and leaning way back in the couch, cradling the back of his head with netted fingers, "we have people who are saying, 'Winner is a dying town.' Um, altogether wrong. We have empty buildings, but we have one two three four grocery stores operating and doing good business. We have a men's clothing store. The town of Winner is only less than four thousand people. The next town as big as Winner," he continued, "is more than a hundred miles away." So they have a hundred-mile trade area that they can take care of and sell to. They have a good hospital with — the one clinic has one two three four doctors and two surgeons. And now they're just building a new middle school and grade school. Moving the football field. So Winner is not a losing proposition at all.

I pressed my point further: "But all those empty buildings on Main Street: Is it the case that businesses are drawing away from Main Street, and you're losing Main Street?"

Ah, Schramm Furniture used to be up on Main Street, he said. The main reason they came down here to Highway 18 is because the large lot was available, and there weren't any large lots of Main Street. Anyhow, Walt continued, Winner is just a good town. And how about us? Walt Schramm wanted to know. He supposed we had been through a lot of towns with strange names. "What about Wall? Are you going to go to Wall? Wall is a famous town."

Wall! The very place I had decided to avoid at all costs. I thought it might even be rude to say how much I had come to dislike the call of Wall, and so I politely neutered my response. I shrugged and said, "I just figured it was somebody's name."

He didn't know where the name came from, he said, but Wall: Wall Drug. And he didn't know why it's Wall. But it would be a place we'd enjoy seeing. It's not only a drugstore, it also has cowboy music playing, and they have imitation horses that buck and all kinds of stuff. And it's on the Interstate. If we went west to Wounded Knee, he was sure there was a road across to Wall's, about fifty miles east of Rapid City. And he couldn't think of anybody else along the road that would have a name that would be unusual. There was Mission. That was an Indian, more or less, Indian town. And there was Rosebud out west of here. Rosebud had probably a finer hospital than we had in Massachusetts. In any event, that was kind of off the subject. But he was thinking of towns: Hot Springs. They have a swimming pool there, building enclosed. And the water is almost hot. And we could go in there and swim in that hot water and all kinds of stuff. He assumed the place was named Hot Springs because it had hot springs. Now, Hot Springs was two hundred miles west. Then we could go to Rapid City. But if we did that we'd miss Wall, because Wall is back east of there.

Wounded Knee

*S*o that was Winner, and we rolled out of town on a late Saturday afternoon headed west with that simple and satisfying story on our minds.

The full story of Winner, which I later learned from some historical articles Mr. Schramm sent me in the mail, is slightly more complicated. The full story goes like this. After a million acres of land were opened up for white settlement in Tripp County, South Dakota, the battle to shape the wealth of that land began. Lamro, incorporated in 1907, was the first white town in the county, and, with plenty of good water, water power, and a central location, by 1908 it was the locale to be reckoned with. During the county's first contest for temporary county seat, in 1909, Lamro competed with only one other town, Colome. Lamro, almost twice as large, won the contest easily.

But the election for permanent county seat was to take place almost a year and a half later, and the winning town would probably become the dominating commercial center of the full region. The competition over votes turned bitter, involving claims and counter-claims, accusations and counter-accusations, and so on.

The wild card was the railroad. Chicago and Northwestern, slated to survey a route into that part of South Dakota any day, was rumored to be headed for either Lamro or Colome. But the railroad had its own town-building company, the Western Townsite Company, and its own plan. The railroad in cahoots with Western Townsite jumped into the middle of the battle between Lamro and Colome during the summer of 1909, and they made themselves winners by the simple act of buying land and defining a town, and then laying tracks onto their own land and into their own town, which they preemptively named Winner. The railroad's Western Townsite Company began selling lots in Winner by December of 1909, and by the election of November 8, 1910, Winner, already an established commercial center, won the grand prize: permanent county seat for Tripp County.

On the night of November 8, several citizens of Winner, knowing they had won, harnessed up their horses and wagons and raided the county courthouse in Lamro, seizing, after pitched battles with Lamro citizens, all the county record books and hauling them back to Winner. The courthouse itself was next: towed by a steam engine and seventy-two horses all the way across the snow to its new home (only to burn down mysteriously on January 15, 1911). By the summer of 1911, the jig was up. The Lamro post office had closed and virtually the entire town could be seen moving two and a half miles across the prairie. Buildings were simply jacked up onto rollers and skids, hitched to horses and huge steam engines, and dragged like war booty over the grass to Winner.

That's the full or at least the fuller story of Winner.

But where did all the people come from? Lamro didn't exist as a town in 1906 nor, I think, did Colome. Winner was a barren stretch of land in 1908. Those early settlements, rough, chaotic, close to lawless, just appeared. Quite as the white settlers who made them just appeared in Tripp County during those years.

What happened was much the same everywhere on this continent. Old Americans were there first, people of a hundred cultures and three hundred languages who, having crossed the Bering Strait ten to twenty thousand years earlier, spread out and occupied the twinned continents from tip to tip, north to south. Some of them organized civilizations and empires, some lived in settled villages, and some roamed as nomads following their food, but they never tried to possess land in the way the New Americans did. And when the New Americans arrived, numerous and hungry for land, they bought it. When buying didn't work, they tricked and cheated to get it. And when tricking and cheating didn't work, they simply drove the Old Americans off the land, away from an earth and sky they had known since forever. As Black Elk, a holy man of the Oglala Sioux, once said of the newcomers:

> *I had never seen a Wasichu . . . and did not know what one looked like; but every one was saying that the Wasichus were coming and that they were going to take our country and rub us all out and that we should all have to die fighting.*

Out of Winner and rolling west now on Route 18, we traveled in and out of prairie and grazing land, past some small, depleted groves of trees, a tavern or liquor store that seemed abandoned, a few houses and a couple of haystacks, then the rolling prairie grassland again. Sometimes the road snaked through, and sometimes it shot straight ahead. In places, it just about fell apart: suddenly turned bumpy and stripey, like an great big old rubber band that has been stretched and then snapped back too many times. We passed some new farms and some farm land seeming freshly plowed, rich and clean, with a half-dozen horses waving their tails in the late-day sunlight, looking vacantly happy and stepping into a little pool of silvered water.

> *Once we were happy in our own country and we were seldom hungry, for then the two-leggeds and the four-leggeds lived together like relatives, and*

*there was plenty for them and for us. But the Wasichus came, and they have
made little islands for us and other little islands for the four-leggeds, and
always these islands are becoming smaller, for around them surges the
gnawing flood of the Wasichu.*

Soon we entered the Rosebud Indian Reservation, and most of the few
buildings we passed now looked very simple. The fewer businesses looked
even simpler: a farm supply place with a windmill behind it and an old, un-
painted shed behind that, and the B & B Guide Service in a shanty. The town
of Mission included, not surprisingly, an old mission, and it seemed like a decent spot, but very poor and a little shabby. Pretty soon Route 18 took us out
the other end of Rosebud Reservation, and we stayed overnight at a place
called, if I remember rightly, the Maverick Hotel in the small town of Martin. Sunday morning we got up early, breakfasted, and kept on moving west
along 18.

The cartographicus said we were headed toward the Wounded Knee Massacre National Historical Site, but unlike any national monument or park
or site we had visited previously, this one was not marked by an alleyway of
signs and arrows and bright enticements promising trinkets and tourist junk.
In fact, it was hardly marked at all, and the road just rolled on quietly ahead,
narrowing ahead, in my vision, down to nothing, turning quietly past a hillside
of brown-and-white horses all looking in different directions with beside them
a herd of black cows all looking in the same direction.

The road took us past a couple of tiny settlements and then onto the Pine
Ridge Reservation where, after a few miles, we located an intersection and a
simple sign showing the way to Wounded Knee. We turned onto that road.
Soon we came to a roadside pullover, and we pulled over to read a green-
painted bullet-holed sheet metal sign that had been erected (so the words said)
by Oglala-Lakota Parks and Recreation to honor Chief Crazy Horse, who
never signed a peace treaty. He represented the fighting Sioux from 1870 to
1877, and he never was photographed.

*He was a small man among the Lakotas and he was slender and had a
thin face and his eyes looked through things and he always seemed to be
thinking hard about something. He never wanted to have many things for
himself, and he did not have many ponies like a chief. They say that when
game was scarce and the people were hungry, he would not eat at all. He
was a queer man. Maybe he was always part way into that world of his vision. He was a very great man, and I think if the Wasichus had not murdered him down there, maybe we should still have the Black Hills and
be happy.*

We kept going: on a gravely road that wound through grassland and some stubbly patches of already harvested wheat, through treeless hills and past the occasional bullet-holed road sign. I ought to mention here that none of us was feeling so good that Sunday morning. Bayne was sick to his stomach. I had a headache. And Britt was feeling bad, too, I think. And so after I commented that I thought the bullet holes in the signs might be the South Dakota equivalent of East Coast urban graffiti, Britt and I got into an unhappy argument over whether or not graffiti was art, and that turned into an unpleasant debate about whether or not Andy Warhol was a miserable, talentless con man or an artist with vision, with each of us defending the most predictable position.

We moved through a land of bleached and rippling grass on the hills and dark lines of trees in the valleys until finally the road turned into a lonely place, a little community of a few dozen small, bungalow-style houses, clearly government-built and all on the same simple plan: little boxes with peaked roofs. There was also a concrete fortress-style building that said on the side: UNITED STATES POST OFFICE, WOUNDED KNEE, SOUTH DAKOTA 57794.

Away from the village, on top of a small, grassy hill and over to one side now, we could see a simple log cabin with a cross on top, which I later learned was the Sacred Heart Catholic Church of Wounded Knee, and a short distance behind that building, across a short stretch of grass, was a second building, smaller and white with a peaked roof and no cross on top, which I later heard was an earlier version of the church. In front of both buildings were old, grassed-over and fenced-in graveyards; and the graveyard in front of the log church, the Sacred Heart, looked newer and included several simple stone and wooden markers and in the middle of those a larger stone monument. Many colored flags or rags had been tied haphazardly to the fence around these graves, and a strong wind made them whip and tremble.

In a little while we had come to the top of the ridge where, looking to the east, you can see for the first time the monument and the burying ground on the little hill where the church is. That is where the terrible thing started.

But we were looking at the two small churches and graveyards on the grassy hill from a distance and so couldn't see so much; and the road drew us into and out of the small village of tiny box houses before we knew it. We turned around, and the road curled and settled us down into a withered valley and a crooked creek down below the Sacred Heart Catholic Church, down into a hot, dusty little circle. In the middle of the circle stood a big green sheet-metal sign that said at the top MASSACRE OF WOUNDED KNEE and had a long historical explanation beneath that I found hard to concentrate on.

This sign also had lots of old bullet holes in it, but the bullet holes had been filled up with nuts and bolts and painted over. Curiously, the entire word MASSACRE had been patched on with a rectangular piece of sheet metal — and I thought perhaps someone must have just blasted out the original version of that word with bullets.

We followed down along the dry gulch, and what we saw was terrible. Dead and wounded women and children and little babies were scattered all along there where they had been trying to run away. . . . Sometimes they were in heaps because they had huddled together, and some were scattered all along. Sometimes bunches of them had been killed and torn to pieces where the wagon guns hit them. I saw a little baby trying to suck its mother, but she was bloody and dead.

About ten or fifteen yards away from the sign, at the first rise of the small hill where the log-cabin chapel was situated, we saw a small post-and-thatch pavilion having a purpose I couldn't guess. It was empty, and then, when I next noticed, it wasn't. A man was standing there in the shade of the pavilion and hanging up things for sale. You know: Indian art and jewelry and other things to sell to tourists.

He was big, broad-faced, and dignified. Maybe about thirty-five years old. He wore aviator-style shades over his eyes and a black Stetson hat on his head, and down from the hat, down across a bare, scarred chest, all the way down to his waist, his black hair hung in two braids. His name was Anthony Tail, he said, and he wanted to know if I was interested in buying anything.

We talked. He said he was born at Wounded Knee and had lived there all his life. There was blood on the ground right about where we were standing and talking, and there were bodies in the ground, under the grass. The wind moved across the grass there, and maybe it was whispering, so I can't say I chattered lightly with Anthony Tail. But I still tried to ask him some things about the community of Wounded Knee — the church, those few dozen houses, and the one post office over there — and about the name Wounded Knee, which, as I quickly learned, was first the name of a creek there, the Wounded Knee Creek. Anthony had no idea where the name of the creek came from. But the settlement of Wounded Knee had once been called Brenan.

"I think in the beginning it was Brenan. It started out to be Brenan. Yeah. Named after a whatdyacall, Colonel, or something like that."

"But Brenan was a community?"

"Somewhere along the line the name got changed, and if you check that massacre sign it says 'Massacre of Wounded Knee.'"

"When the massacre happened, there were people living around here, in the community? And they came over right after it happened or. . . ."

"During."

"And how do we know that?"

"It was word of mouth, our elders telling us what happened. And there used to be the store over there," he added, pointing vaguely in the direction of the settlement. "And it was called a trading post. Ah, gee. I don't quite recollect when that was put up. But it was put up. And I think the only building that is left from the real old times is that church up there over on the other side, the old white one. That was put up right before Wounded Knee, maybe. And, yeah, I think that is the only building left from way back then."

We talked about several other things, too, and he told me to find a book written by somebody — he couldn't quite remember the exact title — that shows and tells what really happened there, from the viewpoint of the Sioux people. The book is not in print any more so it's kind of hard to find, he said, but there are people who have it. And throughout the world, people know about Wounded Knee, he said. Throughout the world it's known. We talked some more, and I learned that about 540 people live in the community of Wounded Knee now, and one major source of income is leasing out land to farmers.

I said, "I thought I saw some farming when we came — and you're leasing that out?"

"Yeah, different people."

"And then it goes in a community fund."

"No, it don't. No, that's personal. Right. Landowners lease the land out."

As for the future, Anthony would like to see jobs created for the younger generation, so they won't have to go through what his generation has gone through.

I changed the subject: "What's it like living here?"

"Peaceful," he said.

"Beautiful land," I commented.

"Yeah."

"It *is* peaceful."

"And, more or less, I think, that's the way we want to keep it."

"Yeah. Is there any — do you do any hunting around here?"

"A lot of people do hunting."

"For food, or . . ."

"For food. It keeps food on the table."

After talking to Anthony Tail for ten or fifteen minutes, Britt and Bayne and I walked up the hill, along a trail of dust and big fat green grasshoppers that kept popping up all around us, up the hill to the new church, the one made out of logs and called the Sacred Heart Catholic Church. In front of this church was the fenced-in gravesite, with many small stones and crosses and the central stone marker. Right about when we got up there, a priest drove up to the log church on a dirt road from another direction, and he unlocked a door and went inside and started saying Mass, I think. I didn't get the sense that anyone was there inside the church to participate in the Mass, but it was good that he opened the church because Bayne was really quite sick and had to use the bathroom.

From the log church we walked back to the old church behind it, a short distance through a sea of grass and a sea of grasshoppers popping up and out of the way as we walked, past a very old graveyard, fenced off with a few old stones and completely choked out with weeds. The names on the stones were mostly unreadable. The old church, which looked like an old house with an ordinary peaked roof and regular windows and door on one side, was not boarded up. It was just open. The door was gone. The windows were gone, and the little church was completely open, with broken glass on the floor and a couple of church pews cast randomly around.

We went back to the new church. Bayne used the bathroom once again. And then we walked over to the graveyard in front of it, the one with the colored rags tied around on the fence, and spent some time there. The graveyard was about the saddest thing I have ever seen.

It was a good winter day when all this happened. The sun was shining. But after the soldiers marched away from their dirty work, a heavy snow began to fall. The wind came up in the night. There was a big blizzard, and it grew very cold. The snow drifted deep in the crooked gulch, and it was one long grave of butchered women and children and babies, who had never done any harm and were only trying to get away.

I looked up and saw that the clouds above us had slid apart and taken on a rippled quality, like sand in the bottom of a stream bed. I looked in the distance and saw nothing but treeless hills and ridges and ripples of land, then a few pockets of trees and a few galleries of trees in the valleys. The grass on the hills around us looked like the fur of an animal, yellow fur. And after I had looked over the grassy hills, I read the names written on the stones. I stood with my two children there in the hot sun and the strong wind, and the three of us read the names written on the stones. Those were the names of the half-starved and unarmed warriors who, having abjectly surrendered and gathered with two or three hundred women and children in misery down there in the crooked gulch, were murdered by U.S. soldiers standing on the surrounding hilltops and firing two-pound explosive shells out of Hotchkiss machine guns at the rate of fifty rounds per minute. The names of the dead went on and on.

I did not know then how much was ended. When I look back now from this high hill of my old age, I can still see the butchered women and children lying heaped and scattered all along the crooked gulch as plain as when I saw them with eyes still young. And I can see that something else died there in the bloody mud, and was buried in the blizzard. A people's dream died there. It was a beautiful dream.

Then we walked back down the hill to find Anthony Tail still there in the shade of the pavilion, and he was still offering art and cultural products for sale. What I finally bought from him was something he called a "dream-catcher." It was made of a bare willow branch warped and tied into a circle, with a net inside woven in something of a spider-web style and focused into a hole at the center. Tied to the edge of this central hole was a nice white feather. Maybe it was a chicken feather, but let's just imagine it was an eagle feather. Later in our trip, I was to see dream-catchers mass produced and made into trinkets and good luck charms and tie clips and earrings, sold at truck stops and pharmacies and gas stations. They were everywhere, just about, all the way to California, but this one was special—and, since none of us had seen much less heard of them before we got to Wounded Knee, Anthony Tail explained the concept.

A dream catcher is a magical device that you put in a good place, he said, maybe over your bed, for example, or at the window near your bed. Then when you dream at night, your dreams rise up like a mist or a cloud. The good dreams will be caught by the magic of your dream catcher. The bad ones will simply drift right on through and away.

Recluse

Almost immediately after we passed into Wyoming the next morning, so it seemed to me, the landscape became more dramatic and Western. The soil turned a pink or salmon color, exposed brightly where its grassy surface was broken by great lifts and gashes. We made a brief detour to see Devil's Tower, which was nice but not the kind of thing a sane person would climb on. Then we dropped south, crawled west, and started climbing north on a two-laner called 14 and 16. Gillette was the only actual city in those parts, and it seemed hungry for coal, which kept pouring into the town inside endless freight trains with identical cars. There was a suburban housing development at the edge of Gillette, but as soon as we had gotten just a few miles north, suburbia was replaced by cloud shadows, sage, grass, and then clumped red rocks and a few red-rocked buttes.

Part of the original Storyville agreement held that we wouldn't bore ourselves silly watching television in motels, but a couple of nights earlier we had chanced to watch an old John Wayne movie. John and some cowpunching colleagues struggled against odds to drive a herd of cattle across the open range from a place called Sturgis to a place called Belle Fourche. And at that time, in that motel, the movie suddenly made sense to me. Sturgis and Belle Fourche were real places. I could even locate them on the cartographicus magnus, just on the western edge of South Dakota.

So, now here we were in Wyoming, galloping over land that came out of a John Wayne movie. We discussed our laundry situation, which was getting right serious, and then we sat tall in the saddle and rode that long, lonesome highway, following a telephone line that stitched its way out to the sky, sailing across an unspoiled sea of land with a few wire fences crisscrossing here and there. We crossed Rawhide Creek, passed a road going off to the Buckskin Mine, and then started counting all the pronghorn antelope loping daintily but eventually gave up because they were everywhere. We passed some salmon-colored gullies with black cows, a broken-windowed farm house with a rusting tin roof, and a lone windmill turning and pumping water in the middle of nowhere. It had become a hot day, and in the distance now, through a waver of heat rising off the hot, sandy soil, we saw a series of low mountains that looked like petrified giant's teeth.

We turned right onto a road called Recluse Road and followed that through hills and grass for about five miles until we came to a lonesome cemetery, called the Recluse Cemetery, where we stopped to think. A mile or two later, the road pulled us into a lonesome collection of trees and bushes and old farm equipment and beat-up vehicles and buildings on either side. The buildings included barns and sheds and house trailers, an old log cabin or two and a newer shingled building with a picket fence on one side of it. A sign said WELCOME TO RECLUSE, WYOMING, POPULATION 13. Another sign, attached to the shingled building with the picket fence, said RECLUSE POST OFFICE.

We stopped next to the post office, got out, and looked around. Pretty soon a man and a woman appeared from opposite directions, and we started talking to both of them. The man said that the population of Recluse was more like sixteen. The woman said she was the postmaster of Recluse. He was Dick Oedekoven, we soon learned, while she was Connie Oedekoven. They were married.

After I started asking questions about Recluse, she took us up to the log cabin opposite the post office to see her father-in-law, Jim Oedekoven.

The log cabin was an old homesteader's cabin, we learned, that had been moved up there some time ago and then extended with a modern wing. Inside, it was an ordinary pleasant house, long and narrow, and we sat in the kitchen and ate cookies from a cookie jar and talked to Jim and sometimes to Edna, his wife, who kept offering us cookies and soft drinks. Jim moved as slowly as an old man, but he looked as strong as a young one. He was big and barrel-shaped, and he wore a brightly colored shirt and big Levi's hung up with rainbow suspenders. He wore thick glasses, had big hands, and whenever he smiled his face lit up and his eyes closed.

"Recluse," he said, responding to our question about where the name came from. "It really doesn't fit it today, but it's 'a hermit' in the dictionary. And back when it got its name it kind of was. It was an all-day trip with a team and wagon from here to Gillette. And you couldn't drive in thirty, thirty-five minutes like you do now."

Well, that figures, I thought, and I said: "And so that's it."

Not quite, he said. Originally the first Post Office of Recluse in Wyoming was about a mile off the highway on the left. On the side of the road you come by some buildings. Well, that's where the first Post Office was. And Addie Reed was the first Recluse postmaster.

But these Reeds, her and some of the rest of her family had came from over on the Indian reservation in South Dakota, right in that area. They had established a post office on the reservation, and they didn't hardly anybody use it. So it was only in use a year or two, and they abandoned it. So when the post office people asked for this new post office, what they wanted to name it, why, this Addie Reed said, "Gosh, I don't know." She said, "You got any suggestions?" And the post office people said, "Well, we've got one that was abandoned over here in western South Dakota on the Indian reservation. It's called Recluse." She remembered it, so she said, "That'd just be fine." So that's what they took. That's how Recluse got its name to start with, from the post office over there in South Dakota.

Jim said those first early post offices were pretty simple, not much to 'em, because they had so little money to work with. They usually operated in the postmaster's house. And a postmaster got paid either on stamp sales or on cancellation of letters. And it sure didn't amount to a heck of a lot. If they got thirty, forty dollars a month, that was pretty big money.

Jim settled back in his chair, folded his fingers together, and went on. Well then, he said, there were other ways to earn a few dollars. A lot of people used to ride the train to Gillette. And then they'd ride the mail truck out to Recluse. Hide buyers, for example. Jim's dad used to take a lot of coyote hides and muskrat hides and badger hides on peoples' grocery bill at the Recluse grocery, which he maintained. And about once in the winter and again before spring, why, a Sears Roebuck hide buyer come to Gillette on the train. And then he'd ride out on the mail truck to Recluse on Monday morning. This would have been back anywhere through the late '20s and early '30s. And the hide buyer would stay at Recluse with Jim's folks. His dad would get these hides and get them down, and sort 'em and pile 'em on the counter and on tables, and haggle over the price. And when they'd reached an agreement they'd finally wind up and go to bed. And next day then they'd get boxes and package these hides, and the Sears Roebuck hide buyer'd get 'em ready to ship. So they'd put the postage on them, and he'd parcel post 'em back to Kansas City. And then the buyer would drive back in to Gillette on Wednesday morning with the mail carrier, take his hides, and the hides'd go on the mail, and he'd get to Gillette. He'd get on the train and go somewheres else and do the same thing. A lot of the early guys traveled that way, salesmen with hardware companies and that sort of thing'd come in on the train and ride the mail truck to these out-of-the-way places.

There wasn't that much to do in the winter time, so a lot of the old homesteaders would run a trap line, or whenever they saw a coyote might get to shoot one. Back then, a choice hide could bring in five dollars, which would buy a heck of a lot of groceries when eggs were two bits a dozen. And people would come in to his dad's store to buy sugar and salt, pepper and spices, and stuff like that. But as for actual groceries, people tended to grow their own.

"Well then, my dad got the post office in the year 1924," Jim said. "He came out to Wyoming in about 1911 and homesteaded."

That happened because one of his dad's brothers, Henry, homesteaded right south of where we were sitting now. Henry had worked for the calvary in Sturgis, South Dakota, at Fort Meade, as a civilian teamster. Along in about 1909, there were some Indians who got off the reservation over there and came up and were heckling the ranchers on Powder River. The ranchers kept complaining to the government because the Indians were always wanting another beef or wanting some groceries, always wanting a handout. And so the ranchers got tired of this situation and called up the army and said, "Come and get 'em back on the reservation." And so the army sent a detachment to gather up the Indians and escort them back to the reservation. His uncle Henry got picked to drive a bed wagon. He was a teamster, Jim said, and so that's how come they seen this country.

"What's a bed wagon?"

Well, it was a wagon that just packed bedrolls. You had a wagon that carried groceries, and you had cooks, cooks in your grocery wagons. And what Uncle

Henry drove was just a bed wagon. Everybody's bed rolls got thrown in that wagon — but anyhow when they come through that part of Wyoming, Uncle Henry liked the looks of this country, see. So, when he got back to Sturgis, and his brothers and sisters there, he was tellin them about this trip, see. And he said, "You know, I think this fall, we got a little time and the weather cools off a little," he said, "we got any money to file a homestead or can make any money this summer," he said, "I think we should go up there and look at that." He said, "I think it's a good place to go and take a homestead."

There were sixteen children in the family, the Oedekovens, and thirteen of them lived to grow up. In about the fall of that year, Uncle Henry and two more uncles, Lewis and Vincent, came up. They brought a pack horse with them, a bed roll, some groceries, and something to camp with. And they came up there and spent several days looking around. They looked it over and picked out what they thought they'd like in the next couple of days. And then the three brothers went down to the Federal Land Office at Sundance. They had a description of the land they wanted for a homestead off the land survey, and they had forty dollars apiece, which was the filing fee, so they filed on the homestead. And that's how they got settled at Recluse to start with.

They cut logs and built a house first thing. And then finally a barn and some trails, and they just kept working at this. Then in the fall and the winter when the snow was deep, they'd cut logs for stuff they needed and they'd cut fence posts, and they gradually got their homesteads fenced so they could put some cattle on them. And from then on they were in business. But it wasn't so easy as it might sound. The original homesteads were 320 acres, but you could take one and your wife could take another. And then you could get another 320 acres in the hills for what they called a timber permit. His dad took that 320 out in the hills where there were pine trees and cedar. He could cut the cedars for fence posts, and he cut his house logs back there. But he never could get water on it. There was no spring and no nothing, so he could never run any cattle on it —

About here in the conversation, Jim's wife Edna came in and started encouraging us to eat more cookies and also have something more to drink. "What'll you have? Root beer or Pepsi? More cookies? Sure you got enough?"

There was a lull in the conversation, after which we somehow returned to the subject of Jim's dad and the Recluse Post Office. So Jim's dad became postmaster in 1924, and that's when Recluse moved up to the spot on the road where it is now, right in the middle of the Oedekoven land. And the next year, his dad bought some store stuff, including a bacon slicer, and so the Recluse Post Office was combined with a general store.

Jim could remember going out with his dad. Jim was pretty small then, but he could remember going down there on a spring wagon and hauling the bacon slicer and the coffee grinder, one of them old hand-cranked coffee grinders. Everything come in the barrel or sack. And people come into the store, told you what they wanted, three pounds, four pounds, and that's what you weighed up. Put it through the grinder, put it in a paper sack, and tied it up for 'em. And they hauled that stuff up here and put it in the store. The first store was small, and it stuck out the side of the old homestead house. Then Jim's dad took the store off and put it up across the road. That burned down, but it was too small anyway. It was so full of stuff, you couldn't work your way around through it. So he built the bigger one.

Then, after Jim's dad stopped running the post office and store, his mother ran it. In the 1960s, they passed it on to Edna, Jim's wife. Edna had it, oh, for twenty-two years maybe. And from there it's stayed right in the family, passed down all these years. Except that the store is closed now. And the gas pump, too. They used to sell gas. But then the federal government, the EPA, shut them down with new regulations. And they're just so tough with their regulations that in order to comply, to put tanks and pumps in the way they wanted them, and a cement cage around them, it would have cost Jim's son Dick about $40,000 to put the pumps, diesel and gas, in. And they were doing about $2,000 worth of business a year. So it would have taken him twenty years to comply with the EPA before he made a dollar for himself. And so Dick said, "The hell with it." He said, "I'm just going to dig them up and take them out." And, of course, when he did that that killed the store volume. They just finally said, "The hell with it." So that's what happened to the store, and now they just run the Recluse Post Office.

Without the small income from the store now, the Oedekovens mainly survive with the cattle ranching and a little farming. Dick has a herd of about eighty head, and sometimes if they keep calves until they become yearlings they may have a hundred head over the winter. That's enough to make a little money. And for their own meat, he and Edna will butcher one a year, and Dick and Connie will butcher one. Then, of the herd, they sell their calf crop, which is probably about sixty-some head. Well, they've got three markets over on the edge of the Black Hills, and the Oedekovens sell their cattle at two of them: in Sturgis and Belle Fourche.

Sturgis! Belle Fourche! That reminded me: "We saw a movie on television two nights ago that had John Wayne driving a herd of cattle from Sturgis to Belle Fourche!"

Jim laughed. "I seen that one! John Wayne's quite a character."

"Did you ever drive cattle to market?"

"Yeah, when I was a kid. The stock yards were down there on the west edge of Gillette, right along the railroad track."

"How would you get the herd from here to Gillette?"

"Trail 'em. Just like John Wayne."

"A herd of how many cattle are we talking about?"

"Ah, well, that just depends on how many you ship and who's shippin. Now, my dad didn't have that many, but he drove in with two or three other guys and we might make up two three carloads in a bunch. You could probably put fifty head of calves to a car load. But, anyway, we'd make it halfway to Gillette in a day. And then make arrangements to stay overnight somewhere, where they'd have a lot close to the trails that we could put 'em in and feed 'em. And, of course, the first few guys that went with cattle, why, there was lots of grass, and they could just eat and be full. They didn't need nothin at night. But after about the third bunch that went down the road, that grass got kinda scarce. We'd have to bring hay then and feed 'em at night, see. Feed 'em and put 'em in where they was on water. And we'd get them on water somewhere at noon, see. Go into a reservoir or a crick or something—"

About here in our conversation the phone rang. Jim started giving advice on the phone to someone on the other end about butchering. And then he had to go help out a friend somewhere. It was time for us to go, too, so we went. We hightailed it right back down the road to Gillette, where we herded ourselves into a room somewhere and ordered a pizza. Then we brushed our teeth, closed our eyes, and dreamed about courage, self-reliance, and faith in a promised land called the American West.

Ten Sleep

From the northern edge of Wyoming a road took us into the midst of some of the most wild wilderness known to the eye and mind of man, through one million acres of Bighorn National Forest, for example, habitat and downright home for myriad deer and elk and moose, bighorn sheep, black bear and coyote, bald eagle and golden eagle.

Inexorably we nosed up into and through the Powder River Pass at 9,666 feet. Inexorably we nosed down into and through the Ten Sleep Canyon to a depth of fourteen hundred feet right past the very spot where Lord Gilbert Leigh, Anglo-Irish playboy and hunter, when playing at hunting fell in the fall of 1884 to his death.

Following the Ten Sleep Creek as it cascaded relentlessly to a final rendezvous with Nowood Creek, we braked breathlessly to our final what-have-you at Ten Sleep, a soporific spot sitting (as the Shoshone and Crow, the Sioux and Arapaho are said to have said) ten sleeps away from their big camp on the Platte River and ten sleeps away from their big camp on the Clark's Ford River.

Anyhow, I think that's how the road went, judging from what the cartographicus magnus and guidebook tell me. For most of this little trip through the Bighorns, as a matter of fact, I didn't hear or see very much other than the sound of rain beating on our top, a tearing sound of our wheels pulling water away from the pavement below, and the disturbing sight of two bright white eyes in the mirror growing bigger and bigger and bigger, then the shudder of something heavy moving past us, and then the sight of two or more small red eyes at the windshield growing smaller and smaller and smaller.

There was also a lot of darkness that got darker and a good deal of motion, down and up and forth and back, and so we were terminally tuckered by the time the symbols

TEN SLEEP
Pop   311
Elev   4256

appeared.

We spent the night in the Ten Sleep Motel, a stationary train of rooms with iffy lightbulbs, grifty floors, and shifty mattresses — where we drifted and lifted into a misty realm of fens deep and penned sheep and in the morning drove back and forth over the main sweep of Ten Sleep until we ended up for breakfast at The Mountain Man Café. The waiter there, a big man with white beard who called Bayne "short stuff" and seemed tired, took our orders beneath a high stamped-tin ceiling. As the ceiling might suggest, the place used to be the Ten Sleep Hardware until recently, and I think I might have liked it better that way. Now it had romantic photographs of wolves on the walls, a couple of whirly overhead fans, one wolf clock for sale, a television blathering eternally, and a bear trap attached to the wall with a red spot painted on its trigger and a sign that said Complaint Department — For Prompt Attention "Please" Press Red Button.

After breakfast, we sallied across the street to check out Dirty Sally's, an old bank building turned into a soda fountain and souvenir shop as well as a sporting goods store, momentarily closed, and then we walked into the front office of a permanently closed gas station where we met Hayden Blair, drinking coffee and reading his morning paper with the help of a desk light, thick glasses, and a big magnifying glass.

This was Mr. Blair's garage, and now also it served as his home. Had done ever since the Environmental Protection Agency stopped his pumps with new regulations about storage tanks that made it impossible for independent gas station owners to stay in business. So here he was, growing old yet dignified, a little sad maybe, dark-blue baseball cap on his head, wearing a clean white shirt and clean work pants and work shoes, a little sluggish before the coffee kicked in maybe but still ready to pop out of this catatonic nightmare at a moment's notice and get back to pumping gas in Ten Sleep.

Echo (Again)

I started the engine, and we woke up from Ten Sleep. Refreshed and rolling now, we dropped south down 16 and then 20 into Wind River Canyon. Through a slot in steep cliffs, we turned down and down to the sweet smell of sage and the bright sweep of gold and brittle grass, down some more to a river clean, pale green with white scallops and lined by a long stretch of flickering cottonwood. We stopped the car and watched the water make shapes like a cloud, dynamic and churning through a deep channel in the middle, raising bulges and lowering dents to spill occult shapes closer in, and pillowing white among the giant rocks scattered openly along surface and edge.

Britt and Bayne began throwing stones into the river. Then Bayne got ambitious and began making big and bigger splashes with big and bigger stones.

"Uh!" he would groan. Then: ker-splash!

"Oh. Big one!"

Back in the car, we tossed and turned through a narrow course of ledges and edges, boulders and tunnels, eagerly chattering away about the height of the cliffs and the size of the boulders as we drove. "Wow! That's even higher. That's nine hundred feet or maybe, mmmm, six hundred or eight hundred I'd say. Naw maybe six. It's high." "Look at these boulders! Look at these boulders! Wow. Look at that one."

After we got out of the canyon, we came onto a land that was generally flat, with a few rises and a few gullies, with the Rockies in the distance to the right like a wall of gray peaks. Now we passed through some barren badlands, with nothing to speak of except sagebrush and buffalo grass and eroded hills — and now and again a few green valleys and some grazing land.

Ahead of us appeared the grassed-over remnants of the Oregon Trail, which we stopped to think about, and then the Continental Divide, a Bierstadtean stretch over which we leapt after a running start. From there it was about all downhill, except for the weather. The clouds began turning purple! They started looming and dragging big shadows across the highway. Then we saw the rain ahead of us, and it looked heavy. The sky began making angry sweeps and swirls and sending out every few minutes a jagged flash of lightning. Soon we were surrounded by a posse of small but very aggressive storms — to the right, to the left, and right in front of us, with still little open spaces where the sun glowed through like light behind a dark glass. "Look at that area over there! It looks like a tornado or something!" And now they were all around us, floating and raging and moving fast, giant rolling black clouds carrying gray skirts of rain underneath.

We passed a number of horses standing together, alert and excited, anticipating the storm and swishing their tails, smelling the rain.

At Farson, we took a left fork and began rolling down 191 straight for Eden when all of a sudden a storm appeared directly ahead, rolling up 191 and bound like a locomotive straight for us. "According to the map," I was saying, "we just go straight. Whoa! Look at that storm!"

So I made a quick U-turn, sped back into Farson, and turned over to Route 28. Committed onto 28 now, we began running alongside a black sky and a real storm with bright arrows of lightning bursting out. We headed right into and through a land darkened by the shadow of clouds, a gray of rain, and then we were racing a whole swarm of weather right alongside us. I had recently read that a person on foot can easily outrun swarming bees, and, thinking that bees and weather might have a lot in common, I drove faster and faster and faster. There was another big swarm of weather on our left, too, but I thought we might just squeeze through. "I think we've done well," I announced, my foot hard on the pedal, peeling down the highway at a thousand miles an hour. "I think that one's moving in this direction, and that one's probably moving in that direction, and we'll just beat 'em both!"

We got pounded and shaken up a little, but pretty soon we saw a promise of sunlight ahead and, in the mirror, a big truck coming up from behind with exhaust pipes sticking out sideways, like a long-horned steer, honking and arrogant and trailing a great cloud of mist behind it. We paused to let the monster pass and then fell down to the bottom of the state and got sucked into the pipeline of Interstate 80 West.

We gurgled along 80 then until we got to the very edge of Wyoming, ledge more than edge actually, where we paused and teetered and then — as the road suddenly dropped away from under our wheels — zoomed on a roll into Utah. The line into Utah, a thoroughly betrucked six lanes still called Interstate 80, just seemed to go down forever, a steel and rubber and asphalt factory of a road screaming in our ears — along with the noise from a single station on the radio — and no signs of life except for what might be inside the rest of the traffic on the road, just going down and down and down and down and down.

This was a narrow valley, a chute, an amazing pass through some big redrocked mountains rising on either side of us. It felt like we were being poured down a funnel, and so when I saw the sign INFORMATION CENTER ONE MILE, I didn't think I needed information but I did think I needed to stop or at least to demonstrate the capacity thereof. I stopped, and the Information Center turned out to be the Echo Information Center. It was a lodge on a ledge overlooking a gorge and a ridge, with the last patches of sunlight trailing across its red-rocked honeycomb of nooks and crannies, crooks and grannies: a natural echo chamber.

There was a place to park your car, a way to inform yourself in the form of cheery brochures stacked in racks, two pay phones, three steel vaults to offer (after a rattle and sticky muddle) the opportunity for liquid intake, and two concrete rooms to provide (after a waddle through icky puddle) the chance for liquid outgo. It was a busy place, a building poured into circular form as if to emphasize its buzzing busyness. Like a beehive but a beehive for strangers, for bees who don't know each other in the slightest. And so there was a peculiar sort of introverted buzzing and a slow waggle-dance done with downcast eyes and vacant anonymity, as in a big city elevator.

Precisely the kind of place where you wouldn't in a hundred years cup your hands to your face and holler a hollow HELLO to exercise the voice or excite the soul. Something might holler a hollow HELLO back, and wouldn't that, like a booboo in a tutu or a moomoo in a muumuu, just about double your embarrassment? And so we simply stood in front of our car, hot and tired, pausing and drinking our two Cokes and one Sprite, stifling duodenum innuendoes, standing oh maybe five yards from the nearest pay phone and thus, due to some remarkable acoustical quality of the place, eavesdropping effortlessly on one side of a conversation conducted by an overweight guy with a big mustache who was, I believe, wired up to another overweight guy with a big mustache down in Salt Lake City. It was a long exchange, and I only tuned in toward the end of it, which went like this: "Well, I just don't trust you. Nope. Hah? Nope. Just don't trust you. Hah? Trust is just something you earn. I do trust you more than I trust John. Because John, he's only two steps above Sam, and Sam can't be trusted. Because he's even about five places below Joanne. Joanne I don't trust at all—except that's she's a little better than Sally. Now, Sally, she is about as low as you can get. She can't hardly be trusted ever—even though she's still above Peter. Peter? I don't have the *words* for Peter."

Big Rock Candy Mountain

Advance token to Salt Lake City.

Our ultimate goal was Big Rock Candy Mountain down toward the mid-bottom of Utah. But we were still at the top, it was getting late, and we needed a place to sleep.

We dropped back onto the big 80 alley heading down to the great salt valley and were nearly run aground by a roaring pickup piloted by a unsavory-looking little man with a salt-and-pepper beard and five little kids lined up next to him in the cab and two shotguns racked onto the rear window. At about eighteen miles to Salt Lake, the road dropped once again, and we rolled down now like a gumball into a funnel through a tunnel and a really tight pass, and then there was the city.

We treated ourselves to a great hotel, ordered a room service meal, watched a video, and in the morning toured the Mormon Temple.

I like the Mormon Temple, which, with all its assorted buildings and grounds, covers a city block and is surrounded by a high wall with some golden trumpet-blowing figures at the top of it, like a very big birthday cake. The problem is that any visitors to the place are potential converts, and so they become what housewives are to the Fuller Brush man. Our guide was a soft-faced nineteen-year-old from Des Plains who called herself Sister Cook and said she was a missionary. She smiled sweetly and then chattered away with all the infinite joy and friendliness that comes once you've tasted the Truth of the Universe.

226

"Hi, how are you?" she said. We answered, and she said, "Wow, that's nice! And where you are from?" We answered, and she said, "Wow, you're from Massachusetts! Just visiting? That's neat! And where are you going after Salt Lake City?" We answered, and she said, "California! Wow, that's really neat. I love California."

Soon she took us down some stairs into an underground chamber. She turned out all the lights, and a vision of stars and planets appeared on the ceiling, with some asteroids and meteors shooting around. It was surprisingly cool and peaceful in that room, and, in spite of myself, the power of suggestion began to assert itself. The floor dropped gently away. The walls began to fade to lemonade. Then spooky stereophonic sounds of asteroids and meteors shooting around started to play on a hidden tape recorder. The heavenly bodies went whoooooooooooooommmmm and swoooooooooosssssshhhhhh and swisssssshhhhhhhhhhhhhhh and whoooooooooooooommmmmm again.

Sister Cook began spooning marzipan into a microphone. "Now when I come into this room," she murmured sweetly, "I feel important. Because I know that God has a plan for us that can bring us happiness." How do we find out what this plan is? She was going to tell us. Well, the first thing God does is he chooses witnesses that are called Prophets. We can read about Prophets in the Bible, and those were the old Prophets. But in our day God has continued to follow this pattern. Joseph Smith was commanded by God to write more Truths for modern times, and so he wrote the Book of Mormon, which just like the Bible is a record of God's plan for our happiness. This idea is very reassuring to Sister Cook. As a matter of fact, there are a lot of prophecies in both the Bible and the Book of Mormon that in latter days have begun to come true. For example, the Savior's death and resurrection are described in both the Bible and the Book of Mormon. The Bible predicted that Jesus would come and be crucified, and so does the Book of Mormon. And even though you might say that the Book of Mormon was written umpteen centuries after Jesus, it's important to remember that its information has been around forever. And thus Sister Cook has two great sources to read from and understand the Commandments. She knows that God loves her and wants to save her from pain, and so He gives her all the Commandments to show the Way. "I love the Book of Mormon with all my heart, and I'm grateful for the peace it brings," Sister Cook concluded.

The stars and planets were turned off. We went on to other chambers and lessons and powerful suggestions. There was a time for searching of souls, a time for filling out of forms, and a time for asking of questions. One question I didn't ask was this: How come Joseph Smith and Brigham Young got to have about fifty wives each, whereas the rest of us only get to have about one?

At last we came out of the spooky building basement and back into the realm of sunlight and birdsong, a little shaken — and ready to leave Salt and find Sugar. So we quickly got onto Interstate 15, which was big and thickly occupied, like a parking lot for moving cars, and pointed our three tongues thataway: to Big Rock Candy Mountain.

I had no idea what this one was going to be. This was a destination the Research Staff insisted on after having discovered it one day on the cartographicus magnus, and, as Bayne was explaining now, "Candy is cool."

Britt: "Imagine an entire mountain made out of rock candy, and if that's not what it is, I have no idea what it is."

This conversation took place alongside some high and spiky mountains as we rocketed south on 15 at seventy miles an hour, looking for a Taco Bell. Bayne said he was so sick of Taco Bell, but Britt was having her turn in the front seat today, and so she got to make the choice. And then, once we solved the lunch problem and were back on Interstate 15 South, we moved onto the next one, which was the mysteries of the universe.

"What do I think God is? I think it's impossible to know, Bayne, but I don't believe there is a man out there with a long beard who's handing out special favors to the True Believers. And if He did want to talk to us, why bother with words? I would rather not, ah, ah —"

"Downsize the universe."

"Thank you, Britt. Downsize the universe with a human projection. I would rather just face the universe and try to think about it as well as I can and as honestly as I can, and not imagine my little words or anyone else's are going to work very well in defining undefinable things. We're just small creatures who really don't understand a lot, and I think it's a mistake to grasp at the quickest and easiest explanation of things just because you want a security blanket."

Our little vehicle slowly turned past a couple of mountains that needed a bra, and then it fell down into a whole valley of orange grass where the mountains were much lower (though in the distance some rough range stood up like a torn piece of gray paper), and our long, long trail of concrete just kept curving and running slowly downhill as we rattled away and rambled along. Pretty soon, the radio frazzled down to only two stations — EZ Favorites and Cecil B. DeMille Classical — and then it sizzled out altogether.

The reason the radio gave out was that we had crawled into the cleavage of some very big mountains, and now those grand projections began to suggest unavoidably what our next destination was all about. They were big. They were made of rock. They looked like candy. I began to think we had torn the wrapper off Big Rock Candy Mountain.

We turned south again onto a two-lane Route 89, which narrowed and began twisting and winding uphill, and soon we came upon a speeding river at the bottom of a narrow canyon. The river was just having a good time going downhill as we slowly rode uphill up an eroded road into the canyon. The canyon was made of smooth and honeycombed rock, red mostly, until we turned a final corner and then: "That! That must be the Big Rock Candy Mountain!"

A whole mountain side was exposed, frosty white and smoothy brown, more like a melting cone of vanilla and chocolate ice cream than rock candy, but registering high on the saccharimeter nonetheless. And along both edges of the road, among some trees and turquoise sage, we came upon several buildings and about a half-dozen signs. The biggest sign of all, peaked and mounted on its own post and surrounded by light bulbs, announced at the right side of the road:

BIG
ROCK CANDY
MOUNTAIN
RESORT

And next to that sign was a building with log-cabin siding and its own smaller roof sign (edged with colored scallops that looked like jelly beans): CAFÉ. Up the road just a bit was the TRADING POST and ROCK SHOP, and back down the road another bit was a motel with a plastic sign colored in five or six different candy colors with a big bite already taken out at the top:

CANDY
MOUNTAIN
MOTEL
COLOR TV

The café, rock shop, and motel were closed, as were (on the other side of the road) a gas station and a few small cabins by the river. So much for Big Rock Candy Mountain, I thought. A tiny little spot. Tacky, but old enough that the tackiness had begun to develop a sticky charm. There were other signs, multicolored, edged with painted jelly beans, arrows, lights, and so on, and then, erected on a couple of temporary wooden posts, yet another, this one less grand than any of the rest and monochromatic: Real Estate BANKRUPTCY AUCTION: World Famous BIG ROCK CANDY MOUNTAIN RESORT mountain acreage — restaurant — gift shop — rock shop — motel — river front cabins — mineral & water rights 215 ACRES TOTAL to be SOLD ON SITE.

A date at the bottom of the sign indicated that the auction had just taken place last week! We might have placed a bid!

We stopped the car, got out, and thought about that. But while we were standing beside our car and thinking in the deserted parking lot of that abandoned little resort in the middle of nowhere, a young woman pulled up in a beat-up car. She leaned out the car window with a big smile, a gap in her teeth, and a florid tattoo on her left shoulder, and said she didn't know whether Big Rock Candy Mountain had been sold or not. Maybe it wasn't. If we were interested in finding out anything more, we should go into Marysvale and find the mayor, who ran the rug shop.

So we climbed back into our vehicle and continued on along the road. Before we got more than a couple of miles farther down the road, however, we were randomly inspired to stop at the Wooden Nickel Crafts and Antiques Trading Post, an enticing spread of old farm and mining machinery, cow skulls, glass objects, and knickknacks. The woman running the antique shop told us not to bother with the mayor of Marysvale, whose rug shop would be closed anyway. Instead, she said, we should go find the man who created Big Rock Candy Mountain — Pratt Seegmiller — and she gave us the directions to his house.

Pratt Seegmiller's house was situated on the edge of Marysvale, a little mining town started during the 1860s when some enterprising prospectors discovered their own version of big rock candy and so drove out the Indians once and for all. Gold had brought boom times at various times in the past. But right now Marysvale sat out there with a hungry look of dilapidated delapidary abandonment. After turning down one of Marysvale's short roads, we found Mr. Pratt Seegmiller sweating away at some form of arcane wizardry in the workshop behind his house. He had blue eyes, glasses, bristly white eyebrows, curly white hair, a wizened face; and the top three buttons of his brown work shirt were unbuttoned.

After pausing to think about things for a minute, Pratt turned up his hearing aid and told us he started Big Rock Candy Mountain with his brother-in-law, Kent Sayler, in 1937. They began by building a cabin to live in, and it took all summer long because neither he nor his brother-in-law were carpenters.

They moved into the cabin in October and lived there for three years, primarily to get the mineral water out. That was the main objective in those days. Pratt's brother-in-law, Kent, had a store back in Minneapolis, and they shipped the mineral water to him. And they would sell it, and Pratt would also sell it there in Utah. So that's how they started, and Pratt seen of course that it was a very attractive tourist attraction, and he started to capitalize on that a bit, and he built a stand up there by the road and had the mineral water, but most things that people wanted wasn't the mineral water. What they wanted was a post card of the Big Rock Candy Mountain. Something to do with the Big Rock Candy Mountain. So then in 1940 Kent, the brother-in-law, managed to get together $600, sent it out with the plans to build a service station and a little curio shop, so they did that, and that's actually the same building that's there now, only it's been improved and remodeled a number of times since.

Then, unfortunately, Kent and he started having different ideas how to run the place. The brother-in-law wanted to run it one way. Pratt wanted to run it another way. So finally in 1949 he sold his 40 percent share in the Big Rock Candy Mountain, and moved to Marysvale, where he worked at mining gold and then discovered the hottest rock candy of all, uranium. He mined and sold uranium to the Atomic Energy Commission for seventeen years. But after he left the business in 1949, his brother-in-law and his sister run the Big Rock Candy Mountain, oh, they run that place for about twenty years, and done very well. They built it up. They built the motels, and they done very well. Then they sold out to someone who is presently in bankruptcy over it, and he didn't never, seems to Pratt like he was never very good at it. It just went downhill until finally, why, he just went in for bankruptcy.

But the mineral springs were beautiful. The mineral runoff goes down to the canyon down there right by the station, and down there in the bottom. Years ago, when they were first starting, Pratt put a dike in, then faced it with cement, and so it was in the natural rocks with a cement-faced dike. And that winter it filled up. It held like something better than a thousand gallons. It was just a tiny, tiny stream, and so the pool would take about ten days for it to fill up, or more. Then when it filled up, to look at it was just blood red, and then to put it in a glass it was amber. He used to take tourists up there, and if he wasn't too busy he'd walk up with them, and then say, "So this is Lemonade Springs." And if he had a paper cup, which he often did, he'd say, "Well, yes, take a little taste." The water has a sour taste. He'd dip a little in the cup, and the water was clean and the people would sip it, and of course the power of suggestion has a tremendous amount to do with it: "Ah! That tastes just like lemonade!" And it doesn't, of course, not if you take very much of it, but it seems to be a quite a healthful water.

"And people would bathe in it for health?" I asked, still wondering why people came to stay at the resort.

"Not bathe in it! Drink it!"

Guests would come and mostly just stay over one night. But then in hunting season, they'd have a tremendous business with the hunters. Pratt's sister would get up at four o'clock in the morning and have breakfast for those hunters. The hunters would stay in the cabins. She'd have breakfast for them, she'd have lunch if they wanted it. So all they had to do was get up and wash theirselves, get over there, have breakfast. If they wanted a lunch, "OK, here's a lunch."

I said, "That's interesting. But I'm still wondering, how did Big Rock Candy Mountain ever get on the map? It was never a town."

Well, when they first come there, it wasn't on the map, and he tried to get some postcards made of it, and he wrote the post card company in Salt Lake that makes 'em, the Deseret Book Company that made 'em, and they sent him a picture that—it was of a side hill, and it's known as the Quilted Mountain. It don't look anything like, it just *bare-ly* looked a *lit-tle* like Rock Candy. It's got a little color in it. But nothing really like it. So they had a hard time. Finally a fella come by. He was a real good professional photographer, and he said, "I'd like to take some pictures of this," and Pratt said, "Boy, you're just the man I've been lookin for!" So he went out and took a number of pictures. They sent those in, and eventually they was able to get some good postcards made, with Big Rock Candy Mountain on 'em, and finally it just got so it was more famous more famous more famous, and eventually Pratt was happy to see it was on the map.

"It just happened!"

Just happened! And he and his sister and brother-in-law were responsible for it. Still and all, when Pratt and his sister and brother-in-law come in 1937, even then, already, there was already a sign that had been put up right in the pine trees. It said BIG ROCK CANDY MOUNTAIN. There was a little service station in town that put that up, and so Pratt asked the man that put it up, he said, "How come did you put that up?" And the man said—well, they used to have a railroad here. They had that until just, oh, less than ten years ago. The man at the service station said, "One of the guys on the railroad come in one time, and he said, 'Somebody ought to put a sign up there that says BIG ROCK CANDY MOUNTAIN, because *that is it!*' He says, 'I come by in the train. I come by in the train everday, and I look over there, and I *know* that's the Big Rock Candy Mountain.'" And so, the man at the service station says, "I just decided to have a sign painted up there," and so he did.

"What year do you think this was?"

Oh, Pratt and them came in 1937. It was probably about two years before, about 1935. So then of course they put signs up themselves, a lot of 'em. Finally, why, this fellow who worked for them, he was a sign painter, and he said, "I'll paint you all the signs you want, if you buy the material." So Pratt bought a lot of sheet metal and boards, and then there was no law against postin signs on the highway back then, so Pratt went from the south for fifty miles, north for fifty miles. Actually he went almost a hundred miles from here, and put up these signs: BIG ROCK CANDY MOUNTAIN. And so that's what got it on the map.

Well, the conversation went on from there, and after another half hour or so we left, thinking Mr. Pratt Seegmiller was a sweet and gentle man, a pioneering entrepreneur with vision and taste. But I had promised the Research Staff a little candy, and so after that we drove back into the main drag of Marysvale where we did find one convenient place open that happened to sell candy. Not rock candy, but something sweet nonetheless, which we savored all the way north and then east on Route 70 until Richfield, where we stopped at a Holiday Inn and wrapped ourselves up for the night.

Mexican Hat

The way to Mexican Hat looked simple. Just take red 24 south and east and then hop onto gray 95 and drop south. A little note written on the cartographicus magnus alongside gray 95 said: "Carry Drinking Water on This Road." There were also some green splotches as well as blue squiggles and several evocative names: Dirty Devil River, Robbers Roost Canyon, Goblin Valley, Cataract Canyon, Grand Gulch Primitive Area, Muley Point Overlook, Ticaboo, and Valley of the Gods.

But nothing on the cartographicus magnus prepared us for the spectacular nature of those natural spectacles in real life. First, we passed a huge red rock mesa with pipe organ sides, eerie and almost endless. Not long after, we were inching through some kind of vast cathedral of rock, a canyon colored red and salmon and orange and white and gray and bluish gray. Just passing through an amazing vast canyon. It felt like being an ant, I thought, an ant crawling through something or other. I couldn't for the life of me think what the ant was crawling through, so I dangled the metaphor in front of my Research Staff.

"Doesn't our driving through this huge canyon sort of make you feel like you're an ant," I said, "and crawling through a. . . . What is it the ant would be crawling through?"

"A small canyon," Bayne said.

But it was something nevertheless. Pretty soon we spied in the distance some great red rock tables with pipe organ sides, and then farther in the distance some white or whitish vanilla pound cakes, getting big and bigger, becoming huge and huger, just grand and grandoliferous: gigantic flatirons made mostly out of red sandstone with an intermixing of gray and blue and vanilla strata eroded and dropped and chipped and fallen away, and fissured and turreted and honeycombed into incredible formations. This place made us feel very small. And after an hour of feeling very small, we began to think about disasters.

233

"What would it be like to climb on that one?"

"I bet you wouldn't make it!"

"Ah, you could fall from the top of that!"

"How about if it fell on top of you?"

Yes, it was disaster time, and now we weren't going to stop until we had considered all the disasters we could think of. "If you were a weight lifter and lifted four hundred pounds," someone said, "and a fly landed on your nose, what would happen? And if you sneeze and keep your eyes open at the same time, know what happens?"

After another half hour or so—time had begun to grow blurry—we began crawling past the most amazing Big Object I'd ever seen in my life. It looked like an inverted ship, or just a ship, anchored out there by itself with crenellations along the top. The stone on top was pink, and the sides, descending not vertically but angled at maybe forty-five degrees, were gray, and frosted with a yellowish sheen from the sun. The top of this Big Object was made of hard stone cracked and shattered in places, creating the crenellation effect. It was long and narrow, maybe a mile long and possibly a third of a mile wide and another third of a mile to the top.

And as soon as we passed that Big Object, we came up to another, an even Bigger Object. So it went, driving in the land of the Big Objects. Well, it was just too grand and bleak and wild; eventually we turned into a vast desert canyon and broke right into the movies: bleached skull territory, where Hopalong Cassidy used to hop along, where the Cisco Kid used to kid a paunchy Pancho, where the outlaws would ride out to hide out in their hidden hideouts from the maw of the law, and where the cowboys in the white hats used to chase the cowboys in the black hats mercilessly past mesas and mountains and canyons and deserts and mesquite and sagebrush. And like the cowboys in white and black hats we chased around mercilessly, too, our Tin Lizzy snorting and clattering through that dream desert at seventy miles an hour until eventually we headed for a giant wall straight ahead. We missed the wall, the road took a few turns, and then we came upon a sign: NO TRUCKS OVER 10,000 POUNDS OR RVs OR BUSES OR VEHICLES TOWING. GRAVEL ROAD 5 MILES AN HOUR 10 PER CENT GRADE.

"Hmm," I said. "And we were making such good time."

Still, the road didn't seem so bad, a little wavery maybe, and I began to think we had just passed another empty threat. Five miles an hour? We were doing fine at about thirty-five an hour and could probably crank it up to forty-five. No trucks? No RVs? Well, why not?

Just about then the whole world answered back.

Suddenly the road ended—or rather it just fell off the top of a mile-high mesa. Just fell. The road dropped down into a series of hairpin twists and turns down the cliff—with no guardrails at the edge and no stable surface, only a grindingly slippy gravel—and when we met a car slowly coming up toward us on this death trap, I stopped, started to back up to make room, and almost backed off the cliff to our heart-exploding deaths a zillion feet below. None of us said a word. The time for meaningless chit-chat was long past. But I kept thinking to myself: *This is not the Peruvian Andes! How could anyone in America, the USA, allow a road like this to exist? Where are the guard rails? Is there any way out of this other than down? Who can our survivors sue?* It was do-or-die time, and I did and lived a thousand lives, rappelling down the cliff hairpin by hairpin, but inside I died a thousand deaths, going slowly slowly down that tight windy slippery slidey horrifying cliffside until—whew!—we finally graveled down onto a more level angle and came out into a flat desert valley populated regularly with giants, dinosaurs, big horses, gods, and so on, all carved out of stone—and, oh yes, a Mexican hat, which was a thirty-ton sombrero consisting of one big globular stone (like the crown of a hat) balanced on a big flat and circular stone (like a wide brim) balanced on a whole elongated construction of stone (like an unfortunate person wearing a thirty-ton hat). A sign with an arrow alongside the road pointed out what we already figured: MEXICAN HAT ROCK.

But we were just happy to be alive. We came to the edge of the town of Mexican Hat, which consisted of some petroleum pumps, a trailer park, a small church, hay for sale, Indian jewelry, Indian pottery, the Mexican Hat Lodge, a Texaco station, a Conoco station, the Canyonlands Motel, Somebody's Indian Trading Company, the Valley of the Gods Inn, and that was it: a little town and tourist trap like a tasteless drop of water in the desert.

Nothing

Route 163 from Mexican Hat ducked through a door into Navajo and then Hopi tribal lands, bleak and grand, and turned into a long straight desert highway moving past monumental mesas and lone male hitchhikers along the roads. But it was getting dark, the mesas started creating their own monumental shadows, and we were hoping to reach a big hole in the ground before nightfall. The big hole was farther away than I had expected, though, and so we drove for a long time with half a universe of stars overhead, our headlights tunneling along a trail that I knew, because the cartographicus magnus said so, wound along the edge of the world's biggest drop-off.

I had thought there would be more places to stay along the way, but there weren't. Luckily, at around midnight we found an available room at the Holiday Inn right inside the park headquarters and dropped into our beds.

Next morning we peered over the edge into a very deep and rather scary hole. It was exactly as advertised, and the three of us spent some time looking down at the little white river down there and at all the rococo shapes and candle-wax dripping off the walls and cliffs that went from here to there. It was exactly the reverse of what we had gone through the day before, as if all those huge mesas along the south edge of Utah had been forcibly ripped out of the land in northern Arizona. It was an awesome museum of geology and natural history and deep time. I never last long in museums — there's only so much beauty and majesty the human brain can take at one time — but I think Britt reached her saturation point even more quickly than I did. She had bought in the hotel gift shop one of those women's mags she was increasingly buying these days. *Marie Claire* was its name, and so Britt, having soon taken all she could from American geology's greatest expression of deep nothingness, sat at canyon's edge and absorbed herself in one of British journalism's greatest expressions of deep nothingness: *Marie Claire*'s article called "Oh, Rio: Plastic Surgery Paradise."

"Britt," I threatened unreasonably, "if you don't put away that magazine right now and spend a few minutes longer really appreciating the grandeur in front of us, I'm going to write about this."

So that was the Grand Canyon, and we might have stayed longer, but we had Nothing on our minds. Nothing required a sagging zig south on 64, a saltant zag west on 40, and a xerophytic zap on 93 into rocks and dirt and cinder heaps over wavy terrain under the hazy gaze of a glaring sun.

Soon after turning south on 93, we saw a white wooden cross planted in the dirt beside the road. Next to the cross a sign with a little picture of a cross on it said LOCATION OF FATALITY. DRIVE WITH CARE.

I stopped to study the cartographicus magnus. I figured we were now about an hour from Nothing, but on the other hand I hadn't see any signs along the road for Nothing. In fact, there was not a lot of anything at all along the road. Basically it was just desert sprinkled with little bushes.

Soon, we were rumbling impatiently behind a very slow and erratic Ford truck, waiting for our chance to pass. A sign said THERE'S A LAST TIME FOR EVERYTHING. And then another sign showed a crude pictograph of a car crashing and said DRINKING. The sign after that showed another crash and said SPEEDING SLEEPING. But I was still trying to pass the guy ahead of me in the pickup truck. Then another sign with a picture of a cocktail glass summarized the whole shebang: DRINKING SPEEDING SLEEPING DRIVING DON'T MIX. *Fair enough, but I'm still going to pass the guy,* I said to myself. *I haven't been drinking, and I'm not sleeping.* The next sign showed swerving tire marks and said simply: NEXT TEN MILES. But soon after those ten miles I found a break in the double line, and so stepped on the gas and passed the Ford pickup — carefully.

The next sign said USE HEADLIGHTS DAY AND NIGHT.

I turned on my headlights.

Bayne had bought three Mexican jumping beans at a gift shop in Mexican Hat, which he named Beanie, Weenie, and Teenie, and for the first twelve hours they had been in high spirits, very happy to get out of the gift shop, but now, as we worked our way down the nihilistic highway through a shimmering heat, Bayne's beans started to slow down. They had seen what hell was like and thought better of it. And the road kept going deeper into this harrowing land of rubble and stubble with, now, a lot of dangerous looking plants: a cactus that looked like a series of blown-up pineapples welded back together, other cactuses made out of knife blades, and a tree filled with circular saw blades.

The sun drummed onto our car top and bounced up from the road, and the sky carried only a few little clouds that looked like escaped amoebas. And now on either side of the road began to appear more and more weird cactuses looking like big green gloves sticking up.

"If you're ever lost in the desert and thirsty, take your knife out and open one of those cactuses. They're supposed to have water inside, OK? I think you just slurp it," I said. But I was bluffing. Really, I had no idea if any of that was true.

Sometimes the cactuses looked like factory glove molds, fingers sticking up. Other times they just looked like overfed space aliens with somewhere between two and five tubular limbs. And now we started noticing all the fatal accident crosses alongside the road. "Wow! Seven crosses."

We came to a huge garden of cactuses, a whole hillside full of them: younger ones looking like a single green finger sticking up, round and combed and prickly, and older ones sprouting fingers. Then more crosses along the road. At last, we sighted a twinned pair of fatality crosses on one side of the road and on the other side Nothing. Nothing was a shelf of rock and gravel on top of which we parked our car next to about a dozen other cars, some of them being worked on, a tow truck, and a big wooden sign bolted onto four high telephone poles that would probably say

welcome to NOTHING, AZ

if half the sign weren't missing, but because half the sign was missing, it said

welcome to NOT.

Another, much smaller sign had been erected much closer to the road. It consisted of a couple of pieces of plywood supported by a parked horse trailer and painted yellow. The top piece of plywood said **HEY!** And, in a crafted, artistically naïve script, the bottom piece said **Nothing**, with a curled arrow growing out of the end of the "g" like a dog's tail.

Aside from the parked vehicles and that tow truck, there was a small bus, as well as two or three small trailers, a gas pump, and two main buildings. The larger building was a big corrugated tin shed, painted salmon, with a corrugated tin roof, and a black and white legend painted on the front:

GARAGE
OPEN
TOWING.

The garage door was open, and from a dark place inside emanated the eerie, wavering, potent wail of an electric guitar being practiced upon.

To the right of the garage was a smaller building, a roadside convenience store, salmon with yellow trim, made of plywood with a sliding glass door. Out front of this store: some lawn furniture and a barbecue grill. And then to the right sat a salmon-colored trailer marked with the words **OUTDOOR GALLERY** and surrounded by bumpers, hubcaps, grills, brake drums, headlamps, steer skulls, strips of bright plastic sheeting, and so on, all conglomerated in interesting and clever ways and then painted brightly to become totems and monsters and masks and objets d'art.

We walked into the store, which was invitingly cool from air conditioning and distressingly noisy from a TV set and a small number of people watching it, bought some soft drinks, paid our money to a dark-glassed, blond-haired woman at the cash register. We looked at the art on the walls, including an exotic mural of Nothing's Founding Fathers and Mother busy working slot machines, and the portrait of a black-and-white-faced dog, Katie, Queen of Nothing. And then we began asking the cash-registrar about Nothing. Pretty soon we were talking about Nothing to the TV watchers, too. "We just want to know how the place got named, and what's the story behind it, and—" I was explaining.

"Got named by a buncha drunks," somebody said, cutting me short. And then somebody else said we should go out and find James, who was playing his electric guitar out in the garage. James, however, a young man with a mustache and stringy, shoulder-length hair, was busy practicing and thought we really should talk to Buddy who was napping but might be ready to wake up. So someone did wake up Buddy, and he came out soon and greeted the three of us most heartily.

"Howdy howdy," he said, shaking my hand. "And what have we, sir?"

"Are you Buddy?" I said.

"I am Buddy, the great one."

I said we were from Massachusetts and had traveled all the way to Nothing.

"You're livin good then. That is the way to live. Travel. Have fun!"

That's what we were doing, I continued, and then I explained that we wanted to know the story behind Nothing. So Buddy and I sat down in the lawn furniture in front of the store and talked and drank Cokes, while the Research Staff came and went, mostly went. Buddy—his formal name was Richard Kenworthy—wore a purple T-shirt and Levi's suspended by black suspenders, and a yellow-and-white tractor cap that said "Nothing, Arizona" on the front. He was a likable extrovert who squinted and tilted his head as he talked, and he talked forcibly with a mildly blustrified manner.

"The great Nothing, yep," he continued. "Well, for one thing it's nothing. But I come out here in '77 to get outta towwwnnn."

"Which town?"

"Well, any town, tell you the truth, any town. I just wanted to get out in the woods, out in the sticks. I liked the look of these hills. Back then gold was kinda high, so I wanted to check it out, see if there was any gold. I didn't find gold. I found nothing. So, I said, 'There's Nothing here.' Ah, and then I had to make a livin so I just started doin what I'm doin now."

"You buy this piece of land?"

Well, yes, Buddy said, he bought it. Then he found out that he didn't own it. Well, someone sold him the land, but part of it was on government property and stuff, so now he's buying from the government—just an odd little piece of acreage, only five six seven, six seven acres here, all leased to ranchers and stuff, the way they do it. But he and his fellow citizens make a living, and so that is the story of Nothing. They burned out in '88 and rebuilt. Everything here burned down. Well, his brother-in-law had a little trailer backed up to the house. The trailer caught fire somehow or other. They ran down when they seen the smoke, and it was coming out the trailer window onto his— Buddy's—porch. And his whole porch was on fire. There was no fire inside the house. So either he had an electrical or he left a cigarette in there, or something on that order, Buddy didn't know. But they just say "an accident," regardless. Wasn't intentional. But still and all, they really like it, at least Buddy does, living out basically in the middle of nothing. Yes. Long as he can make a living he will stay here. At the great Nothing. He will never leave, except in a body bag.

James the electric guitarist is his stepson, Buddy explained, from his second and current wife. Reba was his first wife who came out to Nothing with him. She died of cancer before the town burned down. After it burned down, his other wife — Betty — came through. The blond-haired woman at the cash register is Betty's daughter, Twila, and James is Betty's son. And there are others in Nothing, including Donny, Twila's son, and a couple of older guys who come out of the desert now and then, including George Brucha, the hermit artist who lives out in an abandoned mine-shack somewhere — no electricity, no running water — whose artwork was being exhibited and sold in the town gallery. They all work here, Buddy declared, waiting for the ax to fall.

"Which ax is that?" I said.

"Well, when the ax falls you go to the grave, right?"

"Oh, *that* ax," I said. "Well, I'll tell ya, seeing all those crosses on the road just getting out here — it seemed pretty ominous getting out here."

"Yeah, I work the road now with my tow truck, picking up the pieces, so I work the wreckage and stuff, so it's pretty bad at times. People get a little careless, little fast, little speed. Some of 'em are drinkin, but most of it's carelessness and speed, I think."

We chattered away about carelessness and speed, then about deserts and cacti, and finally drifted back to Nothing. "No, Nothing just kind of sprang up," Buddy said. "I named it Nothing after I come out here, 1977. We were all drunks then. Whole town was drunks. Four to start with. Yep. We were all drinkers. Now nobody's a drinker here. I quit, we all quit. We had to quit."

"Is that one of the reasons you came out here was to get away from the temptations?"

"Ahhhhhh, yes. That didn't cure it all, however. Over the years — years will cure what discipline can't. Know what I mean? As you get older you will be cured of everything. Eventually. Yeah. You *will* be cured. If you don't have the discipline, the years will take care of that. But the people that come out here enjoy it, like it." So, he went on, no, they don't get bored. They get tired sometimes. Not bored. Too many things happening. James, he goes out but he also plays his guitar, and he helps run the tow truck, and he's pretty satisfied. They don't drink nor none of that stuff, so they're just living their lives. One day they might decide to move out. Who knows what'll happen. We've all got our own minds. We've all got our own lives.

I agreed with Buddy about that one, and, well, we sat out in the sun on the lawn furniture in front of the store, squinted, pulled our hats down across our foreheads and over our eyes, drank Cokes, and talked about a lot of things: Indian pottery shards that he sometimes finds; the old days, before the road came in, when Nothing was danged difficult to get around in and danged easy to get lost in; the time two Bureau of Land Management guys got lost looking for a mine, and one was carried out in a helicopter while the other is buried out there in the sand; and the rattlesnakes. Lotta rattlers. Don't want to walk at night, for sure. Buddy doesn't walk anywhere at night without a light. It would be an emergency-type situation for him to even step outside his door without a light. Of course, during the day they're not around because it's too hot. Yeah. They'll come out at night to do whatever they do, hunt or whatever. For food. Now if you got a real *ni-ice* day where it clouds over and stuff, they will be out. Then you gotta watch. There's a lot of 'em out around Nothing. Buddy'd say he's seen a lotta snakes in the last few years, and he's seen only about six snakes that weren't rattlers, is all. Rattlers. They like it hot. The hotter it is, the lower the elevation, the thicker the rattlesnake gets.

So we talked a lot, as I said, and then George Brucha wandered over, and so the Research Staff and I visited him in his art gallery, admired his art, and talked a lot more with him: wiry and graceful, with longish white hair, white stubble on his chin, missing teeth, a ravaged face, and a quiet, understated manner. George grew up in an orphanage back East and finally came out to the desert to get away from alcohol and also to concentrate on his art; and there was a rarefied, rather wise gentleness about him that I thought maybe was the sediment of suffering refined by the sun. And I thought I was getting into the peaceful mood of Nothing, drinking more and more Coca-Colas with ice, when a loud and possibly self-centered Englishman pulled off the highway in a cherry red car and began prancing about, talking excitedly, and taking photographs.

"Hi theh! Howyadoin!" he yelled, and then he went inside the store and yelled the same thing to Twila at the cash register and to the TV watchers. Buddy and I followed him inside — and Twila, who had long been expecting a journalist and photographer from the *National Enquirer* to write something about Nothing, thought he was that person, since he was obviously insensitive and had a foreign accent.

"You from England or —?" she asked. "You the *National Enquirer*?"

"Yeah," he lied. "I came six thousand miles for this!"

"Australia? New Zealand?"

"England."

"England! I knew it was somewhere's where all the —!"

But the Englishman didn't want to talk about England. He wanted to talk about Nothing. "Whot's heah? Whot's heah?" he demanded.

"Nothing!" came the answer.

"Wait till I tell my dawtah about tha!" he exclaimed.

"You're not from Bristol, England, are you?"

"I'm from the nawth! Nawth of England! I play rock-n-roll music!"

"Are you the photographer that's supposed to be doing the photography work?"

"No, but I'm gonna take a phoe-toe if that's OK."

"Yeah, well, you're in the right place: Nothing."

"It's on the mawp! It's on the mawp!"

"Are you the one who's gonna take the photo?"

"No, that's some other guy. Sorry, I haven't got, haven't got—"

"Where would you want to take a picture, outside or inside?"

"Outside, because I don't think I have the light. I'll have a go."

So that was Nothing, momentarily subtracted from by the inflated presence of a loudmouthed rock-n-roller from Britain. Soon after I thought it was time for us to rock-n-roll out of Nothing and back into something, which in this particular instance was Las Vegas. Las Vegas is a non sequitur, not a Storyville, I know that, but it was our next goal (pedaling hot and hard west on 40 and northwest on 93) for some major rest and relaxation at the home of Fiona, my wife's sister, and her husband, Skip. Like Nothing, Las Vegas started as nothing, but unlike Nothing it became something and then Something, and that's where out of Nothing we betook ourselves: to rest and dream and round our little lives with sleep.

LEG³

Hallelujah Junction

On a leisurely Monday morning we waved good-bye to Skip and Fiona and drove north on a hot highway into a hot desert bound for northern California. The Nevada desert made a person feel like a louse crawling across a dirty carpet in a big and empty room. But by the end of the day we had penetrated Reno, crossed into California, and started a long roll on Interstate 80 out of the mountains, down to San Francisco, and then along the coast to Pescadero Beach where we ran and jumped into the surf and collected sea shells.

After a few days visiting our friends Chris and Mark and their three children in Palo Alto, we turned the car around and launched ourselves up Interstate 80 back toward Reno. Everything looked much the same as it had before only in reverse. Then it got dark and nothing looked the same, but just as I was starting to feel desperate we found a little stone lodge next to a river. In the morning, we reached the top of the Sierra Nevadas at the Donner Summit, where at a small museum we learned the following.

In November of 1844, some risk-taking types demonstrated that a person could drag wooden wagons through the Utah and Nevada desert, across a grassy meadow around present-day Reno, along and across a river, and through a small gap in the Sierra Nevadas around Interstate 80 right where we were situated at the moment even though Interstate 80 wasn't there then. That was the first wagon train to pass from Nevada into California, and it was soon followed by a whole slew, including, two years later, the Donner Party. The Donner Party (a hundred people of several families, including those of brothers George and Jacob Donner) started out in the spring of 1846 at the edge of Missouri.

The Donner train followed well-worn wagon tracks west until they met a fast-talker who declared he had found an easier route to California, with plenty of grass, wood, water, and not many obstacles. The party was induced to take their chances on a left turn into some beautiful landscape in Utah, where Indians raided the wagons and killed a couple of the emigrants, but finally most of them made it alive — if late in the season — over to the other side of the Nevada desert and up to the Truckee River, which they followed and crossed fifty times until they had arrived at Truckee Lake by the end of October, 1846, just a few miles from the pass into California.

It had started to snow, however, and soon the emigrants were snowed in. They built cabins and ate whatever of their cattle they could locate under the snow. But the snow continued to fall, completely burying the cabins. A group of seventeen men and women from this so-called Mountain Camp took a gamble on crossing the mountains on snowshoes in late December, and, after some deaths from cold and starvation with the occasional meal of human flesh and a little derangement thrown in, the survivors eventually stumbled into white settlements in mid-January of 1847 around present-day Sacramento. Nevertheless, some eighty members of the Donner Party remained trapped in snow at the Mountain Camp. A rescue and relief expedition was outfitted from Sacramento in late January, but it was impeded and imperiled by cold and the snow that in places lay up to 160 feet deep. By the time a second rescue operation reached the Mountain Camp on March 1, it was observed that the thigh and leg of the late Jacob Donner had been fetched for dinner by his brother, George, and family. Even so the rescuers could only take seventeen people out, of whom several died in the process. When the final expedition reached the Mountain Camp in April, 1847, only Lewis Kiesburg was still upright and in one piece.

Kiesburg, surrounded by dismembered bodies, explained to his rescuers that he had acquired a preference for human flesh, especially brains and liver, and in fact he had just finished Mrs. George Donner. She was "the best he had ever tasted."

After looking at the Donner Museum, we stopped at the Donner House Restaurant — offering Breakfast, Lunch, Dinner, and Cocktails — but decided against eating there because Britt didn't feel like it. And Bayne didn't feel like it. I didn't feel like it either.

Then we followed the Truckee River through a chasm (the kind of chasm that would be rough on wooden wagons) and then crossed the river, at which point a sign said it was only twenty miles to Reno, and suddenly we were moving fast in a flurry of traffic with a lot of gamblers. You could recognize them by their cars, which were classic antiques, restored and spiffy, with stuffed furry dice hanging from the rearview mirrors. The gamblers also wore wraparound sunglasses. Well, we crossed the state line into Nevada at exactly 11:11, and that is a true fact. Double snake eyes.

"That means that we're going to have to gamble in Reno," I said, only to be overruled by the entire Research Staff at once: "No!"

We reached the desert plateau. There were a lot of little desert shrubs, chaparral and sage and not much else except rocks and a few giant billboards made out of lights: COME ON IN WIN CASH AND CRUISES BOOMTOWN HOTEL AND CASINO WAKE THE DRAGON 1965 MUSTANG IN OUR

SLOT. Other than that it was just basically desert. Desert and gambling, which pretty much defines Nevada as far as I can tell, and our big highway just kept rolling: with right behind us now a beautiful classic 1959 Chevy, cherry red on the outside and with the same color plushed all over the interior. And furry dice hanging from the mirror.

"Oh, cool," Bayne said while he looked it over discreetly through the mirror.

But that wasn't all. We were surrounded by classic cars. Maybe there was some kind of classic car convention going on in Reno. Suddenly we were running neck and neck with souped-up Model Ts and MG roadsters and original XKEs, not to mention '50s-style hot rods and old pink Cadillac convertibles and Eisenhower Chevys and even an Edsel, I think. And they all seemed to have hanging furry dice.

We came to the western edge of Reno, and it still looked like desert but now there were a few houses in the desert and more houses ahead. The houses looked like insect egg clusters laid out on a leaf. Soon we were running out the northern edge of Reno, which looked like the western edge, and then we were in the desert again and passing through a series of rock formations that looked like bubbly saliva.

We saw a sign, HALLELUJAH JUNCTION 19 MILES, which spurred us on, and now I did my best to prepare our party psychologically.

"All right," I said. "Here's the plan now. At Hallelujah Junction we're going to do all kinds of exciting things like buy candy. We're going to buy candy. We're going to try to get some music tapes, and we're going to do all kinds of other things that will make us say 'Hallelujah!' which must be the point of Hallelujah Junction. And maybe we'll arrive singing the 'Hallelujah Chorus,' if I can remember the lyrics, and then we'll try to find out where the name came from." We were still driving across the desert — with gullies and gulches, some long valleys with chaparral and sage comforters, and in the distance a set of bumpy mountains — driving north and watching all the gamblers in classic cars with furry dice driving south, when pretty soon we approached the Nevada-California border at a town called Bordertown, which amounted to a toy store full of identical houses with roofs offered in two optional colors.

We came to an inspection station: ALL VEHICLES STOP.

"Let's try not to look like drug smugglers, OK?" I said, feeling a little nervous for no good reason, but we passed inspection with flying colors and then were back in California again, only it still looked like Nevada. Soon after that we arrived at the junction of 395 and 70, which was Hallelujah Junction.

It wasn't much. Hallelujah Junction struck me as a very disappointing little spot: one modern store and gas station that together called itself the Hallelujah Junction General Store. There were American and California flags flying out front, and in front of the flags a wooden sign had been staked into a small green throw-rug of grass. The sign said HALLELUJAH JUNCTION GENERAL STORE, and it had a wooden coot, an old white-bearded '49er I think, jumping up and clicking his heels and looking ecstatic about the wooden gold nuggets stacked up beside him.

This was a 76 self-service gas station. Very modern operation. Lots of automated pumps and a giant steel roof to fight off the sun. Plus there was the store itself, a big modern log cabin with a green plastic roof. Everything looked new. It was hard to know what to think. The store and gas station were still in the middle of the desert. The land around us was an olive drab with the emphasis on drab, dotted and spotted and speckled with green vegetation in the distance. Well, it was certainly a junction, with Route 395 north out of Reno colliding right there with the eastern end of Route 70 headed west for parts unknown. But why would anyone be inspired to say "Hallelujah" there?

"Uh-oh, I have a bad feeling about this," I said. "Anyway, we'll ask how it got its name."

We walked into the store, which offered a big spread of items like Hostess Cupcakes and potato chips and bagged sandwiches, music tapes for sale on the counter, candy, and a Super Spy plastic dart gun complete with three rubber-tipped darts. There were also cowboys in the store, or at least guys wearing cowboy clothes and looking like cowboys.

We bought some necessities, including an Abba tape and a Super Spy plastic dart gun with three rubber-tipped darts, and started talking with the woman at the counter. Unfortunately, before she could say very much, there was a big noise and commotion outside. The woman turned her head, looked out the plate windows behind her, and said with complete disgust: "Somebody drove off again with the hose in the tank!" She went off to retrieve a ripped-away pump hose, and so our questions were deferred and finally referred to the manager, a pleasant and stocky young man with blue eyes, a big chin, and a big mustache. He was wearing a white shirt with a ballpoint pen in the left pocket, a heel-clicking coot next to the words Hallelujah Junction above the right pocket, and a cream-colored *McMillan Crop Ins* cap on his head.

His name was Michael Oglivie, he said, and, though I think he was very busy right at that time, he very generously acted as if he had all the time in the world to answer our questions. Michael said he had worked at the Hallelujah Junction store for about five years, and, he added, his Hallelujah Junction sells more California Lottery tickets than any other store in the state.

"Really?" I said. "That seems totally weird because you're right next to Reno."

"It's a gambling area," Michael said. "People are addicted to it." In any event, he went on, before this store was at the junction, there used to be another store. There was a guy named Harold Stoy, he set up a little — originally it may have been a brothel — a little landing strip, and Stoy had a restaurant and a bar and a motel, and people used to fly in. He came out with his father in about 1932, and they both started the place. Then when his dad retired to live in Truth or Consequences, New Mexico, Stoy ran it all by himself. But today all that's left of Stoy's original Hallelujah Junction restaurant and bar and motel and airport and possibly brothel, all that's left is underneath the southbound lanes of the highway right now. It's all buried underneath the southbound lane. The state took it over.

And the story of the name is that after the Donner Party fiasco, this half-Negro half-Indian man approached the army and told them about his Indian relatives living over there and said there was a trail that went all the way from outside of Reno down to Sacramento, and it was all downhill. It turns out that he was right. The pass right out of Hallelujah Junction is the lowest pass in the Sierras for crossing over into California. And it worked out pretty good for about four or five trips. This Indian'd pick up the wagon trains in St. Louis and then escort them on out to Sacramento and be relieved at Sacramento.

But he got greedy, and his relatives, an Indian tribe in the area, they started raiding the wagon trains and killing the passengers and stealing everything. So it became a pretty big gamble to go that route and also a big embarrassment to the army which had licensed this guy, and then he went back to St. Louis to get another wagon train, and the wagon master supposedly from the previous train he followed him back to St. Louis and killed him in a bar. At about this time, which would be in the very early 1850s, there was an army captain stationed up in the Modoc region named Captain James P. Beckwourth, and the army became embarrassed when all the newspapers found out that the first guy was actually robbing all the trains, and so they sent down this army officer, Beckwourth, and he took over the operation.

And the story goes that in 1852 a wagon train came through the Nevada desert and Reno to be met by Captain Beckwourth. Beckwourth led them to the present day junction and announced that the pass straight on down — right there ahead of us and now called Beckwourth Pass — would be the lowest and the easiest pass in the entire Sierra Nevada range. In other words (Captain Beckwourth declared to the gathered members of that wagon train), no one would have to take the Donner route directly west out of Reno. And therefore (he continued) no one would have to risk getting caught in the snow and then freeze and starve and be miserable and feel compelled to eat poor old Mrs. Donner again. And at that juncture someone in the wagon train jumped up and shouted: "**HALLELUJAH!!!!**"

Likely

Route 395 north seemed to follow a high desert valley between two walls of mountains. There wasn't much around except for Janesville and Susanville, and we stopped for a late lunch in Susanville in honor of our friend Susan.

But I found that high valley very satisfying. A glacier may have carved it out, I was thinking, but probably the ice melted a long time ago so that was why it had now gotten very hot. It was hot but really a very beautiful rural place, grand and spare with the occasional welding shop and old house with a tower house behind it, a long sweep of valley with pale-green grass and shrub and brush beside the road as well as clumps of weeds and wild flowers. Very pleasant and unpressured, partially because there was no commerce to speak of other than inside the towns and none of your usual roadside lunacy, only the occasional laconic commentary about fundamental things such as loose gravel and low shoulders. It seemed like a likely place to have a prison, judging from the large prison we passed on the road, but we were also passing lots of attractive places of the opposite kind, such as a dreamy little farm sitting in a dry and feathery sea of fluffy grass and washed by willow trees willing weepy branches in front of creaky buildings with tin roofs and old gray wood.

"Just keep your eyes peeled for motels on this side of Likely in case we need to retrace our steps after we get there. Next service is forty-four miles. How's our gas doing?" I said.

We passed some old gray board fences tipping this way and that way, some rusty cars, and some long open fields with sage brush and what looked to be wild grass. It was gorgeous country out there, but aside from the highway in front of us, which had turned into a silvery lake constantly receding, there hadn't been a lot of liquid lately. Mostly there were lots of ranches and then after the ranches, except for the occasional telephone line and railroad track, not much other than leached desert and bleached grass. It was beginning to remind me of Wyoming, in fact, complete with the household garbage piled against a bullet-riddled sign that said NO HOUSEHOLD GARBAGE.

It became desert, but after a while the desert turned back into dry grassland, and then we saw signs of water and also of cattle and pretty soon of Likely. LIKELY 12 MILES it said, and after about ten miles the road descended off a slight hill and came to a pretty place with trees wavering around the edges. We passed a few houses, the Likely Cemetery, and then the sign for Likely proper, which said LIKELY. It also listed a Likely population of 200 and a Likely elevation of 4,447.

Likely was altogether a light locale, a little stretch of houses and business buildings on either side of the highway and beyond that another stretch of a few more houses. Beyond those stretches, the town disappeared into grassland, ranchland, and open land. Likely had a lone main line that was also the highway, and Likely had about one crossroad that crossed the highway. We drove east along that crossroad for approximately three houses past something that might have been a barber shop and a house that said WOODCRAFTS, and that looked like the end of Likely: barbed wire and a man in a ten-gallon hat walking over to a horse trailer and scratching his left leg.

Back on the main drag a lady with looped lobes and long hair in a lazy tail was pulling her baby in a baby pusher. There was a building that looked like probably the Likely Post Office, and it looked like it shared a roof with the Likely Laundrymat. There was the South Fork Assembly church at the far end of town, which didn't look like a church partly because it didn't have a cross; and out past the church we found a large collection of large trucks. Some of the trucks had holes, suggesting they might carry cattle, and others looked refrigerated with pictures of sizzling sirloin on the sides, suggesting they might also carry cattle though less alive.

There was the Most Likely Café and a Likely Garage, a Likely Community Church (which wasn't any fancier than the South Fork Assembly but you don't need to be fancy to be a church), the Likely Saloon offering Spirits to Go, and finally the Likely General Store just across Highway 395 from the Likely Fire Department.

The Likely General Store occupied a stucco building with a Western-style façade and "Likely General Store" painted up there in ornate script. Inside the Likely General Store was a large collection of ladders, lanterns, lariats, licorice, loaves of bread, and a sign that said "The Ideal Gift for a Dad" showing a dad opening a present and finding leather cowboy boots. In fact, three cowboys were in the general store right then, including one lout in leather leggings, so it seemed to me we might in all likelihood have reached legitimate cowboyland.

We bought some ice cream and asked the fellow running the cash register if he knew of anyone from whom we could learn the lore of Likely, and he, after clarifying that we weren't looney, laid out in longhand a list of locals who seemed to have the same last name, which was Flournoy, and suggested we might locate someone on that list.

That would be a good idea, I agreed, but since it was late and I hadn't seen any telephones lately or lodging in Likely for that matter, I concluded that the locating might best be launched from Alturas, which lay just about twenty miles north along the highway. I thanked the fellow at the cash register, and the three of us walked back to the car while licking our Likely ice cream.

We drove north from Likely about twenty miles to Alturas. Alturas was a little city with a little-city feel in a Country and Western sort of way, though large enough to have one hotel and possibly six motels as well as perhaps three or four restaurants. We finally located some low-cost lodging at the Hacienda Motel, I believe it was, and then left to locate a meal. I mentioned Country and Western earlier in this paragraph to foreshadow what we were learning about this part of the world, especially when we left to look for a meal in Alturas, which is the following: We had arrived at where beef comes from.

It was ranching country, and as if to clarify that fact, all the restaurants in town offered beef beef and beef—plus a little leg of lamb or a large lobster at the lower limit of the list. I ordered lobster, and I really don't remember what Britt ordered. I do remember that the sirloin slab Bayne ordered was large enough to feed three normal males for a long time and still have enough left over for a lean Labrador. Bayne simply couldn't finish it, in other words, which seemed legitimate to me but alienated the waitlady, who was loathe to repeal the last of the meal: "Are you sure you want me take this? You know, you didn't finish your steak." In any case, I located one of the Likely Flournoys on the telephone late that evening. His first name was Don and his wife's name was Shirley, and he would be glad to meet us at 10:00 sharp the next morning at his house and tell us everything he knew about Likely. He gave directions to his house, which was about a mile east of the Likely limits on the crossroads, and it was a beige house just off the something road past some kind of a fence or something like that so we couldn't miss it.

We did, of course, which turned out to be an embarrassment for me, because when I say 10:00 sharp I mean 10:00 sharp, but sometimes people say "about a mile" when they mean "like, a mile," and sometimes people say "beige" when they mean "like, green." At any rate, we got lost in Likely and then late but at last located Don and Shirley Flournoy, and they were, just as I suspected they would be, a likeable couple who invited us to linger over a table spread with coffee, tea, milk, and breakfast cakes and cookies on their back porch.

They were a ranching couple, Don and Shirley, straight and hard-working, generous and proud, and Don did most of the talking, though Shirley would pipe in when piping in was called for. Don was actually sort of retired from ranching, looking about sixty years old but being about eighty, even though he just finished haying yesterday and had been running the baler all summer long. But he had, he told us, three sons that basically run the ranch, which amounts to some thirty thousand acres of land plus another one hundred thousand acres that they lease from the federal government. They run a couple of thousand brood cows on that land, maybe a hundred bulls, and a certain amount of replacement heifers. That may seem like a lot of land for only a couple thousand cattle, but it's not really. And the government land they lease, it requires maybe about one animal to fourteen acres. They go out there the first of May and come in about the first of September. Then the cattle're basically on the ranch, the deeded land, the rest of the time. The government has that rule because they want the environment to hold and the grasses to stay constant, which makes sense, and then during the winter when the cattle are off the range they feed them hay. In the winter, of course, the grass stops growing and the temperature drops down to zero. In fact, they've had forty below zero there for six weeks at a time, so even though it might be hot right now at this moment, up here in the high desert it does get cold in the winter.

They're just on the edge of the Nevada desert, as a matter of fact, and only get about thirteen inches of moisture year round. And one reason they can ranch at all out around Likely is that they built a reservoir in 1936 and so supplement their river water with stored water. Otherwise, they'd be out of water now at this time of year.

Now ranching has never been easy, but lately it has been getting rougher, Don Flournoy went on. Rougher. Lots of people are unhappy with agriculture. Especially those environmentalists. They have an organization out there called the Sierra Club. As well as a lot of others. There's the Greenpeace and there's—he didn't know what they call the timber people that don't want any trees cut. And they don't give these timber operations any credit for farming and replacing every tree they cut. Well, then the ranchers have to deal with the animal-rights people that don't think they should even kill a cow to eat. And the environmentalists that think that they're hurting the country by using it, and they don't give you much credit for the fact that ranchers've been there a hundred years and it looks much better now than it did a hundred years ago. It's like the old saying, a preacher came by and told the farmer that between him and God they have a nice place, and the farmer said, "Well, you should have seen it when God had it by Himself."

As for the town of Likely today, it's a real nice town. Of course there *are* a lot of Flournoys. And if we were to live there, we might just think there were too many Flournoys. And, Shirley added, they're away from the cultural things. Plays or theater or what have you. Yeah, Don said, their biggest town is Reno. So that's quite a trip, to go to Reno. That's where the doctors and lawyers and hospitals are, either that or Redding. If you have any serious problems, you'd best get out of Likely. There's a hospital in Alturas, Shirley said, but they're not able to handle any major surgery or anything like that. And they have fly-in doctors that fly in to take care of special cases, but the area is isolated enough that they have trouble attracting good doctors, or good teachers for that matter. It's too isolated.

At this point in our conversation, Don began levitating himself out of his chair to go and fetch some sugar for my tea — but Shirley beat him to it. So he landed back down in the chair and continued.

Yeah, he said, his granddad came here in 1871, and there was not very many white people around here then. Lots of Indians. They called them the Pit Indians. That is the Pit River just outside of Likely, and Don didn't know whether it was fact or fiction or legend or what, but those Indians made pits along the edge of the river for game to fall in. So they got deer and what animals were available for meat, and that was that. That's how they got their name. But they just died off. At first, the calamity that happened to them that Don knew about was in 1917 or '18, they got the flu. And right there in the Likely area, they claim that there's six hundred Indians died. When Don was born, there were quite a bit of Indians in the area, and he remembered they were just like anybody else. They had lots of real good Indian families that they associated with. They worked on the ranch, and he played with the Indian kids. They played their games and they played probably the origination of Cowboys and Indians. But now there's not an Indian left in the Likely area. The last couple they had died, but when he was growing up there was more Indian kids at the Indian school than there was white kids. Three times more.

Anyway, his granddad, John D. Flournoy, came across the Plains in a covered wagon with the rest of his family, and they went to The Dalles, Oregon, and then from The Dalles went down to central California, and about the time they got down there they were having a severe drought. So his granddad, he was nineteen years old then, took a bunch of cattle, left his mom and dad back down in central California, and he came up into the northern California country in 1871 and elected to stay.

He had quite a bunch of cattle, two or three hundred head, and he came up here at nineteen years old and staked his claim here. The original homestead was 320 acres. And then there was an area next to him that Don thought his granddad was able to take up because it was swamp area and he reclaimed it. And another little portion, eighty acres, taken up as a timber claim. Well, he was a tough little guy but pretty pious. He was a Southern Baptist. His family came from France. Huguenots. And then he started as a Baptist in the South. And he came to California and continued as a Southern Baptist, and so Don never heard him ever say a swear word. When he really lost his temper, he said,

"By George!" When he said that you knew he was irate. He lived to be eighty-seven. He got on a horse at eighty years old, bareback, no saddle. And the horse bumped him off. That shook him up a little bit, but that would give us just an idea of how active he was right through the very last.

His grandfather, John D., had four boys. One of his four boys was named Arthur, and Arthur had ten children including Don. Don could remember now when he was about Bayne's age, there was a pool table in the Likely Saloon, and they used to like to sneak in there and play pool, and his dad, Arthur, came in there and caught them, and: "You boys get out of here!" He told the proprietors, "If I catch my boys in here again," he said, "I'm going to burn this place down!" So, needless to say, the Likely Saloon was off-limits to Don and his brothers. For quite a few years. His dad was not too much on drinking either.

Still, he wasn't a Southern Baptist or anything like that. He just had his own religion. And he believed in the Golden Rule, but he said he couldn't believe that this Almighty was here because of the suffering. So he just believed in treating your fellow men as you'd like to be treated. And Don remembered his dad was watching television, and the Brooklyn Dodgers were playing somebody. It was on a Labor Day weekend. So the two of them were sitting there watching the ball game, and his dad says, "I think I'd like to go to the hospital." And Don said, "You feel bad?" "No, but," his dad says, "you got to go someplace to die. I don't want to die here in the house." And Don got excited, and he says, "Well, come on. We'll get it going." "No," his dad says, "I want to take a shower and clean up. When I leave here," he says, "I'm going to leave clean." Don helped him take a shower and bath, and he had a housekeeper and a daughter-in-law who happened to drop in, too. They were there. So when they finally got ready to leave, why he just waved, offhanded like he did. He said, "I'll see you girls in the Great Hereafter." Then they went out the door. And it was a hot, hot spell, almost like what we're having now, and so when they got outside Don says, "It's pretty hot out here." And, his dad says, "Oh, probably not half as hot as where I'm heading!"

Don took him into the hospital in Alturas, and they put him in bed and gave him a little oxygen mask to kind of perk him up, and he stayed there overnight and about ten o'clock the next morning, some of the other family members were in there, and they said he just took that mask off and set it aside, and that was the end of it. He died. He was eighty-seven. And his wife lived to be eighty-seven. Both of them ate beef about three times a day.

But back to the story of grandfather John D. Flournoy, who came up to the area in 1871. After he had been there in the area for a time and had started homesteading, then some other settlers came into the valley until it was finally enough people that they concluded they would like to get on the postal service route. This area is located on the South Fork of the Pit River. And so the settlers sent in the name, South Fork, for a post office name. And the postal authorities came back and said that there was too many South Forks in the United States already and would rather they look for something else. And so they had a meeting in the store. The general store at that time was owned by Don's granddad. They were all sitting around the stove and discussing different names or maybe whether there was any point at all in even having a post office, and—his granddad was from Virginia and Missouri before he came to California—he said, in the languid style of someone from Virginia and Missouri, "Well, there's *likely* to be a town here someday."

The rest of them said, "Well, let's just call it Likely."

That was the story of Likely, a likely story or, if one may be excused for a liking of labored litotes, at least not an unlikely story. And so, after finishing our cookies and cakes, tea and milk, and thanking Don and Shirley Flournoy most sincerely for their time and generosity, we took our leave and left Likely at last.

Boring

The bottom of Oregon looked like the bottom of any state except that it was covered with trees.

We drove hard north on Interstate 5.

We reached the southern edge of Portland near the top of the state late that same day.

In reality, it was late the next day, but now I can't remember how it took us almost two days to get from the bottom of Oregon to the top, so why don't we just pretend it was one?

Next morning, we headed east on Route 212 with Mount Hood growing bigger in front of us.

Then a sign said BORING.

We were in Boring, which seemed like a quiet little community on a Sunday morning.

There was approximately one significant street in Boring, which amounted to the highway.

256

There were about a dozen business modalities in Boring, including one big sawmill, half tucked away behind the strip of commercial buildings lining the highway.

There seemed to be a big hair-cutting place in Boring as well, situated across the highway from the sawmill.

The hair-cutting place had a sign made out of a two-foot-diameter circular saw blade with the words HAIR MILL written on it.

But it was a Sunday morning, as I said earlier, and so Boring was kind of quiet.

Some guy had parked his car back by the entrance to the Boring sawmill, and now he was sprawled out with the car doors and windows open, trying to catch a Boring snooze and a Boring breeze simultaneously.

Zigzag

Zooming out of Boring, we pegged a right onto Route 26 following four cars, all of them loaded with bicycles. Route 26 was a four-laner headed into the Cascade Mountains, Mount Hood in particular, and we were already moving into some nice forests. We zipped past the Big Foot Motel, and I thought it was great to think that Big Foot could have a place to shower and catch some Zs if he wanted. Mount Hood kept looking bigger. There was beaucoup de snow at the zenith, we could see that, and now it looked like there might be some super slippery zones for the sledding zealot.

We zigged past the Mount Hood Village, which had a couple of camping resorts and a café, and then we zinged into the Wildwood Recreation Site. There was a barber shop and a motel and a Whistlestop stop, and I thought it bizarre because here we were in a big forest and yet driving in line with a zillion other cars and suddenly passing antlers, antiques, gifts, espresso, a video store, real estate, snack shack, the Panda Panda Chinese-American Restaurant, the In-between Store, another espresso bar, so on, until we saw the sign that said only one more mile to Zigzag.

Zigzag! So we were about there, but Route 26 was still a straight and powerful four-lane highway. No zigging or zagging there. It went gradually uphill but pretty much straight right up to the sign ZIGZAG indicating Zigzag proper. And Zigzag proper seemed to consist of a brief zone of business along the road with, at the end of it all and off to the right, the Zigzag Ranger Station of Mount Hood National Forest. Nobody was home at the ranger station, however, because it was Sunday, so we turned around and prepared to cross the highway and go back, only to find ourselves stuck there with all the endless Sunday afternoon traffic going zip zip zip zip zip zip zip zip zip zip.

We zipped ourselves finally across the highway and stopped at the Zig Zag Mtn Store on the other side. Oh, the traffic was so intense there, I had to fight just to park the car. Inside the Zig Zag Mtn Store worked two young women who were no help at all. The one only worked there, and the other said she didn't know a thing about Zigzag, name or place. She acted as if I were brazen to quiz her about the obvious. *Zigzag? Well, zig and zag.*

We zagged back, after a long wait for a traffic gap, onto the other side of the Zigzag zone and stopped at a log cabin promoting the Generation-X zeitgeist. This was a new log cabin with perfectly round logs, a red metal roof, and a big mural of a zany zombie wearing bug-eyed sunglasses and his hat on backward. Inside, they sold not only snowboards, skis, and video madness but also nachos and pizza. Several people were buzzing around inside that place but only one of them seemed to be over eighteen years old. He wasn't much help either. "The only thing I can tell you about Zigzag," he said, "is I don't know where the name came from." He said we should zip just up the road to the Zig Zag Inn.

We zipped up to the Zig Zag Inn and zapped a parking zone there. The Zig Zag Inn was a complex red-and-white building based on an old cabin at the center. Inside, it was log-cabiney and decorated in a style midway between Switzerland and Zanzibar with a touch of zoophobia. A giant fish and several huge deer heads had been nailed up in high places, and four ornate deer antler chandeliers dangled from the ceiling. There was a wooden Indian with a sign that said "Please Wait to be Seated" and a pizza spatula sign that said the same thing. There were model cars all over the place and a model log cabin hanging down with lights inside and its own Zig Zag Inn sign. There were booths and a bar and video games and a pinball machine called "Swamp Thing Pinball." A frazzled young woman worked the phone right at the restaurant entrance, said, "Good evening, Zig Zag Inn," and organized orders for pizzas. And an older woman who owned the place came up and said her name was Linda Trickel. She wore dark slacks and a light blouse and had unfrizzled brown hair. She was nice and solved a lot of things including the Zigzag puzzle.

Zigzag, she said. It's called that because right there across the road behind the Zig Zag Mtn Store the Zigzag River zigzags.

Zig Zag Inn, where we were, was obviously named after the village after the river. And an original denizen, Bill Lenz to be exact, an outdoorsman and hunter, a musician and log-cabin builder with a zest for life, came through and built the Inn seventy years ago, in the late 1920s. Bill Lenz also built the Barlow Trail Inn, which is that tavern just down the road. The Barlow Trail was an extension of the main Oregon trail. The old Oregon Trail stopped on the other side of the Cascade Mountains, right at the Columbia River along The Dalles. That was opened up with the first big wagon train in 1843. Then in 1845, a fellow named Sam Barlow arrived in The Dalles on one of those wagon trains and decided he could make money by building a toll road across the base of Mount Hood, thereby taking all those wagoneers stuck in The Dalles through the mountains and out to the good farmland on the other side. The Zigzag River was there even then, and it was even called the Zigzag. We could find it named in Sam Barlow's original request to the Oregon Territory for permission to build his toll road. And the original Zig Zag Inn was famous for its chicken dumplings, but the gas station was probably the primary draw. In those days, to get out to the wilderness here was a two-day trip from Portland. Of course, these days, it's only an hour and a half, which would account for all that traffic out front currently sizzling.

Zig Zag Inn she's owned for about fifteen years, Linda Trickel continued, and it's gotten busier and busier over the years. As civilization moves this way, they're getting busier and busier. But they could seat two hundred people, and they have a big downstairs. Now the new bar was upstairs, and over there was the old front porch, as we could see. And this, where we were standing, was the main structure of the original log cabin. And the fireplace, which was there, used to be over there. We could see where it was razed, moved stone by stone when, in the '40s, the highway department pushed them back. So this was the original log structure right here, and out back was the old chicken coop, which had been revised into an extension. Those deer antler chandeliers, she gazed on those at a gallery in Sandy. Finally her husband and she agreed they could afford them and so had them custom-made by the young man in Bend who makes them. And they made sure they were even and all the same size because they wanted their zoomorphic things zygomorphic too.

Zig Zag Inn she owns, as she said, and the Barlow Trail Tavern down there, she used to own that, too, and it was built a year after the Zig Zag Inn by the same builder, Bill Lenz. It was a brothel for the fellows working on the forest service. She didn't know if we had gone into their dining room, but there's a balcony inside there. The prostitutes used to walk along the balcony, and the fellows would pick out the girl they wanted for the hour and whatever. Some old local Forest Service men told her this, as did Billy Lenz, son of Bill Lenz.

Zigzag used to have a post office. It used to be across the street in the Zig Zag Mtn Store, but because of the unique name they had too many requests, so the post office divided the territory. And the Zigzag River is right out there. Oh, right across the street. As you go out, well, you go down that dirt road next to the Zig Zag Mtn Store. The first creek that runs under there is the Zigzag. I asked, "Does it actually zigzag?"

"Zigzag? Oh," Linda declared, "you bet it does." During the last floods two years ago, it took down a lot of trees. A couple of houses went into the river. And did I want her to show me that Portland brew? They named a beer after Zigzag.

Zigzag Beer: It's a popular beer now, and they just came out with it about three months ago. She gave me a bottle, which I did indeed treasure. "Well, that's neat. That's great. Thanks," I said, and then, after we paused for another hour to eat pizza and listen to Country and Western jazz on the juke, the Research Assistants and I zagged back across the busy highway once more and zinged right down the dirt road next to the Zig Zag Mtn Store. We parked the car at a hazardous squeeze and climbed down to a rocky little river—or creek—in a rocky maze. A couple of giant logs were fallen across the way, and several deep pools looked like good trout rendezvous. The river or creek seemed like a nice place to put your feet in if you were wanting to put your feet in somewhere, and after examining it even more, looking up and looking down, I could see that it did actually zig and zag—and in a flood it might go crazy. Altogether it was an attractive little stretch of water, the Zigzag, though I wouldn't want to get stuck there at zero degrees or sneezing in a freezing blizzard.

Discovery Bay

We came out the other side of Mount Hood into a farming valley and drove all the way up to the Columbia River Gorge, where we turned right. The Columbia River Gorge was a spectacular slice of river through earth, lined with round hills and curtains of rock. "Wow," we said, and we hoped to discover my aunt at the end of it.

"Let's just look for the exit sign that says AUNT EVELYN'S PLACE," I said, but really I had no idea how to find her place except randomly to take the second exit into The Dalles, stop at a gas station, and use a telephone.

We finally did discover Aunt Evelyn, who showed us a great time in The Dalles, where she has lived longer than she would like me to write about, and then after a couple of days we took off again, following the trail of Lewis and Clark west before turning north again and driving into Washington State.

We leapt past Mount St. Helens, swam through the city of Olympia, and then shivered into a skyline of forests on a road that ran along the Hood Canal, which wasn't a canal so much as a straight, deep, long arm of water carved out some time back by a single-minded glacier.

We continued north until we got to the top of the road, where we discovered that the arm of the Hood Canal was replaced by a little finger and next to that a dot on the cartographicus magnus called Discovery Bay. Discovery Bay may have been a bay, but it was also a town, starting around Fat Smitty's.

Fat Smitty's was located in a white wooden building with a blue roof and red ornate trim. The place had a great big FAT SMITTY'S sign as well as an eight-foot-high wooden Coca Cola bottle in front and an eight-foot-high double-decker wooden hamburger with all the trimmings. There were also wooden hens, a wooden eagle, and a wooden chef clutching a wooden Pepsi Cola lid to his chest. Also a wooden man with a wooden cup handle on his wooden nose, and a wooden fork, spoon, and knife. And a wooden mosquito squatting as well as a wooden Mr. Potato Head and a wooden Sasquatch or something, and a wooden ice cream cone and various other wooden figures, not to mention a couple of wooden toadstools.

Fat Smitty's was OPEN, a neon sign said.

"Let's go inside," we said to each other, and we went in and ate hamburgers and fries for dinner. Fat Smitty cooked the hamburgers, and he wasn't fat. He was big. He had oily brown hair, oily glasses, an oily white shirt, and he was busy cooking hamburgers. He didn't know much about Discovery Bay, however, and he told us to go up the road until we discovered Discovery Grocery.

Discovery Grocery was situated along with Frank's Surplus Sales at the near end of a long white series of wooden buildings, two stories and rotting away. The grocery had a front porch roof covered with moss, half-collapsing and barely held up by chains and surrounded with Christmas light bulbs. It was depressing, and we went inside for about thirty-seven seconds. After the grocery and surplus, the rest of the building seemed abandoned.

Basically, the whole area looked like a wreck, with the most viable concern a small log cabin just down from the white buildings. This was an actual log cabin called Log Cabin Espresso, and it included an open side window being pointed at by an L-shaped arrow sign that said "Drive Thru."

A ten-foot wooden lumberjack with a checked shirt and red cap guarded the front door.

Inside the Log Cabin Espresso we discovered two actual lumberjacks, both of them retired. I'm only guessing about one, who may have merely looked like a lumberjack. He was husky, square-jawed, and a little gruff but now was sneezing on his hand and handing out ice cream, candy, snacks, and various espresso-style concoctions. I bought one of the latter for myself and some sweets for the Research Staff, and then we talked to the other lumberjack, who was sitting in a chair inside the cabin and socializing because he was in that kind of mood.

His name was George Brown. He was seventy-five years old and recovering from a heart attack about three weeks previously. That was a warning, and he had to be careful and lose some weight, which he was doing. He had a small white mustache and whitish-grayish hair, and he wore a light green-and-white checked shirt, black pants, black socks and shoes, black suspenders, and '50s-style black-rimmed glasses. He looked big. He had very dark eyes, a grizzled stubble on his chin, and a tough face that was possibly roughened and puffened as a consequence of his recent hospital experience.

George was tired as much as retired, he said. He logged up until about 1975 or 1973, he guessed, and when he cut trees he always worked by himself. He was independent. No partner. He worked as a single guy. It wasn't really dangerous: He's still here, ain't he? He figured he cut fifty thousand trees. He'd fall the full-length tree. When it hit the ground, he went with the chain saw and cut it in sections. And then he got the next tree. And somebody else pulled it out with cables. These were Douglas fir, white fir, hemlock, cedar, pine. The fir was what you went for. They were, oh, anywhere from a foot through to the biggest one he ever cut was twelve foot and four inches in diameter. He did that with a forty-two-inch bar. And it was very rotten down the center. When it hit, it broke into great big slabs, five-foot slabs. Split like a ribbon. Absolutely beautiful. It would have been an excellent piece of timber if he could have saved it. Well, it was saved, but it shattered. He had no idea how old it was. Probably a thousand years old. But it was dead. He didn't know how old it was.

The Discovery Bay Fire District is about four hundred people, George went on to say, and it takes in the little town of Gardner, up the way. They have the espresso stand, the video store, grocery, Fat Smitty's, the Snug Harbor restaurant up the road. George has lived in Discovery Bay for fifty-five years, he noted, and the place is pretty much the same as it's always been, though there's less people now than there was in 1960. That's because the town was timber-oriented. At one time they had two sawmills, and then the timber dried up. Sure, they've replanted, but it takes a forty- fifty-year period for the trees to grow back. But still and all the trees are recovering now. Oh, yeah. All this stuff that he cut out when he was young is starting to grow back. Like the mountain up there, all covered with forests now. When he was young, George could see clear up the mountain. He could remember running in and grabbing his old man's field glasses and looking for deer out there, when he was a kid. That's all grown up since he was a kid.

Discovery Bay got its name, George continued, because in 1672 Captain George Vancouver anchored in the bay while he was discovering this whole part of America and after he had discovered a crick in the bay. He needed to get fresh water for his ship from the crick. His ship was called *The Discovery*, so that's that. That's where the name came from. And if we were to drive down there, well the road is washed out there, but if we wanted we could discover the crick that they bailed the water out of. Actually, he didn't know whether we could drive down there or not, but now thinking about it he thought not.

Chicken

We stopped to work up an appetite in Seattle for a few days with our friends Susan and Steve and then drove north to the port of Bellingham, almost in Canada, where we ditched the rental car. Then we opened up the menu to ponder and settle down for our next big meal, with Chicken as the main course.

Of course the soup came first, a thousand miles' worth. We jumped into it at Bellingham on the Alaska State Ferry and climbed over the waves until we were slurping noisily across a long blue surface that pulsed and swayed and gleamed, a surface of rippled dimples. Soon there were dark forested islands everywhere and, at night, a moon drawn by its long sparkling chain in the water. In the morning we were woken up at 5:30 by semihelpful announcements over the PA, such as: "Pod of killer whales off the starboard bow." By the time I had gotten out of my bunk, dressed, and figured out which side was starboard, the killer whales were long gone.

But I loved that boat. For one thing, I didn't have to drive. Bayne liked it too. As he explained on the first morning at breakfast: "You can shake your leg under the table and nobody notices."

Bayne and I got to sit out and watch the pure wilderness roll by off the starboard or port bow, one of those, on what we called "the private deck," a short deck at cabin level that for some reason only a few other passengers discovered. Britt got to sleep late and lie on her bunk and read Salman Rushdie's *Midnight's Children* without having to deal with us or a schedule. Britt was grown up by then, as I knew very well, and Bayne and I gave her lots of space and privacy as well as time to take long showers and read. When she had finished *Midnight's Children,* which took a day, she moved onto highbrow literature from the ship's store: *Self, Glamour, Redbook, Cosmopolitan.* I could barely stifle my immature alarm at the contents promised on their covers, and after a while I started to become really concerned. Here we were passing through one of the most spectacularly wild and beautiful places in the world, in the universe probably, and Britt was missing it. "I'm kinda bored," she admitted at dinner on the second day.

"Bored?" I said. "How can you possibly be *bored* in one of the most beautiful places on earth?" She looked up blankly behind insect-eye sunglasses and nailed me: "It is beautiful, but I'm not mature enough to ingest it all at once."

Me, I would have died before admitting boredom. Even if I were bored. I could have sat out on the private deck and watched the scenery roll by all year long. I had a good set of binoculars in front of my eyes and was looking for eagles, killer whales, nice whales, big seals, big otters, big jumping fish, and anything else big that might happen to appear. Now we were passing through a narrow channel at the bottom of a giant V of sometimes forested and sometimes rock-studded mountains. Then we were cutting past vast stretches of undisturbed forests with a rich piney scent, riding on a hissing cradle of white fingers. There were button islands filled with trees, mountains made of bosoms and buttocks, and a sky filled with gray mattresses disguised as clouds.

There are one hundred thousand glaciers in either the world or Alaska, I forget which—even though I took good notes during the lecture on the main observation deck—but only about 250 have been named. Nameless glaciers started to appear in front of us, and the mountains began to grow and grow and grow. Within a day the mountains had become massive slabs of rock with sheets of snow on top, and the glaciers were appearing as long whitish arms reaching out of the clouds and down the mountains and pouring milk into the water. Over a cold milky-green water past glaciers and gigantic rocks up a gigantic trench we sailed until finally we reached the very end of it, just about, at the town of Skagway, where we disembarked.

So much for the soup. Next the antipasto, five hundred miles of it starting with a quick nibble at Skagway. Skagway exists because in the summer of 1896 Robert Henderson happened to notice several flakes of a glinty material in his pan along a creek in the upper Yukon Territory near the merge of the Yukon and Klondike Rivers. He opened his mouth and said, "GOLD!" Robert

Henderson was not smart enough to keep his mouth shut, and thus within a short time he was a poor man while the entire Klondike region was swarming with feverish prospectors intending to strike it rich. In the summer of 1897, a steamer from Alaska steamed into the port of Seattle carrying sixty-eight suddenly wealthy men who possessed altogether the better part of a million dollars' worth of Klondike gold, fabulous money in those days, and the news, particularly coming as it did at the end of a four-year economic slump, created a frenzy in the United States.

Within the next year and a half, more than a hundred thousand people, single men primarily but plenty of women too, set out for the Klondike. Half of them made it. Most of these Klondikers were from the United States, as a matter of fact, and many of *them* took the very route we were taking now on our own personal rush of the Storyville kind: by boat from the Seattle area and off at Skagway, where we were now.

Skagway was a slab of mud and ice in the winter of 1896 and '97, but, by the end of that summer, it was a thriving tent city. By the next year, Skagway was a thriving town, with mud and ice streets along with wooden sidewalks and hotels and dance halls and saloons. Soapy Smith and his thugs ruled the place, successfully fleecing the incoming newcomers in numerous ways until Soapy got sudsed in a shootout. Although Soapy was long dead by the time we got there, someone did a good job of preserving the original wooden buildings, and so you could walk along the main drag of town and imagine you were about to be fleeced by Soapy Smith and his thugs until seven big tourist boats pulled up and disgorged a thousand tourists from Peoria navigating by video camera.

A hundred years ago the Klondikers were eager to escape Skagway because of Soapy Smith and gold, so they walked out the back of town and climbed a rugged mountain with a thousand pounds of grubstake on their backs. They negotiated the treacherous Skagway Trail up the mountain forty-five miles to White Pass at the edge of Canada, and most negotiated the trail more than once because who can carry a thousand pounds at one time? Fortunately, we were traveling lighter than the Klondikers did, especially considering that we had left our main laundry bag back at a motel in Oregon. Fortunately also, we rode the Skagway train. The railroad was blasted through those mountains around the turn of the century on special order from the big mining companies, and the tracks are still there as well as the train, which still runs daily even though it's creaky squeaky and leaky.

When we got there, White Pass was a cold and lonely place of swirling granite, dwarfed trees, and a thin carpet of moss and lichen and tiny white wildflowers.

After passing White Pass, the Klondikers paused to pitch their tents at the source of the mighty Yukon River. The Klondikers paused because they were waiting for spring to come and the ice to melt. When the ice melted, they built rafts and boats and floated down the Yukon a few hundred more miles to Dawson City and the Klondike gold fields. We didn't have to wait for spring because it was already late summer. Also we didn't have to float down the Yukon because at the end of the train was a bus. The bus took us down a road beside the river to Whitehorse, the capital and population center of Yukon Territory, where we found a hotel run by Swedes and also a good place to eat called the Pasta Palace.

Whitehorse was named after the swirling white rapids there, which looked like either galloping white horses or the flapping white manes of galloping white horses, I'm not sure. The place used to be a portage and recharging place for all those Klondikers floating down the Yukon River to Dawson City, as it was for us. A person could, we discovered, rent a Canadian car in Whitehorse and ride it downriver all the way to Dawson City. Canadian rental cars are like American rental cars except they're more nondescript and expensive, especially when you're intending to take them across the border to Fairbanks. Canadian rentals also turn you into a more polite driver. You linger at intersections to wave another driver on, who is busy waving you on, and you say, "After you, Alphonse."

Politely, therefore, we drove our nondescript vehicle through an indescribable landscape until after two hundred hard-to-describe miles the road dropped into a bowl between mountains and we fell at last into the Klondike boomtown of Dawson City, situated on a bland slice of mud at the edge of the grand Yukon. Like Skagway, Dawson City was created by an inordinate appetite for gold. In 1896 it was empty. Nothing there. In 1898 it was a heaping community of twenty thousand people, salted with Jack London and Robert Service and peppered by Diamond Tooth Gertie and Snake Hips Lulu.

We stayed at the JJJ Hotel, a tastefully restored old-fashioned building with a sign at the desk that said, "We are looking forward to the chance to meet with each and every one of you to tell you about the city and its heritage." Aside from keeping many of the original buildings and the Yukon River intact, the historic preservationists at Dawson have very smartly kept the streets in their original condition: mud. Think about it. Other than spreading around horse manure, what better way to recreate the flavor of life a century ago? It was raining and drizzling and raining again while we were there, and since all the hotel and restaurant employees in town wore turn-of-the-century clothes, we got to see what really happened to the bottoms of all those long, lacy dresses in the olden days. Another authentic thing about Dawson City was they didn't have

a broom. They said they were originally from Pennsylvania but that he, Bill, had always dreamed of coming to Alaska, so they came up thirty years ago. He had been a bricklayer in Pennsylvania, but in Alaska he got working for a mining company in the Chicken area and so did that until ten years ago. These days he traps during the winter, and during the summer he and she run the shop for tourists at Chicken. So that was Chicken: a tourist stopover. And when they said the shop was built only ten years ago, my stomach turned down in disappointment.

Only ten years! That seemed *way* underdone.

Disappointed and still hungry, we hit the road — only to find a short way down the road three signs stacked on top of each other and pointing with three arrows to a second Chicken on the left. This second Chicken promised to be more of the meal I had long ago ordered in my mind. The signs looked official, and they said

2/10 Mi.   DOWNTOWN CHICKEN
2/10 Mi.   CHICKEN CREEK CAFE
2/10 Mi.   CHICKEN GAS STATION.

My stomach turned up as I turned the wheel and the car turned off the road there and drove two-tenths of a mile down a dirt alley between low trees until the alley ended at a small parking area with a couple of gas pumps and a pair of his and hers outhouses along with four old-and-weathered-looking wood buildings. The buildings were fronted with a rickety boardwalk, flat Western-style façades, and a smattering of nailed-on moose and caribou antlers, pick-axes, old saws, old signs, and various other old whatnot. So I thought we had found the right Chicken at last. Well done, just like I ordered!

The sign over the building to the far left said CHICKEN MERCANTILE EMPORIUM, while the other three buildings were the CHICKEN LIQUOR STORE, the CHICKEN CREEK SALOON, and the CHICKEN CREEK CAFE. We walked into the Chicken Creek Cafe first, where on the other side of a squeaky screen door were some tables and a counter with a regular grill and refrigerator behind the counter. We ordered burgers and fries and chicken-noodle soup. The chicken-noodle soup was good, I thought, as was the fresh-baked pie we had for dessert. But the girl behind the counter who cooked the burgers and ladled out the soup and served the pie said she didn't know a lot about Chicken. She was young. She had big glasses and was wearing a T-shirt with a picture of a hen on a nest and the caption, "I got laid in Chicken."

She didn't know a lot about Chicken, she repeated, but she thought her stepmother, who did know a lot, would talk to us.

As it turned out, her stepmother, Susan Wiren, was about to take a nap but hadn't yet begun and so would be willing to sit out on the front porch of the Chicken Creek Cafe, drink tea to my coffee and the Research Assistants' pop, and tell us all she knew about Chicken. Susan Wiren had long brown hair that was kind of sun-streaked. She looked lean and athletic. She had a sharp nose, blue eyes, and a tanned face. She wore a shirt that said "Pie Lady" and had a child's picture of a pie.

Susan had been in Chicken for ten years, she told us, and expected to remain for another five. Originally when she came she said to herself it was a ten-year sentence. Now it was looking like a fifteen-year sentence. Actually, she liked it there. Originally, yes, she thought of living in Chicken as like a prison sentence. But it was better than where she was before, which was fifty miles from Chicken living subsistence.

She wound up living subsistence in Alaska in the first place because her husband is an adventurer. They still love each other. They've been married ten years. But originally they lived in Pennsylvania, and he wanted to move to Norway and live in a hut and hunt fox and geese. They had a boat and sailed their boat up to Norway, but when he wanted to live there she said, "They don't speak English up there! You can't work legally, and I just don't think I want to do that, Gregory." He said, "Where else can we go?" And then he said, "Let's do some research on Alaska." Her husband is a firm believer in research. So they did a lot of research on Alaska, and they read the pros and cons and decided to sell everything they owned. They just got rid of the boat. But they brought the anchor with them because you never know. They had an anchor, and she brought her sewing machine, and they were going to live subsistence. And actually if she didn't have children she might have been just fine. But they immediately started popping out children. They have two natural and one adopted and one step. So they have four, in other words.

So anyway, Susan and Gregory came to Alaska to live subsistence. They lived in a cabin on the Forty Mile River which is fifty miles from Chicken on the way to Eagle. Living subsistence means you live off the land. Gregory became very adept at killing small animals and skinning them. Specifically martin, which are turned into sable coats. Since then they sort of changed their attitude about killing small animals for their fur, but at the time it was a way to make a living, and Gregory also gold-mined. He was a diver for a suction dredge. In other words, using scuba gear. So he worked for a local miner, and she was there alone pregnant with sled dogs eating her cat. It was just a "wonderful experience," she said, using a bland tone to nail those ironic quote marks on. She would go out blueberry picking with a 30.06 over her shoulder. And actually it was good, but once she got kids, she just thought that this was not — everybody around her seemed to have a lack of teeth and a lot of people on welfare. A lot of people on welfare, and her father was a Republican, and she just couldn't bear it. She paid taxes. She worked hard. She and Gregory weren't on welfare. But most people around who lived that kind of lifestyle, they definitely got food stamps.

The nearest neighbors were five miles up the river. And she had a 30.06 on her back because of bears. Bears are a problem. They killed two grizzlies up there a month ago. No one in Chicken that she knew about historically anyway had been killed by a bear. And she thought that the attitude to bears in Chicken is: "If it comes really close." Bears can really, really move. They can really cause a lot of damage in your life. They tear apart buildings.

The first winter in subsistence was really awful. They didn't have a radio except for a short-wave. They used to listen to Radio Moscow. And they got mail whenever they got into Eagle, which was about once a month. It was very, very cold. She couldn't go outside for very long at all. She was not used to the lack of contact with other humans. It was really hard for her. It was sixty-five to eighty below for six weeks straight that winter. It was really cold. And they lived in a valley with big ridges, so they never saw the sun. They had light but never saw the sun. Here in Chicken they see the sun. It's low in the winter, but it goes up and it sort of goes around and they see the sun. And Susan came to realize that it was important for her to be able to see the sun.

Winter solstice, which is the 21st of December, the sun is up at eleven and down at three. They do have a fairly long dawn and dusk, but it's pitch dark by 4:15. There are a lot of people who just can't take it and get depressed, but actually a lot of people commit suicide in the spring there, because they've been looking forward to spring and then their life is just as terrible. She knew four suicides personally, which did seem like a lot. She never knew any suicides when she lived in Pennsylvania, whereas, she meant, it was just so common there in Alaska.

So they lived subsistence for one year, and then they bought Downtown Chicken. As for how Chicken got its name, there are two different stories. The first is that in the old days Chicken Creek had gold nuggets as big as hens' eggs laying right out there on the creek. And you could just walk out there and pick up all these hens' eggs, the gold nuggets shaped like them. The second story is that the local miners wanted to call the town Ptarmigan because that was the name of the local bird they were eating a lot of, but they weren't sure how to spell "ptarmigan," so they named it Chicken instead. Personally, she believes the second story is the true one.

The first residents came out to Chicken in the 1880s, and even though this is still part of the Klondike gold area, it was obviously a few years before the big strike near Dawson City. Actually, the population of Chicken has been sort of the same over the years. A small winter population. Last winter it was four-teen. And today half of the population is children, and most people make their living in a tourist-oriented business. Robin, who runs the Chicken Post Office, gets her money from there. Her husband is a gold miner. And Toad, whose real name is Don, is another resident. Toad has been there about twenty-five or thirty years. He's actually a really nice guy. Strange, but nice. They're all a little idiosyncratic in Chicken. It comes with the territory. Now, the summer popu-lation, at one point there were seven hundred people living on the creek, gold mining. And then when they got the strike in Dawson in 1896 all those min-ers just packed up and went to Dawson. But there was still gold here, so there were still miners at Chicken. They started to have postal service in 1903. In 1906 they had a hotel there even though there weren't any roads. It was a gold-mining community and still is. There was a cabin over at Chicken Creek be-fore the Klondike gold rush. And the town is owned by a rather large gold min-ing concern—

At this point, I realized I was confused, so I interrupted Susan in midsen-tence: "Which town is owned by a gold mining concern?"

"Chicken. Old Chicken."

Well, I thought we *were* in Old Chicken!

"Where is Old Chicken?" I said. And she patiently explained that Old Chicken was the real and original Chicken. Across the road. That's where the original cabin and the old schoolhouse and the old hotel and haybarn and things were. And where we were, Downtown Chicken was just a business, a tourist stopover she and her husband bought ten years ago that was built about nine years before that for tourists.

Only nineteen years old! I thought to myself. *Another Chicken underdone!*

But, Susan went on, she does have an agreement with the gold-mining com-pany to take people across the road to the original Chicken, the Old Chicken. The tour starts at Downtown Chicken every day at 1:00, and even though to-day's tour was over and done, she might be able to put off the nap she really needed long enough that Evelyn, who was working at the Chicken Mercan-tile souvenir gift shop, could take us across the road to Old Chicken. Evelyn was her adopted daughter from France.

"We do need to do that," I said.

While we were waiting for Susan to replace Evelyn in the Chicken Mercan-tile and tourist souvenir gift shop, I stepped into the Chicken Saloon to meet Toad, because Susan had said this was mail day and therefore Toad would be drinking. Toad never drank during the winter, she added. He was too smart for that. But he did drink on mail days during the summer. The Chicken Saloon had five thousand men's hats as well as a lot of women's underwear hanging down from the ceiling. A jukebox played heartrending music, and old Toad in work clothes with a big hat on was sitting at the bar, drunk and rude and finishing a can of malt liquor. I bought him another can of malt liquor, which made him drunker and ruder, and then I left the Chicken Saloon and came out to find Evelyn and the Research Assistants talking together and getting ready to cross the road.

Why did we cross the road? To get to the other side where, after steering along a trail through some bushes and underbrush and so on, we came to an extended collection of wonderfully ancient and disintegrating log cabins that represented true Chicken. Evelyn, who was recently from France, was saying with a French accent that in the old days when Chicken was first founded all the old gold miners had a lot of Tommy guns.

I stopped to tie a shoelace. "Tommy guns?" I said, amazed, since I thought Tommy guns weren't used until Prohibition days.

"Yes, Tommy guns," she said. They ate a lot of Tommy guns, which tasted a lot like chickens. So they wanted to call the town Tommy Gun, but no one knew how to spell "Tommy gun" so they finally decided to call it Chicken. And, Evelyn continued, there were about seven hundred people in Chicken mining until in 1968 the company decided to stop mining because there was not enough gold any more, and everybody left at that time and it became a ghost town. Before it used to be a pretty nice place. So a lot of people come up now especially to see the Tisha schoolhouse. Tisha was the teacher, and she came to Chicken in the 1920s to teach school.

OK, Evelyn continued, she was going to give us a quick tour because Susan was waiting and needed that nap. Mostly up there, she said, pointing to a small tight cube of a log cabin on log stilts, was where the food cache was. You try to keep your food away from your cabin so the grizzlies don't come and bother you.

And now she said, as we walked down a trail between trees and bushes, we were heading down to see the schoolhouse. Originally it was a hotel right there. It was a two-story building, and it burned down. Evelyn thought it was because of a wood stove. If you don't really pay attention to it, it might get red hot and catch on fire. So it burned down. Then they built this building right there, she said, and that was used as a schoolhouse until 1929. I could look through the double pane windows. There was a school room, and here was where they had their parties.

"Oh, what parties?" I said.

"At Tisha's time. No dance or nothing wild."

OK, that was a log cabin there. And as we could see on this side when you build these cabins and then heat them in the winter, the permafrost starts to melt and then the building sinks. That's why the windows were so low. Because this building had sunk. And then we had an outhouse and a building right there and a food cache right behind it. OK, then this was the original road to Eagle. At first, every ten days they would bring the mail in by a mule pack. Then later on with sled dogs. Today it is by airplane twice a week. Sometimes there are moose here at Chicken, and they had a bear trying to get into the Downtown Chicken Cafe a few years ago. He wanted to eat the pies. He was terrorizing people for two days. He was hiding, coming out, hiding. He dug a hole in the door, and the owner shot him. And his head is mounted in the Chicken Saloon. Now all the bears around they just are in the woods somewhere. And if we wanted to know something about what Chicken was like during the 1920s, we should after we got back to the Mercantile in Downtown Chicken get a copy of *Tisha*, the autobiography of Anne Hobb, who taught school there during the 1920s.

I did get *Tisha*, in fact, and I heartily recommend it, but not as much as I recommend Chicken, the real Chicken, which I tasted at last and found to be just right.

Old Man

Two days later we were standing in the Fairbanks International Airport trading in our Canadian car for an American one. The only problem was, when the woman at the car rental place found out where we wanted to go next—north on Route 11—she wouldn't rent me a car. "That's the Haul Road," she said decisively.

Even the cartographicus magnus represents Route 11 as a questionable enterprise. The cartographicus calls it "the Dalton Highway" as well as "the pipeline road" and portrays Route 11 as a single five-hundred-mile stretch of narrow black alternating with narrow white that follows the trans-Alaska pipeline due north from Fairbanks through the Arctic Circle to Prudhoe Bay and the Beaufort Sea.

At least, I had thought, it would be hard to get lost on Route 11, since no other roads go up there. But here was the rental car lady getting huffy and refusing to rent us a car.

As luck would have it, though, the woman in the next rental car booth over, having eavesdropped, leaned across and declared that she would rent me a car to go on the Dalton Highway. It would have to be a four-wheel drive, she noted, which was more expensive. But they had one. All I had to do (wink, wink) was sign a statement promising (wink, wink) I wouldn't go on the Dalton Highway.

The instant we got out of Fairbanks everything turned into forest, except for a stretch of pipe peeking out from behind the trees. It was a big silver pipe about four feet in diameter that, suspended up on steel legs to stay above the permafrost, looked like an extremely long and silver centipede.

At about twenty miles or so out of Fairbanks, the road turned into a dirt and gravel surface, and the pipe now looked like a silver stretch of silver rope. We drove into a little aspen and birch forest that was growing in the middle of things, and the leafy trees were quite tall with a lot of their leaves starting to turn yellow or yellowish. So it was a very pleasant little forest until we came to the end of it and turned into white and black spruce forest. Then the black spruce shrank and turned into its own little stretch of forest that became so stunted in places it looked not much taller than a cornfield.

Then we were looking over a large expanse of forested hills going all the way out to a giant gray and purple mountain in the far distance that looked like the fist of God. And listening to our Abba tape as we went. Britt had her turn in the front seat that day and therefore had become the music czar. She announced that today was going to be Abba day. We were going to play the Abba tape until we got to Coldfoot.

"Ooooh, let's not," Bayne said from the back seat. Bayne said he didn't like Abba anymore.

We were listening to endless Abba and bumping merrily along over that dirt and gravel road that actually had a pretty good surface until it ended and a rougher surface began. A sign said All Vehicles Proceed With Lights On Next 426 Miles. Another sign said Speed Limit 50 Next 426 Miles. A third sign, sprinkled with a few bullet holes, said James W. Dalton Highway.

So now we were officially on the Dalton Highway, still following the pipeline and passing through normal forests, dwarf forests, little fields, and beautiful little lakes edged with yellow velvet. Alongside the road were lavender streaks of fireweed punctuated here and there by white fatality crosses. And every once in a while from around the corner would turn a giant truck hauling a giant yellow grader or some kind of giant yellow insectlike earth-moving equipment, with the big truck moving on giant tires spewing and spitting rocks into the air and threatening us with imminent collision and our own white cross. Occasionally we would see a beautiful little purple wildflower alongside the road and then look up again to notice the silver pipeline, which had started to look like a Chinese dragon.

We crossed the Yukon River, the one we had ferried across who knows how many hundred miles earlier at Dawson City, but now the river was about half a mile wide and looking very deep and strong, sweeping along through the northern wilderness.

We crossed No Name Creek and came out into another area of tiny lakes and ponds, fields, and then an entire valley of miniature black spruce, some of them a couple of feet high, with occasionally a quaking aspen or quivering birch alongside the road waving us on with great enthusiasm. There was a great dome of sky with amazing dramatic things going on everywhere among the clouds, and then we came to a sign that said Finger Mountain and a mountain with dramatic things going on there as well, including a battle of big fingers and one gigantic granite hand and finger that gave the following advice: "Go south, young man."

Instead, we continued north down the other side of Finger Mountain and entered a huge tundra-scape, a vast valley with about half a dozen small lakes in the middle reflecting the blue off the sky and the rest of the valley a camouflage carpet of alternating yellowish orangish goldish splotches with streaks of maroon and interrupted here and there with a few clutches and clusters of bogged and besogged black spruce. The pipeline zigzagged along into the valley until it collided almost with a tiny cluster of cabin, shed, and prefab house as well as a clothesline with clothes, a couple of old camper shells, a trampoline, a bulldozer, a canoe, and various other things. All these artifacts were deposited in a narrow flat between the pipeline and the highway, and a sign out front declared them to be part of the Arctic Circle Bed and Breakfast Inn and Gift Shop at Old Man, Alaska. That was about the first sign of human habitation we'd seen in fifty miles or so, and Old Man, even though it was nowhere to be found on the cartographicus magnus, sounded to me like a Storyville.

We stopped.

It was chilly now, and when we got out of the car a sharp wind brought us up short. We walked through the mud to the Gift Shop, which was part of the main prefab building. A sign said OPEN so we walked inside. No one there. We said, "Hello? Hello?" No one there. So we left the Gift Shop, walked through the mud back to a cabin with the skin of an unfortunate bear nailed to it and a sign that said Coffee Soda, and knocked.

"Oh!"

We had surprised a young girl in the Coffee Soda cabin who hadn't heard us drive up. I think she might have been reading a book or possibly fixing herself lunch in one room, and the crackle of wood burning in the potbellied stove in the other room must have masked our approach. Yes, she said, she could make some coffee or tea. Sandwiches? Crackers? Would we like a soda or orange juice?

Her name was Stacey Burroughs, she told us, and she was thirteen years old until April 19, at which point she would be fourteen. Stacey right at that moment happened to be the only official resident of Old Man. Her mom and dad, she said, were right now up at Coldfoot doing some end-of-the-summer employment. Her dad was doing carpentry, and her mom waitressed at the truck stop in Coldfoot. Would I like some cream with my coffee?

So she was now basically running the place by herself. Of course, they don't really get that many customers. We would be the first ones, she thought, today. Well, traffic had dropped off now that the season was almost over. Yesterday, they got one person. Sometimes her mom made pies and cakes and things. And she was normally around. This was the first time she'd left. It was like, bam: You get sick of doing dishes. This was the first time Stacey had run the place by herself. It was also the first time being by herself without being told what to do. And it was kind of weird.

Old Man, Stacey went on, didn't exist in its present form until her family bought the property six years ago and put in the buildings. They moved from Wiseman, north of Coldfoot. She grew up in Wiseman. But her mom and dad bought this place because they wanted to get out of Wiseman. With a population of about two dozen, Wiseman was a little crowded there for her mom and dad. Stacey didn't understand that, really. But anyway, here in Old Man, it was a population of about three.

Old Man used to be the name of a construction camp for the pipeline during the 1970s. It was the Old Man Camp. Where the name Old Man came from originally she wasn't entirely certain, but she thought it came from the Kanuti River. That was three miles away. Kanuti apparently means Old Man in the native language, so maybe there used to be an old man around there somewhere. Or maybe they thought the river was an old man. But when her family first came down from Wiseman, there was nothing there. Her mom and dad bought four acres, and her dad bought the house they have out there. He bought it in Fairbanks. This guy had a taxi company in Fairbanks, and he owned the house units. They bought them, had them hauled out. The building wasn't in good shape now. During the haul from Fairbanks to Old Man it kind of got bounced around majorly.

Stacey was a sweet-looking girl with blondish-brownish hair cut in bangs at the front. She had blue eyes, creamy skin, and a quiet gentle smile. I saw her blue eyes because she momentarily removed the dark glasses she wore. Then she put them back on and said she had to wear them or suffer headaches.

That, in fact, was why she preferred winter to summer, she said. Because in the winter there wasn't much sun, and so she didn't have to wear glasses. It did get cold in the winter, Stacey went on, but she just didn't go outside much when it got really cold. Last winter the coldest it got was fifty below, but then they were never there because they did Thanksgiving, Christmas, and New Year's in town with her grandpa. In Fairbanks. So they just took a vacation from Old Man in the middle of the winter, but actually they were not going to do it this year because they were going to have some dogs. They had dogs before. They just got rid of them. They sold them away. She didn't even know it was going to happen. One day it was like, "Where are the dogs, dad?" "I got rid of them." It was like, "Oh great." Didn't even get a chance to say goodbye to her favorite dog.

They used the dogs for mushing, mainly. Whenever her dad went trapping he would take them because it's a lot easier than using a snowmobile. Dogs don't break down. But they needed to get away, and with dogs you can't. You gotta give them food every day. But they needed to leave Old Man for a while because some family problems came up. They were gone for, well, three months out of one year and three months out of another. Because her brother died and her uncle got shot. So like too like many memories there, so they had to get away. Her brother was eighteen. He just graduated. Yeah, there were some other kids with him, a car crash. That was a pretty bad year, '93. And that's when they sold the dogs, around there. But now her dad was going to get more. That would be nice. She loved puppies, Stacey said.

"Nobody can resist puppies," I said.

"Nobody can resist puppies," she agreed.

Actually, Stacey said, they plan to teach people, cold weather visitors to Old Man, to mush. That way instead of people always having to ride in the sled — that's really boring — they can drive the sled. Stacey herself learned how to mush at an early age, and when she was very young they had a humongous dog. His name was Ben. At a year old, he could just set his head onto the table and look around like, "Where's the food?" He got into trouble about that a couple of times. He got a little smack on the butt and slept outside. He didn't like that much. Did I want more coffee? Did Britt and Bayne want more soda?

We were still all sitting at a round table next to the potbellied stove inside the Coffee Soda cabin. Stacey poured me some more coffee, and at that point I happened to look out the back windows of the cabin with full attention for the first time and notice how surprisingly close we were to the pipeline. We were sitting within an easy stone's throw of the thing!

When I expressed my surprise, Stacey said that when they bought the land at Old Man, actually, the pipeline corporation threw a hissy fit. They hadn't realized the land was for sale. They came down with helicopters, and they came out. There were two security men. Stacey could just barely remember it. The guy comes out and he says, "What are you doing?" "Well, we are on our land." "Oh, OK, bye." So he left. But then one of the guys with the pipeline, a friend of theirs, did some research to see if they really owned it. They did. He went back to his boss and said, "I can't kick them out. They own it."

In fact, Stacey went on, they're so close to it, she's got her own hammock out there hanging from the pipeline. The only place she can hang it is on the pipeline, since there are no big trees around.

We took our coffee and sodas in hand and walked along a path out back, and there was Stacey's hammock. It was a nice big hammock, white cotton mesh, strung up and hanging from the bottom of one of the giant pipeline support structures. Stacey climbed into the hammock and lay back while Britt took her photograph. While Britt was taking the photograph, I asked Stacey if she thought that the Alaska pipeline people minded her hanging her hammock on their big silver dragon. She said she didn't think so because when they were out there a few years before, she was a cute little girl and they kind of liked her, she thought. So they didn't mind.

Coldfoot

We hit the Arctic Circle a few miles later. The circle was thin enough that we couldn't actually see it, and the only reason we knew we had hit it was the roadside rest-stop and marker. This, I believe, represented the only significant public facility on the entire highway, and it was nice: picnic tables, Port-a-Potties, and a big wooden sign with a top view of the globe and the words ARCTIC CIRCLE.

We listened to Abba for the next hour, dropped into pristine valleys, crossed bright red or sometimes maroon tundra, entered spruce forests and some cottonwood and birch forests, passed mirrored lakes and beautiful rivers, and drove onward with some far gray raggedy mountains forever around us. We listened to Abba until we reached a sign that said COLDFOOT with an arrow pointing to the right and symbols for gas, telephone, bed, and food. The sign also said: Next Service 244 miles.

So we turned down a short dirt track into Coldfoot, which looked like the rough little Arctic outpost it was. It consisted of a big stretch of mud with some gas and diesel pumps, a few wooden sheds, some metal sheds, a couple of slabwood cabins with moose and caribou antlers nailed on. Most importantly, Coldfoot had a hotel and a café. The hotel was on the far side of the mud flat, and from the outside it looked like a gigantic motor home. The front section was built of wood and had a flat roof, but the rest of the hotel was a long metal shed, like a train without wheels or a tunnel with windows. The hotel was an imitation pipeline for people, in other words, only it was rectangular instead of round.

It looked like it'd be just right for cold and snow, and we checked in at the hotel to get our own little metal cubicle before walking across the mud to the Coldfoot Café. To the left of the café was a series of gas and diesel pumps and to the right stood a huge metal barn that, I was now thinking, must have been the main Operating Room for eighteen-wheelers, a couple of which in fact were right now vibrating nervously, smoking fitfully, and grumbling heavily just outside the place.

The café itself was an old wooden building with a steeply pitched roof, and right in front of it were parked half a dozen pickups, including one that had just pulled up as we were walking up. In the back of this pickup were some big bloody pieces of meat and a mammoth set of antlers. In the front of the truck a young hunter, short, handsome, and heavy-jawed, was in the process of climbing out. When I commented on the size of the antlers, he said, "Oh, I did real good!" He grinned and then added as an afterthought: "The sun shines on a monkey's ass once in a while." Then he paused as if trying to think of what to say next, but he couldn't think of anything and I was too busy trying to unravel the meaning of his analogy to say anything, so wordlessly we walked into the café together.

He had the waitress fill his thermos with coffee, said he was headed out to camp somewhere, and then dashed out the door.

The waitress who filled his thermos, meanwhile, was Sandy Burroughs, Stacey's mom from the Arctic Circle Bed and Breakfast at Old Man. Sandy and I had a nice little chat about things before the Research Staff and I found a table and placed our orders. Burgers fries and Cokes seemed to be the most promising items on the menu that day. The Coldfoot Café, in fact, was a perfectly good café. It had a dog sled hung up over the cash register, and at the moment it was catering mainly to truckers. Big dirty rough truckers. Nice guys,

I'm sure, who came in with grease on their hands and faces and clothes and sat down dog tired at the tables to gossip about trucks, roads, brakes, and so on.

In short, Coldfoot seemed like a very authentic place, and all three of us enjoyed our dinner at the Coldfoot Café and even had a pleasant extended chat with the biggest, toughest-looking trucker of all, a giant named Pat Davis. Big Pat everyone called him. He was a trucker, all right, and he wore dark greasy pants and a cream-colored T-shirt the size of a tent. He had a wild head of dark hair. He had legs the size of pillars. He had arms the size of my legs. He had a huge, roughly handsome face that was red and decorated with a full whiskbroom mustache and a sledgehammer chin. And he drove a big truck, an eighteen-wheeled 1990 Extended Hood Peterbilt 379 with a 302-inch wheel base, 18-speed transmission, and a 425-horsepower Cat engine — for Black Gold Express out of Fairbanks.

For the last eight years, he told us, Pat had driven the Dalton Highway, round-trip about twice a week, hauling back and forth equipment and supplies to Deadhorse and the Prudhoe Bay oil fields. Well, right now he was returning to Fairbanks with a piece of paving equipment on his back, which had been used to pave an expansion of the Deadhorse airport. Naturally, he carried everything he needed right on the truck. Fuel? He carried three hundred four hundred gallons, which was normally way more than enough. But of course during the winter you would want to keep that engine running the whole time. If you shut it down, it might not start again, yeah.

The winter is the best time to make the drive, Pat went on. Yeah, the road is a lot smoother. Actually in the wintertime when it gets down to thirty, forty below or even zero, the road becomes just like asphalt. But then when the temperature gets up around thirty or so, you better best be chaining up because the hills are so steep up there. The hills are so steep up there you can wind up going backwards. That's happened to him once or twice, Pat said, and it's a feeling like you've never felt before. Well, the trip takes about eleven twelve hours in the wintertime. That is, if you don't get any blows. If you get into a blow, you might sit in one place for four days waiting for the road to open again, because the state boys don't come out until the storm is over. The longest blow he'd ever been in was eight days. So you just sit there with your engine running.

But the weather can just change so fast. It can change in an hour up there. It can be sunny, and then an hour later you can't see a thing. When it storms, it storms. When it blows, it blows. He once drove up there in a 120-below wind chill. But you ever get down to about forty below and have a sixty-mile-an-hour wind, when it gets really cold your tires go flat. There are trucks parked out there at Coldfoot for about four days, several trucks, yep, tires are flat. And of course, at the Atigun Pass you have to watch out for that occasional avalanche. He was on top of the pass when they had an avalanche. He heard someone yell, "Avalanche!" It took one truck over the guard rail and halfway down the mountain. The cab tore off the frame, but the driver just had a bump on the head. Another truck it lifted it up in the air and turned it right upside down. An avalanche is kind of like rippling water. It come down and lifted that truck up, and it pushed two other ones against the guard rail. That was probably the worst he'd seen so far. Some of the truckers that were already down below, they walked across and got—Harold Mallory was his name—pulled him out, got him out. Then the state crew came out with snow blowers, and they started plugging away at the avalanche.

Well, we actually chatted for a nice long while with Big Pat, and then, after dinner was over, Britt wandered back across the mud to the hotel room where she rested and read while Bayne and I stayed at the Coldfoot Café to attend a concert given by Snowshoe Scott and his Magic Squeezebox.

The café had an annex at the far end, I forgot to mention, a newer section built of plywood with four whirly fans overhead and chairs around several tables with artificial flowers in real vases. This section of the café was called "the cabaret," and it obviously had been built for the tourist business. Although there were no tourists in Coldfoot at the moment, Sandy Burroughs explained (as Bayne and I waited for Snowshoe Scott to appear), a bus of them was due to arrive from Fairbanks any minute.

Snowshoe Scott had red hair, a red beard, a high-bridged narrow nose, and a gap between his front teeth. He was dressed to entertain, with a modified generalized Forest Service uniform: black hat, black shoes, dark olive pants, khaki shirt buttoned at the neck and tightened with a bola tie clasped by a pair of miniature snowshoes. He had a friendly smile and a pleasant confident tenor voice that, along with his magic squeezebox, produced a couple of hours' worth of first-rate entertainment.

Snowshoe Scott was a professional. When it was starting time he started playing to an empty house, almost, with just Bayne and me as his entire audience. And when the tourist bus finally pulled in half-an-hour late and the cabaret began to fill up with a busload of tired, hungry, and occasionally grumpy video camera–toting tourists from Peoria, he just kept right on playing, reciting poems, performing, and giving little historical anecdotes. An audience of two or forty-two, it didn't matter to him, and he played sweet sentimental favorites like "Let Me Call You Sweetheart" and "Bye Bye Blackbird," all of which were a great hit with the tourists, who applauded and said things like: "You're doin the right songs from the right era!" One tourist even stopped to find a better hearing aid. He had a box full of hearing aids, like a carpenter's box of graduated drill bits, and he carefully selected the right one.

After Snowshoe had passed his hat at the end of the show, Bayne and I persuaded him to sit down at our table and talk to us, and so we learned his real name, which was Tony Scott Pearce. He got his stage name the very first time he went into an Indian village. He went to a village during Spring Carnival time, so it was in the first part of April. He went to this village, and to make a long story short they were having dog races and a snowshoe race. He got in the snowshoe race, and he won. So they kind of said, "Hey! Who are you? Snowshoe? Snowshoe Scott?" And it didn't really stick at that time, but every time he went back to the village, they wouldn't recognize him. When he'd go into the village, he was just another white guy. So he started using the name Snowshoe to kind of cut through that half-hour of introductions every time he met somebody, so they'd remember who he was. And then it just kind of stuck. He got in more snowshoe races, and he never lost. So it kind of stuck that way too. The name was kind of out there, and he grabbed it.

"How come you never lost a snowshoe race?" I thought to ask.

"I'm fast," he said.

Now, Snowshoe said, how Coldfoot got its name happened in the following way. In 1898, there was the gold strike in this area. It was a strike right at this creek, right out the window there. This was Slate Creek. It was up about six miles with the creek coming in from the north called Myrtle Creek, and that's where the first gold settlement was. In 1898, a guy named Newt Ellington discovered gold there. And the town of Coldfoot was set up as a supply point for miners who were in the area.

Most of the miners who traveled here were what they called "a sniper." They just traveled with a shovel and a pick and a gold pan. They were far away from anywhere. And they had to just carry whatever they could on their back to do their mining. They would build little ditches and shovel their dirt into these ditches. And then they'd have the creeks wash the dirt along, and they could get their gold from the bottom of the ripples in these ditches. It was a tough country to mine in. There were some miners that tried to spend a winter up here. They only got as far as about into October, and then they left. They got "cold feet." And that's how Coldfoot got its name of Coldfoot. And Coldfoot, the old Coldfoot, was really around for about only about eight years nine years ten years.

During its heyday, Coldfoot had like a couple of saloons and three or four whorehouses. They had four or five hotels, a couple of stores. Maybe a couple hundred people. There was a bunch of different towns just up and down. You had thousands of guys here. Thousands of guys here and when wintertime came, they kind of congregated rather than roam around. And when they congregated they gave their place of congregation a name, and then when the spring came, they were gone and the town was gone. So some of these towns were just a flash in the pan. Coldfoot was around longer than that, but in 1907 or thereabouts there was a larger gold strike up out of the present-day town of Wiseman. And so people went up there. Then, finally about 1940 or so, the last of the remaining structures in Coldfoot were moved up to Wiseman. That's the way it was. And this was nothing for a long time, and then in '74 or '75 this road was built. They built this entire road in five months.

Before this road, everybody who came up here had to come overland or down one of the rivers. In the winter when they froze, you could travel them by snowshoes or by dog team. So you didn't have towns away from rivers. Period. That's the way it was. There was no road. And then the road, the Dalton Highway, was built for the pipeline. That was in '75. And then, once they put in the highway and then, finally, opened it up to the public, they had to put in a place where you could stop and get gas, food, and so on. So there were two areas set up for travelers to get service at. One was at the Yukon River, and the other was at Coldfoot. As for the old Coldfoot, the old original Coldfoot, there are still some remains. There's not a whole lot there, but we could see some remains, and it was interesting, Snowshoe said.

He drew a map and gave a warning: "Just watch out for bears."

After talking with Snowshoe for about an hour, Bayne and I trudged back across the mud to our room in the hotel and called it a night. We had a hasty early breakfast at the café next morning, pulled out into a miserable chilly rainy drizzle, crossed the highway, and followed on a rougher road Snowshoe's map to the original Coldfoot. It was good to have four-wheel drive out there, and before we got completely stuck in the mud I parked the vehicle and walked the rest of the way.

I made the Research Staff stay in the car, since it was raining thoroughly now and I was still remembering Snowshoe's warning about bears and feeling cold-footed myself about the whole enterprise. I followed a track down to a dark area of dense trees until I saw on one side an old, half-collapsed log cabin and on the other side an old, half-collapsed plank cabin. That was it. Completely overgrown with trees and hunkered down darkly in the pelting rain like a couple of unhappy bears. I didn't want to go any farther in there because I figured I wouldn't be able to run fast in the mud if a bear started chasing me. I wasn't even sure if running was the best idea. Weren't you supposed to play dead or was that just with grizzlies? So I stopped when I saw the edges of the place. I'm not sure whether there were any other cabins or not, but I had glimpsed a part of the original Coldfoot and after that glimpse in the cold rain I hotfooted it back to the warm car, and we churned through the mud right out of there.

Deadhorse

The drive north from Coldfoot was harrowing enough that I never did keep good track of the time. I think we spent about seven or eight hours on the road transversing the nearly 250 miles to Deadhorse, and during much of that drive I entertained myself by calculating the distance driven divided by an estimate of the gas consumed in order to decide whether or not we were going to make it. It was cold and rainy most of the way, foggy much of the way, and it got worse at the end.

We passed through some extensive forests, crossed a number of roiling streams and rivers, and arrived at a giant wall of marble with a hill of forest that rolled right up to the wall. It was spectacular. And then for a long time we were moving through a beautiful river valley and following the pipeline.

As we drove north, the deciduous trees became more and more yellow until they lost their leaves and after that the trees themselves got lost, and we drove into a treeless tundra.

It was Bayne's turn in the front seat that day, and Bayne had already proclaimed it a silence day. No music. And the silence after a while combined with the rain and fog, the humming of our defroster fan, and the rhythmic bumping and splashing and rattling across the road to put us to sleep. Two of us, at least, with the third touch and go there for a while. Both members of the Research Staff were sound asleep by the time we reached the Atigun Pass and the first sign I had seen since Coldfoot, just about. It said AVALANCHE AREA DO NOT STOP NEXT 44 MILES. The road twisted into a maze of jagged gray snow-covered mountains that had recently shot up all around us.

This was the Brooks Range. The mountains were all snow-covered at the peaks, and the peaks were poking into the clouds while the clouds were peeking into the peaks, and it looked from where we were as if the clouds were snowing into them as well. The mountain peaks were bright white where they merged into the clouds, and the clouds looked as white as the peaks, and the whole thing was rising up beside us like the lost city of Atlantis rising magically up from the ocean with the briny ocean dripping away from its high towers and battlements.

The trees had definitely disappeared by now, and as our little precarious road began to turn and twist out the other side of the mountains, we began to roll over into nothing but alpine tundra with splotches of red and orange and yellow and gold. When the fog dissipated, the vista before us looked spectacular, with a river running through a valley and the snow-covered mountains on either side.

The rain finally left, and the sky cleared up, and the road got slightly better. I was driving along in silence, watching the odometer, watching the gas gauge, and keeping a regular calculation of gasoline mileage, when (a) a passing truck threw a rock at us that cracked our windshield and (b) we got swallowed up by another fog. So now we were driving with a big star in the windshield down the gullet of a white fog, moving steadily downhill now, surrounded by a small circle of red orange and yellow tundra and covered by a steadily moving dome of chalk white fog. We had already been driving, I supposed, three or four hours, something like that. I didn't have a watch. I was saying to myself, "There's nothing, no restaurant, gas station, motel, nothing until we get to Deadhorse."

"And," the odometer added, "we aren't even halfway yet to Deadhorse. Not even halfway!"

The engine said, "Sure, we can do it. No problem. It's all downhill now."

And the gas gauge said, "Um, let me think about this. Can I put you on hold?"

The fog cleared up, and now we were moving into another tundra valley, with waving swells of land covered with orange carpet and, in the far distance, another set of massive jagged mountains. These looked bigger than the last set, and come to think of it, this valley looked bigger than any I had so far seen. It was a game or a trick: the farther north we went the bigger things became. That had been true of pancakes in restaurants, and now it was true of mountains and valleys.

We saw some musk oxen down by a river, and through the binoculars they looked like big shaggy blotches.

We were hit by another stretch of fog, and the tundra turned into a waving desert surrounded by a hemisphere of chalk. We drove until the fog got even thicker and started to swirl, and when we came out again we had finished with the slope, more or less, and seemed to be rolling onto a flat coastal plain. But the fog came back, and that made the drive, which had already been tiring, even more so, especially when those giant trucks came our way and loomed out of the fog with their two yellow eyes. It was almost like coming to the end of the world there, and then the wind started to blow, and we were going down-hill once again, a gradual slope that went on for an hour or two hours, with some very strong winds sweeping across the road in front of us.

I had a feeling we were going to drive right into the sea, and during the last fifteen minutes, come to think of it, we had seen a lot of seagulls. Meanwhile, the yellow eyes of a truck appeared in front of us moving up fast and I saw it coming. It was like a bullet, really, flying from behind the truck, a big irregular rock spinning up in the air and slowly then fast turning our way until BAM it hit the windshield and created a big white flower. That was the second crack in the windshield.

The road turned to pavement, and it became a paved causeway through the tundra. It was dreary and eerie out there, and we turned and came into a great cold and foggy world of cranes, mud, trailers, more cranes, more mud, more trailers, sheds, barns, trucks, and a lot of grim-looking foul-weather friends such as giant cockroaches on eight-foot rubber tires and a six-foot high chain-saw on tank treads.

It was about seven o'clock in the evening but still light outside, as it would be for another four or five hours. Light, however, can be relative, and in this case it was dark light. The sky had a dirty chalkboard color, and it reflected into the slick of the road and the puddles over the tundra until that reflection melted back into the denser white of the fog which seeped back into the sky where it became a dirty chalkboard color and started the whole thing all over again. But there were informational signs along the road, and we followed the signs to a foggy drift of the road lined by some low tunnel-like trailers coagulated into distinctive units. We came to one coagulation of trailers with a sign on the side saying PRUDHOE BAY GENERAL STORE US POST OFFICE VIDEO RENTALS. And next to that was another coagulation of gloomy-looking trailers with a sign saying ARCTIC CARIBOU INN.

It was a hotel! I parked on a piece of mud, and we got out. It was downright cold outside of the car, with a sharp wind blowing and a chilly drizzle persisting. Our car was caked with mud half-an-inch thick, the windshield was obviously beyond repair, but we smiled and told ourselves we were just happy to be in Deadhorse.

At the door to the Arctic Caribou Inn a note told us to watch out for bears.

Some four-hundred-pound grizzly cub orphans had been wandering around the parking lot lately, the note said, and even though they were cute, we should keep in mind that they were dangerous.

I quickly looked around for four-hundred-pound grizzly cub orphans in the parking lot, didn't see any, and so walked through the double-doored airlock into the hotel. The inside of the hotel was dreary in a troglodytic way, but by then dreary and troglodytic seemed fine, in any case certainly better than being eaten by cute four-hundred-pound grizzly orphans.

I stopped to wipe the steam off my glasses. It was actually steamy in there. I could smell dinner being cooked, and I was pleased to learn from the woman at the desk that they had a room available. This hotel consisted of a series of interconnected prefab units, as I've already suggested, and we were given a room in the C wing, which was one major wing away from the back of the whole thing. We unloaded the car, washed up, and wandered back to the front part of the hotel, where there was a dining area and a series of windows leading to the kitchen.

Food had been arranged at the windows, and it was kept warm in steam trays with heat lamps. Signs above the trays explained what the food was. There was Arctic Caribou Stew, Chicken Prudhoe, North Slope Something Salmon, and so on. I don't remember what I ate, but I do remember eating a lot of it and also shouting my compliments over to the chef, who every few minutes appeared out of the cave of the kitchen, stooped through the food windows, and called out to people sitting in the dining room: "How do you like my food?"

He was very serious about his cooking, and his name was Barry Rodriguez.

An hour or two later, when the food was all tucked in for the night, the Research Staff and I located Barry Rodriguez as he was just locking up the kitchen. Barry was from Florida, he told us, and I would guess he was twenty-nine years old. He had dark eyes and a regular face with receding dark hair on the top offset by advancing dark hair on the bottom. He looked pale, as if he hadn't been out of the cave very much, and his eyes seemed red around the edges, as if he were overworked.

He was. He said he worked from six in the morning to usually eight o'clock nine o'clock at night. That was how you made your money, he added. All overtime. On an average day, Barry said, he spent the whole time indoors except for he might go out for a walk, and how long did that take? Thirty minutes, maybe. He might take a walk out back and look for bears or whatever. Walk up to the Prudhoe Bay Hotel, shoot a game of pool or whatever, something like that. Sometimes he watched TV, but he was still working all day long.

He preferred that. He usually worked two three months at a time and took two three weeks off. That was seven days a week, fifteen sixteen hours a day. So it was crazy up there, but he loved it. He liked the money. He liked the job. He liked the hours. He liked the people. Aah, he really didn't have friends, but who does anymore nowadays? And he didn't have a girlfriend either because the kind of girl he wanted doesn't exist any more. He was a solitary kind of guy. For entertainment, he worked. He always tried to create new dishes. He lay in bed at night thinking, "What can I do with this? I think this would be pretty good." And he was usually pretty inventive on some of the stuff he came up with. For example, he invented Bleu Cheese Halibut au Gratin, and he has had raves on it. He was going to make that tonight, but the bread crumbs they sent were small and he wanted the big ones. But he invented food and what have you, and he cooked with heart instead of cooking for profit.

Barry was trained as a chef at the School of Hard Knocks. Self-taught. But he had always worked in real nice restaurants, and he'd been into cooking since he was ten years old. He used to live in a resort in Florida, and they used to go out on the docks to catch catfish and bring the catfish into the back kitchen, and the old black man, he was very, "Mess o' catfish! Oh, Freddy's going to love you tonight!" Barry still remembered the name Freddy. "Freddy's going to love you tonight." And Barry would say, "Can I help with the prime rib?" So that's where he learned to cook. He became a chef, worked at some very fancy places, and then, one day, he decided to come up to Alaska. He told his girlfriend, "I'm going to Alaska to work up on the slope." When he first stepped off the plane, it was January 3, 1990. Minus eighty-seven degrees with the chill factor.

As Head Chef at the Arctic Caribou Inn, Barry got to plan all the menus, do all the cooking, set the pace. The caribou steak we were offered at dinner? Actually it was reindeer. Which is the same animal, but it's been domesticated. It was still caribou but it's just fed different and raised different. A lot of people liked it, which was a surprise. Barry had to force some people to try it. One lady one day, "Oh, I just can't eat it." Barry said, "Ma'am, you ever been to a foreign country?" "Yeah." "Well, have you ever tried their foods?" "Well, yeah." "See. Now you have to try this." So they'll try it and come back: "Oh, this is my second helping, I love it."

So just about everybody liked his cooking. Barry thought even the grizzly bears in back of the hotel liked his food. They were eating it, and that was proof the food was good. Out of the dumpster, yeah. People did try to chase the bears off, but the bears come back. People put sirens on, they had guns. Not real guns, but they were like cap guns, loud cap guns. But nobody was actually going to kill a bear in Deadhorse or Prudhoe Bay, oh no, not unless the bear was attacking somebody. There used to be twenty or thirty of them up there, all over the place. But people had kind of chased them off, so now Barry guessed there were like maybe four or five bears running around Deadhorse. And then the bear population will go up again, and then it'll go down, go up and down.

But Deadhorse, no, he wasn't sure where the name came from. People say Deadhorse is different from Prudhoe Bay. For example, Deadhorse is right here, this side of the guard shack. Prudhoe Bay is on the other side of the guard shack. And this side, this is all of Deadhorse, and it included the post office and the general store as well as the hotels. He guessed there were three hotels in Deadhorse. And then there were camps. As a rough guess, the population of Deadhorse alone he was guessing five hundred. But it picks up in the wintertime. Wintertime, this would be a busy place. That's when everything gets moving, because the tundra is frozen. You can drive across the frozen land, and it won't hurt the tundra. No tracks or nothing. It's smooth. It's ice-covered, and you can drive on it.

There are all kinds of stories about the name Deadhorse, and Barry wasn't sure anyone would ever really know the true origin. But he was guessing it was some sort of runway they built after oil was discovered in 1968, and they used horses to clear it off or something like that. Horses died, and they had to haul 'em out. Hence the name Deadhorse.

The D wing at the far end of the hotel was what Barry called "the ghetto." No one stayed back there other than Barry, who preferred having a room in the ghetto because it was quiet and he could go to bed early without being disturbed. All the other rooms were empty, though, some with unlocked doors and a couple of the unlocked ones with windows providing a good view of the white field behind the hotel where the dumpster and the bears were. Barry showed us the best empty open room with the best view of the dumpster, and so that night we bear-watched until darkness took over at 11:30 or so. The bears weren't there.

Two bears came very early the next morning, though, and I thought they weighed much more than four hundred pounds each. They lumbered around like delinquent monsters, chased away the seagulls, climbed into the dumpster, and had a great time rummaging through Barry's food.

After breakfast I left the Research Staff in the hotel to relax and went out looking for gas. The hotel provided a little map of Deadhorse and Prudhoe Bay, and with the help of that map I got completely lost. Deadhorse only consists of a few interconnecting roads, so getting lost ought to be difficult, but the roads are longer than the map explained, and furthermore I think some of them were not on the map. Moreover, I could see why Barry liked to stay inside at the Arctic Caribou all day long. The lady at the desk of the Prudhoe Bay Hotel, just down the mud a quarter of a mile from the Arctic Caribou, said she really liked to work in Deadhorse because she could be there for months and never have to go outdoors. She had everything she could want right in the hotel.

I was talking to her because I was trying to buy a ride out to the Arctic Ocean. Even though the ocean or sea was a mere five miles from where we were, the road would take us into the oil fields: private property. We couldn't drive there. We had to take the tour on a bus or van run by one of the oil companies. And the lady at the desk sold me three tickets for the 10:00 AM trip out there.

So we checked out of the Arctic Caribou and went over to the Prudhoe Bay Hotel to wait for our tour.

Unlike the Arctic Caribou, the Prudhoe Bay had many oil workers staying there, and we watched shaggy men with weight-lifters' arms and dirty boots smoke cigarettes, shoot pool, watch TV, and write lying letters home. When two tourists did show up, they looked small and Victorian next to the oil workers, but they were our tourists as it turned out, so we all greeted one another, and then we all walked out to the front of the hotel and climbed into a van driven by a soft-spoken young man named Eric Goode.

Eric Goode wore a warm-looking North Face fleece vest over a white polo shirt, and his head was protected by a white baseball cap with a set of sunglasses wedged at the front, as if the cap needed to see too.

When Eric first came up there (he told us, as we headed toward the Arctic Ocean) he thought to himself: "Holy cow, there's no way I'll do this." He said, "Sure, for the summer, but then I'm going to school." But the more he did it the more he actually enjoyed it and realized that it was a pretty good concept. As long as you get on with a company that's loyal to their employees you could be up there for a while. His primary job, he's a carpenter. Yeah, then he drives truck for the hotel also, and he gives the tour to the Arctic Ocean and the oil fields. Pretty much everything. He has learned a lot working up there. It has turned out to be a good opportunity. He hasn't went to school, and yet he's making a lot more money than people with degrees. It's not a bad deal. For now anyway. It'd be hard when you had kids. It's true that a lot of the class of guys up there, Eric found them hard to stand. They have no morals or scruples. They would have a wife back home, and then they meet girls up there and just forget what they have back home. The divorce rate is pretty high.

Right now the population of Deadhorse and Prudhoe Bay would be around twenty-four thousand people, Eric went on (as we bounced through the muddy foggy main drag of Deadhorse) but of course a lot of the contracting companies have their own quarters. The oil reserves were discovered in 1968 by Arco. In 1973 they started construction of the pipeline, and it was completed by '77. First oil flowed down through the pipeline on June 20, 1977. Eleven pump stations. They have the capability to shut down the whole pipeline in six minutes. Eric was pretty sure they did it once. He couldn't remember the circumstances. Anyhow, the oil comes out of the ground with a natural heat of about 160 degrees. They cool it at the pump station to about 130. By Valdez, it will have gotten down to about 100. Right now they are putting around one million barrels per day down the line, even though it has the capacity for two million barrels — at forty-one gallons per barrel. It takes eight days for oil leaving Prudhoe Bay and going down the pipeline at 6.5 miles an hour to get to Valdez.

We were driving through Deadhorse right now, Eric said, up until we reached the guard shacks, the security check point. After that was into the Prudhoe Bay oil fields. Up until those shacks was considered Deadhorse. And Deadhorse was not actually a town it was just Deadhorse, developed to accommodate contracting companies who were affiliated with the oil fields. It was just all industrial.

The hotel we had departed from was probably eight miles away from the ocean, and the guard shack that we were headed for, which signified the end of Deadhorse, would be five miles away from the ocean. The guard shack, really what those signify is they, of course, keep track of the personnel that's on the fields and they know where they're at in case anything happens, and it just also means that you've entered Prudhoe Bay.

And as for the name Deadhorse, there are a couple of myths, but the true story is that there was this young fella, his father left him an inheritance of $6 million, but he couldn't claim it until he was, Eric thought, thirty-five years old, so he went to Alaska and bought into this trucking company, asking his father for an advance on the inheritance. His father didn't really want to fund it, and in the meanwhile the trucking company was going bankrupt, so the father said, "I don't want to put money down to feed a dead horse."

So the son called his trucking company Deadhorse Haulers.

After oil was found in 1968 and they started to build the Prudhoe Bay facilities, Deadhorse Haulers got one of the first contracts up there to build the runway and to do some work up there, and the name stuck. People started calling the runway and then the larger area Deadhorse. The name just stuck. And the guard shack that we were stopping at right now, Eric said, that marked the end of Deadhorse.

Roads End

To the guard inside the shack, looking us over through his now-open window, Eric said, "How we doin?"

"Good."

"A little nicer today."

"A lot nicer."

And the guard waved us onto the largest oil field in North America. There was a total of nine fields up there, and we were on the largest field in North America right now and that was Prudhoe Bay oil field. It was 250 square miles, and they drilled at about nine thousand feet deep, Eric said. The permafrost there was two thousand feet deep. And when they first started up there, it was predicted that there would be thirteen billion barrels of recoverable oil. Just this year they reached the nine billion mark, so Eric thought they were definitely on the decline.

"But natural gas, there is such an abundant amount of it up here," he was saying. "There's so much natural gas it pushes up. There's no pumps of any sort, it just pushes up through pressure, and then it sets in the manifold building in the middle. That's the larger green building over there."

It was less foggy now, and I could see the larger green building he referred to. We drove past it and through the tundra until the road reached the water. That was the road's end, and I must say things would have been just about perfect if it were other than what it was: a drop-off into icy fog and freezing water.

Fortunately, however, I had had a feeling this was going to happen, and so a few chapters back while we were still in California I bought my own little Storyville: a place called Roads End. Roads End had been sitting down there in the middle of southern California not doing anyone any good. It was not much to look at, in truth, but I bought the place anyway, using that big advance I knew I was going to get for this book. Then I had the entire town disassembled piece-by-piece in California and packed and shipped up to Alaska, so that when our vehicle pulled up at the end of our road, I and the Research Staff could step out into a metaphor or even a complete chapter called "Roads End" before facing the eternal expanse of milky sky and milky water on a cold and gravelly little jut.

We had arrived at the East Dock, Eric told us. The whole bay out there was six to eight feet deep, so it was really shallow, and they only had two months out of the year when the ice was clear and the harbor could be used.

We sat in the van with the heater on and the wipers flicking slowly back and forth to clear a condensing fog, while Eric assured us it was more comfortable now that the mosquitoes were gone. It was also better now than it would be in a month when the ice pack moved in and the polar bears jumped off.

"I want to go out and get my feet wet. I don't know about anybody else," I said, and I climbed out of the van, soon to be joined by almost everyone else.

Everyone but Eric took off shoes and socks, rolled up pantlegs, and walked down the gravel to the water. We tested the water with our toes, and looked out into the fog. The water was freezing! We looked at the fog for ten or fifteen minutes until we were bored with looking at the pale white end of the world, at which point everyone shook hands with everyone else, smiled, and climbed back into the van, which Eric then started up and turned around.

THE END

Acknowledgments

This is a work of nonfiction and therefore everything in it is kind of true, but I would still like to acknowledge where I drove my prosaic vehicle under the influence of a poetic license. More particularly, I've presented this journey as though it were a single summer's lark with two members of my Research Staff; in reality it is based upon three major trips we took during the month of August for three summers — with three or four minitrips added at later dates to patch up on places we skimped the first time around.

I have tried to describe, quote, paraphrase, and otherwise represent the people we met along the way as accurately as possible in the text; and I do hope I've succeeded and also expressed my sincere gratitude for all the wonderful assistance given. Since, though, I was unable to name everyone who helped — or even every Storyville we passed through — I would like at this point, with a slightly expanded itinerary, to thank *all* of those ordinary heroes and Good Samaritans who responded to our requests for direction and information with such superb and surprising hospitality.

Thanks, then, to Billy Whitten and Mrs. Fred "Dolly" Sapp (of Start, Louisiana); Preston Green, Helen Wells, and Mayor Leon Saunders (of Plain Dealing, Louisiana); Charles Glover and David and Aaron Applebaum (of Uncertain, Texas); Marshall Ivey and Linda Starkey (of Cut and Shoot, Texas); Ruby E. Tyler and "Pee Wee" Garland Bock (of Magnet, Texas); Pastor Matthew Van Hook, Glen Sandusky, and other members of the Noodle Baptist Church congregation (of Noodle, Texas); Allene Edmondson (of Loco, Oklahoma); Roy and Norma Reed, Seth Timmons, and Arleen Thompson (of Hogeye and Bug Scuffle, Arkansas); Mr. and Mrs. B. McCollum Jr. (of Greasy Corner, Arkansas); Mary Ann Fava, A. V. Anderson, Bruno Fava, and Homer Lathan (of Alligator, Mississippi); Milburn J. Crowe (of Mound Bayou, Mississippi); Mayor Tom Turner Jr., Shirley Ferrell, and Nellie Blankenship (of Belzoni and Hard Cash, Mississippi); Larry Cline (of It, Mississippi); Judy and Herbert Harper (of Hot Coffee, Mississippi); Kathy Procker, Janice Hearn, Gerry Green, and Laurence Ingram (of Soso, Mississippi); Charles Wilson, George Brown, Samuel Slaughter, and Adolphus Murphy (of Equality, Alabama); and Miss Frances Thompson and Lois Stowe (of Between, Georgia).

Thanks additionally to Edna and Lonnie Harris, John Ray Campbell, and James Smrye (of Harmony, North Carolina); Jane Braswell with Chelsea Rose and Levi (of Whynot, North Carolina); Dee Smith (of Bottom, North Carolina); W. D. Rogers (of Pinch, West Virginia); Mr. Carper and Rita McKawn (of Left Hand, West Virginia); Rosie Smith Moon (of Accident, Maryland); Michael Smith (of Detour, Maryland); Frank L. Weaver and David Fidler (of Bird-in-Hand, Pennsylvania); Stephen Scott (of Intercourse, Pennsylvania); Anne Foster and Wolfgang and Jessie Bauer (of Climax, New York); Clayton Fuller (of Onset, Massachusetts); Raymond Damon (of Old Furnace, Massachusetts); Martha Ivins (of Lawyersville, New York); Mr. and Mrs. Harold Dodge (of Index, New York); Brian Bergquist (of Horseheads, New York); Ray Underwood, Janice Weisenfeld, and Ann Sherwood (of Painted Post, New York); Robert R. Lyman (of Roulette, Pennsylvania); Russ Lineman (of Big Shanty, Pennsylvania); Mr. Hechler (of Brandy Camp, Pennsylvania); Myrtle Shirey and Viola Lamadue (of Needful, Pennsylvania); Dorris Allison, Chris, and the little yellow-and-white dog (of Panic, Pennsylvania); Ruth Crist (of Home, Pennsylvania); Nellie M. Cogley (of Echo, Pennsylvania); and Jim Allen and Frank L. Doverspike (of Distant, Pennsylvania).

Thanks as well to Chief Daniel J. Simecek (of Twinsburg, Ohio); Officer John B. Flint (of Reminderville, Ohio); Marion D. Mardis (of Newcomerstown, Ohio); Herb Linger (of Crooked Tree, Ohio); Beth Day (of Getaway, Ohio); Don Brown (of Dog Walk, Kentucky); Gene Holtzclaw and Raymond Duvall (of Preachersville, Kentucky); Jeanette Stephens, Donita Dyer, and Lovy Garmon (of Marrowbone, Kentucky); Dorthy Garmon (of Subtle, Kentucky); Stanley and Jo Nell Ferguson and Jeff Reese (of Chicken Bristle, Kentucky); James Alexander, Ella Mae Russell, Walt Kinsey, and Frank Oliver (of Monkeys Eyebrow, Kentucky); Robert "Horsefly" Bean (of Muddy, Illinois); Ray Hines (of Equality, Illinois); John Ebert (of Goofy Ridge, Illinois); Clayton Spires and Ed Shefey (of Normal, Illinois); Mr. Robert J. Kretche (of Dilly, Wisconsin); Roland "Charlie" Fowler and Buzz and Elaine Schultz (of Embarrass, Minnesota); Alan W. Krueger (of Young America, Minnesota); Connie Apton and Sally Timm (of Sleepy Eye, Minnesota); Howard Nelson (of Crooks, South Dakota); Adrian E. Dalen and Patches the cat (of Buffalo Trading Post, South Dakota); Sandra Schmidt and Walter C. Schramm (of Winner, South Dakota); Anthony Tail (of Wounded Knee, South Dakota); James Oedekoven (of Recluse, Wyoming); Kathleen Smith and Myra Spellman (of Spotted Horse, Wyoming); Harry J. Johns (of Story, Wyoming); Hayden Blair (of Ten Sleep, Wyoming); Pratt Seegmiller (of Big Rock Candy Mountain, Utah); and Richard "Buddy" Kenworthy and George Brucha (of Nothing, Arizona).

And more thanks to Shirley and Mel Paolini (of Birds Landing, California); Bev and Doug Pickell, Karen Prust-Mangino, Eleanor Keene, and Dorene and Larry Fisk (of Cool, California); Mike Ogilvie (of Hallelujah Junction, California); Don and Shirley Flournoy (of Likely, California); Kay Phillips, Lois Campbell, and Charles Powers (of Igo, California); Nettie Clevenger, Mary Cole, and Nola Jean Shoup (of Ono, California); Willard Boring, Jeremiah C. Leach, and Gordon and Karen Watkins (of Boring, Oregon); Linda Trickel (of Zigzag, Oregon); Bambi Beck and Kim Petitjean (of Duckabush, Washington); George C. Brown (of Discovery Bay, Washington); Toni Makinaw and Joni Miller (of Startup, Washington); Bill and Mary Morris and Susan Wiren (of Chicken, Alaska); Stacey, and Sandy and Bryan Burroughs (of Old Man, Alaska); Pat Davis and Tony "Snowshoe Scott" Pearce (of Coldfoot, Alaska); Jack and Roma Reakoff (of Wiseman, Alaska); and Barry Rodriguez and Eric Goode (of Deadhorse, Alaska).

In addition to all the ordinary heroes and Good Samaritans we met along the way, several other people, including family and friends, served very generously as hosts. They put us up. They took care of us. They amused and fed us. For the hosts, a special thanks to my sister-in-law Bea and niece Leslie (in Texas); my brother Dwight and sister-in-law Marti (in South Carolina); my sister, Debbie, and her husband, Milan, as well as niece and nephew, Katie and Robbie (in Maryland); my brother Doug and sister-in-law Joanne (in Pennsylvania — had they been home); my nephew Andrew (in Maine); friends Phil and Carol (in Massachusetts); my brother David, as well as Mary Beth, Kris, Jon, Davey, and Debbie, and also cousins Richard and Irene and Aunt Amy (in Illinois); friends Mark and Alison (in Minnesota); sister-in-law Fiona and her husband, Skip (in Nevada); friends Chris and Mark, as well as Julia, Elissa, and William (in California); Aunt Evelyn (in Oregon); and, of course, our friends Susan and Steve (in Washington).

There were other friends as well, most notable in this context for helping us along the conceptual highway. Thanks, then, to Harry Foster, who thought Storyville was a good idea and so encouraged me regularly and significantly. It's not his fault that I misunderstood the situation in Hogeye. For general advice and hints about the hidden places of Mississippi, I am indebted to Tom Rankin, of the Center for the Study of Southern Culture at the University of Mississippi in Oxford and to Stephen Young, editor of the *Southern Quarterly*, at the University of Southern Mississippi in Haddiesburg. Tom Rankin told me about an amazing place called Mound Bayou, for example, and the route to an elusive little Storyspot in Mississippi called It. Katherine Steele of Greenwood, Mississippi, gave a lot of good general information and advice about the Delta; I am sincerely grateful to her. And I must thank Rob Amberg, of Marshall, North Carolina, for setting us on the path to Harmony. Rob also gave me a lot of good general information and advice.

Most of the best information about Storyvilles was given openly and on the spot by our generous informants, and I tried as much as possible to avoid second-hand information — from books, libraries, and museums. Neverthe-less, a number of background sources proved critically enlightening. The newspaper articles partly quoted in the chapter on Greasy Corner, Arkansas, include Michelle Hillier's "Mechanic-chef Left His Mark" in the *Arkansas Democrat Gazette,* "Welcome to Where the Name Tells Town's Tale" in *The Commercial Appeal,* and Christopher Sullivan's "Ol' Man River Filled with Mud, Memories" in *The Jonesboro Sun.* I supplemented my hazy knowledge of the Delta Blues (for Alligator, Mississippi) by reference to Len Lyons's *The 100 Best Jazz Albums* (New York: William Morrow, 1980) and Michael Erle-wine's *All Music Guide to the Blues* (San Francisco: Miller Freeman, 1996). And I was able to locate Hot Coffee, which is not on most maps, with some as-sistance from Kathy Kent's *Welcome to Lickskillet: And Other Crazy Places in the Deep South* (Birmingham: Crane Hill Press, 1996). Sean Dolan's *Pursuing the Dream* (New York: Chelsea House, 1995) proved essential for my brief discussion of the Civil Rights movement in the Equality chapter. I found my knowledge of Climax, New York, considerably deepened by a little book of local history, *Climax Recollections,* provided by Anne Foster. And I had some additional help learning the history of Painted Post from the following sources: Beverly G. Alsen's *Painted Post Centennial 1893–1993,* Thomas P. Dimitroff and Lois S. Janes's *History of the Corning Painted Post Area* (Corn-ing: Bookmarks, 1991); Charles H. Erwin's *History of the Town and Village of Painted Post, and of the Town of Erwin* (Painted Post: Times, 1874); and Sam Roberts's "Yes, a Small Town Is Different" (*New York Times,* Aug. 27, 1997). My knowledge of the Finnish log constructions found in Embarrass, Min-nesota, was broadened by leafing through Suzanne Winckler's *Testaments in Wood* (St. Paul: Minnesota Historical Society, 1991). And I supplemented my historical understanding of Sleepy Eye by reference to Elizabeth Scobie's *Sleepy Eye: A History of Sleepy Eye, Minnesota* (1994; Sleepy Eye: Herald-Dispatch, 1972). Mr. Schramm of Winner, South Dakota, mailed me copies of articles on the history of Winner written by Rosland Jordan, Winner E. Keller, Dennis B. Lyons, and Robert Maule, all published in *The Tripp County 50th Anniversary Book* (1959). And Anthony Tail of Wounded Knee pointed to an excellent book, James H. McGregor's *The Wounded Knee Massacre: From the Viewpoint of the Sioux* (Rapid City: Fenske Printing, 1940), which I used for historical reference along with the better-known work by John G. Nei-hardt, *Black Elk Speaks: Being the Life Story of a Holy Man of the Oglala*

Sioux (1961; Lincoln: University of Nebraska Press, 1932). My knowledge of Ten Sleep, Wyoming, was expanded with Anita M. Hinton's *Ten Sleep Through Peepsights* (Ten Sleep: Medicine Wheel Studios, 1992). My minor understanding of the history behind the Donner tragedy and Hallelujah Junction was made slightly less so by reference to James J. Rose's *Sierra Trailblazers: First Pioneer Wagons Over the Sierra Nevada* (Lake Tahoe Historical Association, 1995) and Thornton J. Quinn's *Camp of Death: The Donner Party Mountain Camp 1846–47* (Silverthorne, CO: Vistabooks, 1996). Discovery Bay discoveries included details from William H. Schweizer's *Solemn Silence: The Complete Guide to Hood Canal, by Land and Sea* (Seattle: EOS, 1992). Finally, I developed my comprehension of the Klondike Gold Rush in northern Canada and Alaska with help from Michael Cooper's *Klondike Fever: The Famous Gold Rush of 1898* (New York: Clarion, 1989) and Robert Sprecht's *Tisha: The Story of a Young Teacher in the Alaska Wilderness* (New York: Bantam, 1976).

Deadhorse and Roads End were the end of our trip, but not of the book. Afterward there was the little problem of writing it — and I had technical help from Lynnette Simon and also Rosalie Prosser and her associates at ADS. Then there was the less little problem of getting it into print; and here I must thank my agent at Sterling Lord Literistic, Peter Matson, for his wisdom and steadfastness, and my editor at Georgia Press, Barbara Ras, for her bright and buoyant enthusiasm.

My wife, Wyn Kelley, as always, sustained me throughout the doing and the writing; she remained the anchor for a wandering and sometimes drifting ship of exploration. I am always grateful. Finally, and with the deepest appreciation, I must now acknowledge and thank my two Research Assistants, Britt and Bayne, who, with strong attention, good spirits, genuine humor, unfailing energy, and astonishing patience, kept us moving even when I felt stuck. They were my companions and advisors, my consultants and my counselors. They were my eyes and ears. In West Virginia they even tied my shoes and stood me upright. *Storyville, USA* wouldn't exist if they hadn't made the whole shebang happen, from Start to Roads End.